# YAMAHA

## WORKSHOP MANUALS
## AND
## ILLUSTRATED PARTS LISTS

## YA5 1961-1963 & YA6 1964-1967

A Floyd Clymer Publication
This edition published in 2020 by
www.VelocePress.com

All rights reserved. This work may not be reproduced or transmitted in any form without the express written consent of the publisher.

## Introduction

Welcome to the world of digital publishing ~ the book you now hold in your hand, was printed using the latest state of the art digital technology. The advent of print-on-demand has forever changed the publishing process, never has information been so accessible and it is our hope that this book serves your informational needs for years to come. If this is your first exposure to digital publishing, we hope that you are pleased with the results. Many more titles of interest to the classic automobile and motorcycle enthusiast, collector and restorer are available via our website at www.VelocePress.com. We hope that you find this title as interesting as we do.

## Note from the Publisher

The information presented is true and complete to the best of our knowledge. All recommendations are made without any guarantees on the part of the author or the publisher, who also disclaim all liability incurred with the use of this information.

## Trademarks

We recognize that some words, model names and designations, for example, mentioned herein are the property of the trademark holder. We use them for identification purposes only. This is not an official publication.

## Information on the use of this Publication

This manual is an invaluable resource for those interested in performing their own maintenance. However, in today's information age we are constantly subject to changes in common practice, new technology, availability of improved materials and increased awareness of chemical toxicity. As such, it is advised that the user consult with an experienced professional prior to undertaking any procedure described herein. While every care has been taken to ensure correctness of information, it is obviously not possible to guarantee complete freedom from errors or omissions or to accept liability arising from such errors or omissions. Therefore, any individual that uses the information contained within, or elects to perform or participate in do-it-yourself repairs or modifications acknowledges that there is a risk factor involved and that the publisher or its associates cannot be held responsible for personal injury or property damage resulting from the use of the information or the outcome of such procedures.

## Warning!

One final word of advice, this publication is intended to be used as a reference guide, and when in doubt the reader should consult with a qualified technician.

## Page Numbering

As each of the individual factory publications in this manual have their own index, the page numbers corresponding to that index are printed exactly as they appear in the original publications. The page number to the upper corner is the page number within the manual and is used in the section index below.

## Main Section Index

| | | |
|---|---|---|
| YA5 Workshop & Service Manual | Pages | 1 to 112 |
| YA5 Illustrated Parts List | Pages | 113 to 160 |
| YA6 Workshop & Service Manual | Pages | 161 to 220 |
| YA6 Illustrated Parts List | Pages | 221 to 292 |

# YAMAHA YA5

# WORKSHOP MANUAL

## PREFACE

YAMAHA is proud to present the completely new "YAMAHA 125 Model YA-5". The single cylinder engine is new! The body styling is new, and each separate part has been improved. The rotary valve engine is the greatest single feature of the YA-5, with power almost equal to the more expensive twin cylindered model.

No matter the superiority of the product, ultimate satisfaction to our clients depends on your service. This manual is for your use in furnishing the very best service possible to insure understanding and cooperation between manufacturer, dealer and customer.

YAMAHA 125 MODEL YA-5 SERVICE MANUAL
1961 EDITION

Published by YAMAHA MOTOR CO., LTD.
Hamamatsu, Japan.
Printed by SHINWA PRINTING CO., LTD.
Tokyo, Japan.

Reprinted in 1964

# YAMAHA 125 MODEL YA-5

## "SERVICE MANUAL"

## CONTENTS

### CHAPTER 1    INTRODUCTION

| | | |
|---|---|---|
| 1—1 | Outstanding Feature of the Model YA-5 | 1 |
| 1—2 | Specification of the Model YA-5 | 2 |
| 1—3 | Completely New Mechanism of the Model YA-5 | 5 |
| 1—4 | Tools for the Model YA-5 | 12 |

### CHAPTER 2    ENGINE

#### 2—1  OVERHAULING ENGINE ............ 14

| | | |
|---|---|---|
| 2—1—1 | Attaching and Detaching Engine | 14 |
| 2—1—2 | How to Disassemble Cylinder | 15 |
| 2—1—3 | How to Disassemble Crank Case Cover (Left) | 15 |
| 2—1—4 | How to Disassemble Crank Case Cover (Right) | 15 |
| 2—1—5 | How to Disassemble Crank Case | 16 |
| 2—1—6 | How to Disassemble Kick | 16 |
| 2—1—7 | How to Disassemble Mission Change | 17 |
| 2—1—8 | How to Disassemble Crank and Valve | 17 |

#### 2—2  ASSEMBLY ............ 18

| | | |
|---|---|---|
| 2—2—1 | Crank Case Assembly | 18 |
| 2—2—2 | Attaching Rotary Valve | 21 |
| 2—2—3 | Attaching Crank | 23 |
| 2—2—4 | Assembling Transmission | 26 |
| 2—2—5 | Attaching Kick | 34 |
| 2—2—6 | Assembling Right and Left Crank Cases | 35 |

2—2—7    Attaching Change Driving Mechanism ................................ 36
2—2—8    Attaching Clutch ................................ 48
2—2—9    Attaching Cylinder, Piston and Piston Ring ................................ 41
2—2—10   Attaching Dynamo and Ignition Timing Control ................................ 43
2—2—11   Attaching Left Case Cover ................................ 44
2—2—12   Attaching Inlet Cover, Carburetor, Air Cleaner and Carburetor Cover ................................ 45

# CHAPTER 3    FRAME

3—1    Frame ................................ 48
3—2    Steering Handle and Wires ................................ 49
3—3    Front Fork ................................ 51
3—4    Rear Arm ................................ 53
3—5    Rear Cushion Unit ................................ 54
3—6    Fuel Tank and Saddle ................................ 55
3—7    Foot Rest, Main Stand, Side Stand and Brake Pedal ................................ 57
3—8    Drive Chain System ................................ 58
3—9    Front and Rear Wheels ................................ 60
3—10   Tires and Tubes ................................ 65
3—11   Brake Assembly ................................ 65

# CHAPTER 4    ELECTRICAL EQUIPMENT

4—1    Electrical Equipment of the Model YA-5 ................................ 68
4—2    Component parts ................................ 68
4—3    Explanation of parts ................................ 69
4—4    Explanation of parts ................................ 69
    A    Ignition System ................................ 69
    B    Starting and Charging System ................................ 73
    C    Lighting and Signal Systems ................................ 79
    D    Battery ................................ 84

# CHAPTER 5    PERIODICAL INSPECTION

5—1    Carburetor ................................ 87
5—2    Air Cleaner ................................ 88
5—3    Ignition Timing ................................ 88
5—4    Spark Plug ................................ 88

5—5   Contact Points ········································································· 89
5—6   Battery················································································· 89
5—7   Carbon Brush ········································································· 90
5—8   Front Fork············································································· 90
5—9   Removing Carbon ··································································· 91
5—10  Lubrication ··········································································· 91

## CHAPTER 6   TROUBLE SHOOTING

6—1   Failure to start ······································································· 93
6—2   Speed is slow, Engine Power is lower than usual ·························· 94
6—3   Engine overheats ···································································· 96
6—4   Clutch does not work well ······················································· 97
6—5   Speed Change is inadequate ···················································· 98
6—6   Engine makes noise ································································ 98
6—7   Handle is unsatisfactory ·························································· 100
6—8   Bad Cushion ········································································· 101
6—9   Brake does not work well ······················································· 102
6—10  Charge is insufficient······························································ 102
6—11  Self-starter does not turn························································· 103

# CHAPTER 1. INTRODUCTION

## 1—1 OUTSTANDING FEATURES OF THE MODEL YA-5

YAMAHA's distinguished creation, the YAMAHA 125 Model YA-5 possesses an excellent newly designed engine, a smart body styling and a first class mechanism beginning a new phase in the motorcycle industry. Moreover, the Model YA-5, easy to handle motorcycle, has the highest power of the single cylindered cars and can compare with double cylindered ones.

Its main features are described below.

### (A) SUPERIOR PERFORMANCE MOTORCYCLE WITH HIGH-POWERED ENGINE (New devices as rotary valve and third port have been adopted)

Because of the adoption of the rotary valve and the third port, the Model YA-5 has sharply increased its horsepower. In addition, the single cylinder device results in easier operation and simplifies the rotary valve mechanism.

As compared with the Model YA1-3, the YA-5 reaches a higher level of performance from a mechanical and technical standpoint. For example, maximum output and maximum torque on the Model YA-5 are 10 ps/6500 rpm and 1.2 kgm/4500 rpm respectively, while on the YA-3, they are 6.8 ps/6000 rpm and 0.96 kgm/4500 rpm.

Since the single cylindered engine, moreover, permits an increase in its output without excessive rotation and raises the torques in lower rotations, the YA-5 provides an excellent performance. As the result of the output increase, maximum speed is increased from 85 km/h (YA-3) to 100 km/h (YA-5), and acceleration of 0—400 m requires only 19 sec. Therefore, YA-5 is suitable for all kinds of purpose.

### (B) HIGHEST STARTING PERFORMANCE
### (Large capacity starter dynamo and carburetor with starter have been adopted)

The starting dynamo is of the large capacity which has improved the dynamo of YA-3. For example, just turn the starter lever and press the starting button, and the engine may be smoothly started at any time. Because the starter mechanism is built in the carburetor.

### (C) MISSION OF SEESAW CHANGE

The seesaw change has been adopted instead of the pedal-kick. It excels the conventional type in easy handling and riding comfort. In relation to the shifter cam, as the conventional plate cam has developed into the drum one, the smooth operation is secured at all times.

### (D) EXCELLENT SUSPENSION SYSTEM

The front fork is of the telescopic type. As it acts as spring and shock absorber, the stability, the steerage and the riding comfort has been remarkably improved.

### (E) SIMPLE MAINTENANCE

The electrical equipment housed in the center of the frame results in easier inspection and maintenance. In addition, the engine mechanism is of the simple construction because of the single cylinder. Therefore, even the beginners can assemble and disassemble it easily.

## 1—2 YAMAHA YA-5
### —SPECIFCATIONS—

**NAME:** YAMAHA
**MODEL:** YA-5
**DIMENSION:**

| | |
|---|---|
| Overall Length | 1870 mm |
| Overall Width | 680 mm |
| Overall Height | 955 mm |
| Wheel Base | 1250 mm |
| Load Clearance | 130 mm |

**WEIGHT:**

| | |
|---|---|
| Net Weight | 110 kg |
| Seating Capacity | 2 persons |
| Weight Distribution | |
| At no load Front | ········ 50 kg |
| Rear | ········ 60 kg |

**PERFORMANCE:**

| | |
|---|---|
| Maximum Speed | 105 km/h |
| Stationary Fuel Consumption | 65 km/$l$ (35 km/h) |

| | |
|---|---|
| Actual Fuel Consumption | 48 km/$l$ |
| Climbing Ability | 1/3 |
| Braking Distance | 12 m (50 km/h) |
| Minimum Radius of Turning | 1900 mm |

**ENGINE:**

| | |
|---|---|
| Type of Engine | YA-5 |
| Cooling System | Air-Cooled engine |
| Cylinder | Single Cylinder System |
| Displacement | 123 cc |
| Bore × Stroke | 56 × 50 |
| Compression Ratio | 6.75 |
| Maximum Power | 10.5 HP/6500 rpm |
| Maximum Torque | 1.2 kgm/4500 rpm |
| Minimum Fuel Consumption At Full Load | 340/ps-H 600 rpm |
| Equipped Engine Weight | 31 kg (including muffler) |
| Engine Dimension (length) | 448 mm |
| Engine Dimension (width) | 392 mm |
| Engine Dimension (height) | 353 mm |
| Starting System | Dynamo Starter and Kick |

**IGNITION SYSTEM:**

| | |
|---|---|
| Ignition | Battery Ignition |
| Ignition Timing | 2.6 mm (24°) before upper dead point |
| Starting System | Dynamo |
| Spark Plug | Hitachi M-44-W, NGK B-7H |
| Angle-Advancing Device | Equipped |
| Point Gap | 0.3~0.35 mm |

**STARTER DYNAMO:**

| | |
|---|---|
| Manufacturer of Dynamo | Hitachi |
| Dynamo System | DC shunt dynamo |
| Dynamo Output | 90 w/14 v 1600 rpm |
| Type of Starting Motor | Starter Dynamo |
| Model | GS-113 |
| Voltage Regulation System | "Tirrill" regulator |

**BATTERY:**

| | |
|---|---|
| Manufacturer | Furukawa YU 252 |
| Model | BSP 3-12 MBH 3-12 |
| Capacity | 10 AH. |

**CARBURETOR:**

| | |
|---|---|
| Manufacturer | Mikuni |
| Model | M 21 S 1 |
| Type of Air Cleaner | Steel Wool |
| Tank Capacity | 8.5 $l$ |
| Lubrication System | Lubrication oil mixing |

## Model YA5, view from four sides

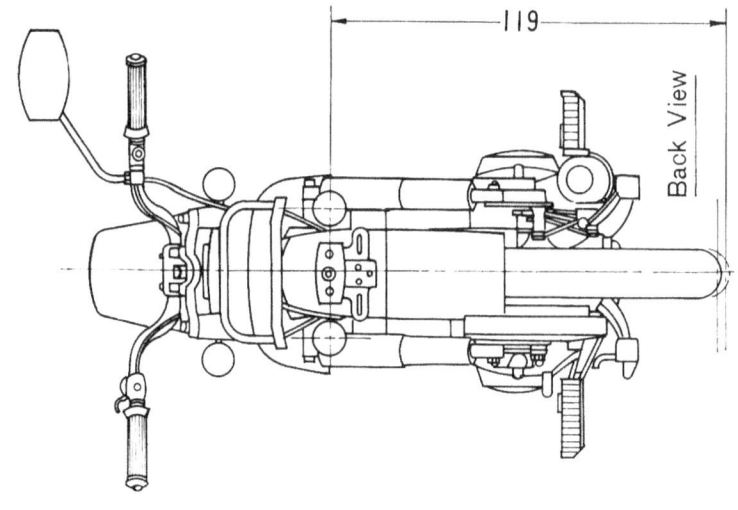

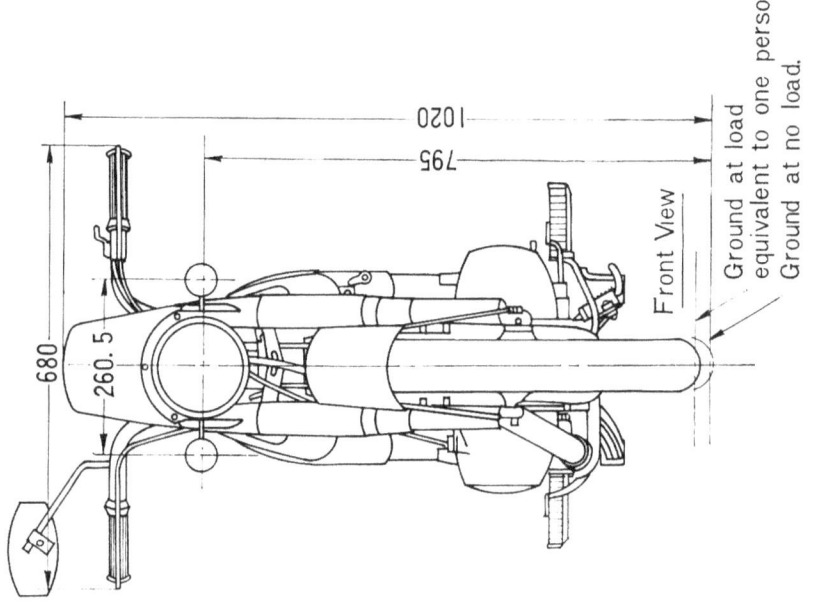

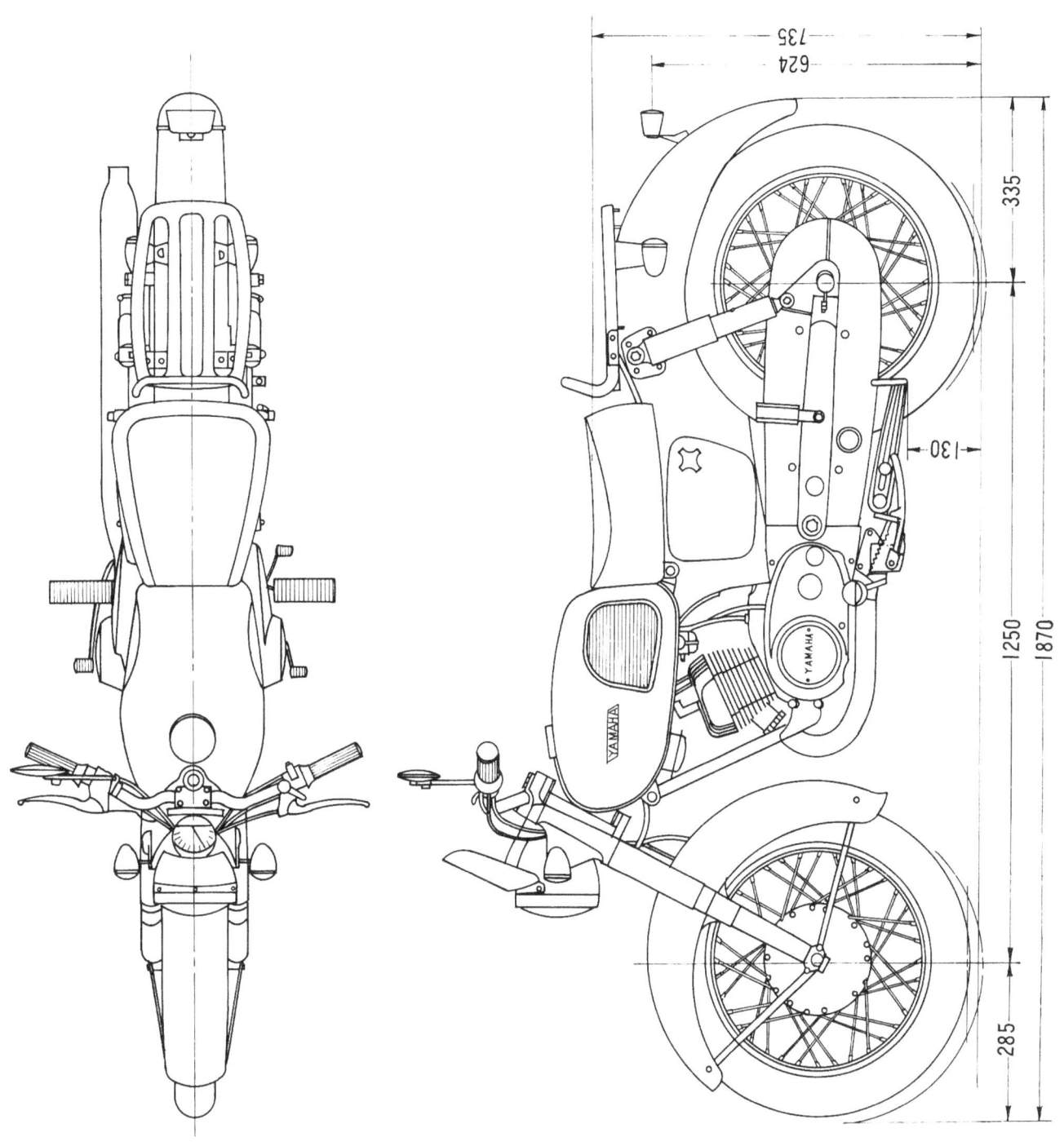

| | |
|---|---|
| Fuel Ratio (gasoline : oil) | 20 : 1 |

**CLUTCH:**

| | |
|---|---|
| Type | Wet multiplate clutch |
| Position to be Attached | Transmission main shaft |
| Material of Clutch Disk | Mould Cork |
| Primary Reduction System | Chain |
| Primary Reduction Ratio | 2.785 |

**TRANSMISSON:**

| | | |
|---|---|---|
| Type | Constant mesh (four steps gear) | |
| Operation System | Left Foot Pedal | |
| Gear Ratio | (low gear) | 2.965 |
| | (2nd gear) | 1.794 |
| | (3rd gear) | 1.291 |
| | (top gear) | 1.000 |

**FINAL DRIVE:**

| | |
|---|---|
| Type | Chain |
| Reduction Ratio | 2.733 |

**FRAME:**

| | | |
|---|---|---|
| Type | Monocock | Backbone |
| Suspension | Front | Telescopic Fork |
| | Rear | Swing Arm |
| Cushion unit | Front | Coil Spring |
| | | Oil Damper |
| | Rear | Coil Spring |
| | | Oil Damper |

**STEERING SYSTEM:**

| | |
|---|---|
| Type of Handle | Pipe |
| Steering Angle | R & L 45° |
| Caster | 63° |
| Trail | 93 mm |

**TIRE:**

| | |
|---|---|
| Front | 300-16-2P |
| Rear | 300-16-4P |

**BRAKE:**

| | |
|---|---|
| Type | Internal Expanding |

**LIGHTING SYSTEM:**

| | |
|---|---|
| Head Light | 35W/25W 12-16V |
| Tail Light | 20W/5W |
| Stop Light | 20W/5W |
| Direction Indicator | 8W × 4W |
| Pilot Light | 2W |

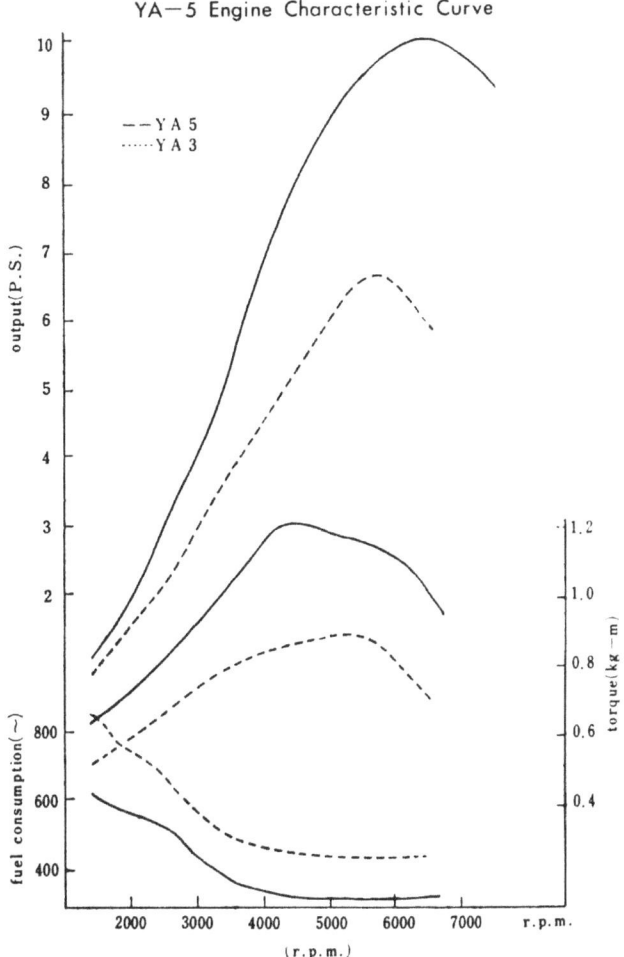

## 1—3 COMPLETELY NEW MECHANISMS OF THE YA-5

### 1—3—1 Rotary Valve

#### (A) THE REASON WHY THE ROTARY VALVE HAS BEEN ADOPTED

The today's 125 cc motorcycle shows a tendency to increase the engine power by adopting the twin cylinder casting system. However, when popularizing the motorcycle, its double cylindered engine encounters a difficulty in the aspects as construction, durability, operation and price.

For the above reasons, our technical staff have made every possible effort in creating more excellent type of machine than the double cylinder engine. The rotary valve applied to the single cylinder one is the fruit of our collective achievement. It excels the double cylinder engine in power and speed.

#### (B) WHAT IS THE ROTARY VALVE?

In the engine of the ordinary motorcycle, the valve means the device for controlling the suction and exhaust in the four cycle engine. To be exact, this is the poppet valve. There are various kinds of valve. One of them is the rotary valve.

The poppet valve moves up and down, i. e. in the straight direction, while the rotary one takes a rotary motion. Hence the name.

The rotary valve is considered as the device which controls the suction and exhaust that the poppet valve of four cycle and the cylinder port of two cycle do. Usually it serves chiefly to control the suction.

The exhaust is controlled by the piston valve.

Now the mechanism of the rotary valve. The plastic disk with a notch is attached around the crank shaft, and as the crank revolves, it rotates to open or close the inlet port in the crank chamber. Unlike the conventional valve, the fuel enters directly into the crank chamber. For this purpose, the carburetor is built in the crank case.

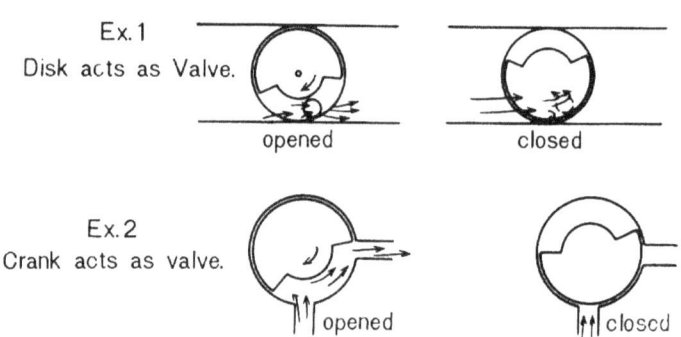

Example of Rotary Valve

Ex. 1 Disk acts as Valve.
opened    closed

Ex. 2 Crank acts as valve.
opened    closed

### (C) WHY DOES THE ROTARY VALVE IMPROVE THE PERFORMANCE?

In case of two cycle, the suction and exhaust are controled by opening or closing the cylinder port by means of the cylinder drum. This method is very good, but its unsatisfactory port-timing is one serious draw-back.

In order to keep the engine in the best condition, the sufficient fuel should be sucked. For this purpose, the suction time should be prolonged. In addition, if its start is not early and its finish also is not early, it has little effect. Because the gas in the case is compressed near the end of the suction.

The conventional valve is inconvenient in the above point. For example, assume that the beginning of the suction is 50° before the upper dead point, and its end is 50° after the upper dead point.

To correct this defect, the rotary valve has been adopted. It controls the suction timing not by the piston stroke, but by the revolution of the crank shaft. In the rotary valve, it is possible to adjust the suction timing freely by

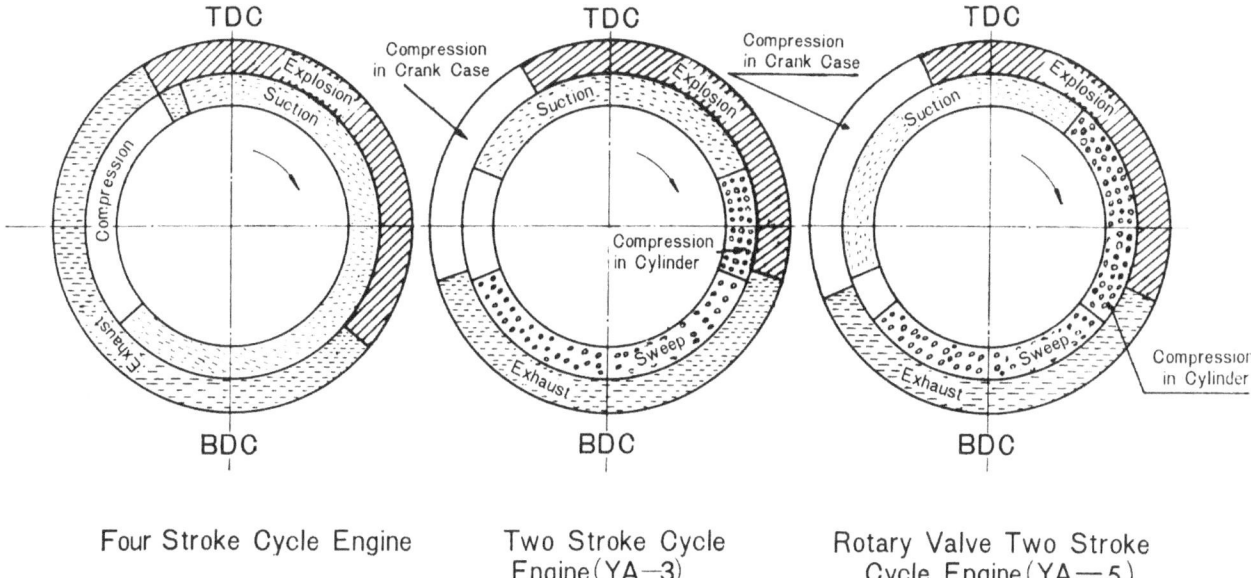

Four Stroke Cycle Engine     Two Stroke Cycle Engine (YA-3)     Rotary Valve Two Stroke Cycle Engine (YA-5)

## PARISON IN PORT TIMINGS

changing the notch of the disk. The timing of the suction and exhaust of YA-3 and YA-5 is illustrated by the diagrams below.

As shown by the diagrams, the timing of YA-5 is the most excellent.

The improvement in the suction timing results in the increase of the suction efficiency and the possibility to enlarge the inlet port. Thus, the rotary valve has made it possible to increase the power remarkably.

### (D) OTHER ADVANTAGES OF THE ROTARY VALVE.

1. Improvement in performance at low speed.

As the rotary valve makes it possible to quicken the end of the timing, the low speed performance has been improved.

2. Improvement in fuel consumption.

As the end of the timing is quickened, the fuel is smoothly supplied.

Another advantage is to make it possible to adopt the third port described in the next sub-section.

### (E) DURABILITY OF ROTARY VALVE

As the rotary valve rotates at high speed, the inaccurate engineering work causes the compression leakage. However, since the valve of YA-5 is made of plastic, it resists heat and wear to a high degree.

The results of measurement of the resistance to the wear at trial running is given below.

    Abrasion after     10,000 km.         70～80 km/h

Case 0.04~0.06 mm
Valve 0.02~0.06 mm

# YA—5 ENGINE (ROTARY VALVE) DIAGRAM

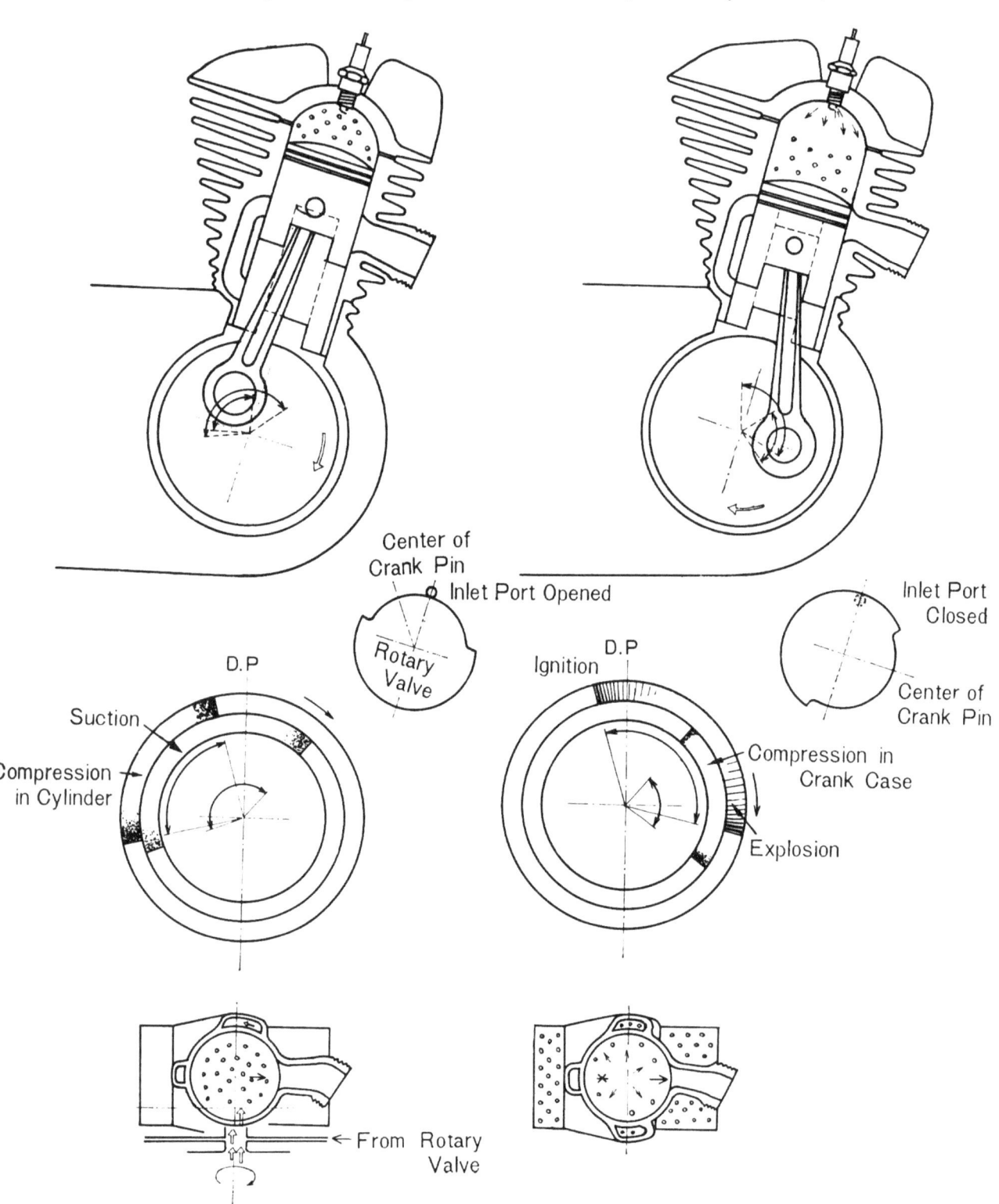

# EXHAUST / EXHAUST·SWEEP

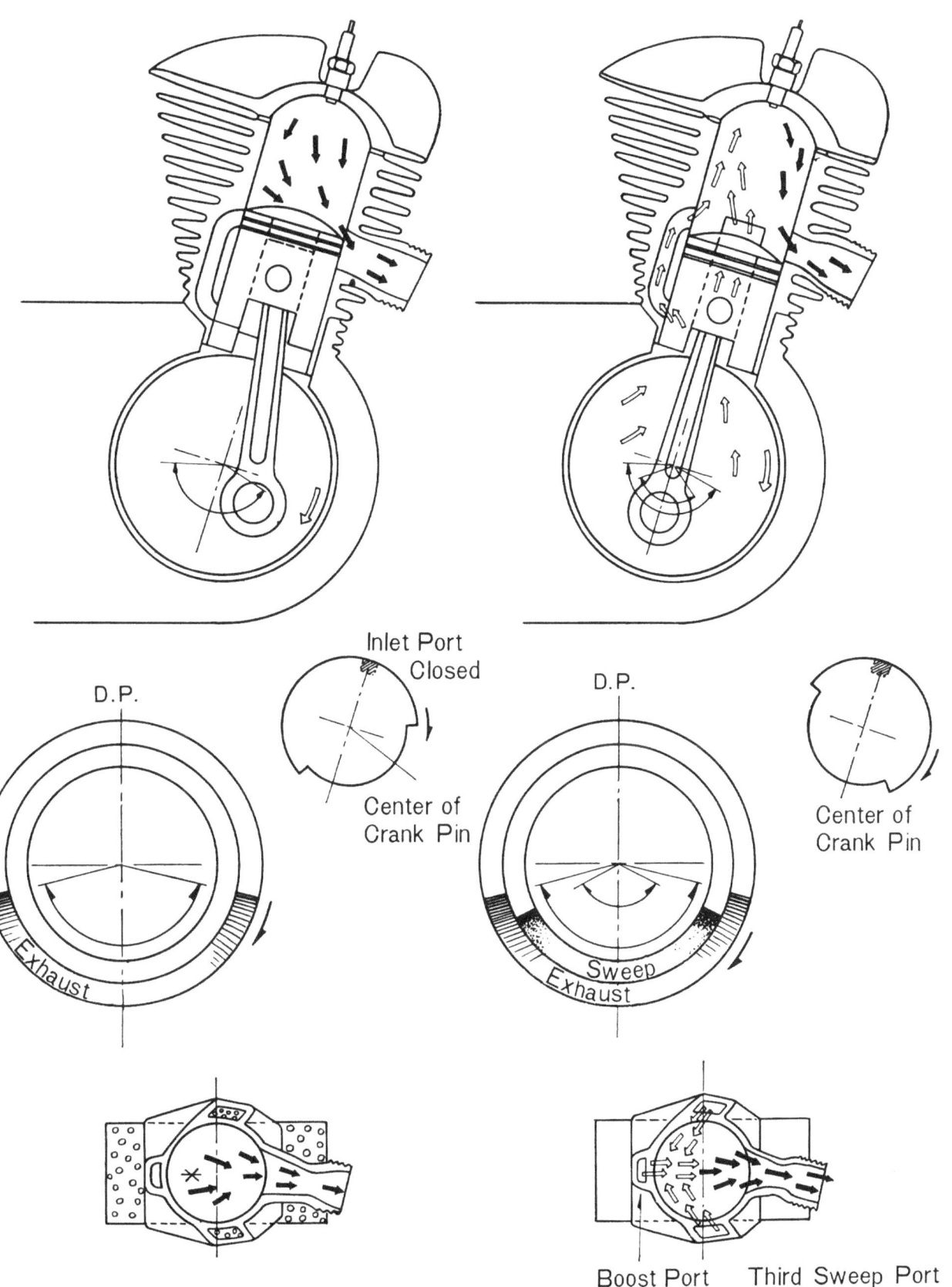

### 1—3—2 THIRD SWEEP PORT

The rotay valve has permitted to attach the carburetor to the crank case.

Therefore, the inlet port of the cylinder has fallen into disuse.

Intead of it, the sweep port has been applied. As the result, not only the sweep efficiency has been remarkably increased, but the performance has been sharply improved.

### 1—3—3 CARBURETOR WITH STARTER

The carburetor is the apparatus supplying the fuel to the engine.

The efficiency depends upon whether it satisfies the following three conditions.

1. The carburetor should supply an adequate amount of the mixture gas of the fuel and air to the engine according to its running condition.
2. The fuel should be vapourized as completely as possible.
3. The above operation should be automatic.

### A) Features

1. The driving at low speed is stable because of the special score system and the fuel consumption goes well than the conventional carburetor.
2. The special mechanism of the starting system results in more reliable and easier starting than the conventional choke and tickler system.
3. As the air breather has been adopted for the main system, not only the vapourization of the mixture gas, but also the acceleration has been improved.
4. The prolonged durability keep the performance unchangeable for any length of time.
5. Because of the simple construction, even the beginners can maintain the machine easily.

### B) Construction of starter

The starter serves as an apparatus making dense mixture gas suitable for starting when the engine is cold and its construction is as same as for the little carburetor. The air enters from the inlet port to the engine side through the starter plunger. At this time, the negative pressure acts on the end of the breather pipe. Then, the fuel spout out of the breather pipe through the starter jet, and it is mixed with the air supplied from the inlet port. Lastly, the appropriately dense mixture gas enters the engine.

C) **Starting**

a: Starting under freezing temperature:-

1. Open the starter valve to its full width, and fully shut the throttle valve, (idling opening)
2. Press the starter button.
3. Open the throttle valve after making sure of the engine starting.
4. Start to run, after making sure that, as the throttle valve is opened wider, the revolution of the engine is increased.
5. The starter valve should be closed after the engine is warmed up.

The conventional carburetor having the tickler and the shutter often did not

# DIAGRAM OF CARBURETOR WITH STARTER

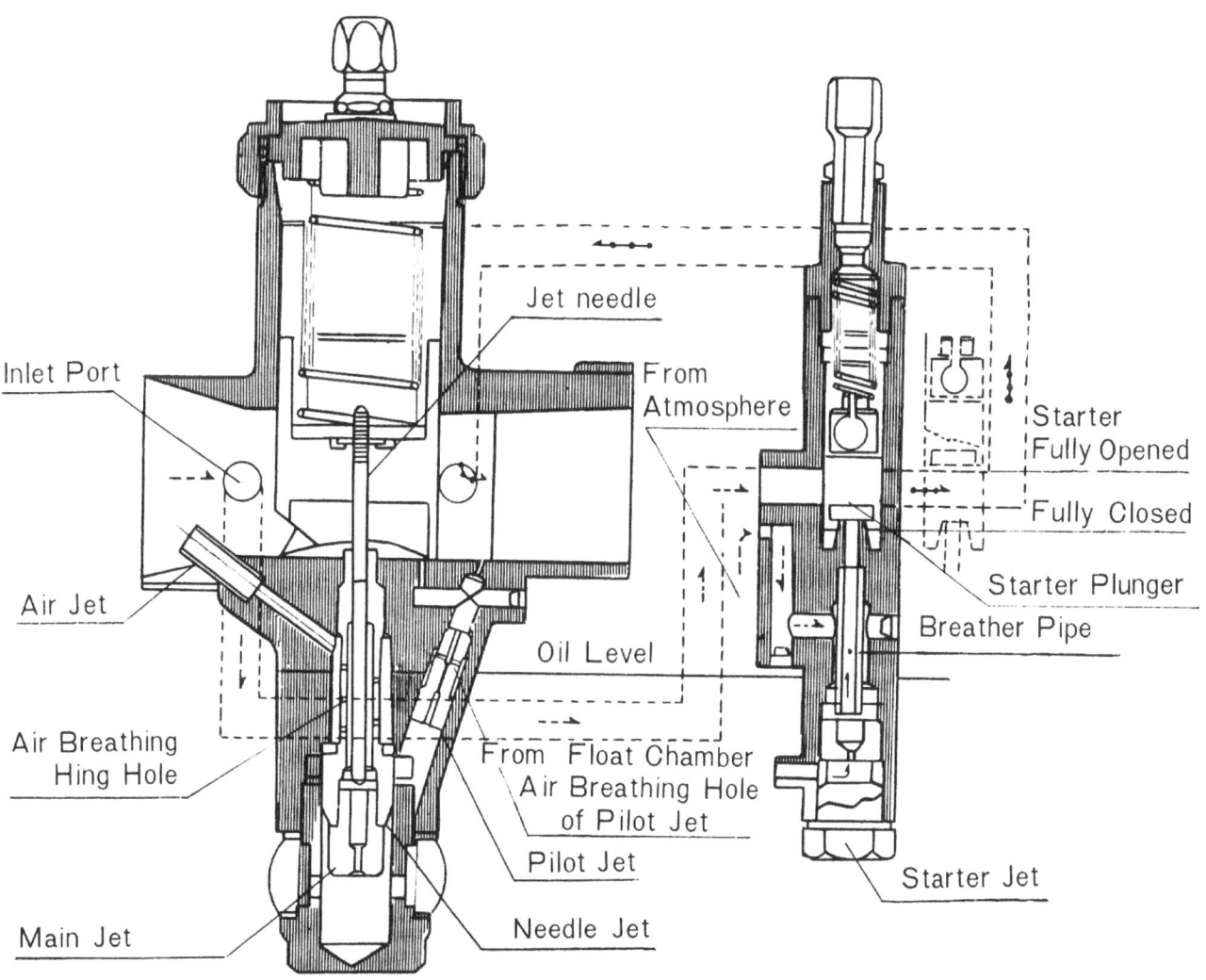

start promptly, for the mixture gas was too rich. But this carburetor with the starter works smoothly.

b: Starting when engine is warm

When the engine does not start by pressing the starter button, open the starter valve. After the starting of the engine, open the throttle valve. After making sure the revolution of the engine has been upped, close the starter valve. Then, start to run your machine.

## D) Adjustment

As the carburetor has underwent the rigid factory test and its every parts has been adjusted by the experts, its adjustment is not permitted except the following cases. When the engine is cold, tighten the air screw about 1/4 turns to smooth the fuel consumption. In summer, loosen it as much.

## 1—4 TOOLS FOR THE MODEL YA-5

As YAMAHA YA-5 has been designed in due consideration of YA-3 and YD-2, it is possible to maintain and care your machine with few tools.

The special tools for YAMAHA is described below.

### A: Tools for engine

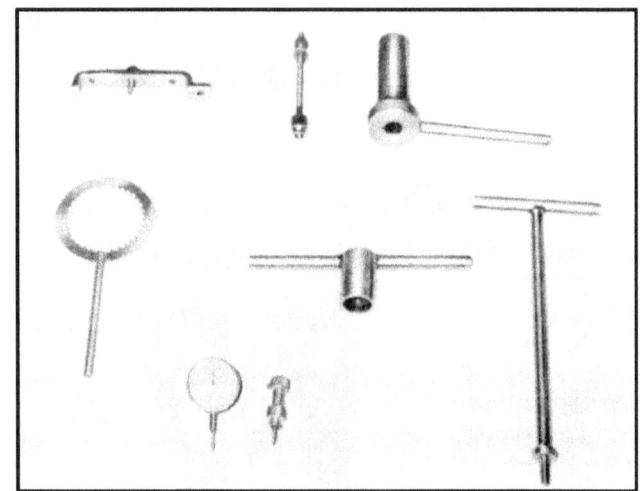

a. Valve cover pulling tool (served as the locating tool, too). (Left in the upper row in the picture)
b. Crank attaching tool (For the inner sleeve alone. For the outer sleeve MFI should be used). (Right in the upper row)
c. Tool for stopping rotation of clutch (Left in the lower row)

The above three items make one set. In addition, the crank case assembling tool, the dial gauge, the dial guage stand and others are necessary, but the tools hitherto in use serve the purpose.

### B: Tools for body

a. Front fork attaching-detaching tool (right in the lower row)

b.  Front fork disassembling tool (middle in the lower row)

## C: Testers

The electro-tester and the engine speed tester (tachometer) should be used as before.

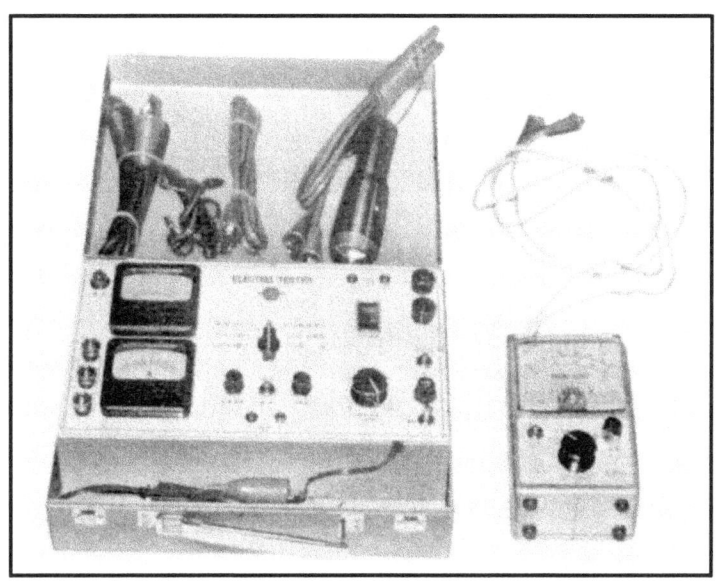

# CHAPTER 2. ENGINE

## 2—1 OVERHAULING ENGINE

### 2—1—1 ATTACHING AND DETACHING ENGINE

**How to detach**

a. Loosen the exhaust pipe lock nuts and remove the exhaust pipe.
b. Dismantle the carburetor cover, Then, remove the throttle wire and the starter one.
c. Remove the inlet-cover, then the fuel pipe.
d. Remove the kick pedal, then the change pedal.
e. Loosen the left case cover screws, and dismantle the cover.
f. Remove the starter dynamo wiring. At the same time, remove the neutral switch cord without fail.
g. Unscrew the chain case lock bolts, and remove a lower part of the case.
h. Remove the chain clip, then the chain.
i. Remove the four bolts holding the engine, and the engine is detached.

**How to attach**

Attach the engine in the reverse order of the above instructions.

When making a trial run just after attaching the engine, make sure there is mission oil.

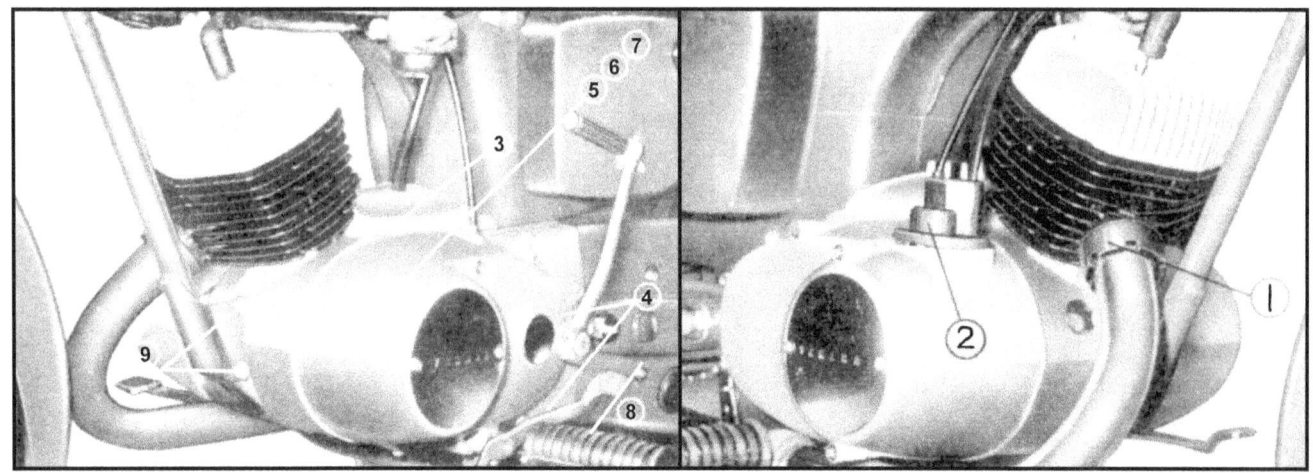

## 2—1—2  HOW TO DISASSEMBLE CYLINDER

a. Unscrew the cylinder head nut with a 14mm box spanner, and remove the cylinder head. Then, pull out the cylinder head packing. Lift the cylinder, and it is detached.

b. After packing the wess in the crank case so that the gudgeon pin clip may not fall in the crank chamber, remove the clip with a prier.
Next, remove the piston pin with a soft hammer and the piston is detached.

## 2—1—3  HOW TO DISASSEMBLE CRANK CASE COVER (LEFT)

a. Unscrew 6 bolts holding the left case cover.
Dismantle the case cover, and remove the clutch wire from the clutch lever.

b. Remove the dynamo lead from the distributor cap.
Unscrew the armature lock bolts, and remove the governer.
Unscrew 2 bolts locking the dynamo yoke, and remove the dynamo yoke from the crank case.

c. Remove the armature with an armature pulling tool.

d. Loosen the drive sproket lock nut (left handed).

## 2—1—4  HOW TO DISASSEMBLE CRANK CASE COVER (RIGHT)

a. Unscrew the crank case cover lock bolts, and dismantle the case cover with a soft hammer.

b. Unscrew 4 clutch spring caps (left handed) with a driver. Then, pull out the spring and its sleeve.
At the same time, pull out the clutch pressure plate and the clutch disks.

c. Pull out the push rod.

d. Loosen the clutch lock nut when holding the clutch boss with a clutch locking tool. Then, remove it.

e. Loosen the primary sproket lock nut when holding it with the clutch locking tool. Then, remove it.

f. Remove the boss.

g. Remove at once the primary sproket, the clutch housing and the primary chain.

h. Pull out the main shaft spacer, then the adjusting washer.

i. Remove the clips of the shifter shaft and the change shaft. Then, remove the shifter pawl holder, the change lever spring, the shifter segment and the collar washer.

j. Unscrew 4 screws holding the crank case bottom plate.
Then, remove the bottom plate.
If the bottom plate is not detached easily because of the adhesive, remove it with a soft hammer.
Do not gouge with a driver. If do so, it will result in oil leaking.

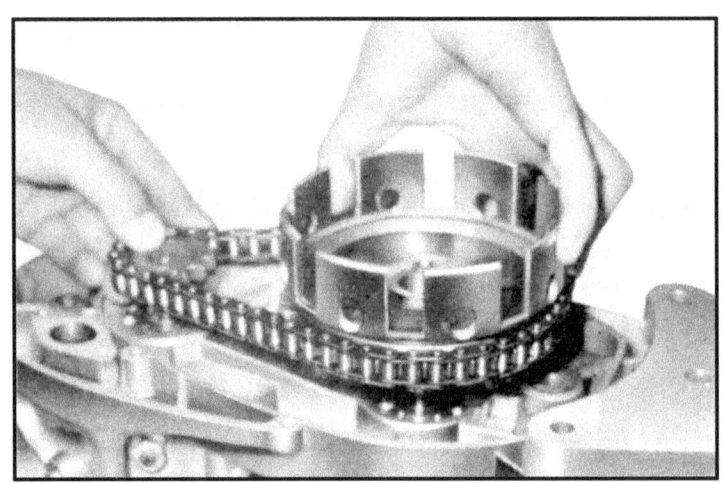

### 2—1—5 HOW TO DISASSEMBLE CRANK CASE

a. Remove the crank case lock bolts.

b. Plant the bolt at the end of a crank case disassembling tool in the exclusive bolt hole in the dynamo locking section of the left crank case.

c. Disassemble the case turning the handle of the tool. Adjust the position of the case with the soft hammer from time to time, and disassemble it.

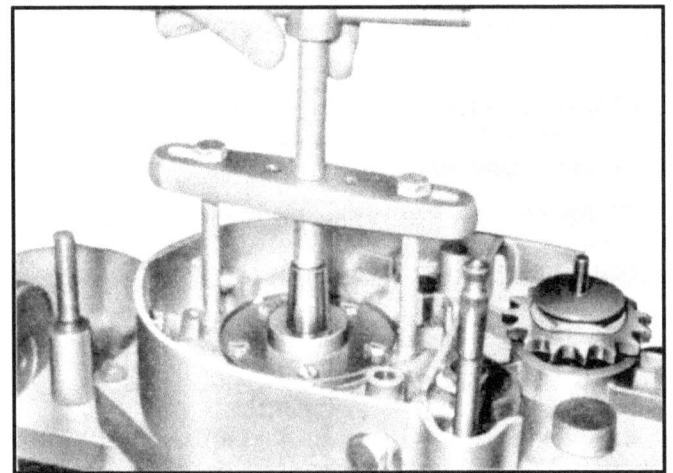

### 2—1—6 HOW TO DISASSEMBLE KICK

a. Remove the kick shaft clip.

b. Remove the kick shaft spacer, and pull out the spring.

c. Remove the clip, and pull out the kick gear.

## 2—1—7 HOW TO DISASSEMBLE MISSION CHANGE

a. Remove the change shaft clip, then the change shaft.
b. Remove at once the transmission gear and the shifter.
c. Remove the main shaft with a soft hammer.

## 2—1—8 HOW TO DISASSEMBLE CRANK AND VALVE

a. Remove the crank out of the right crank case with a crank pulling tool.
b. Dismantle the valve cover with a valve cover pulling tool.
c. Remove the valve spacer from the clutch side with a soft hammer.
d. Remove the valve.
e. Unscrew 4 screws holding the oil seal housing of the left crank case. Then, remove the housing.
f. Pull out the left crank shaft bearing toward the crank.
g. Push out the right crank case bearing No. 16005 toward the clutch.
h. Pull out the valve cover bearing No. 6304 toward the crank.

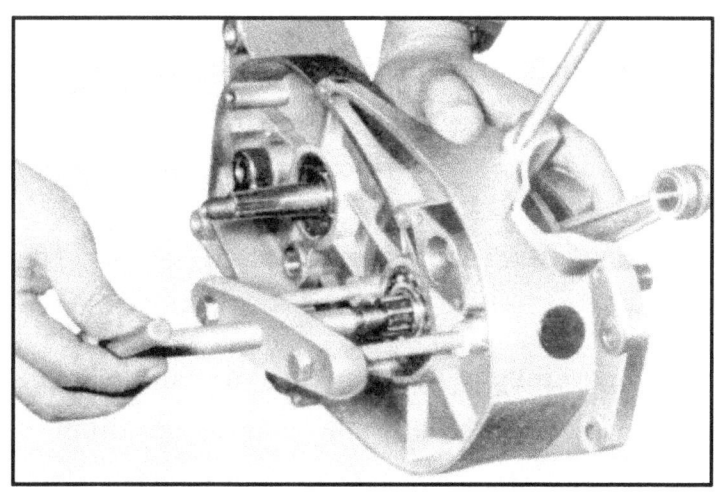

## 2—2  ASSEMBLY

### 2—2—1  CRANK CASE ASSEMBLY

The YA-5 possesses the aluminium alloy die-cast crank cases. They are devided into the right and left cases, which are adhered by adhesive (Araldite) and secured bolts.

Component parts of the crank case assembly are shown by the diagram below.

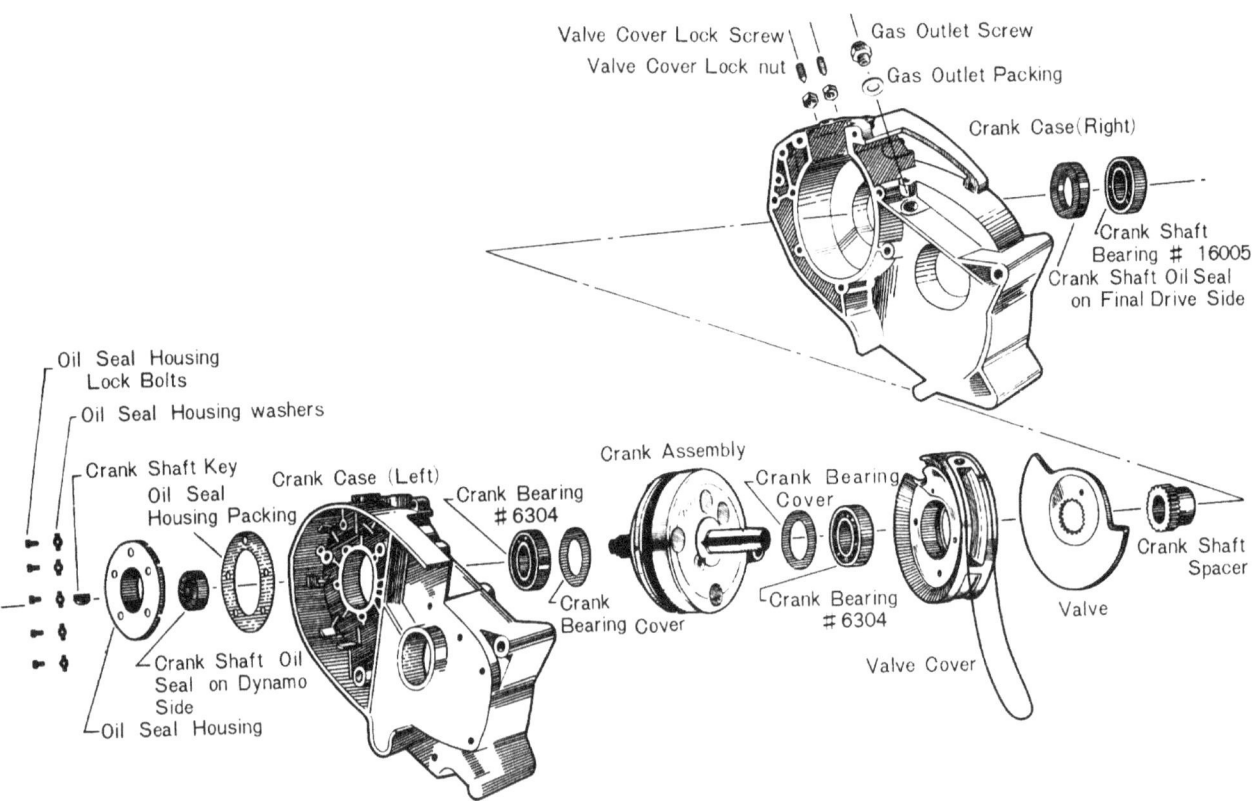

### Inspection

Make sure the contact surface of the crank cases and of the crank case covers have not a score. Note that the score causes oil leaking. If there is a score, repair it.

### How to assemble (insertion of bearing oil seal)

### WASHING:

Rub away "Araldite" carefully with a spatula or sand-paper soaking the crank case in washing oil. Then, wash the crank case in gasoline or alkaline abluent, and wipe it with a clean wess.

## INSERTING CLIPS:

The clips to be inserted are indicated below.

| | | |
|---|---|---|
| Left crank case | Main shaft bearing clip | 1 piece |
| Right crank case | Crank shaft bearing clip | 1 piece |
| | Main shaft bearing clip | 1 piece |

## Attaching bearing and oil seals around shaft:

Make sure that the contact surfaces of the bearings have not a score and that the oil seal housing is planed off.

If there is a score or the latter is insufficiently planed off, attach them after repairing. It is advisable to attach them arround the shafts with the aid of a press after heating the crank case up to about 120°C.

## SHAFTS TO ATTACH BEARINGS AND OIL SEALS:

### Left Case

| Where attached | Name of Parts | Size | Number of Parts | Remarks |
|---|---|---|---|---|
| Crank shaft | Crank shaft bearing | #6304 C2 | 1 | Make both outer sides of bearing and crank case even. Face side with bearing number to crank. |
| Main shaft | Main shaft ball bearing on sprocket side | #16005 | 2 | First, attach one bearing around shaft with hammer until it touches clip, then spacer. Next, attach another |
| | Main shaft ball bearing spacer | | 1 | Face side with bearing number to the inside of case. |
| | Main shaft oil seal | SD 60×47×7 | 1 | Face side with bearing number to secondary chain. |
| Kick shaft | Oil seal | S 20×30×7 | 1 | 〃 |
| Change shaft | Oil seal | S 12×22×7 | 1 | 〃 |
| Intermediate shaft | Intermediate shaft bearing metal | Oil-containing alloy | 1 | |

# Right Case

| Where attached | Name of Parts | Size | Number of Parts | Remarks |
|---|---|---|---|---|
| Crank shaft | Crank shaft bearing on final drive side | #16005 | 1 | Attach bearing on the outside of case. Face side with bearing number to primary chain. |
| | Crank shaft oil seal on final drive side | SW 25×47×8 | 1 | Face side with number to primary chain. Attach it on the opposite side of bearing, i.e. on valve side. |
| Main shaft | Main shaft bearing on clutch side | #6303 | 1 | Attach bearing around shaft with hammer until it touches clip. Face side with number to the inside of case. |
| Intermediate shaft | Intermediate shaft bearing metal | Oil-containing alloy | 1 | |

Lastly, drive one crank case pin into a pin hole at the rear section of the right crank case.

## Measurement

When replacing the crank case, it is advisable to take an accurate measurement of the distance from the contact of the cases to the following points: crank shaft bearing, main shaft bearing, intermediate shaft bearing and shifter cam shaft bearing.

## DISTANCE:

### Distance from contact surface

| | |
|---|---|
| to crank shaft bearing of left case | 25.40~25.60 mm |
| to crank shaft bearing of right case | 25.40~25.65 mm |
| to drive pinion of left case | 28.90~29.20 mm |
| to main shaft bearing of right case | 32.00~31.75 mm |
| to intermediate shaft bearing of left case | 38.05~38.05 mm |
| to intermediate shaft bearing of right case | 31.30~31.35 mm |
| to shifter cam shaft bearing of left case | 53.00~31.35 mm |
| to shifter cam shaft bearing of right case | 38.00~38.00 mm |

## 2—2—2 ATTACHING ROTARY VALVE

The newly adopted rotary valve is one of the most delicate component of the engine assembly.

### Inspection

a. Lay the valve on a surface plate and check whether there is warp. If a warp is found, replace the valve.

b. Make sure the valve is not damaged, replace it.

c. Fit on the valve spline to the spacer and see if there is not a play. If there is a play, replace it.

d. Measure the undersize of valve thickness. If it is over the normal valve, replace it.

Thickness of valve: 4mm $\begin{smallmatrix} -0 \\ +0.05 \end{smallmatrix}$ limit for correction: 0.4mm

### Care in handling valve

As the valve is made of plastics and very delicate, handle it with care. Do not lay it on the metal. Do not put a thing on it. Because it warps. In addition, it is badly effected by moisture. Therefore, supply oil without fail after washing in gasoline.

### How To Attach

### A. Valve

a. Insert the crank shaft spacer into the crank shaft bearing of the right case till it reaches the outer end of the bearing.

On this occasion, face the spline side of the spacer to the crank chamber. Not that the excessive insertion of the spacer causes harm to the oil seal.

b. Set a carved mark on the valve to a mark on the spline side of the spacer. Then, fit the valve in the spacer spline. In this case, face the side with the mark to the crank chamber.

c. After attaching the valve, make sure it holds a correct position against the case. If not, correct it.

### B. Valve Cover

a. Hammer the crank shaft bearing No. 6304C3 into the valve cover, when facing the side with a bearing number to the crank.

b. Fit the O-ring in the valve cover groove.

c. Locate the valve cover with a locating tool (it also serves as a valve cover pulling tool), and fit on the cover with a plastic hammer. In this case, do not strike the bearing.

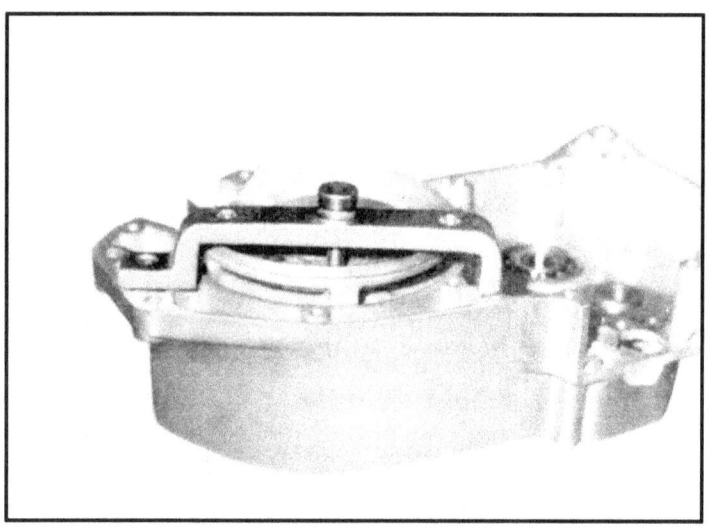

If you have no locating tool, it is advisable to attach the cover as follows. Adjust the crank case inlet port, the valve cover inlet port and the bolt hole for locating the valve cover, and bring them in a line. Then, attach them. And you will have a good result.

d. After attaching the valve cover, make sure that the valve cover inlet port is brought in a line with the crank case inlet port and that the hole of the crank case for a valve cover lock screw with the taper hole of the valve cover.

e. Hold the valve cover with 2 lock screws from the outside of the crank case. Then, tighten the valve cover lock nuts.

## 2—2—3 ATTACHING CRANKS

The cranks and the crank shaft are joined into one unit. The right and left cranks are connected with each other by the crank pin.

The sides of both cranks bear not only the carved serial number, but also 2 pieces of aluminium and 3 pieces of lead to balance them.

### Inspection

As the cranks require considerably high accuracy and has the elements to be worn out, in case of the engine overhaul, be sure to inspect it as indicated in the table below.

Component parts of the cranks are shown by the diagram below.

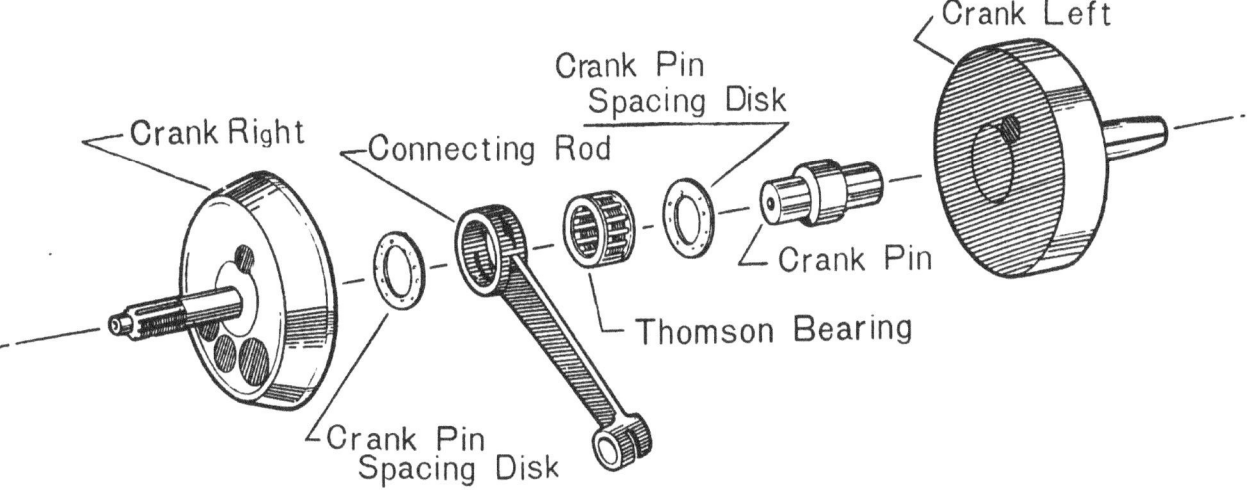

| | Inspection item | Criteria | Remedy |
|---|---|---|---|
| a | Fitness of piston pin to connecting rod small end. | When touching piston pin end, connecting rod should be lightly turned. | In case of loose fitness, replace bush. In case of tight fitness, adjust it with reamer. |
| b | Measurement of wear and tear of connecting rod big end by means of swing of small end. | Swing of connecting rod small end should be below 3 mm. | If it is 3 mm and over, disassemble crank, and check connecting rod and roller pin. Then, if faulty replace it. |
| c | Score or abrasion on crank shaft surface. | Allowance of abrasion should be below 0.05 mm. | If crank is worn out more than criteria, replace it. |

When disassembling the crank, check the crank pin as indicated below.

If the crank pin roller slide has a score or the undersize of the diameter is found to be above 0.05 mm in the maximum worn out section, replace the crank pin.

## The point in disassembling and repair of connecting rod

The radial clearance of the needle bearing in the connecting rod big end should be adjusted by the combination of the connecting rod and the crank pin listed in the table below.

|  |  | A | B | C |
|---|---|---|---|---|
| Outside diameter allowance of connecting rod | $23\phi \begin{array}{l}+0.013\\-0\end{array}$ | $+0.013$ / $-0.010$ | $+0.009$ / $-0.005$ | $+0.004$ / $-0$ |
| Inside diameter allowance of crank pin | $23\phi \begin{array}{l}+0\\-0.009\end{array}$ | $+0$ / $-0.003$ | $+0.004$ / $-0.006$ | $+0.007$ / $-0.007$ |
| Radial clearance |  | $+0.016$ / $-0.010$ | $+0.015$ / $-0.009$ | $+0.013$ / $-0.007$ |

By the above combinations the radial clearance* should be adjusted within the range of 0.007~0.016 mm.

\* Clearance perpendicular to radial axis

As the molicular coat lubricating oil is used for the needle bearing, do not wash it when assembling, except that it is considerably dirty.

## Accuracy test

After assembling the crank, check the motion and the play of the connecting rod. At the same time, take an accurate measurement of the following points.

a. By applying the dial gauge to the connecting rod small end, check whether the swing of the connecting rod small end is within 0.8 mm.

b. Check whether the axial play of the connecting rod big end is within the range of 0.1~0.2 mm. In this case, after pushing the connecting rod against one crank, measure with a thickness gauge the clearance between another crank and the lower end side of the connecting rod.

c. Measure with a micrometer the width and the inside width of the crank assembly, then check whether the obtaind values are equal to:

Width of crank assembly $51^{+1}_{-1.1}$

Inside width of crank assembly $9^{+1}_{-1.1}$

d. Support the crank assembly with two V-shaped blocks, and revolve it. Then, take an accurate measurement of the swing at the position shown in the diagram.

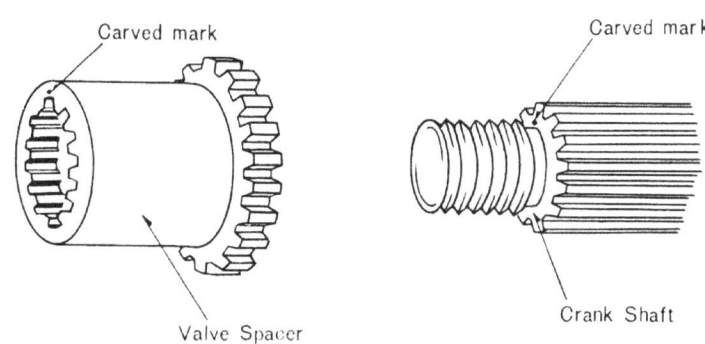

a) With of crank assembly
   $50{+0 \atop -0.1}$ mm
b) Swing of crank
   Readings of dial gauge;
   ① Within 0.02
   ② ″     0.06
   ③ ″     0.06
   ④ ″     0.02
   ⑤ ″     0.03

△Fulcrum

## Attaching crank

a. Wipe the crank with a wess, or clean it by giving blows.

b. Attach the bearing cover to the right and left cranks respectively. In case of the cranks built in the crank cases, a play of the cover is to be within the range of 0.15～0.2 mm. It is advisable to make use of the bearing cover served up to this time.*

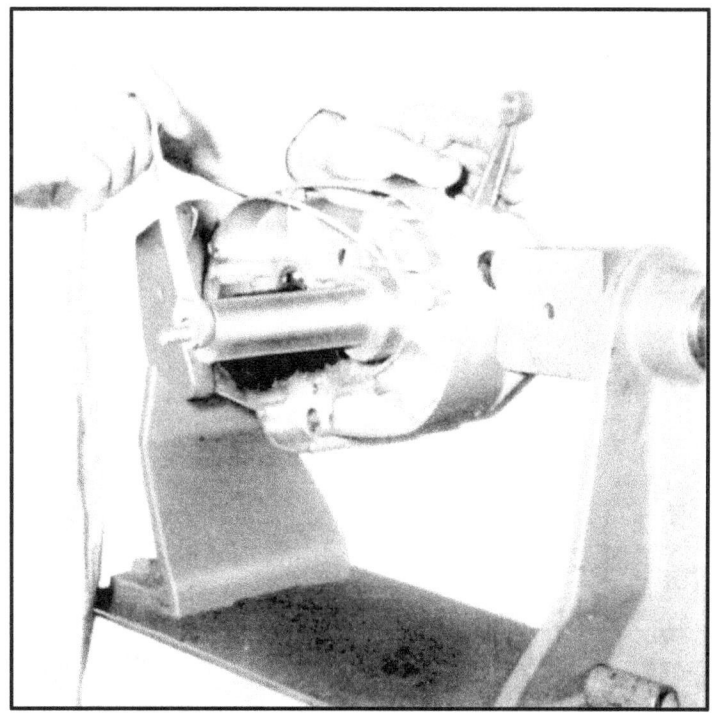

c. Insert the right side of the crank shaft (side with spline) into the right crank case, then interlock spline so that a carved mark on the outer side of the valve spacer and that of the crank shaft coincide.

d. Attach a crank fitting tool to the crank shaft head, and put the connecting rod on the cylinder locking hole. Then, turn the tool to the utmost. The crank being completely inserted, you will feel the spanner weighted.

---

* The crank shaft bearing cover is usually used without replacing. However, when replacing the case or the crank, it is necessary to newly determine the width of the cover by means of the obtained values and the expression below.

Width of bearing cover =
$$\left(\frac{\text{inside width of crank case-width of crank assembly}}{2}\right) - \text{Play } (0.15-0.2)$$

Then, remove the tool.

When making use of the tool, see if its outer sleeve reaches the crank shaft spacer. If not, the oil seal bearing is likely to be damaged, for the spacer becomes unstable.

e. After attaching the crank, make sure it works smoothly. At the same time, check the rotation of the valve.

f. At last, attach the crank shaft bearing cover to the left crank shaft.

## 2—2—4 ASSEMBLING TRANSMISSION

The transmission of the Model YA—5 is of the constant mesh type (four steps gear). The transmission is roughly devided as follows:

```
┌ Shifter mechanism ─┬ Shifter cam mechanism
│                    └ Shifter cam driving mechanism
└ Transmission gear mechanism
```

The next sub-section covers these mechanisms.

**Structure**

### A. Shifter cam mechanism

This mechanism conists of the following components: shifter A which drives a sliding gear of the main shaft, shifter B which drives a sliding gear of the

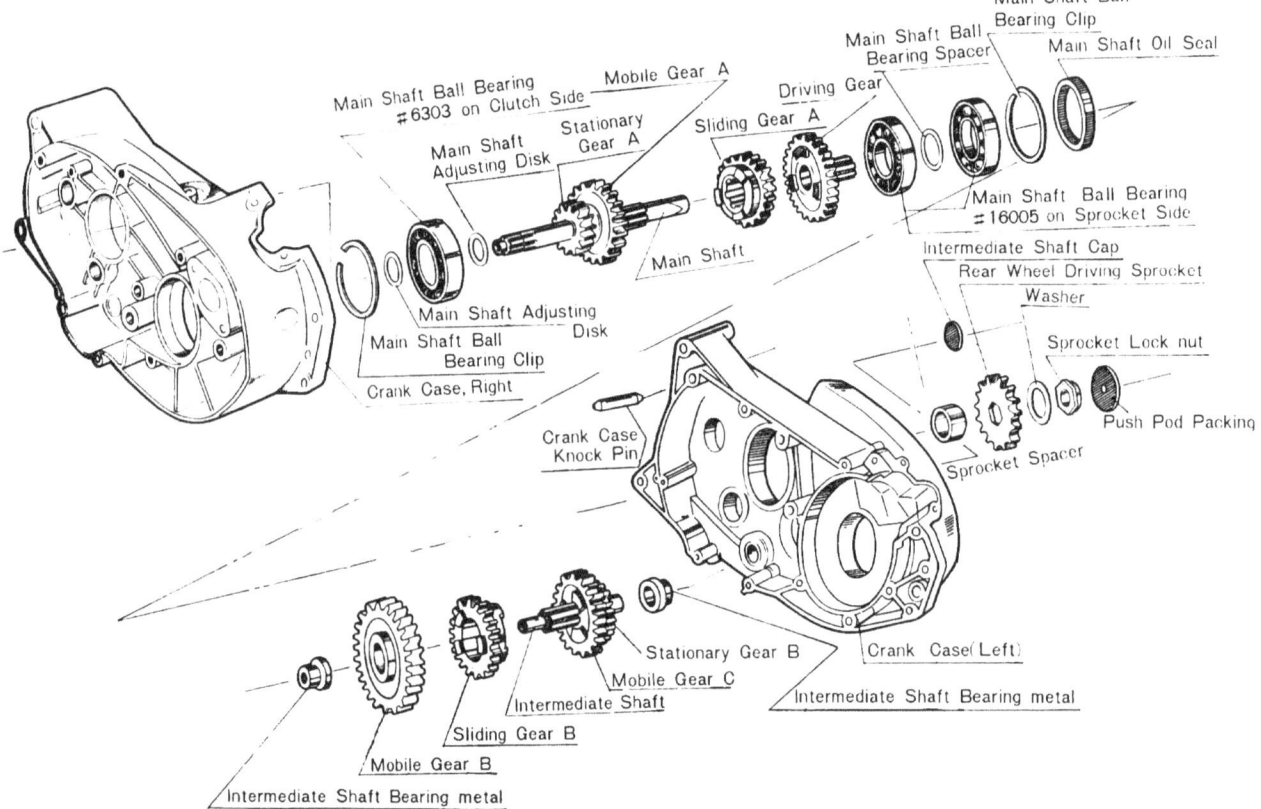

intermediate shaft, shifter cam shifter guide pin which guides the shifter and stopper pin which controls the shifter cam.

The shifter cam has a cam groove in which two shifters are fit by the guide pin.

Now, revolve the shifter cam and the guide pin will slide along the groove, while the shifter will do in the axial direction. The shifter cam makes one-fifth turns, i. e. 72° in case of neutral, low, 2nd, 3rd or top gears respectively, when each position is controlled by the stopper pin.

On the other hand, the shifter cam moves regularly owing to the cam groove.

The position of two guide pins in each steps, or relationship between the shifter movement and the cam groove, is shown in figure.

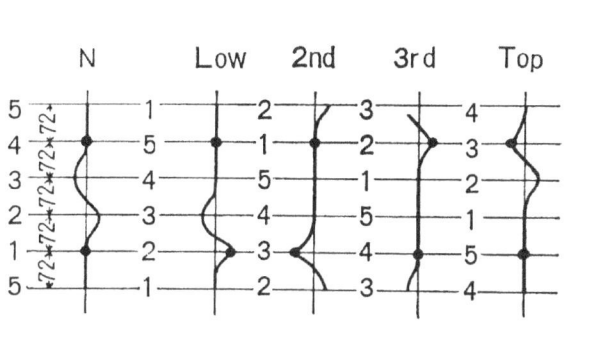

The figure shows that according as the shifter cam turns in the direction of arrow, its movement becomes speed-up or speed-down.

On the Model YA-5, the guide pin has a roller at its and so that the shifter may work smoothly.

## B. Shifter cam driving mechanism.

This mechanism gives rotation to the shifter cam through the movement of the change pedal.

In order to move the shifter regularly, it is necessary to revolve the shifter cam at regular intervals. On the Model YA—5, shifter cam makes one-fifth turns (72°) at each tread of the change pedal.

When treading the change pedal, the shifter pawl holder and the change shaft move simultaneously in the same way. Through this movement, the shifter pawl pushes a tooth of the shifter segment. At the same time, it gives rotation to the shifter cam connected with the above shifter segment.

The very moment the shifter cam has made 1/5 turns, the stopper pin stops it to move.

The shifter pawl holder is stopped to move by the stopper pin, while the

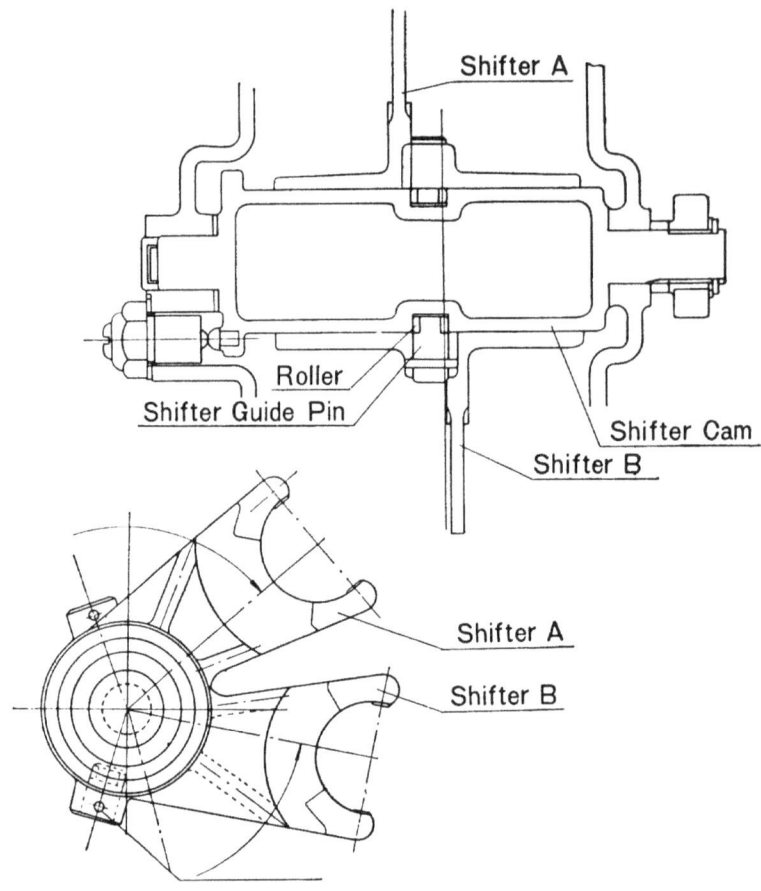

returning spring which has been opened by the spring cap connected with the holder returns the holder and the change lever to their place. In this case, the shifter pawl returns to its place sliding inside the holder and escaping from shifter segment.

By repeating this action the shifter cam is given rotation.

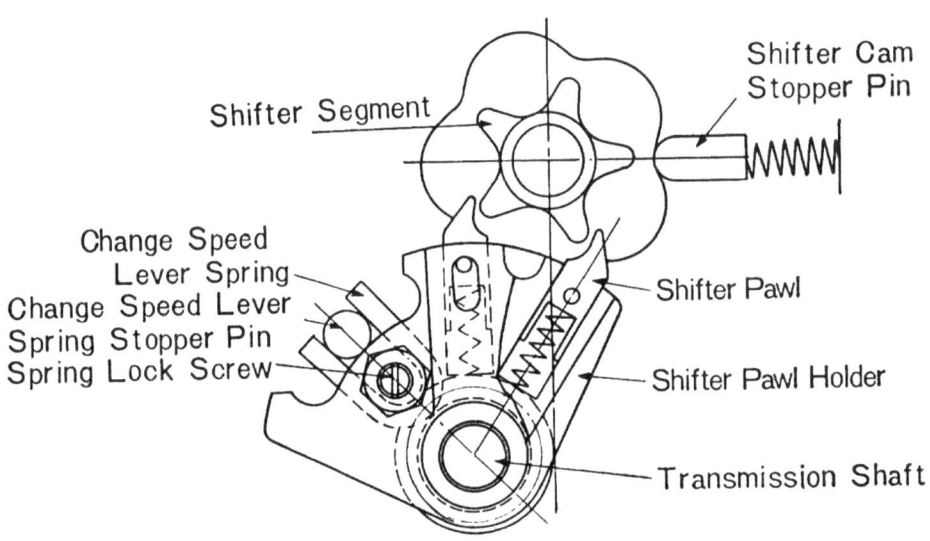

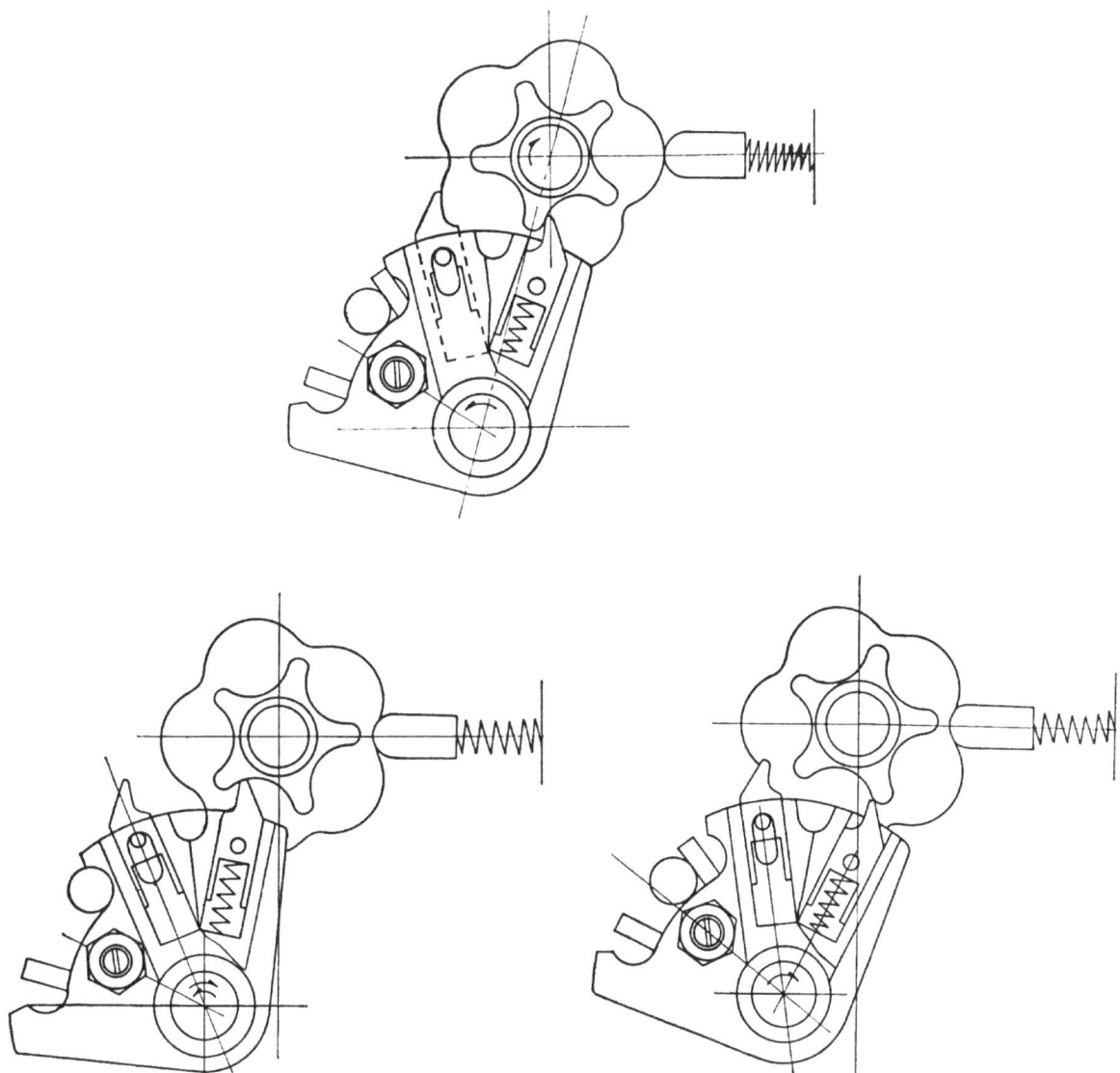

## C. Transmission gear

The transmission gear consists of 8 gears in addition to the drive sprocket. The motive power is transmitted into the main shaft through the primary and the dependent sprocket joined to the clutch housing, and then through the drive sprocket attached around the drive gear of the main shaft into the secondary chain.

The sliding gear (B) and the mobile gear (B) interlock, and the motive power generated by the engine is transmitted as follows:

Main shaft—stationary gear (A)— mobile gear (B)— intermediate shaft —stationary gear (B)—driving sprocket

$$\text{Reduction ratio} \quad \frac{31}{18} \times \frac{31}{18} = 2,965$$

# DISPOSITION OF TRANSMISSION GEARS

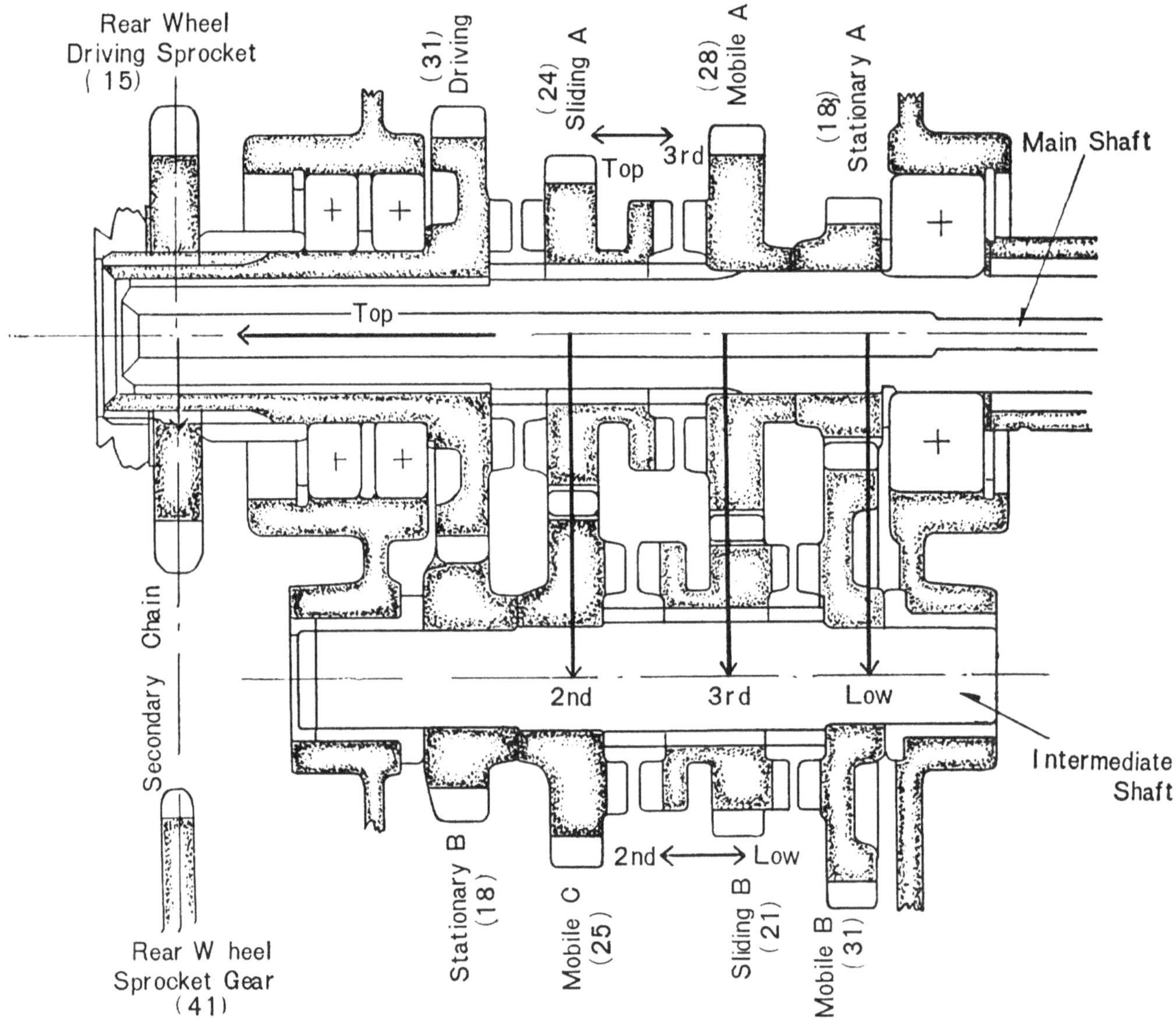

The sliding gear (B) and the mobile gear (C) interlock, and the power is transmitted as follows:

Main shaft—sliding gear (A)—mobile gear (C)—sliding gear (B)—intermediate shaft—stationary gear (B)—driving gear—driving sprocket

Reduction ratio $\dfrac{21}{28} \times \dfrac{31}{18} = 1,794$

The sliding gear (A) and the mobile

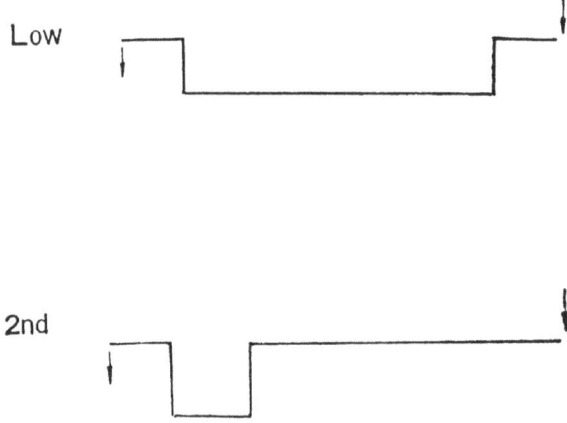

gear (A) interlock and the power is transmitted as follows:

Main shaft—sliding gear (A)—mobile gear (A)—sliding gear (B)—driving sprocket

Reduction ratio $\frac{21}{28} \times \frac{31}{18} = 1.291$

The sliding gear (A) and driving gear interlock and the power is transmitted to the driving sprocket along the main shaft.

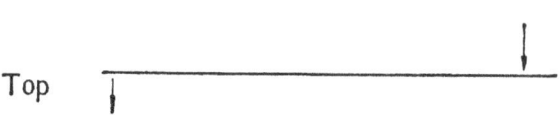

Reduction ratio      1.000

As the primary sprocket has 14 teeth and the dependent sprocket has 39 teeth. Therefore, primary reduction ratio is given as

$\frac{39}{14} = 2.715$

As the rear wheel driving sprocket has 15 teeth and the sprocket wheel 41 teeth, secondary reduction ratio is given as

$\frac{41}{15} = 2.73^*$

## Assembling

### A. How to assemble shifter cam

a. Insert the neutral switch contact point in the shifter cam.
b. Attach the shifter (A), and then the shifter (B) gently.
c. Attach the roller to the shifter guide pin with the planed off side upward, and fit the shifter boss in the cam groove.
   On this occasion, holes for the pin should be brought in a line.
d. Attach the guide pin. After making sure of smooth rotation of the shifter, secure it from both sides.

---

* General reduction are given as follows:
  First speed    $2.785 \times 2.965 \times 2.733 = 22.568$
  Second speed   $2.785 \times 1.794 \times 2.733 = 13.654$
  Third speed    $2.785 \times 1.291 \times 2.733 = 9.826$
  Fourth speed   $2.785 \times 1.000 \times 2.733 = 7.611$

### B. How to assemble shifter pawl holder.

a. Insert the spring and the pawl in the shifter pawl holder. Make sure the shifter pawl slides smoothly up and down.
When the shifter pawl slides down to the bottom, it should hide itself completely in the holder.

b. Insert the pawl stopper pin from the side with a long hole of the holder. On this occasion, if the stopper pin is inserted too deeply, its action becomes worse.

c. Attach the change lever spring lock screw from the side having the boss of the shifter pawl holder, then tighten it with a nut.

### C. How to assemble transmission gear

a. Attach the mobile gear A to the main shaft, and the mobile gear B to the intermediate shaft. Here, make sure that the clearance between the mobile gear and the stationary gear is within the range of 0.1~0.15 mm.

b. Heat the fixed gear up to 13°C~150°C, and attach it to the shaft with a press.

c. Measure the assembly width of the main and the intermediate shaft from each stationary gear to the outer side of the spline, and make a note.

### How to attach

### A. Main shaft

a. The main shaft adjusting washer inserted between the stationary gear A and the main shaft ball-bearing No. 6303 should be as thick as for the disk used up to this time.*

b. Insert the main shaft in the right crank case.

---

\* This adjusting washer is used without replacing. If the main shaft is renewed, its thickness is given by the expression below:
Thickness of main shaft adjusting washer =
(width of crank case) width of main shaft-clearance (0.05~0.20 mm)

### B. Shifter and sliding gear A

a. Turn the shifter groove of the sliding gear A to the right case, and fit the shifter A in it. Then, insert the shifter cam shaft (serrated side) in the right case.

At the same time, attach the sliding gear A to the shaft.

b. Attach the shifter cam adjusting ring around the shifter shaft on the side having the neutral switch.

### C. Intermediate shaft

a. Put the mobile gear B on the intermediate shaft bearing metal of the right case.

b. By facing the shifter groove of the sliding gear B to the left case, fit the shifter B in it.

c. Attach the intermediate shaft to the position where the spline groove of the sliding gear B and the intermediate shaft slide well. Then, insert it in the bearing metal through the mobile gear B.

d. Lastly, check whether the intermediate shaft works smoothly.

When the shifter competes with the sliding gear B, the intermediate shaft may not turn smoothly. If it turns simultaneously with the main shaft when out of gear, it means that the mobile gear does not work smoothly.

### D. Change shaft

a. Fit the snap ring in the groove of the change shaft.

b. Insert the change shaft ring in the snap ring (serrated side). Then, attach the change shaft to the right crank case.

### Inspection

After attaching, they should be inspected in the following order.

a. Adjust pawls of the gears by turning the main shaft. Then, by truning the shifter cam, check whether the shifter works smoothly.

b. Make sure the sliding gear A and B lie exactly in the middle of the adjacent gears when the shifter cam being in neutral position.

The clearance between pawls is 1.25 mm.

c. The depth of the gears is 3.75 mm.

If the depth is insufficient, correct it with the adjusting washer of the main shaft.

---

\* You need not replace this ring when reassembling.
If the shifter assembly should be replaced, its thickness is given by the next expression.
Thickness of shifter cam adjusting ring =
   crank case − width of shifter assembly − clearence (0.15~0.20 mm)

## 2—2—5 ATTACHING KICK ASSEMBLY

### How to assemble

First, heat the kick gear up to 130°~150°C. Second, insert the kick shaft in the gear from the side having the boss.

On this occasion, bring the end of the kick shaft in a line with that of the kick gear. Besides the relation between the position of the hole in which one end of the spring is fixed and the kick device position should be kept as shown by the right diagram.

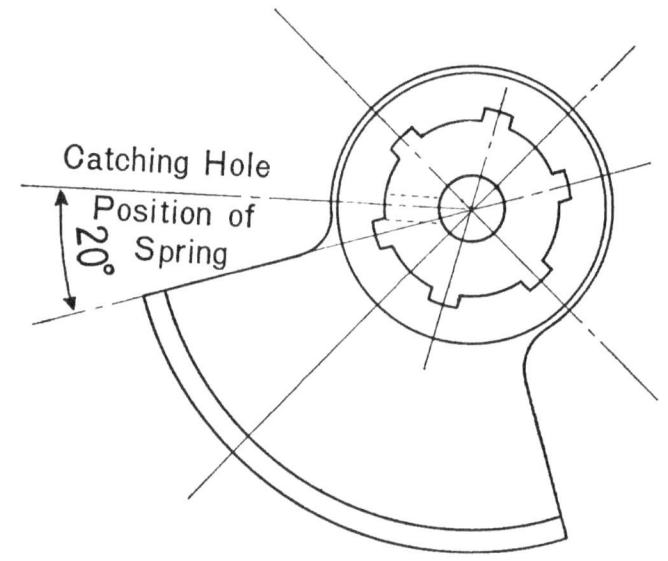

### Inspection

a. Make sure the teeth of the kick gear are not faulty or damaged.

b. See if the kick shaft is not bent.

### How to attach

a. Insert the kick shaft in the right crank case from the outside (clutch side) and secure it with the kick shaft clip.

b. Attach the kick spring arounnd the kick shaft and fix one end of the spring in the hole of the crank case.

c. After twisting another end of the kick spring with a kick spring fixing tool (used for YD) till it gets about

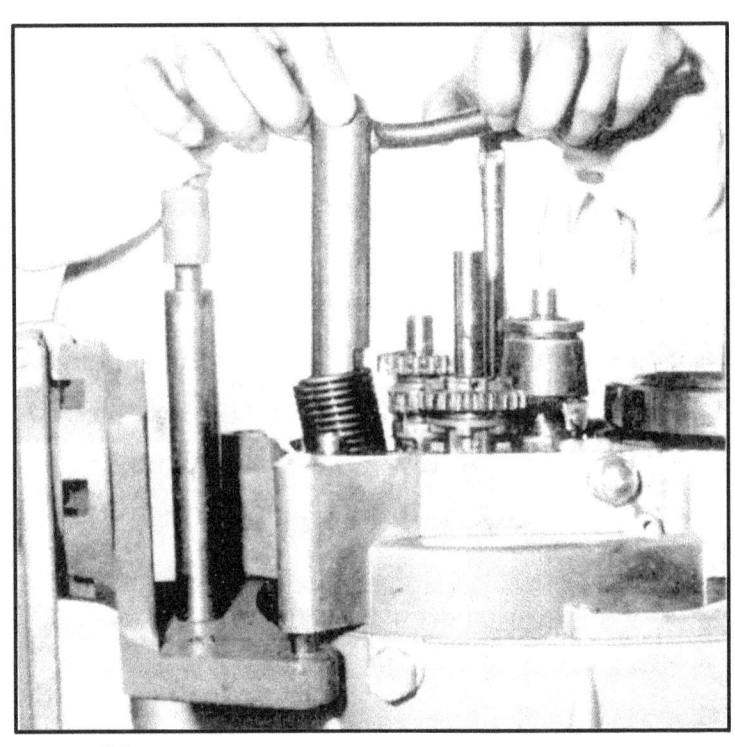

120°, insert it in the hole of the kick shaft.

d. Insert the kick spring support in the kick shaft, then fit the end of the kick spring in the groove, lastly, secure with the clip from the upside.

## 2—2—6 ASSEMBLING RIGHT AND LEFT CRANK CASES

After all the parts (crank, valve, transmission, and kick shaft) have been attached in the crank cases, the right and left crank cases are joined together.

**How to assmble**

a. Clean the contact surfaces of the right and the left crank cases.

b. Make sure all the parts have been inserted. In particular, the crank shaft bearing cover and the main shaft adjusting ring are likely to be omitted.

c. Dissolve "Araldite" * in the hardener, * and stir up them with a spatula. The correct ratio of "Araldite" and the the hardener is given below.

Araldite 10 : hardener 2~3

d. Spread "Araldite" on the contact surface of the left crank case with a finger tip.

e. Make sure the front and rear sections of the case contain the knock pin, and check with a plastic or wooden hammer whether the surfaces to be adhered are parallel with each other. Then, after revolving the rear wheel driving sprocket till gears stop to compete with each other, adhere the case closely.

f. After the cases have closely adhered each other, secure it with the case lock bolts below.

**Bolts**
 YS 12-6 25-15   2 pieces
 YS 12-6 40-15   4 pieces
 YS 12-6 45-15   2 pieces
 YS 12-6 58-15   4 pieces
 YS 12-6 68-15   1 pieces
 washer              11 pieces
 gasket               2 pieces

Tighten bolts in symmetrical order, and repeat it. Two bolts at the center of

---

\* Araldite—A kind of adhesive
  Hardener—If Arardite is dissolved in the hardener, it hardens with time and makes it possible to adhere more firmly.

42

lower part of the case should be tighten with a gasket.

g. After tightening bolts, clean the cases, especially the cylinder part.

h. See if the crank works smoothly. If it does not revolve smoothly, adjust the clearance between the crank case by tapping crank shaft with a plastic hammer.

## 2—2—7 ATTACHING CHANGE DRIVING MECHANISM
### Attaching
### A. SHIFTER CAM STOPPER PIN

a) Insert the shifter cam stopper pin in its hole situated in the left case, then the shifter cam stopper pin spring.

b) Attach a packing to the shifter cam stopper screw, and tighten it. Next, fit the stoppor pin in the stopper groove by revolving the shifter cam.

### B. SHIFTER PAWL HOLDER

a) Attach the change lever spring stopper pin to the right case.

b) Insert the change lever spring in the boss of the holder assembly, and hold the spring lock screw between ends of the spring.

c) Insert the holder assembly in the change shaft serration from the boss side, and hold the spring stopper pin between ends of the spring.

d) Hold in place the end of the change shaft with a clip.

### C. SHIFTER SEGMENT

a) Fit on the shifter cam shaft spacer to the shifter cam shaft of the right case.

b) Make sure that the stopper pin is fit in the stopper groove of the shifter cam.

c) Insert the shifter segment in the serration with a due regard to the position of the teeth.

d) Insert shifter segment spacer, and hold it in place with a clip.

e) Adjust the clearance between the shifter pawl and the segment tooth by turning the screw for looking the change lever spring. After the adjustment, tighten the screw and nut firmly without fail. If not, the change driving mechanism gets out of gear.

## D. NEUTRAL SWITCH AND PACKING

a) Attach the neutral switch to the left case. On this occasion, insert 1mm. packing in between.

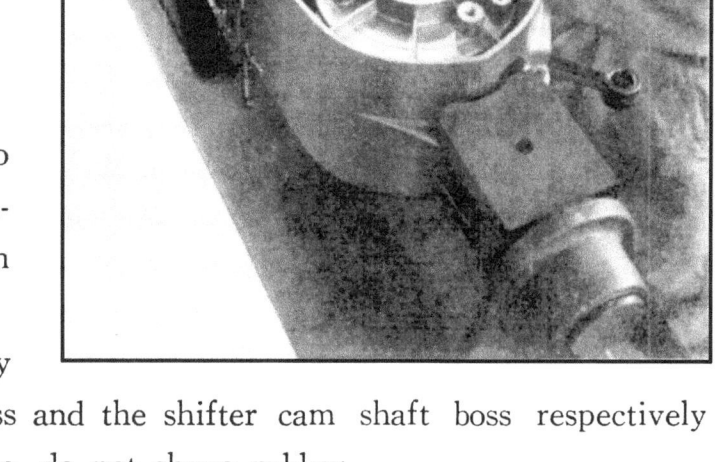

b) Attach the caps horizontally to the intermediate shaft boss and the shifter cam shaft boss respectively with a hammer. In this case, do not shave rubber.

## INSPECTION

After attaching the change pedal to the change shaft, observe the inner part of the crank case from a peep hole and check the engine action in the following order by revolving the driving wheel and treading the change pedal toward front and rear.

a. Tread the change pedal up and down, and release it suddenly. Does it return to its former place?
b. Is the shifter segment driven regularly?
c. Does the shifter pawl work smoothly?
d. Does the shifter work smoothly?

## ATTACHING BOTTOM PLATE OF CRANK CASE

After the inspection of the change mechanism, attach the bottom plate.

a. Attach the packing for the crank case bottom plate with adhesive, then the crank case bottom plate.

b. Hold the bottom plate tightly with 4 screws and 4 gasket.

c. Attach the oil drain packing and the oil retainer screw to oil drain port in the bottom plate.

## ATTACHING GAS DRAIN PLUG

Attach the gas drain plug and the packing to the gas drain port in the upper part of the crank case.

## 2 2—8 ATTACHING CLUTCH

The clutch is of the wet multiple-disk type which consists of 5 friction disks of mould cork.

The clutch housing is connected closely with the primary drive sprocket in addition to the kick pinion. The primary drive is transmitted by the roller chain DK 328 (54 pitches).

As the primary sprocket has 14 teeth and the dependent sprocket has 39 teeth, the primary reduction ratio is given as

$$\frac{39}{14} = 2.715$$

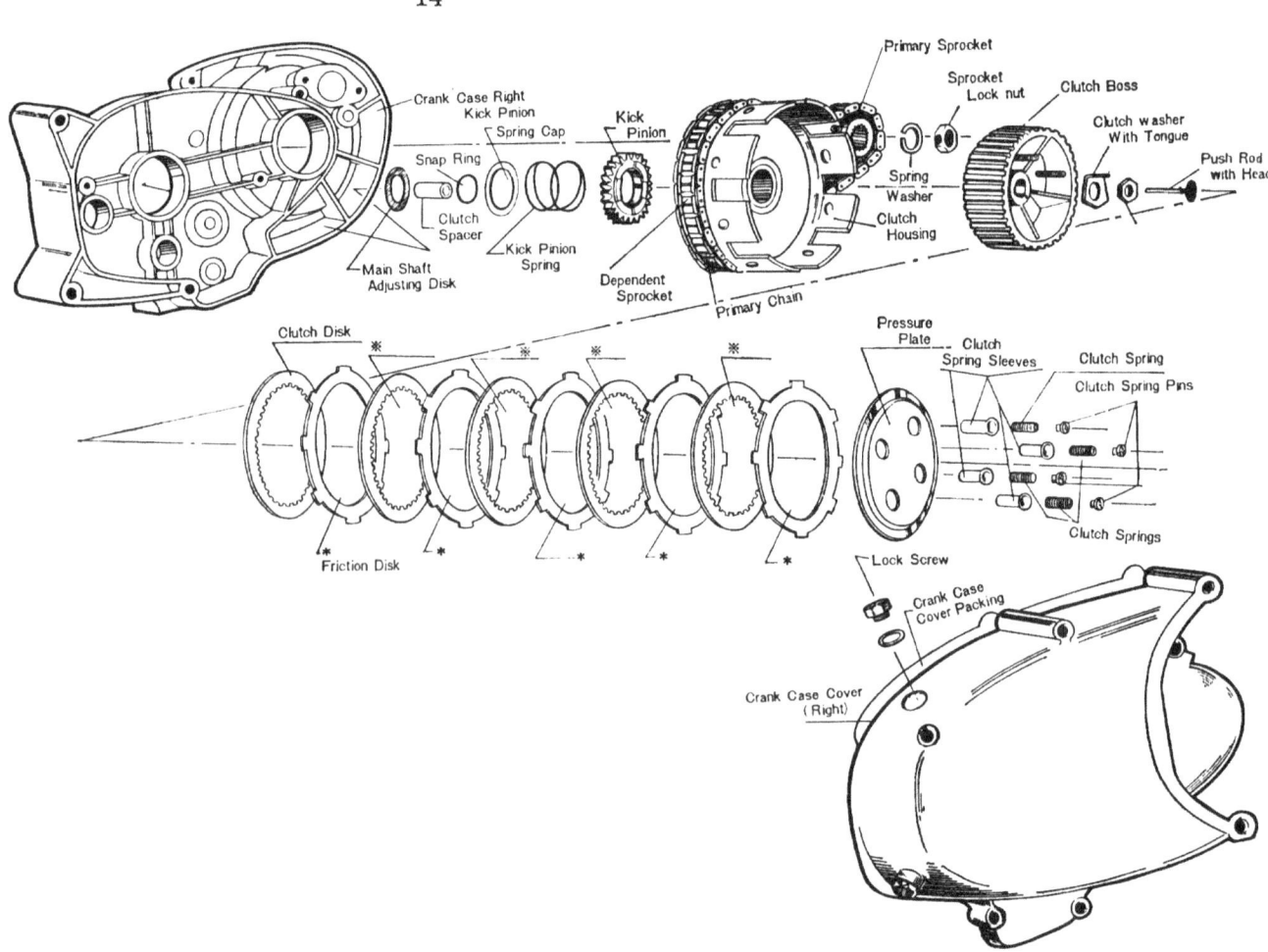

### Assembling kick pinion

Face the pawl side to the boss, and attach the kick pinion to the clutch boss. Then, attach the kick pinion spring and its support. Lastly, hold the spring support with the sanp ring.

### Attaching clutch

a. Attach the adjusting disk and the clutch spacer to the main shaft. After attaching, supply oil to them.

b. Fit the primary chain, including the primary sprocket, on the clutch housing. Then, attach them at once to the crank shaft and the main shaft.*

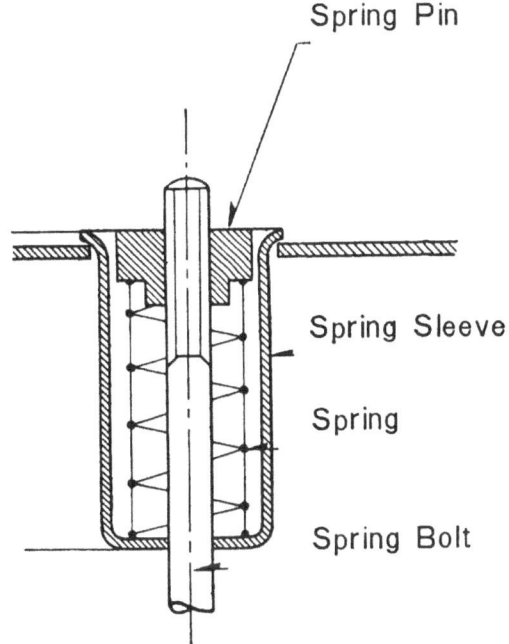
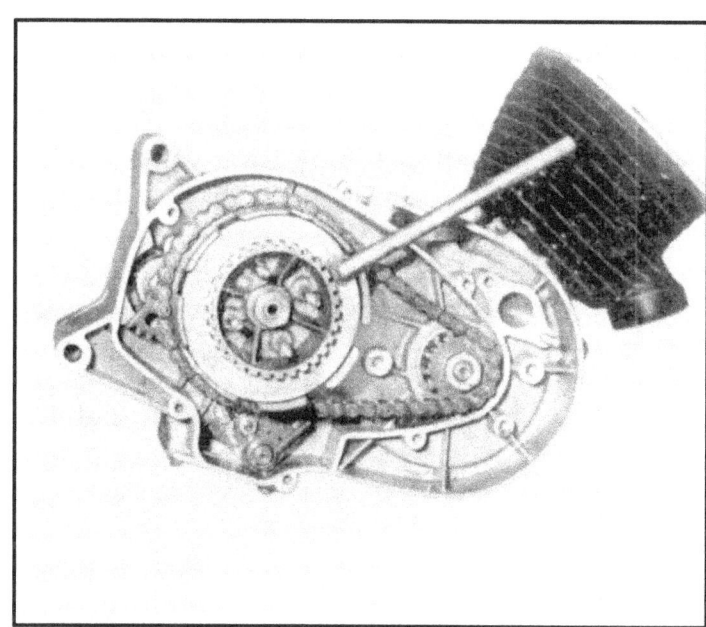

c. Attach the clutch boss to the main shaft.

d. After the housing has been stopped to move by a clutch retaining tool between the housing and the boss, insert the spring washer (for the left handed screw) in the primary sprocket, and tighten the lock nut. Note that this is a left-handed nut.

e. Attach the clutch washer with tongue to the main shaft without removing the clutch retaining tool, then tighten the nut (same as primary sprocket lock nut).

f. Insert the push rod in the main shaft.

---

* It is advisable to attach the housing to the shaft after the primary sprocket and the crank shaft spline have been put together in advance. It may be, however, not easy to attach the housing. If necessary, tap its inner part with a plastic hammer.

g. Attach clutch disks and friction disks one after another, then the pressure plate closely connected with the last clutch disk.
h. Attach the clutch spring sleeves to the pressure plate. Then, insert the clutch springs into their sleeves.
i. Screw the clutch spring caps into their sleeves as shown by the diagram below.
These spring caps are left-handed ones.

**Inspection**

a. Check whether the primary chain is tightened correctly.
If there is over 15 mm slack in the center of the chain, replace it.
b. If the roller of the chain is damaged, replace it.
c. Make sure there is no play between the clutch disks and the clutch boss spline, between the friction disks and the housing notch.
1mm clearance is appropriate for that between friction disk and housing. The clearance of 0.4~0.5 mm makes a noise.
d. If the abrasion of the friction disk is over 0.5 mm, replace it.
e. If the length of the no-loaded clutch spring is shortened over 10 % of the normal length, replace it.

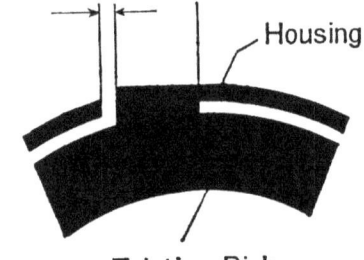

0.4mm and below
Housing
Friction Disk

**Attaching right case**

a. After cleaning of joint surfaces of the right case and its cover, apply liquid packing (Three-Bond No. 2).
b. In addition, attach a case cover packing to the joint surface of the cover. Then, join them together.
c. Case cover lock bolts are:

    YS 13-6, 20-14  2 pieces
    YS 13-6, 35-15  2 pieces
    YS 13-6, 72-15  1 piece
    YS 13-6, 80-15  1 pieces

d. After the cover has been mounted, insert the oil level plug packing, and tighten the plug.
e. Wipe the liquid packing away.

## 2—2—9 ATTACHING CYLINDER, PISTON AND PISTON RING

What distinguish the cylinder of the YA-5 from the conventional one lies in the facts which it is made of special cast iron and possesses the boost port for sweeping instead of the outlet port. Because of the above features, the engine power has been remarkably increased.

Unlike the conventional piston, the piston of the YA—5 is made of high-silicone and it has the sweep port on its back.

In addition, the bore and stroke is improved from 52mm × 58mm to 56mm × 50mm (same as for YDS).

### INSPECTION

As the cylinder-piston is "the heart" of the engine assembly, it should be inspected with special care.

a. Take an accurate measurement of the cylinder with a micrometer or a cylinder gauge.
   The measurement is taken at 8 points illustrated by the diagram. After the measurement, find the maximum remainder between them. If it becomes 0.05 mm and over, the boring is necessary.

b. Measure the outside diameter with a micrometer at 10 mm distance from the bottom in the direction perpendicular to the piston skirt boss, then the inside diameter of the bottom of the cylinder.
   Next, take the latter from the former. The remainder means the clearance between the cylinder and the piston.

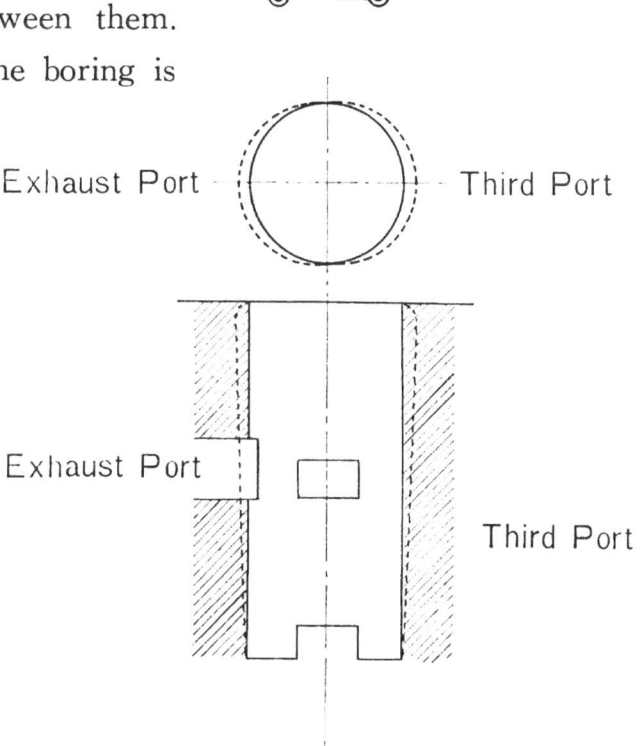

Minimum clearance between cylinder and piston should be adjusted to
0.025~0.030 mm.

c. Insert the piston ring in the cylinder, and keep the horizontal psition. Then, measure with a thickness gauge whether the clearance has the following value or not.

In case of the first ring    0.15~0.30 mm
In case of the second ring   0.10~0.25 mm

d. Check with a thickness gauge whether, the clearance between the piston ring and the piston ring groove is
0.02~0.05 mm

**Correction**

a. In case of the boring of the cylinder, the boring limit should be 0.1 mm.
b. After the boring of the cylinder, the horning is necessary.
c. After the horning, the error of inside diameter at each point should be adjusted to be
within 0.01 mm.
d. when correcting the cylinder, the resultant inside diameter should not exceed the standard diameter
over 0.4 mm.

**How To Attach**

a. Attach the second ring (Parkerized ring) and the first ring (chrome ring) to the piston. On this occasion, the side having a mark TP should be directed upward.
b. Insert the gudgeon pin clip in the connecting rod small end. Then, make sure it revolves smoothly.
Remarks: excessively loose insertion will cause a play during the drive and hasten the wear of the rod. On the other hand, tight insertion also will make troubles.
c. Insert the gudgeon pin in the piston to the degree which it catches about 1mm in the rod small end. After directing an arrow on the piston head toward the front, attach the piston. After attaching, the movement of the piston should be inspected.
d. Fit the gudgeon pin clips correctly in tne groove from right and left sides respectively.
e. Screw the cylinder lock bolt into the crank case.
f. After making sure the cylinder packing is clean, attach it to the port.

g. See if the cylinder is clean. After the ring and the knock pin have been correctly joined together, attach the cylinder with a due regard to the cylinder packing.

h. Insert the cylinder head packing, and attach the cylinder head. Lastly, fasten it with the spring washer lock nut.

## 2—2—10 ATTACHING DYNAMO AND IGNITION TIMING CONTROL

### How To Attach

a. Put the dynamo side bearing cover on the outer race of the left crank shaft bearing.

b. Apply liquid packing on the oil seal housing packing. Then, put it on the position to be attached of the left crank case.

c. Attach the dynamo side oil seal (SW 20×36×10) to the oil seal housing.

d. Adjust the oil slot of the oil seal housing to the oil hole of the case. Then, hold the oil seal housing with five bolts. On this occasion, the washers with tongue should be used for them. After tightening, fit one end of the washer in the housing notch, and lock the bolt with another end.

e. Attach the crank shaft key (half-moon shaped key) to the crank shaft.

f. Insert the dynamo locating knock in the hole of the crank case with a hammer.

On this occasion, insufficient insertion causes poor charging because of the unstable yoke.

g. Attach the armature to the crank shaft.

h. Pull up 4 brushes of the dynamo yoke, and adjust them to the knock of the crank case. Then, attach them.

i. Tighten the dynamo yoke lock bolts.

j. Fit the cam of the automatic angle-advancing device to the armature notch. Then, fasten with armature lock bolts.

k. Push down the brushes.

**Spark Control**

### A. Preparation

a. Tester (electro-tester or pocket tester)
b. Dial gauge and its stand.
c. Dynamo spanner or thickness gauge.

### B. Hints on control

Adjustment of point gap.

Find the position of maximum point gap by revolving the crank shaft.
The maximum point gap should be adjusted to

0.35 mm.

**Spark control**

a. Attach the dial gauge to the cylinder. Then, find the position of the upper dead point, and set the gauge to 0.
b. Set the tester to the measurement of continuity. Next connect the terminals with the point arm and the crank case.
c. Loosen a screw locking a stand of the contact breaker. By moving the stand, control the continuity so that it is broken within the range of 2.3～2.8 mm before the upper dead point.

## 2—2—11 ATTACHING LEFT CASE COVER

### How To Assemble

a. Attach the clutch assembly to the clutch bush.
After measuring the angle, insert it gently in the case cover with a hammer, and pull out the lever. Then, insert the bush to the utmost. The position of the clutch lever is shown by the right diagram.

b. Attach the clutch lever to the bush. Then, attach the steel ball, the clutch abjusting screw and the clutch adjusting nut from the outside of the crank case. Supply sufficient grease to the push screw and the steel ball.

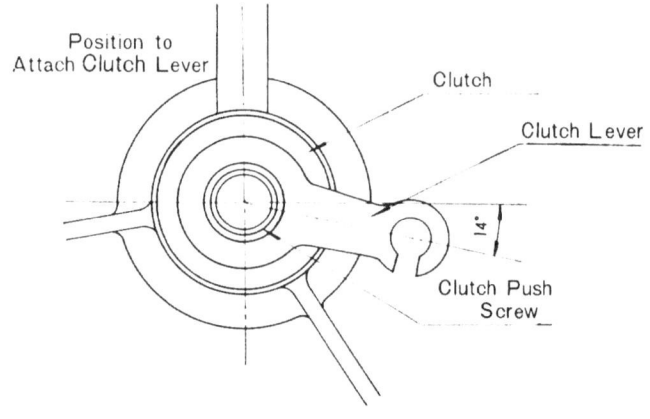

c. Insert the spring hanger into the case cover with a hammer. Then hang the spring on the clutch lever and this hanger.

d. Attach the case cover lid and the dynamo cover packing.

### How To Attach Drive Sproket

a. Attach the drive sproket around the driving wheel shaft with the retaining washer and the lock nut.

b. Insert one steel ball into the main shaft, then the push rod. Lastly, hold them with the rubber packing.

### How To Attach Case Cover

Now, attach the case cover.

The following lock bolts should be used.

**YS 13-6, 90-15-2 pieces**
**YS 13-6, 62-15-2 pieces**

## 2—2—12 ATTACHING INLET COVER, CARBURETOR, AIR CLEANER AND CARBURETOR COVER

The Model YA-5 has adopted a new device for the carburetor: the starter.

The starter has more outstanding feature than the tickler and the choke adopted for the conventional carburetor. Just pull the lever attached to the handle and the cylinder may be supplied with mixture gas suitable for starting under freezing temperature.

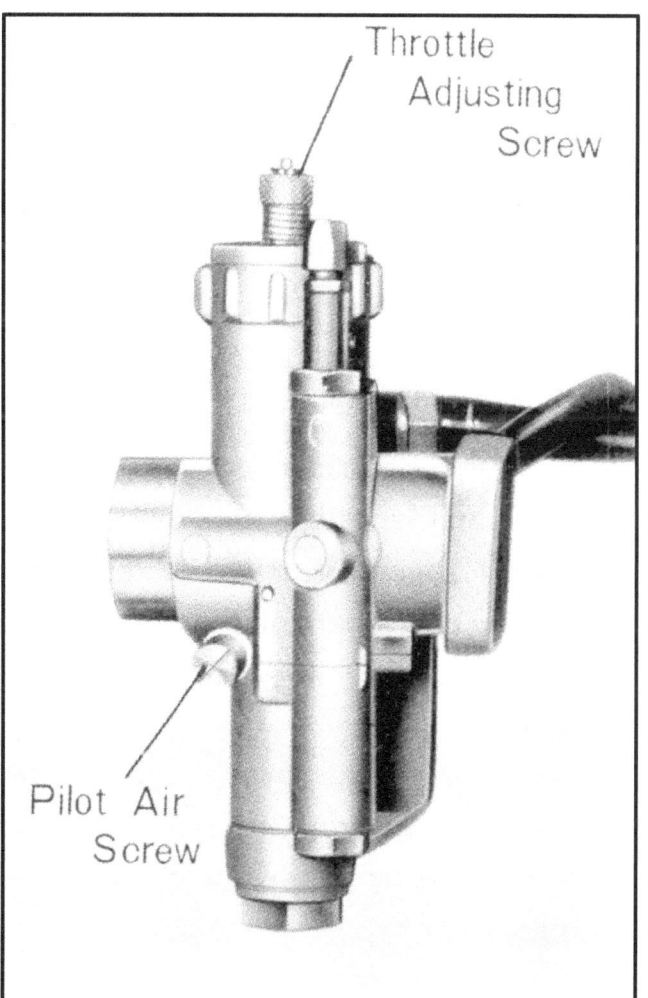

SPECIFICATIONS OF CARBURETOR

| Type | Mikuni M21 S1 |
|---|---|
| Main Jet | #120 |
| Jet Needle | 22M3-3 |
| Throttle Valve | #15 |
| Pilot Jet | 20AB |
| Pilot Outlet | 0.6 |
| Air Cleaner | reversing $1^3/_4$ turns |

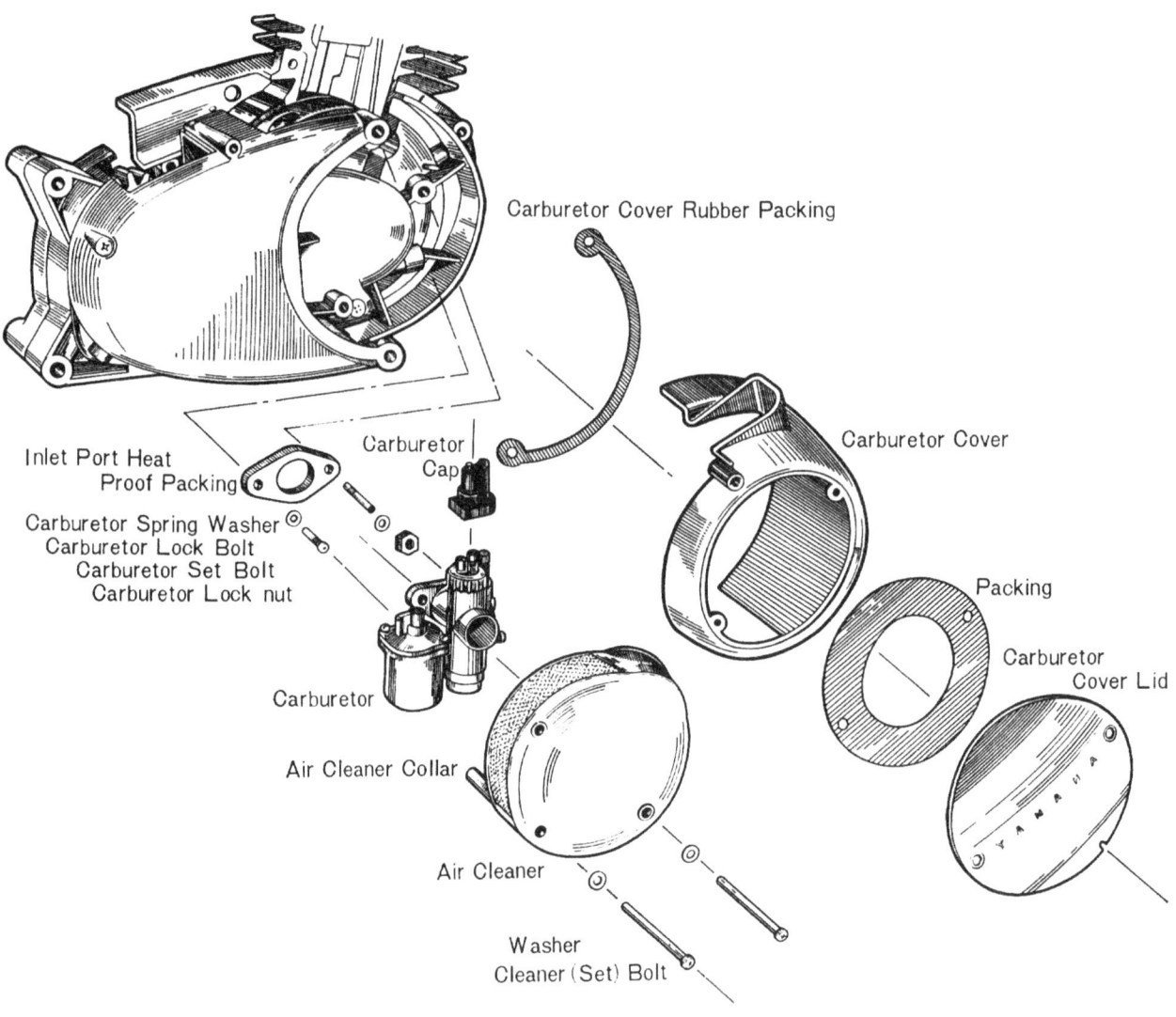

## How To Attach

a. Place the carburetor lock shaft A (15 mm) in the right crank case inlet port.
b. After attaching the heat-proof packing to the inlet port, attach the carburetor. Then, fasten it with the lock nut, the look bolt B and the washer. As the upper part of the heat-proof packing differs from the lower one, care should be taken to adjust it to the shapes of the carburetor and the inlet port.
Note that, if the position of the attached carburetor is not perpendicular, this has a harmful effect on the performance.
c. Mount the air cleaner on the carburetor. Then, hold it with lock bolts and collars.
d. Attach the carburetor cover lid and its packing to the carburetor cover.

Then, attach them to the crank case cover.

    Lock bolts    YS 13-6, 40-20,    2 piece

**How To Attach Inlet Cover**

Drive a knock into the inlet cover. Then, attach it to the crank case upper part.

# CHAPTER 3.  FRAME

### 3—1  FRAME

The frame of the YA-5 is of the stressed skin construction of pressed steel. This type of the frame, fruit of the collective achievemet of our technical staff, had the most outstanding feature from the standpoint of dynamics. Therefore, it excels the conventional frame in durability and weight.

As the head pipe welded in the front section of the frame contains the ball races and the steel balls, the YA-5 provides excellent steering characteristics.

Besides, as the head pipe and the frame are welded through the rigid stiffener plate to which the down-tube is attached, the YA—5 not only secures to hold the engine firmly, but improves the flexural and torsional rigidity of the frame.

The electrical equipment is compactly housed in the vibrationless section, center of the frame. Consequently, you can keep its performance in the best condition and handle it easily by removing the right and left side covers.

There are a battery bind and a tool box under the right side cover. This is convenient for the prompt use of a tool. On the other hand, the regulator and starter switches are housed under the left side cover.

**Inspection**

After the engine and other parts been removed by the instructions described in the preceeding chapter, the frame itself should be inspected in the following order.

a. Check whether the pipes and the pressed section from the head pipe to the rear fender are damaged or deformed. In particular, the frame of a motorcycle having a record of collision or other grave troubles should be carefully inspected without fail. If a damaged or deformed part is found, replace or repair it.

b. Note that the distortion or the eccentricity of the head pipe section causes harm to the stability and the steering of the motorcycle. If the head pipe is excessively deformed, replace it.

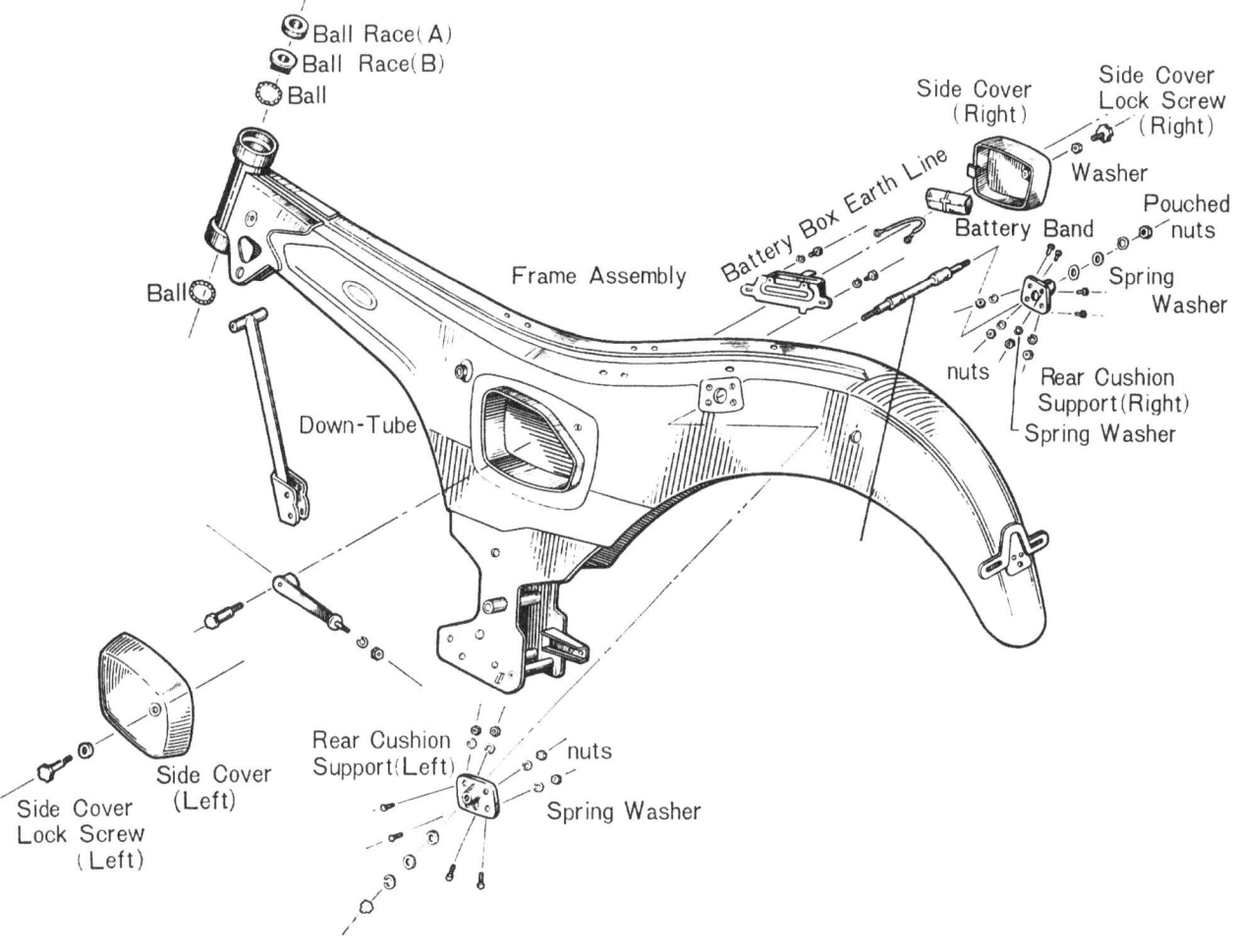

c. The ball races and the steel balls should be carefully checked, especially in case of a time-worn car. In particular, as the one-side wear or the crack of the ball causes harm to the steering, when finding a faulty one, replace not the one, but all the balls and races.

**Assembling**

A combination of new balls and old races, or of old balls and new races, should be avoided. Therefore, even if only one piece is faulty, replace all without exception. The balls and the races which have gotten through the inspection or the new ones should be carefully washed and supplied new grease when assembling. Besides, care should be taken to prevent them from sand, dust and other impurities.

### 3—2 STEERING HANDLE AND WIRES

The steering handle is the pipe one which possesses the throttle grip and the front brake lever on its right side, the clutch lever and the start lever on its left side. The throttle wire alone and is passed through the pipe. The front brake wire and the clutch wire are arranged so that you can grease up them. The handle is held with four lock bolts through the handle bar crown and the handle holder. Its position slides freely up and down.

**How To Disassemble**

a. Detach the throttle wire, the clutch wire, the front brake wire and the start wire;
b. Remove the head light;
c. Remove the cord connected with the wire harness;
d. Unscrew four bolts holding the handle; and the handle is detached.

How to take the handle to smaller pieces is given below:—

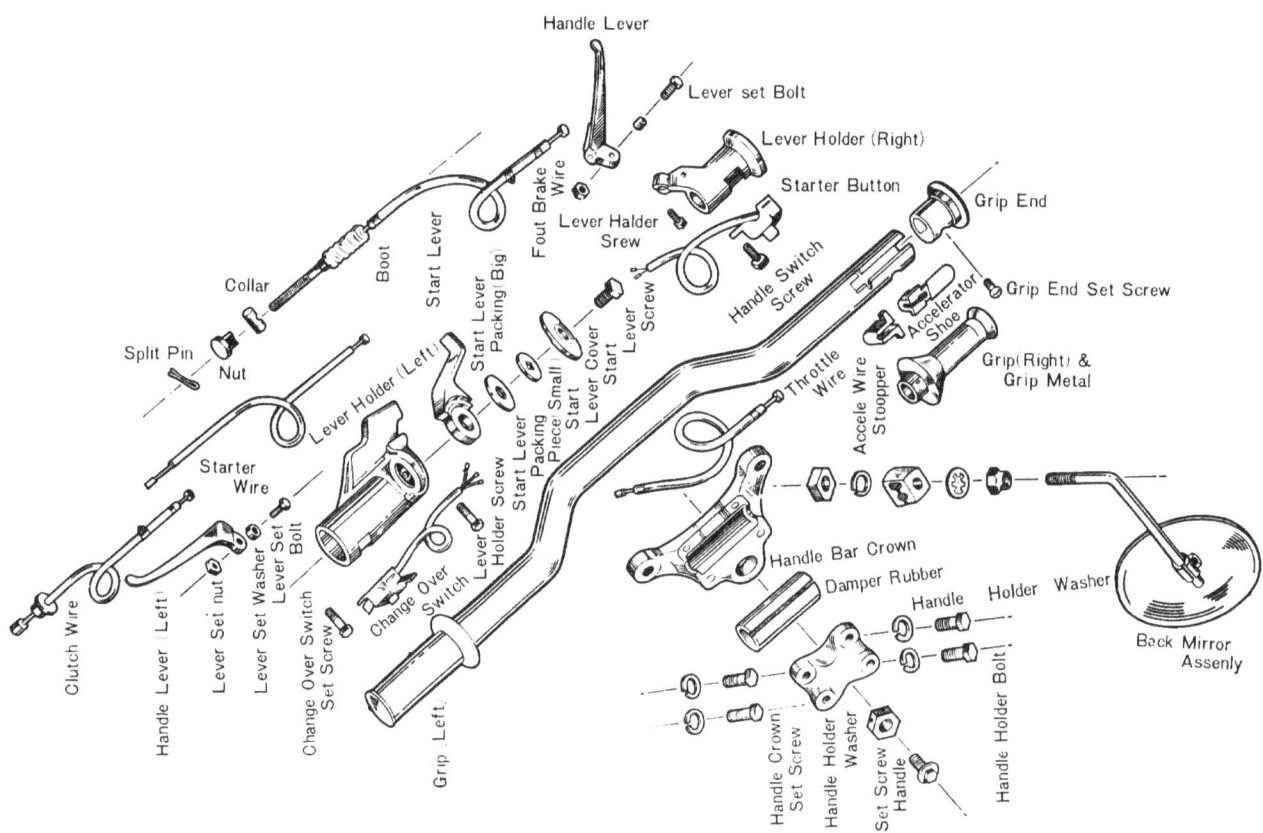

a. The front brake wire should be removed by detaching the right handle lever.
b. The clutch wire should be removed by detaching the left handle lever.
c. The start wire should be removed by detaching the start lever.
d. Throttle wire may be removed in the same way as for YA-3: first, remove the grip end; second, pull out the grip metal twisting it; third, remove

the wire stopper and the accelerator shoe; lastly, pull the throttle wire out of the steering handle.

### Inspection

a.  If the covering of the throttle wire, the clutch wire, the brake wire or the start wire is worn out or damaged, tape or replace it.
b.  In case of the above wires, if the inner of the wire does not work well because of the excessively bent outer or the broken one, replace the wire.
c.  Supply oil sufficiently to the inner of the above wires.
d.  Apply grease to the accelerator shoe and the grip fitting, and reassemble them.

### How To Assemble Handle

The handle should be assembled in the reverse order of the above instructions.

## 3—3 FRONT FORK

The front fork is of the same telescopic type as the YD-2 adopted. It possesses the round head lamp, the front fender and the handle lock key. The lower part of the steering shaft is connected with the inner tube through the under-bracket; the middle part is connected with the head pipe having ball races (because of them, this part is the most important of the steering system); the upper holds the inner tube by means of the handle bar crown. Thus, the front fork features the rigid construction.

### How To Disassemble

a.  Care should be taken of the oil contained in the inner tube. In order that the oil may not flow out of it, it is advisable to erect the front fork when disassembling.
b.  Remove the front wheel, the front fender, the head lamp and the handle.
c.  Unscrew the bolt and the lock nut in the center of the handle crown, and the front fork may be detached as an assembly. On this occasion, attention should be paid not to scratch the fork cover and the steel balls.

d. Remove the steering key
e. Loosen the dressed bolt and the under-bracket bolt. Then, remove the lower part of the front fork then the inner tube.
For this purpose, it is advisable to use a front fork detaching tool.
f. Hold the axle metal end firmly with a vice. Next, turn the inner tube gently, and the stopper pin fits in the slide metal groove.

Besides, the slide metal and the inner tube interlock. Give another turn (left-handed), and the slide metal comes out pushing the oil seal out.
g. Remove the outer tube, then the inner tube.

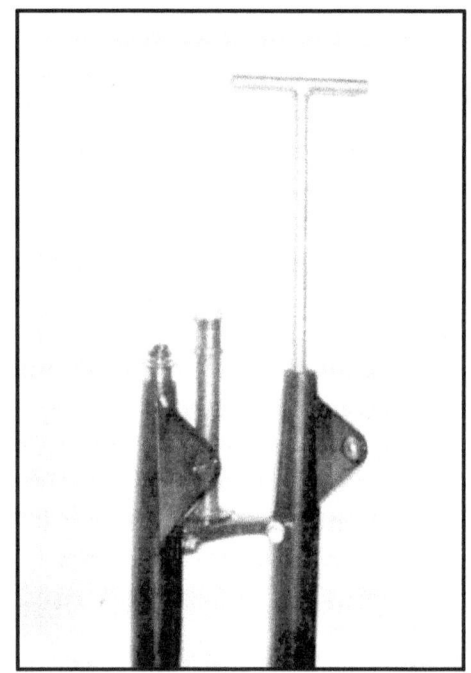

### Inspection

If the spring or the washer or the oil seal is faulty or deformed, replace it.

### How To Assemble

The front fork may be assembled in the reverse order of the above instructions for disassembling. Some remarks, however, are necessary. First of all, clean every part carefully.

a. Put together the outer tube with inner one, and insert the slide metal. Then, fix them. On this occasion, it is advisable to use a front fork assembling-disassembling tool.
b. Insert the washer (A) and the oil seal. In particular, this washer should be inserted without fail. Because, if not, it becomes very difficult to disassemble it again. As the outside of the inner tube is of the mirror finished surface plated with chromium, care should be taken not to score it when disassembling. Because such a score causes oil leaking.

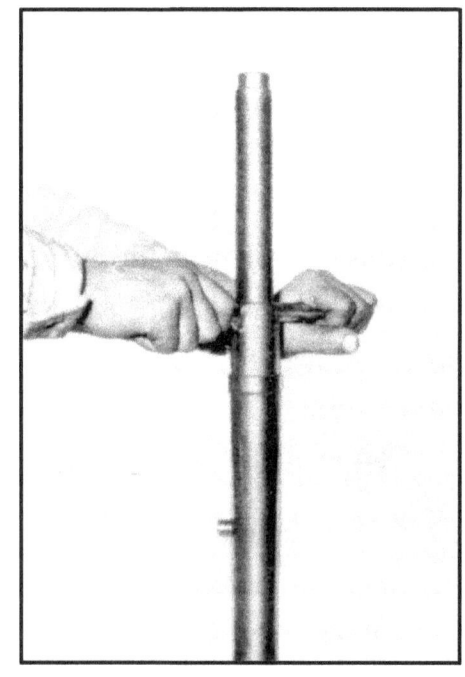

c. Pour oil. KAYABA No. 2 working oil of 170 cc. should be used.
It is possible to substitute a mixture of mobile oil No. 30 and spindle oil No. 600 in the ratio 5 : 5.

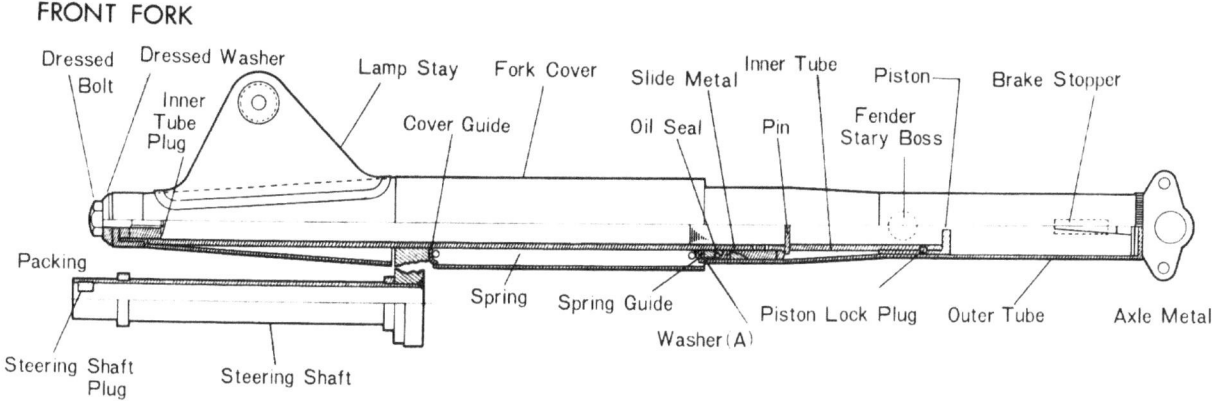

## 3—4  REAR ARM

The rear arm is of the swing arm construction of which the rear arm shaft serves as a central axis of the motion. The rear end is supported by the frame itself through the rear cushion unit.

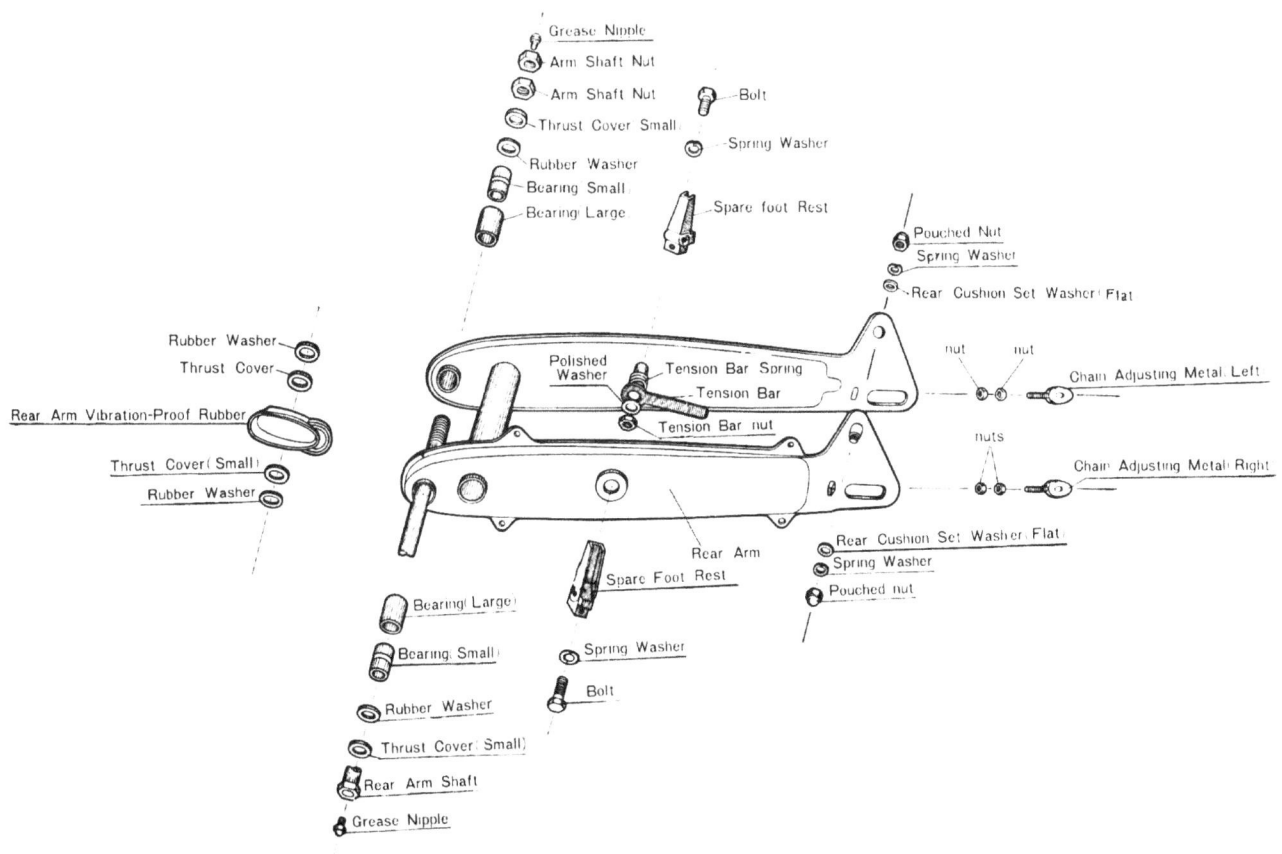

### How To Detach

a. Remove the rear wheel and the tension bar;
b. Remove the upper and lower chain cases, then the chain;
c. Remove the cushion, and loosen arm shaft nut, and pull out the shaft; And the rear arm may be detached.

### Inspection

a. If the vibration-proof rubber is damaged or worn out, replace it.
b. If the rubber washer on the rear arm shaft is worn out, replace it. Moreover, if the big or the small bearing is excessively worn out, renew it.
c. See if the rear arm is distorted or deformed. If it is faulty, replace it.
d. If the tention bar hole is enlarged or the tension bar spring is faulty, replace it.

### How To Assemble

First, attach the big bearing around the rear arm shaft, then the vibration-proof rubber little by little from the backside of the arm. Next, adjust the rear arm to the pipe for passing the rear arm shaft through (this pipe is situated in the frame), and pass the rear arm shaft through it, and secure with nuts.

On this occasion, the small bearing, the rubber washer, the thrust cover (small) and the vibration-proof rubber should have been inserted in the rear arm shaft in advance.

Second, attach the rear arm to the rear cushion, then the chain case to the rear arm. The vibration-proof rubber should have been adjusted to the chain case without fail.

## 3—5 REAR CUSHION UNIT

The rear cushion unit consists of two components: the suspension spring that absorbs a shock given by the ground and the shock absorber that damps the vibration caused by the shock.

### How To Disassemble

a. Pull out the pin;
b. Push the outer shell (A) down;
c. Set a spanner to the lower part of the piston rod;
d. Loosen the eye and remove it from the piston rod;
e. And the outer shell (A), the suspension spring, the outer shell (B), the

spacer and the spring guide are detached.

Note that the bumper rubber and the washer come off at the same time.

f. The shock absorber, including the piston rod tube, should not be taken to smaller pieces, because they are indivisible.

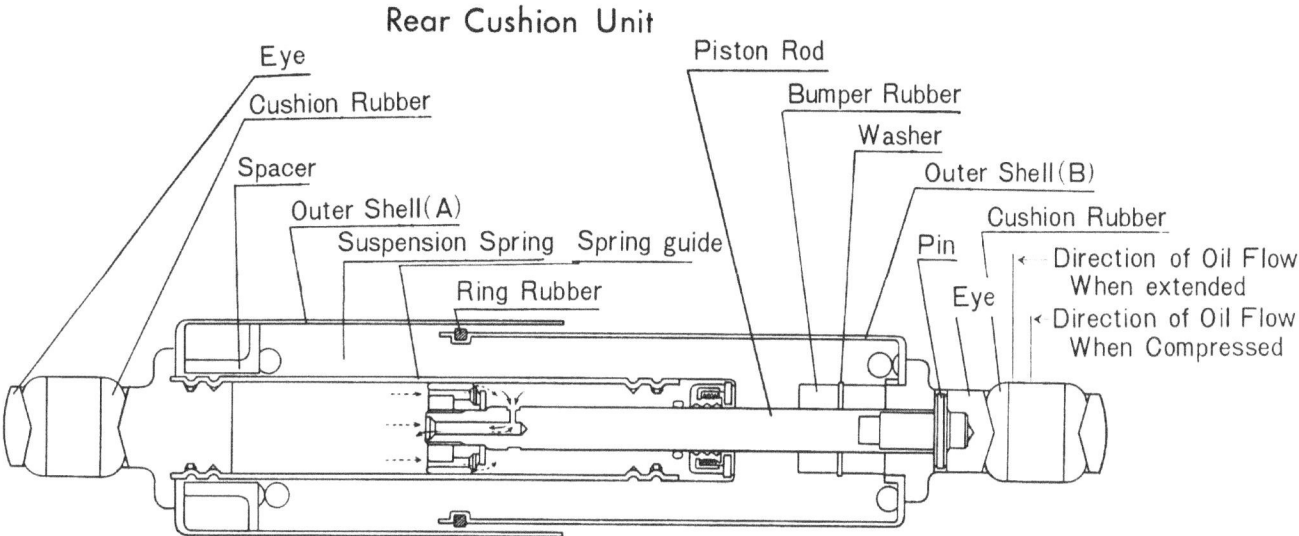

Rear Cushion Unit

## Inspection

a. Measure the length of the spring. If its overall length is under 246 mm, replace it.

b. If oil leaking of the absorber is remarkable, or the piston rod is damaged or deformed, replace the shock absorber assembly.

c. If the bumper rubber, the washer, the spring guide or the ring rubber is deformed, damaged or faulty, replace it.

d. Replace the deformed or damaged cushion cover of the upper or the lower eye.

## How To Assemble

The rear cushion unit may be assembled in the reverse order of the above instructions. After assembling, make sure the spring and the outer shell work well when adding your body-weight and giving a stroke.

### 3—6 FUEL TANK AND SADDLE

The front section of the fuel tank is put together with the down-tube, while the rear section with the saddle.

The front of the saddle is put together with the fuel tank, while the rear is held by nuts on the saddle attaching plate.

**How to detach**

Detach one side of the level pipe, and unscrew the lock bolts out of the front and the rear section. Then, lift the fuel tank and it may be detached.

Unscrew the front section lock bolts and the rear section lock nuts. Then, lift the saddle.

Remove the strainer cup, then the packing with care. Next, unscrew three screws (5mm) and the cock assembly comes off.

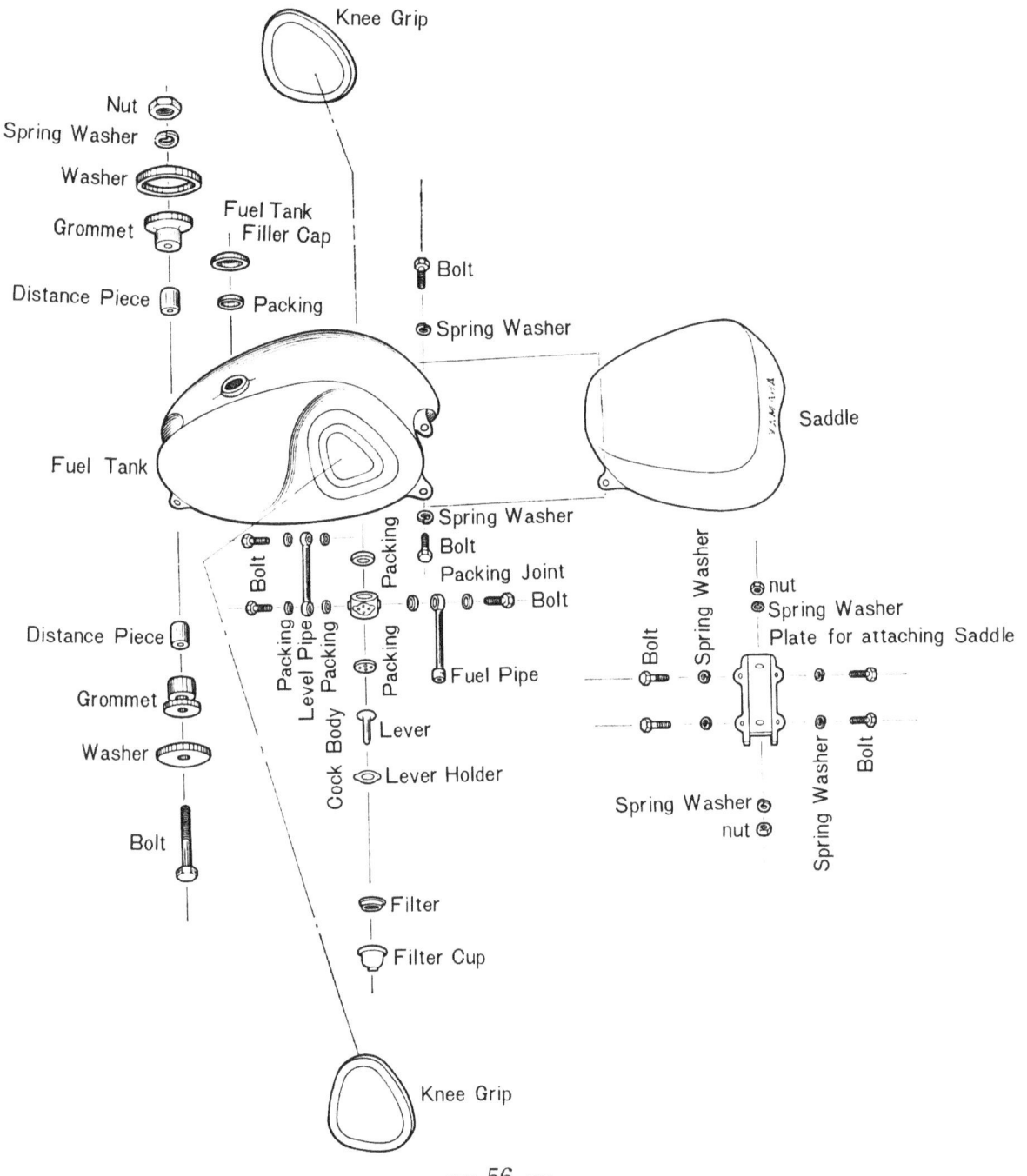

**Inspection**

a. If the fuel tank grommet is faulty or damaged, replace it.
b. If oil leaks out of the fuel tank, replace it.
c. Replace the faulty or damaged tank cup packing.
d. When attaching the fuel pipe and the level pipe, care should be taken of the position of the joint.

### 3—7 FOOT REST, MAIN STAND, SIDE STAND AND BRAKE PEDAL

**How To Disassemble**

a. In case of the side stand, remove the lock nut from the backside, then the side stand lock bolt and the spring. And it may be detached.
b. In case of the main stand, remove the main stand spring, and pull out the main stand lock bolt.
c. In case of the brake pedal, remove the E-shaped stop ring and its washer.

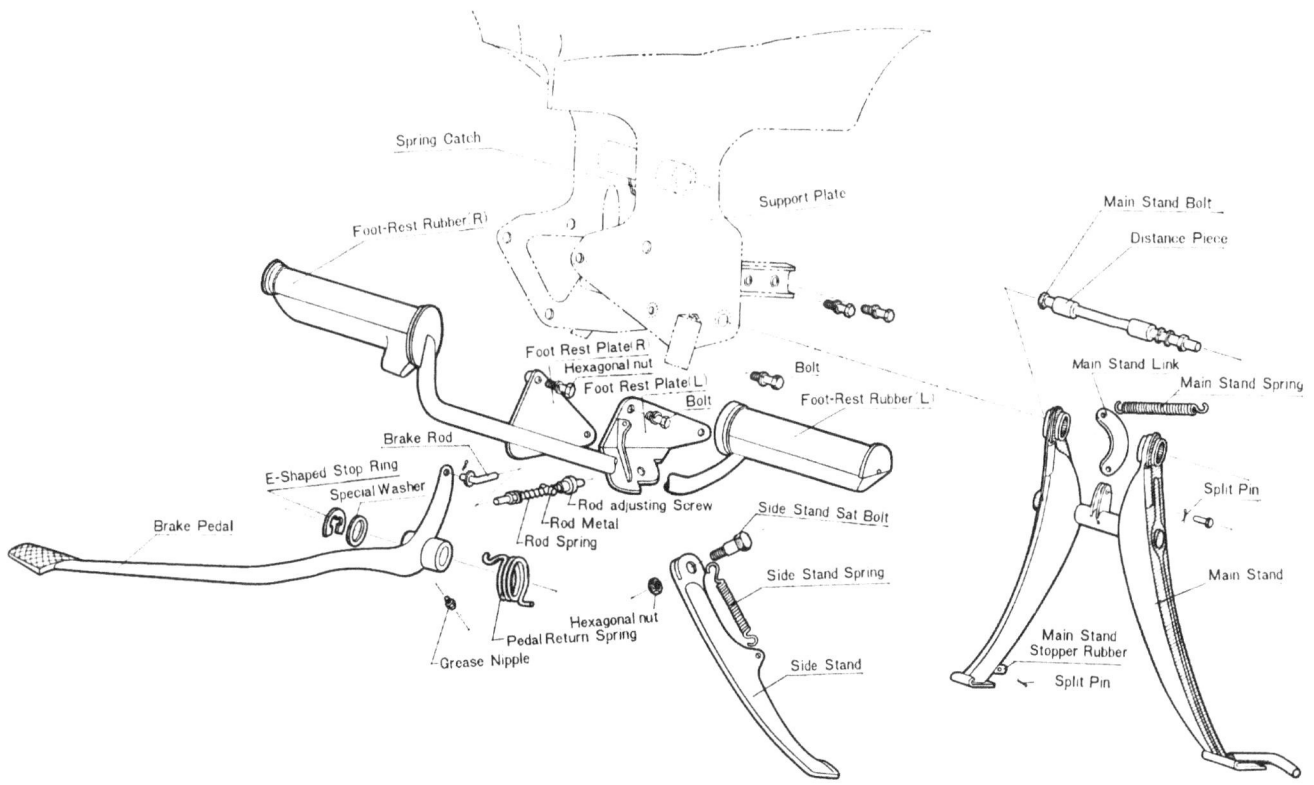

**Inspection**

a. If the brake pedal is bent or it has an excessive play, replace it.
b. If there is an excessive play between the main stand and its spacer, replace the latter.

Replace the faulty or worn out stopper rubber.

c. Renew the remarkably deformed or rusty spring.

**Care in Assembling**

When assembling, wash them carefully, especially their working section, and supply grease sufficiently.

### 3—8 DRIVE CHAIN SYSTEM

The motive power generated by the engine is transmitted through the chain from the rear wheel driving sprocket to the rear wheel sprocket gear. Acting as the damper through the damper rubber, the sprocket gear transmits the rotatory power to the rear wheel. The section from the rear wheel driving sprocket to the sprocket gear is covered up with the chain cases. They keep it from dust and prevent from wearing out in the early stage.

#### A. Chain cases

Remove 6 little screws of 6 mm (4 pieces on the outside, 1 piece on the backside and 1 piece at the rear end) and the chain cases are divided into two parts: upper and lower.

#### B. Chain

DK428 chain with 79 pitches has been adopted. Remove the left crank case of the engine, then the change joint clip, and the chain is put out of gear. If it is difficult to detach the chain, remove the chain cases. When the chain adjuster reaches its adjusting limit, it is advisable to remove one link to shorten the chain. However, you must renew it for the second time.

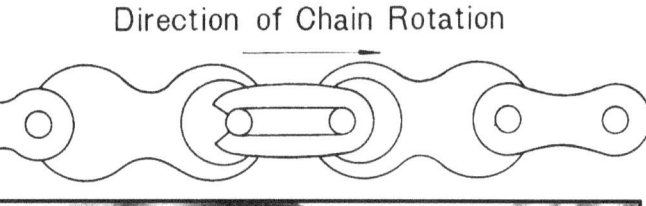
Direction of Chain Rotation

Sprocket Wheel
Damper Rubber

When replacing the chain, check the front and the rear sprockets. If they are remarkably worn out, replace them.

Important: The chain clip head must face in the direction of the chain rotation.

## C. Sprocket Wheel

Four ribs of the sprocket wheel fit in the grooves of the damper rubber attached to the rear hub. Thus, the sprocket wheel transmits the motive power. On this occasion, the elasticity of the rubber prevents knocking.

### How to disassemble

a. Remove the chain cases and put the chain out of gear. Next, unscrew the rear wheel nut, and pull out rear axle, and remove the rear hub.

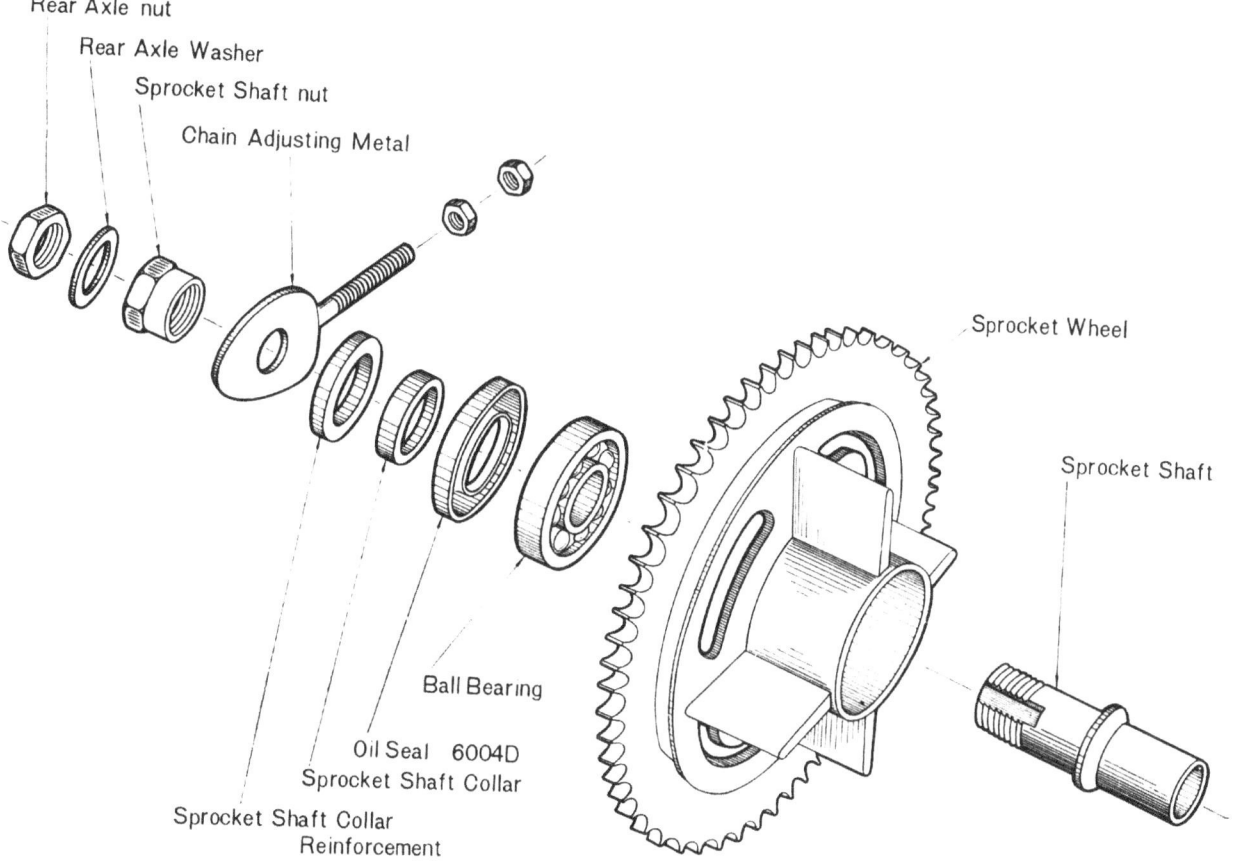

b. Unscrew the sprocket shaft lock nut and the sproket wheel comes off.
c. Pull the sprocket shaft, the bearing, the oil seal and the sprocket shaft collar out of the sprocket wheel boss, and clean them.

### Inspection and assembly

a. When holding the ball bearing (6004D) in your hand and revolving its outer race, if it does not turn smoothly or it has an excessive play, replace it.
b. If the lip of the oil seal SD 26-42-8 is remarkably deformed or worn out, replace it.
c. If the teeth of the sprocket wheel are remarkably worn out, replace it.

After filling the ball bearing with grease, insert the sprocket shaft in it. Next, insert them in the sprocket wheel boss, and attach the oil seal.

> Remarks: Attention should be payed to the position of the ball bearing and the oil seal. It is desirable to use a guide when inserting them with a hammer.

Next, attach the sprocket shaft collar and its shifter plate. Lastly, attach the assembled drive chain to the rear arm loosely, and fasten it gradually tightening the chain.

## 3—9 FRONT AND REAR WHEELS

The front and the rear wheels have the tire of 300×6 2P and 300×16 4P respectively.

The rims of both wheels are of the steel square type which have been lightened and strengthened by the seam weld. Each wheel has 36 strokes in sets of 4 (No. 10 straight type) All the strokes are equally tightened by the nipples.

When further tightening the stroke, tighten with a nipple spanner so that it has the same tension as others.

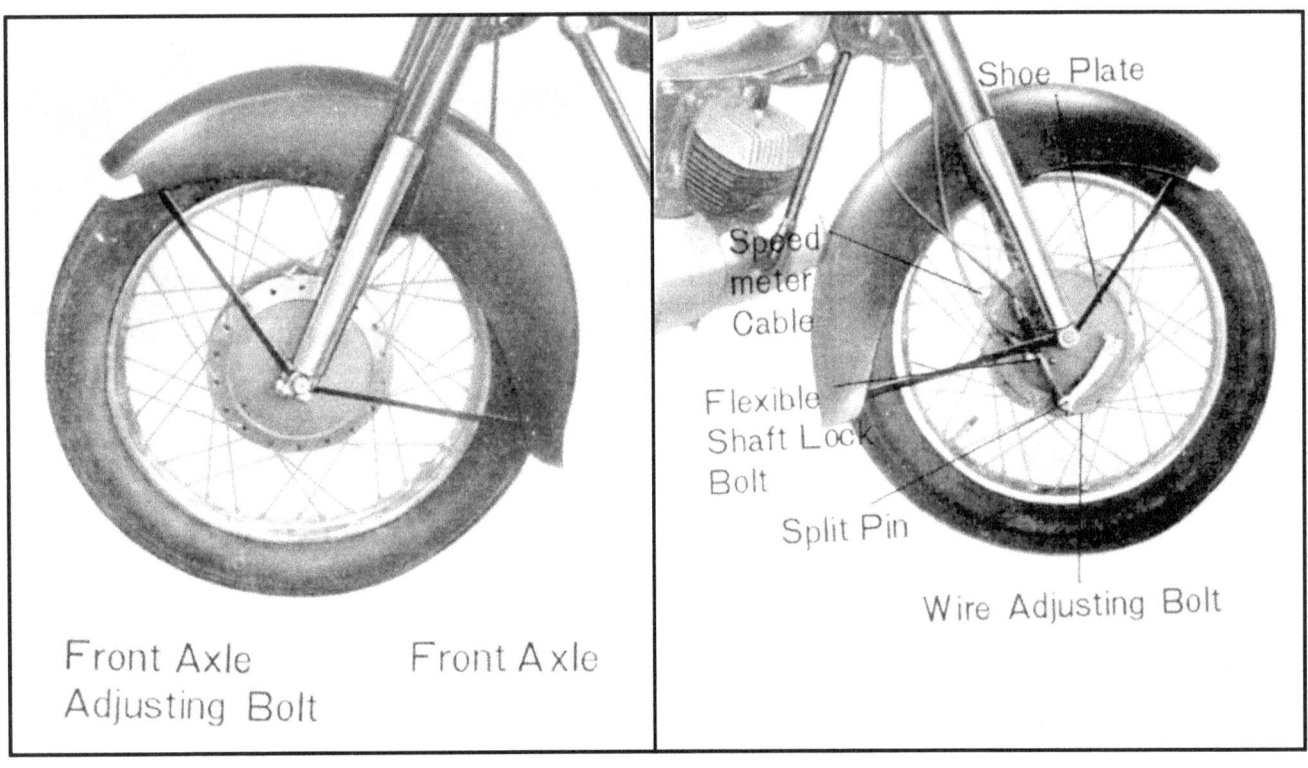

## A. Front wheel

### How to disassemble

The front wheel should have been lifted in advance when disassembling. Remove the parts of 1-7 in the following numerical order and the front wheel with the shoe plate may be detached. If it is lifted higher, it is possible to detach without removing the parts of 1-5.

1. Split pin;
2. Wire adjusting nut;
3. Wire adjusting bolt;
4. Flexible shaft bolt;
5. Cable for speedometer;
6. Front axle lock bolt;
7. Front axle;
8. Front shoe plate.

In case of removing ball bearing 6202 DD, push it out with a hammer through the spacer detaching hole.

If possible, it is desirable to use a tool shown in diagram below.

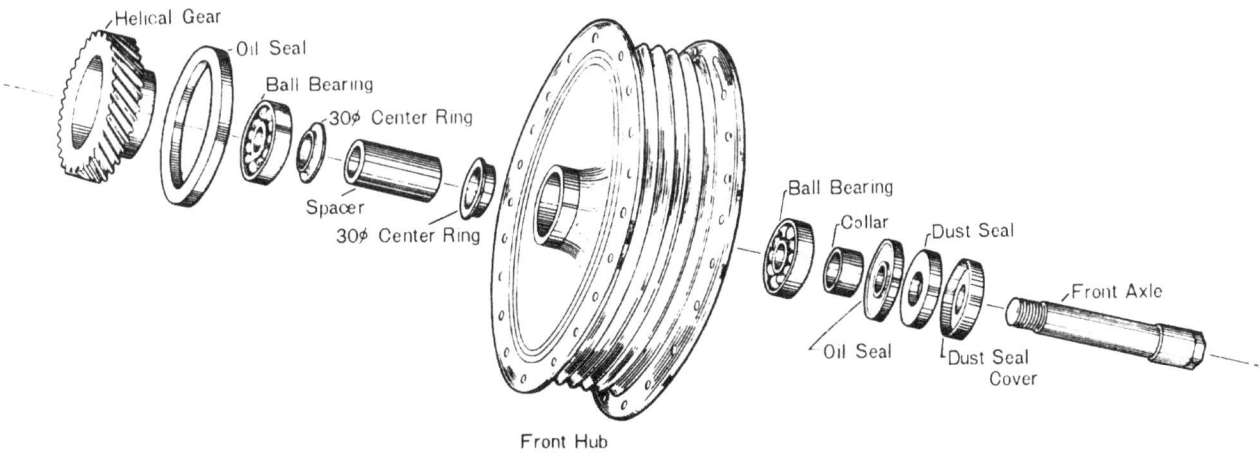

**Inspection**

a. Check the swing of the rim. A method of measurement of the swing is indicated by the illustration. **The rim swing should be adjusted to 3 mm and below.**

b. Check the spokes. If they are slack or bent, replace or adjust them.

c. If the tire pattern is excessively worn out, repleace the tire.

d. Check whether the tires are damaged or not. If necessary, mend or renew them.

e. If the bearing (6202 DD) has an excessive play or it does not run smoothly, replace it.

f. Replace the remakably bent or damaged front axle.

g. If the tooth surface of the helical gear is remarkably worn out, replace it.

h. Check whether the lips of the oil seals (SD20-35-7 and OS47.5-60-7) are damaged or deformed. Replace the faulty one.

i. Replace the faulty dust seal.

j. If the brake surface of the hub has a harmfull score, repair or replace it.

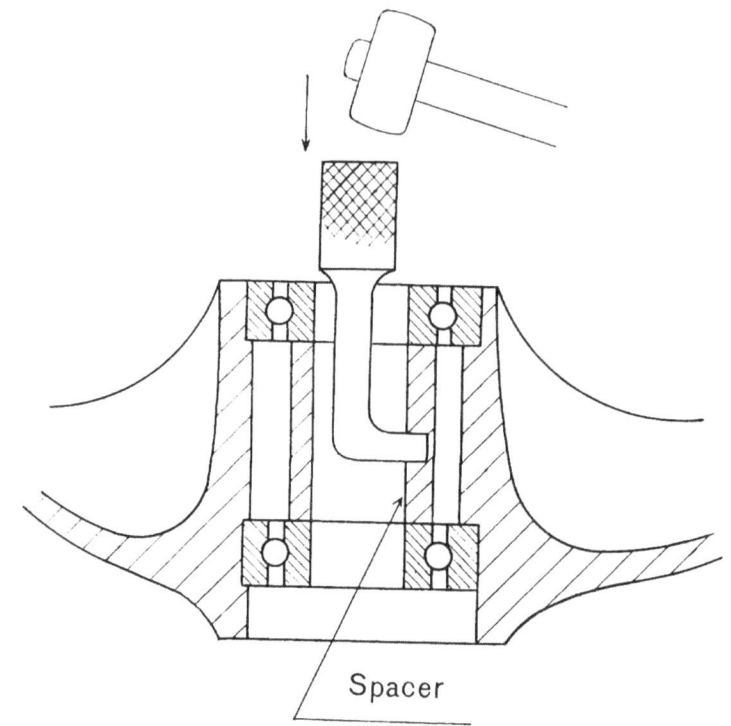
Spacer

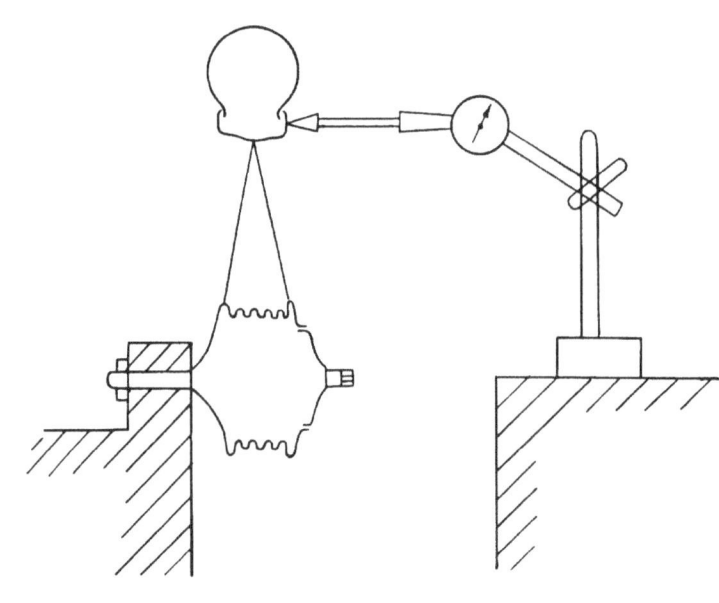

**How to attach**

The front wheel may be attached to the body in the reverse order of the above instructions.

The front axle torque should be adjusted to 7.5~8.5kg-m

a. When replacing the bearing, care should be taken to attach it in parallel with the suface to be inserted and to give no load to the inner race.
b. When replacing the helical gear and the oil seal, supply the specified grease sufficiently.
c. Keep the braking surface of the hub clean.

## B. Rear wheel
### How to detach

The rear wheel may be detached, if its components are removed in the numerical order indicated by the following diagrams.

The ball bearing 6202D is removed in the same way as for the front wheel.

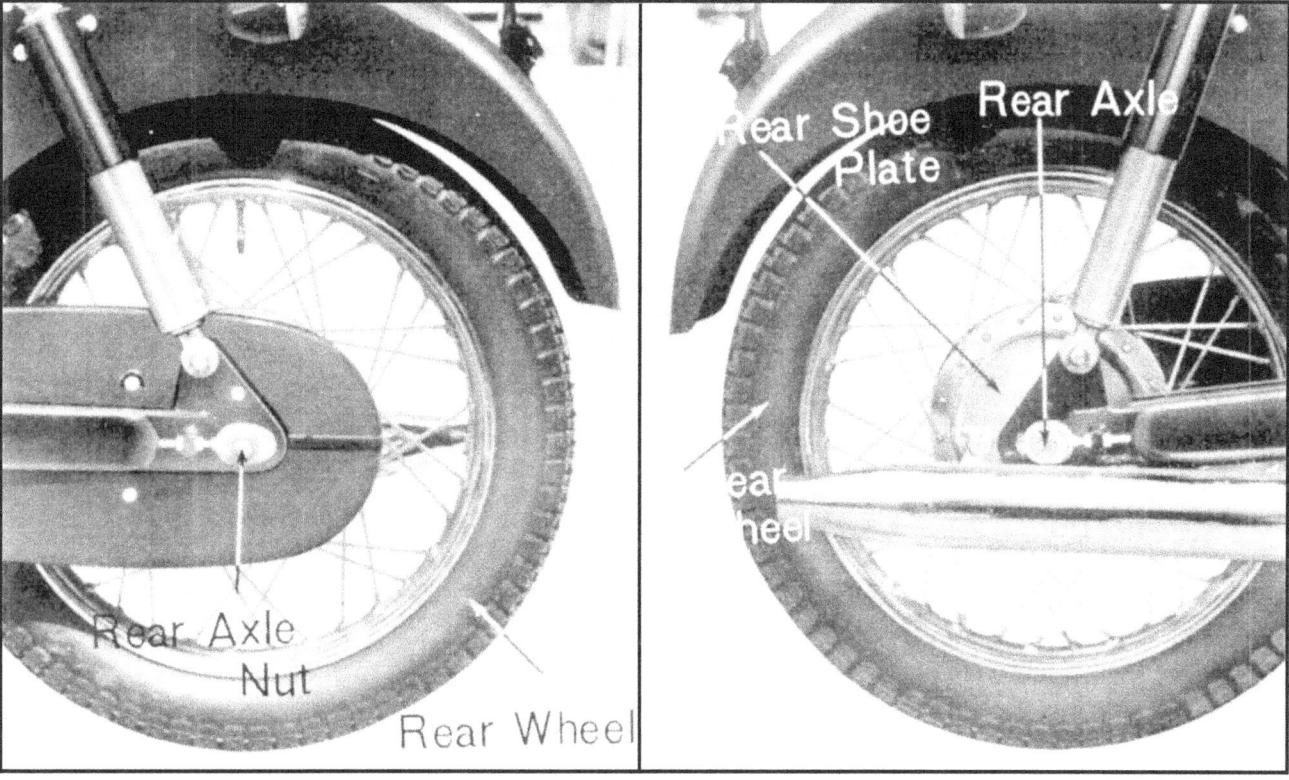

1 Rod adjusting nut;
2 Torque adjusting clip;
3 Torque adjusting nut;
4 Tension bar;
5 Rear axle nut;
6 Rear axle;
7 Distance piece;
8 Rear shoe plate;
9 Rear wheel.

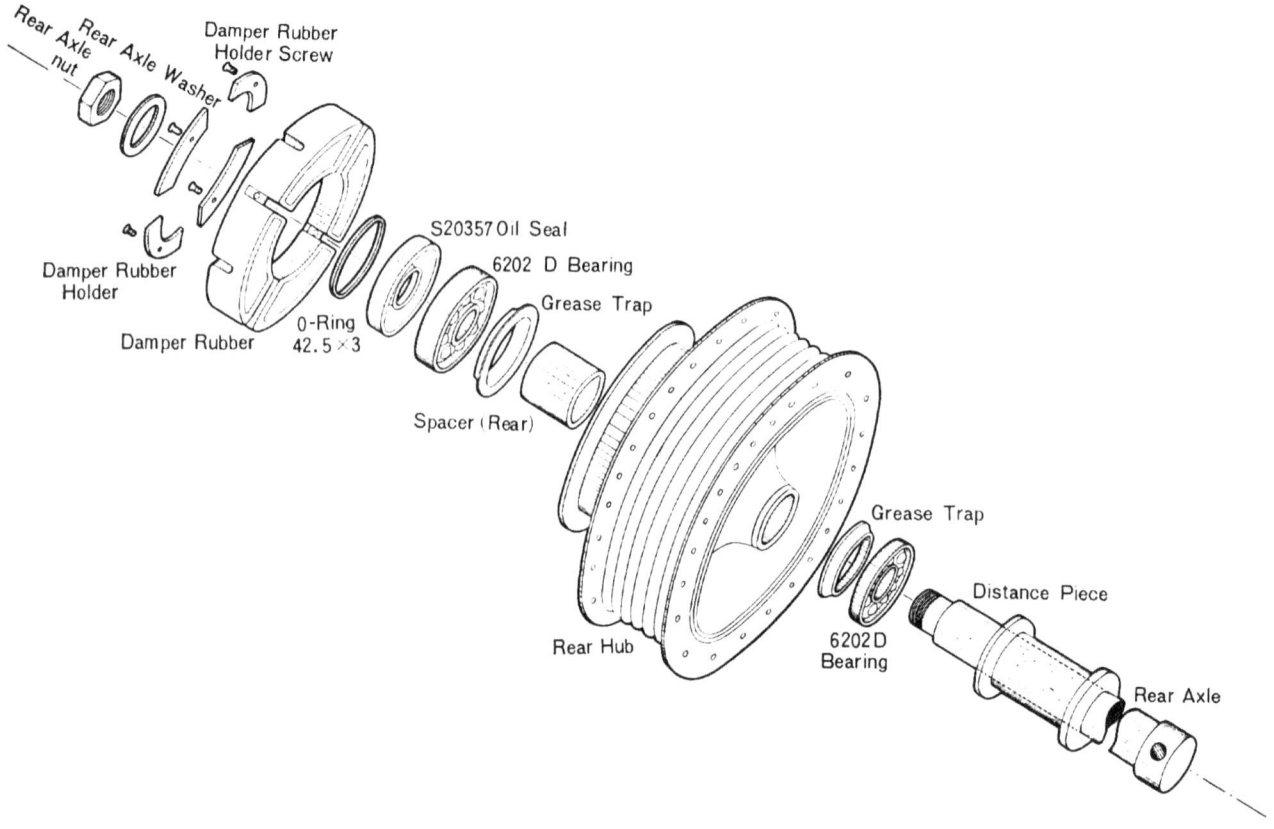

## Inspection

a. The swing of the rim should be measured in the same way as for the front wheel and corrected to the same value.

b. The spoke also is measured in the same way as for the front wheel. The slack spoke should be tightend.

c. If the tire or the tire pattern is worn out or faulty, mend or replace it.

d. If the ball bearing 6202D has a remarkable play or it does not run smoothly, replac it.

e. If the lip of the oil seal S2035-7 is damaged or deformed, replece it.

f. If the brake surface of the hub has a harmfull score, repair or replace it.

**How to attach**

The rear wheel may be attached to the body in the reverse order of the instructions for detaching.

The front axle torque should be adjusted to 7.5～8.5 kg-m.

a.  When replacing the bearing, care should be taken of the points described in the precceding sub-section.
b.  Keep the braking surface of the hub clean.

## 3—10 TIRES AND TUBES

When mouting and dismouting the tires, care should be taken not to damage the rims and the tubes. The tire should be pumped up not at once, but little by little adjusting the position of the tubes.

a.  When replacing the tires or the tubes, the correct size ones should be selected.
b.  Normal tire pressure:

        Front wheel      1.6 kg/cm$^2$ (22 lbs/in$^2$)
        Rear wheel       2.0～2.2 kg/cm$^2$ (28～32 lbs/in$^2$)

The tire pressure varies somewhat depending on whether the load is heavy or light.

## 3—11 BRAKE ASSEMBLY

The brake assembly is of the expanding type which makes the brake shoe adhere closely to the drum by turning the cam mechanically (in case of the rear brake) or with a wire (the front brake).

The brake linings are completely glued to the shoe by the special adhesive and the rivets.

**A. Front Brake**
**How to disassemble**

Remove the front wheel and the shoe plate according to the precceding instruction under the section 9 in this chapter. The structure of the of the brake is shown by the next diagram.

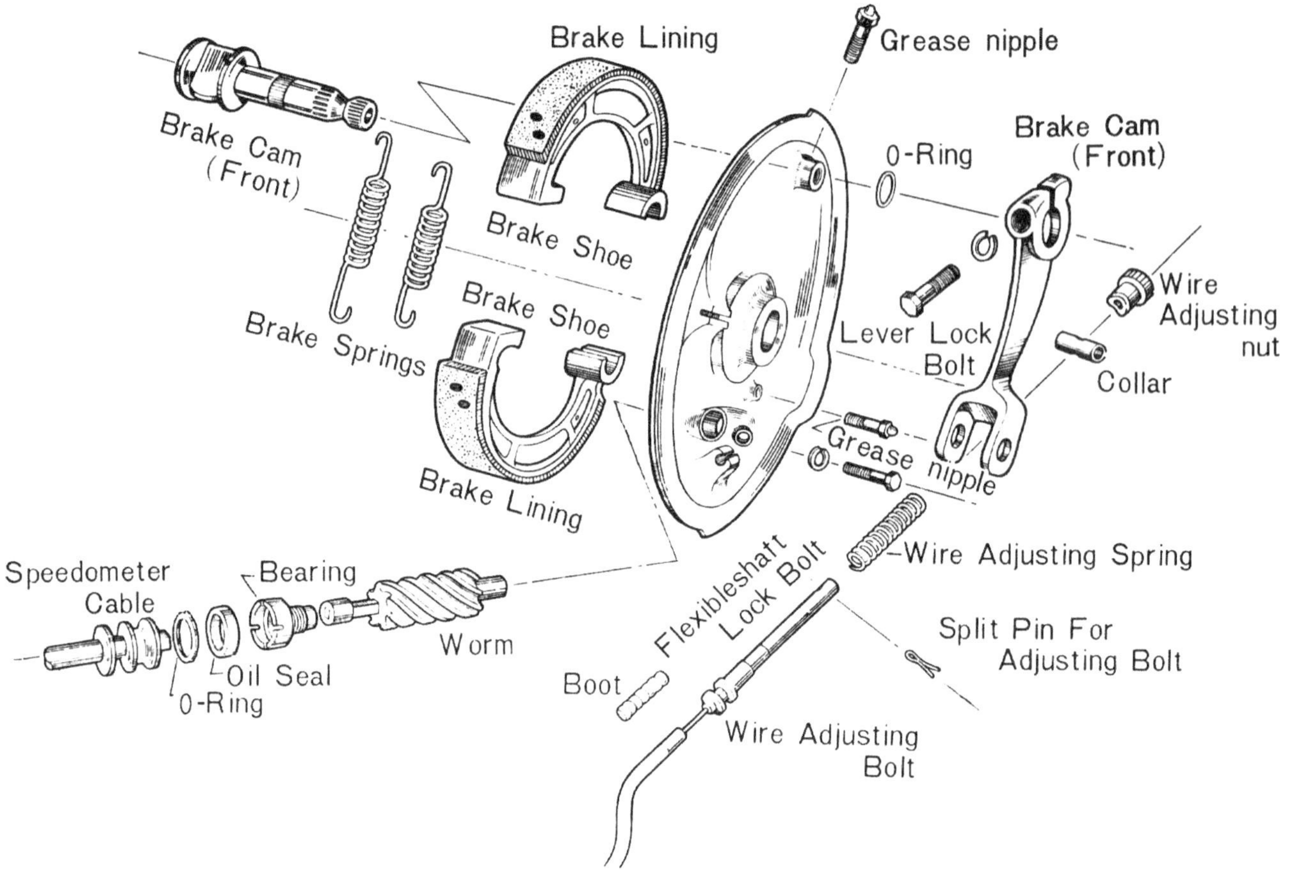

### Inspection

a. If the thickness of the linings reaches the limit of utility, replace the shoe assembly.

    Utility limit of lining = minimum thickness 2 mm

b. If the cam's working section in the shoe or the cam section of the cam pin is remarkably worn out, replace it.

c. Replace the faulty shoe spring.

d. If the worm and the bearing is worn out or the oil seal SO 7-14-4 inserted in the bearing is faulty, replace it.

### Hints on assembling

a. When assembling the front brake, supply specified grease sufficiently to the worm, the oil seal and so on. On this occasion, keep the lining from the grease.

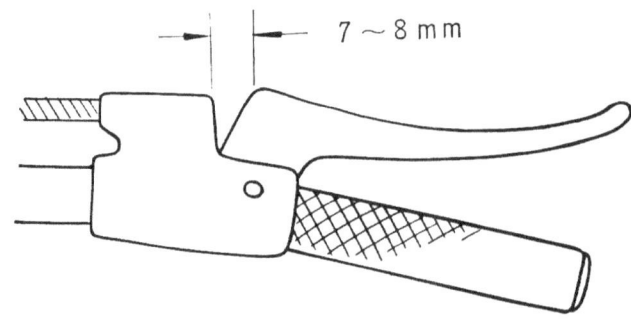

b. There should be a play of 7~8 mm for the front brake before it being put into action and effect. See the diagram.

## B. Rear Brake

The method of disassembling and inspection and the hints on assembly are same as for the front brake.

The play of the brake pedal should be adjusted as diagram below.

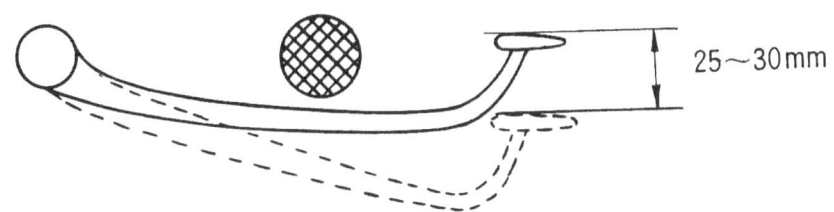

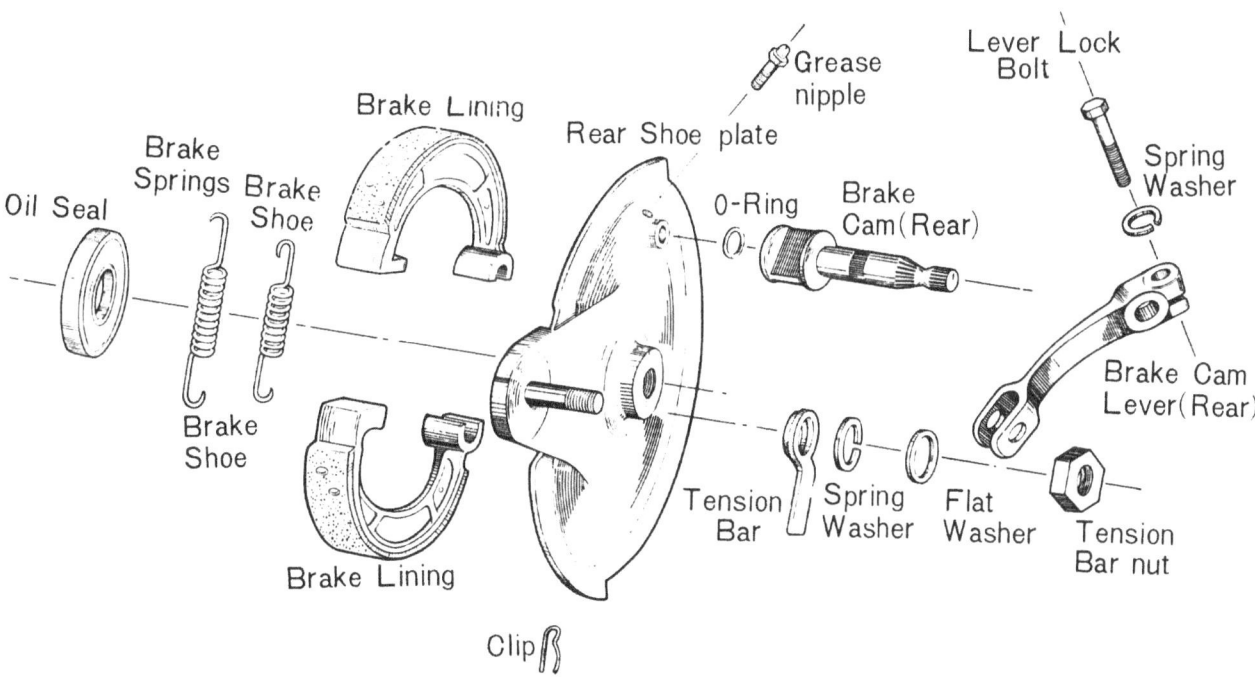

# CHAPTER 4. ELECTRICAL EQUIPMENT

## 4—1 ELECTRICAL EQUIPMENT OF YAMAHA YA-5

The electrical equipment of the the YA—5 has been designed and manufactured on the bases of the YA—3's excellent starter dynamo and the valuable data which its over two years production has furnished. YAMAHA is proud to present it our user.

As compared with the YA—3, the starter dynamo has been improved from $120\phi$ to $134\phi$ according to the high-powered engine. On the other hand, the maximum output of the dynamo shows a decrease from 26 km/H to 24 km/H. For the above reasons, the battery have had an ample scope and the battery capacity has been improved from 11 A/H to 10 A/H (12V. single subustance).

Our technical staff has attached the regulator, the starting switch and other in the box on the left side of the body to simplify their inspection and, in addition, adopted the MF I type inner mechanism for the speedometer.

The other features are described in the section headed "Explanation of Parts".

## 4—2 COMPONENT PARTS

The principal parts of the electrical equipment are attached to the four section below.

| Part | Maker | Type |
|---|---|---|
| ENGINE: | | |
| Starter Dynamo | Hitachi | GS-113 Type Torque 1.3 kgm and above Output 14V 90W 1600 rpm |
| Neutral Switch | Asahi | YNS-5 |
| Spark Plug | Hitachi | M 44W |
| FRAME: | | |
| Battery | Furukawa | BSP3-12 12V 10AH |
| | Yuasa | MBH3-12 12V 10AH |
| Regulator | Hitachi | T107-11 |

|  |  |  |
|---|---|---|
| Starting Switch | Hitachi | A104-15 (same as for YD2) |
| Fuse Holder | Kanazawa | 20A×3 (same as for YA3) |
| Ignition Coil | Hitachi | C11-04 (same as for YD2) |
| Stop Switch | Asahi | YS5 |
| **FRONT:** | | |
| Head Lamp | Koito | H-114 |
| Speedometter | Yasaki | LSC |
| Main Switch | Asahi | YAM-5 |
| Flasher Relay | Shashin | 12T-1 For 14V·16W (same as for YA-3) |
| Front Flasher Lamp | Kinsen | MLF-5 |
| Handle Switch (right) | Asahi | YBS |
| 〃 (left) | 〃 | YCS |
| Horn | Kinsen | BM-2 |
|  | Mitsuba | MB-3A |
| **TAIL:** | | |
| Tail Lamp | Koito | H-115 |
| Rear Flasher Lamp | Kinsen | MLR-5 |

The wire harnesses connect one part with others.

## 4—3 EXPLANATION OF PARTS

The ignition, the starting, the lighting, the signal and the battery systems are described below.

### A. Ignition System

The ignition system starts combustion of the mixure gas compressed in the cylinder with the electric spark and makes the engine work smoothly.

The ignition system consists of the following components.

a. Contact Breaker (It belongs to the starter dynamo).
b. Condenser (It belongs to the starter dynamo).
c. Ignition Coil.
d. Spark Plug.
e. High Tension Cord.

## a. Contact Breaker

Connection Diagram of Ignition System

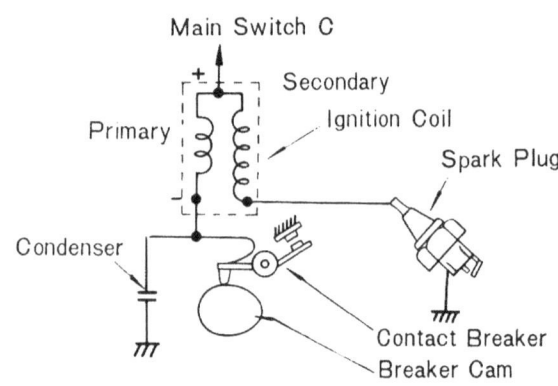

Construction of Contact Breaker

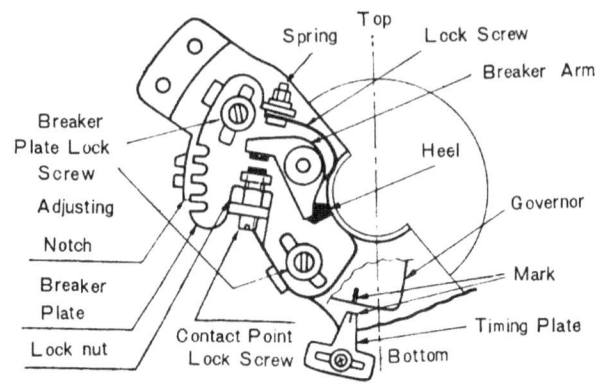

### Function

The contact breaker is the device which interrupts the primary current of the ignition coil and causes high tension to the secondary coil.

The contact breaker attached to the starter dynamo is illustrated by the above diagram.

### Adjustement

1) **Point Gap**

   The point gap should be adjusted in the position where the brake cam pushes up the heel. It should be adjusted to 0.3~0.35 mm with the contact point lock screw and the lock nut.

2) **Ignition Timing**

   The ignition timing should be adjusted to 2.6 mm (tolerance of $-3, +2$) before top dead point by attaching the dial gauge to the plug hole in the cylinder head. The relation between the piston stroke and the crank angle is shown in the left figure.

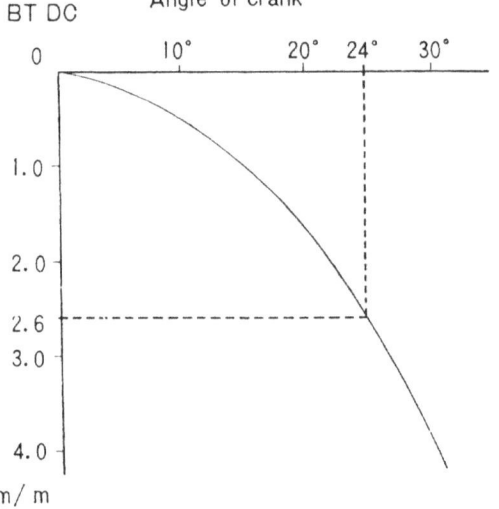

Relationship between Stroke and Angle of crank

## b. Condenser

### Function

The condenser absorbs the spark which is about to be emitted between the contact points and prevent the contact point of the contact breaker from burning with the spark.

### Position To Be Attached

The condenser is attached to the breaker attaching plate of the dynamo. Its lead is connected with the lead-in line of the breaker at the terminal I.

### Inpection

The condenser lead should be detached at the terminal I. The insulation test should be given by the 500V megger or the YAMAHA service tester. If the resistance is above 3MΩ and the capacity is 0.22 μF (±10%), the condenser is all right.

### c. Ignition Coil
### Construction

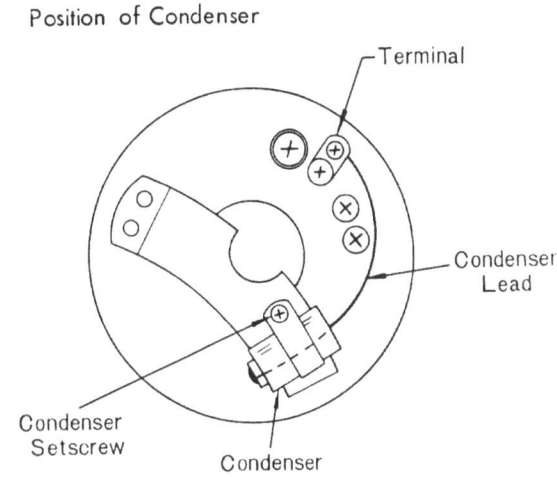

Position of Condenser

The ignition coil acts as a kind of transformer of which the turn ratio of the primary and the secondary windings reaches about 1 : 50. If the primary current is interrupted by the contact breaker, the high tension of 150~300V is brought about in the primary coil by the self-induction. Then, this tension is boosted to 7,500~10,000V by the secondary coil and causes the plug to spark.

The coil is available at all the YAMAHA models except YDS—1.

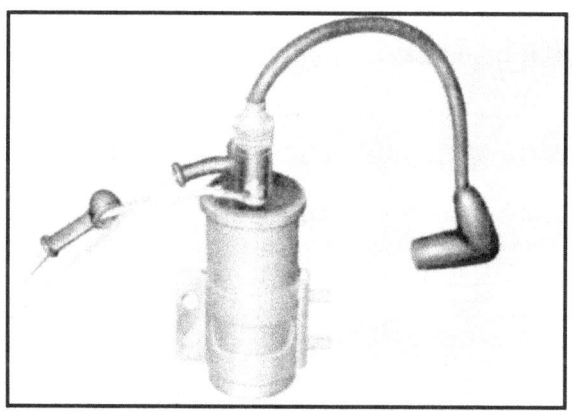

### Inspection

First, the resistances of the primary and the secondary coils should be inspected. If normal, the spark test should be given by the YAMAHA service tester.

If the spark is 6 mm and over, the coil is completely normal.

## CONSTRUCTION OF IGNITION COIL

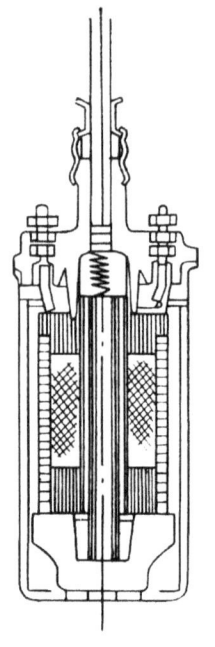

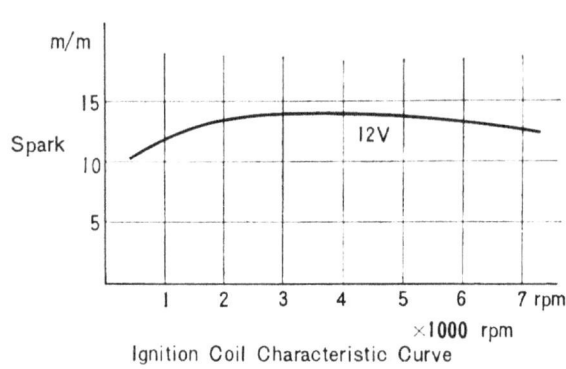

Ignition Coil Characteristic Curve

### d. Spark Plug
**Function**

The spark plug ignites the compressed mixture gas with the spark.

The hot type plug is recommended to the user who drives at low speed, while the cold type one is recommended to the user who drives at high speed or in the hill country.

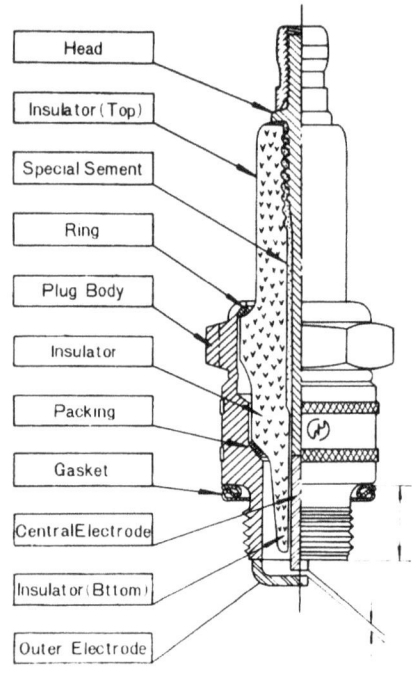

### Selection of Plug

In case of NGK plug, the last letter of the name (H in case of YA-5) and in case of Hitachi plug, the first letter (M in case of YA—5) mean the lenght of the lock screw. When replacing, care should be taken to select the correct plug.

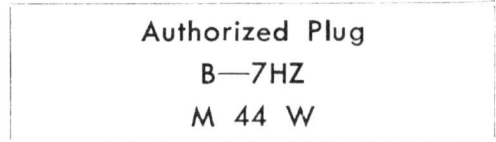

### Inspection

The ignition plug should be inspcted

every 3,000 km to clean the electrode and the leg and to correct the gap. It is possible to use the plug up to 10,000 km under the normal condition.

### e. High Tension Cord

The high tension cord transmits the high tension to the spark coil.
It is of the same rubber mould type as for MF-1.

## Inspection Standard

| | Item | Inspection standard | Inspection time |
|---|---|---|---|
| **BREAKER** | Point gaps | 0.3~0.35 mm | Every 3,000 km. |
| | Point pressure | 500~700 g | When engine does not run smoothly at high speed. |
| | Condenser capacity | 0.22μF ±10% | At irregular firing |
| | Ignition timing | 24° (2.6mm) | Evrey 3,000 km |
| **COIL** | Primary resistance | 4.9 Ω (20°C) | At irregular firing |
| | Secondary resistance | 5.5KΩ (20°C) | " |
| | Spark characteristic | 6 mm and over 1,2v | " |
| **GOVERNER** | Angle-advance characteristic: beginning | 5° about 1,200 rpm | When engine does not run smoothly |
| | finish | 24° about 1,600 rpm | |
| **PLUG** | Spark gap | 0.6~0.7 mm | Every 3,000 km |

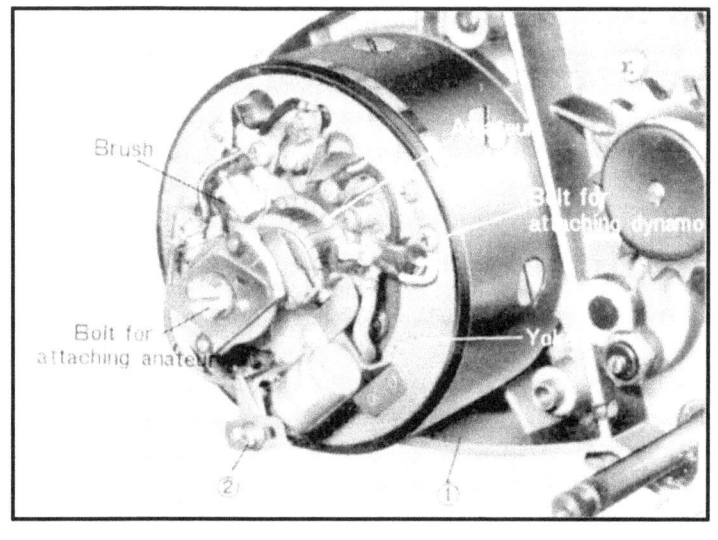

## B. Starting and Charging Systems

The starting system is the apparatus which the electric motor revolves the crank instead of the hand or the foot.

The charging system charges the battery which is the power source necessary for starting and supplies the power to any load when the engine is running. Consequently, the former differs from the latter in function and performance. On YA—5, however, the starter and the dynamo has been joined into a unit. For this reason, both system is explained in this section.

The starting system consists of the following components.
a. Starter Dynamo.
b. Starting Switch.
c. Starter Button.

The charging system consists of the following components.
d. Starter Dynamo.
e. Regulator.
f. Fuse Holder

### a. Starter Dynamo

The starter dynamo characteristics are given in the figure below. As shown in the figure, when the compression pressure is normal (8 kg/cm), the v.p.m. of the crank is about 600 vpm and the current is about 30A.

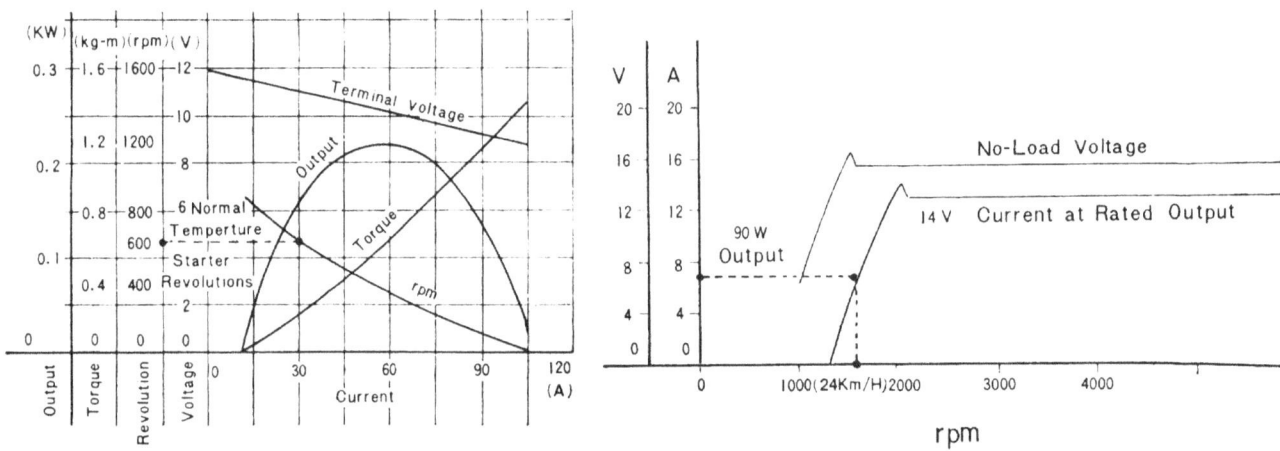

When the r.p.m. of the dynamo is over 1600 r.p.m. or the car speed is over 24 km/h at top gear, the dynamo becomes the rated out put of 90W. Therefore, it is desirable that our agencies or our dealers recommend the user to drive over this speed,

### b. Regulator

**Function**

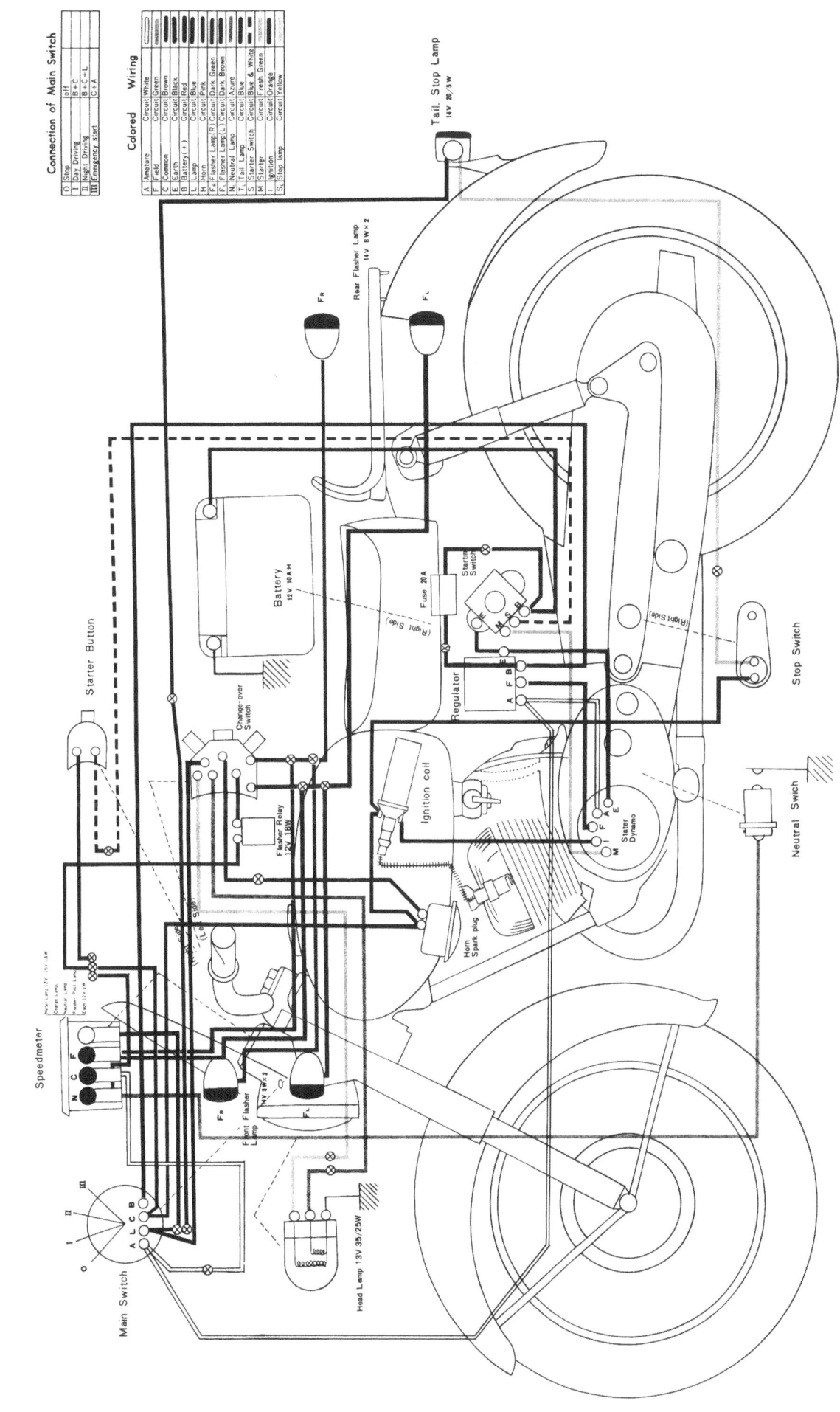

# MEMO

The regulator controls the current in the shunt coil of the dynamo by means of the constant-voltage relay and keeps the voltage constant. Besides, the charging relay pervents it from flowing back from the battery to the dynamo while the voltage in the dynamo is 0 or lower than the battery voltage —while the engine stops or idles.

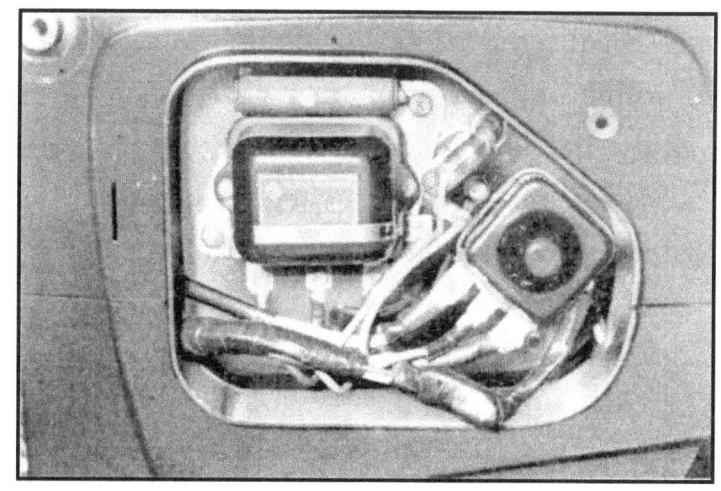

### Inspection

The inspection of the no-load voltage shoud be conducted by removing the wiring from the regulator terminal B after engine starting and by connecting the voltmeter instead of it. If the above instructions are too troublesome, it is advisable to adopt the following easier method.

#### Preparation
1) DC Voltmeter (20~30V).
2) Engine Tachometer (Pulse Tachometer) etc.

#### How to inspect
1) Connect (+) of the voltmeter with the regulator terminal B and (−) with the frame body.
2) Start the engine, then keep it 3000 rpm.
3) Break the connecter of the fuse holder, and measure the voltage.
4) If the voltage is within the range of the rating (14.8~15.8V), the regulator is normal. If not, adjust it.

HOW TO INSPECT VOLTAGE

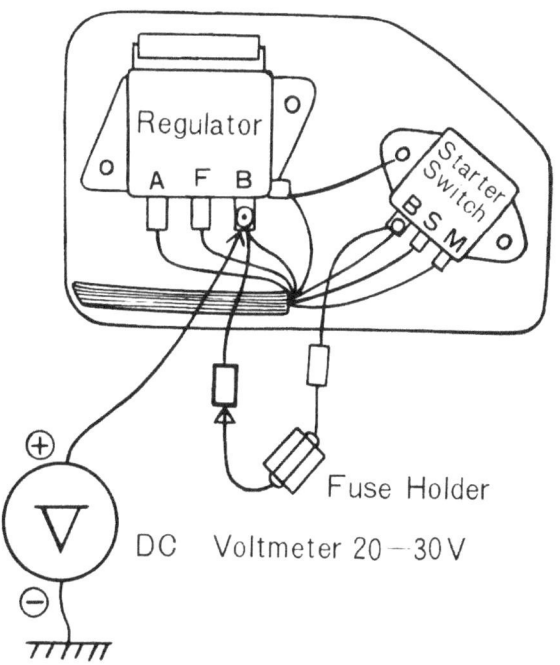

#### Adjustment
1) Measure the voltage by the above inspection method. If it is not within

the range of the rating or the riding conditions, make it almost impossible to charge the battery, adjust the voltage by means of the adjusting plate of the voltage relay. Gaps of each section of the voltage relay are shown in the left diagram.

For the inspection and the adjustment, the gap gauge should be used.

2) The charging relay should be adjusted by the adjusting plate similarly to the voltage one.

Connect the voltmeter (DC 20~30V) with the regulator terminal A and the frame body, and gradually increase the running of the engine. If the contact point is closed at voltage of 12.5~13.5V, the charging relay is normal. If not adjust it by bending the adjusting plate. Usually there is no need for adjusting this relay. Gaps of each section are shown in the diagram.

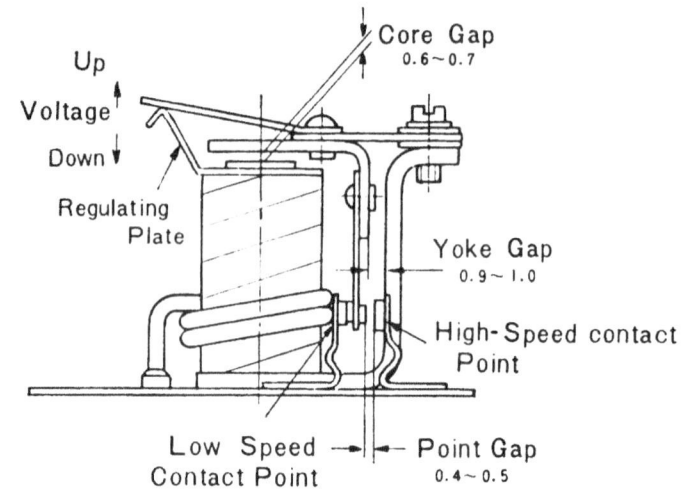

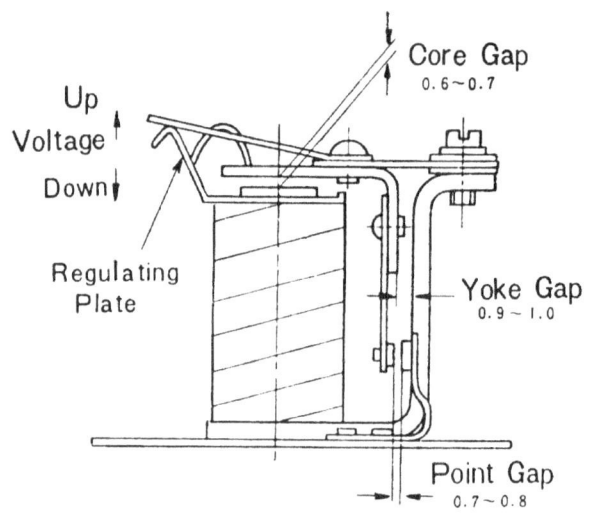

### c. Starting switch

The starting switch makes and breaks the electric circuit connected with the starter. This switch is operated by the starter button.

### Inspection

The contact at the contact point should be measured.
1) Connect the voltmeter with the terminals M($-$) and B($+$).
2) Press the starter button, and measure the voltage drop at the contact point.
3) If it is lower than 0.3V, the starting switch is normal. If not, remove the cover, and file the contact point with sand-paper (No. 00).

If the starter button does not click when pressed, inspect the connection between the terminals S and E. If the resistance reaches about 5Ω, the wiring is not broken.

### d. Starter Button

The starter button turns on and off the starter switch. Press the button and the terminal C is connected with the terminal S, and the current flows to the electro-magnetic coil of the starting switch.

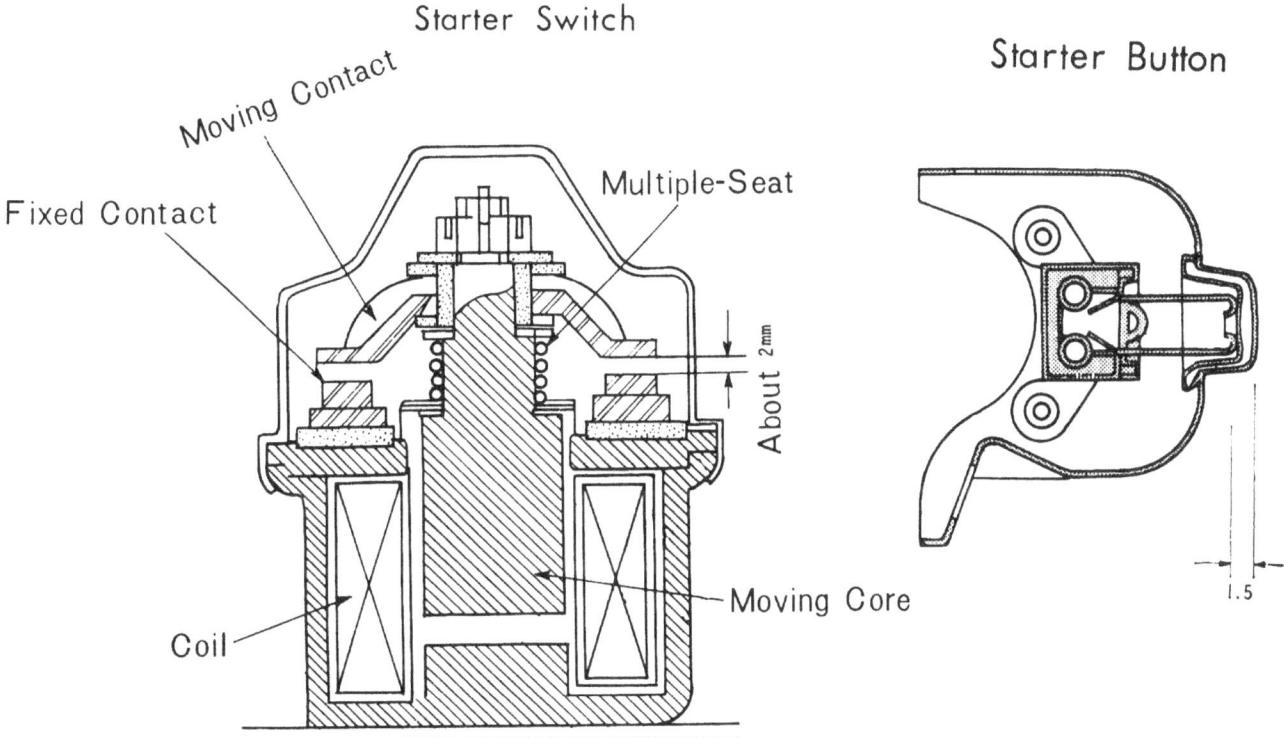

## Inspection standard

| | Item | | Inspection standard | Inspection time |
|---|---|---|---|---|
| **STARTER-DYNAMO** | Field | Number of poles<br>Resistance : shunt<br>　　　　　　　series | 6<br>6.8Ω (20°C)<br>0.0145Ω (20°C) | At unusual voltage |
| | Brush | Whole length of brush<br>Utility limit (in length)<br>Force of spring<br>Material<br>Number of brushes | 20 mm<br>11.5 mm<br>400~560 g<br>MH 33<br>4 | After 6,000 km<br>Every 3,000 km |
| | Commutator | Diameter of commutator<br>Wear limit<br>Mica under-cut<br>　〃　　limit<br>Difference between maximum and minimum diameter | 37.5φ<br>35.5φ<br>0.5~0.8 mm<br>0.2<br><br>below 0.05 | Every 3,000 km |
| | Breaker | Contact point gaps<br>Contact point pressure<br>Condenser capacity<br>Ignition timing:<br>　befor angle-advance<br>　after angle-advance | 0.3~0.35 mm<br>500~700 g<br>0.22μF±10%<br><br>5°<br>24° (2.6 mm) | Every 3,000 km |
| | Others | Air gap<br>Armature taper | 0.3<br>20φ×$^1/_{10}$ | |
| **REGULATOR** | Voltage Relay | No load voltage adjustment<br>Load voltage of ignition coil<br>Resistance of voltage coil<br>Resistance of field coil<br>Air gap | 15.3~16.1V<br>15~15.8V<br>70Ω (20°C)<br>10Ω (20°C)<br>See diagram | Every 12,000 km |
| | Charging Relay | Cut-in voltage<br>Resistance of voltage coil<br>Compensating resistance<br><br>Air gap | 12.5V~13.5V<br>10Ω (20°C)<br>12.5Ω (available in voltage relay)<br>See diagram | |
| **STARTING SWITCH** | Contact Points | Pressure<br>Resistance<br><br>Correction limit:<br>　on mobile side<br>　on fixed side | 1.7 kg<br>0.2V/100A and below<br><br>0.3 mm<br>0.5 mm | |
| | Electro-magnetic Coil | Resistance | 5Ω (20°C) | |
| **STARTER FUSE** | Fuse | External dimensions<br>Capacity | 6φ×26 mm<br>20A | |
| **STARTER BUTTON** | Contact Point | Contact resistance | 0.1V/10A and below | |

## C. Lighting and Signal Systems

The lighting system is the complex whole of the lighting equipments for night driving and the signal one conveys information or direction to another car or pedestrian.

### Lighting system:
a. Head Lamp.
b. Tail Lamp. (licence plate lamp)
c. Meter Lamp.

### Signal system:
d. Speedometer and Cable Gear Unit.
e. Flasher Lamp and Relay.
f. Tail Lamp (tail lamp, brake lamp and reflex reflector)
g. Charge Lamp.
h. Horn.
i. Switches. (Main switch, Handlebar switch, Stop lamp switch and Neutral lamp switch)

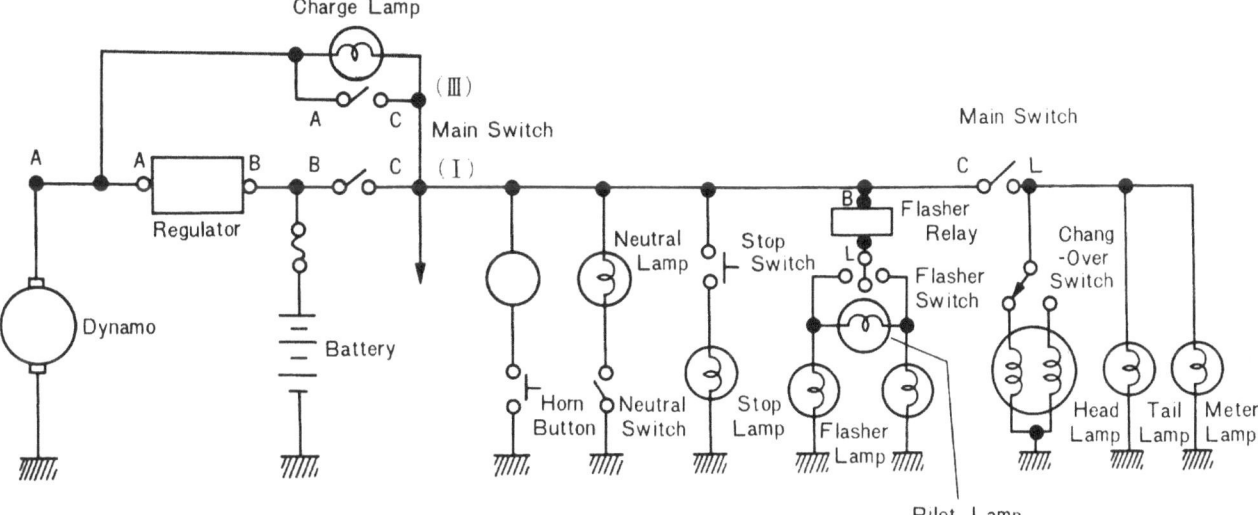

Connection Diagram of Signal & Lighting Systems

### a. Head Lamp

As shown in the illustration, the head lamp is designed to give sufficient light for safe riding. Light-rays is collected by means of the reflector and emitted through the lens.

The socket holder is not of the ring nut type of YA—5, but of the rubber cover one.

## b. Licence Plate Lamp

This lamp throws light on the licence plate. As the traffic regulations provide that the licence plate lamp should be white, the lower part of the tail lamp lens is transparent. The bulb of the licence plate lamp is available in that of the tail lamp.

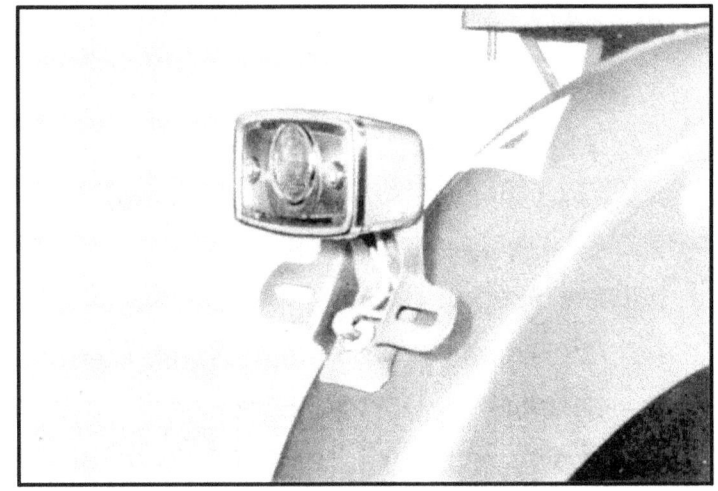

## c. Speedometer

The speedometer indicates the speed at which the cycle is moving. The gear section built in the shoe plate transmits the revolutions of the front wheel to the speedometer through the meter cable. As shown in diagram, the magnet is attached to the shaft which is directly connected with the meter cable and its revolutions produces the eddy current, which turns the indicator.

## d. Flasher lamp and Relay

The flasher lamp is connected with the relay which flashes the signal lamp for indicating the direction of turn.

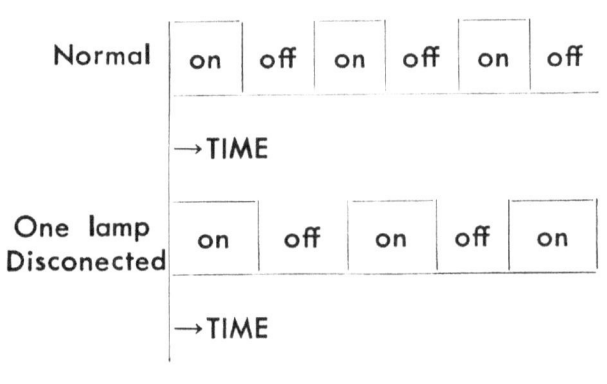

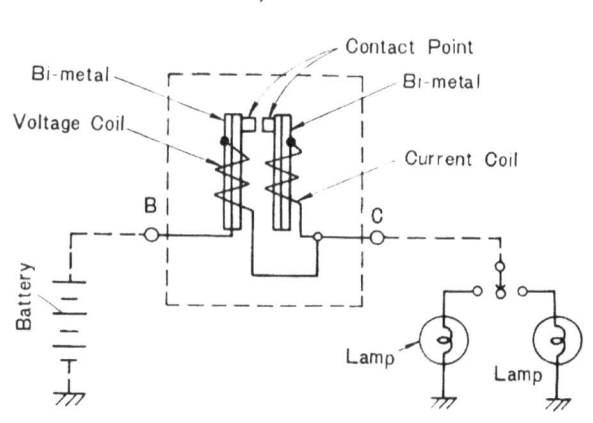

The front flasher lamps of YA-5 are different from those of YA-3 in their attaching section. If the globe is loose, adjust it with its nut and shaft. The rear flasher lamps are secured by the lock bolts of which diameter has been increased from 8 mm (YA—3) to 10 mm.

The flasher relay is of the bimetal type. The internal connection is illustrated by the right diagram.

The working time of the flasher relay is adjusted according to the bulb to be used, so the specified bulb must be used. If the relay does not turn on and off the light regularly or it takes long time to start, replace it.

Its working time is given in above figure. As it shows, when the filament of one of the rear flasher lamps has burned out, the lighting time of another lamp is prolonged over two times.

### e. Tail Lamp

The tail lamp signals the existence of your cycle to the driver who follows you. The reflex reflector attached according to the new traffic regulations acts as the tail lamp when stopping or the filament of the tail lamp has burn out.

The brake lamp conveys your intension of stopping or braking to the driver who follows you. Its filament is built in the bulb of the tail lamp.

### f. Charge Lamp

As shown in the connection diagram, the dynamo terminal A and the main switch terminal C is connected with each other. When the dynamo does not generate electricity, the electric pressure of the battery acts on A-C, and the charge lamp is turned on. When the dynamo starts, the potential difference becomes 0, and the lamp is turned off.

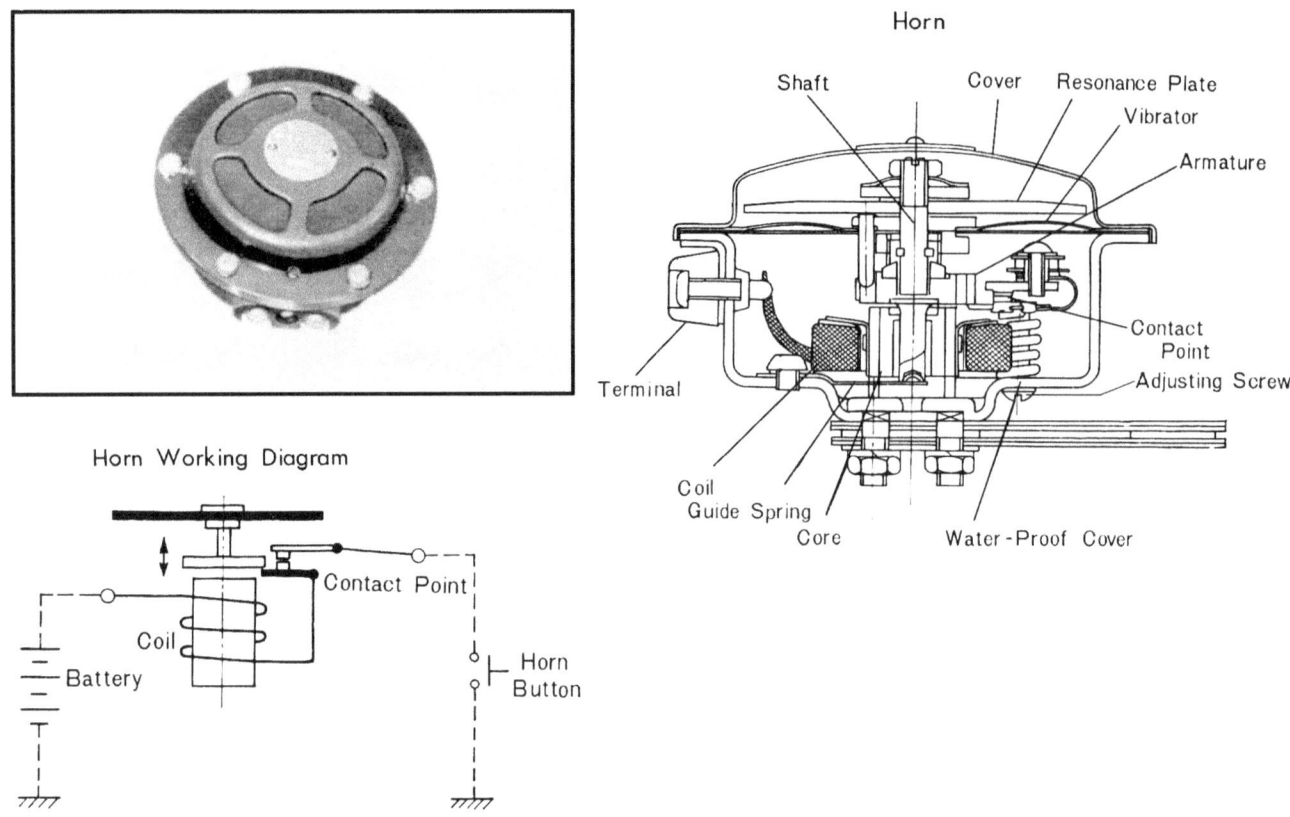

### g. Horn

The horn arouses another driver's attention. The electric horn of a microphone type is in use.

As shown in diagram, the principle of the horn is same as for the electric DC buzzer. If the horn makes no sound or bad one, unscrew the horn lock bolts (2 pieces of 8 mm bolt), and remove the horn, and adjust the sound by turning the adjusting screw right or left. If it still makes no sound or grave one, its inner part is faulty.

### h. Switches

#### 1) Main switch

The main switch makes and breaks the circuits of ignition, starting, lighting, and signal.

As shown in diagram, the switch part of a slide type and the cylinder key part are joined together.

If the connection between terminals B.C.L and A is broken as listed below, replace the switch assembly.

The mascot keys comprise 20 varieties in all.

## 2) Handlebar switches (left)

The handle has switches consist of three: first for exchanging the head light, second for sounding the horn and third for lighting the direction indicator lamp. They are same as for YA-3 except the cord.

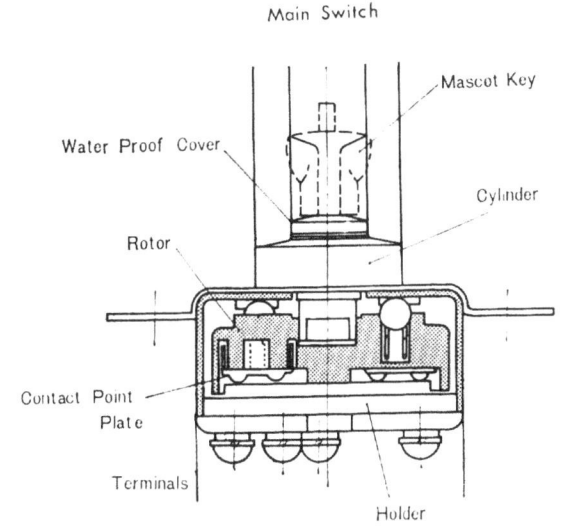

Remove the switch assembly from the lever holder, and push the flasher switch toward the lever side. And the handle switch is detached. If the lamp does not light when switching on, the contact point should be filed by the sand-paper No. 00.

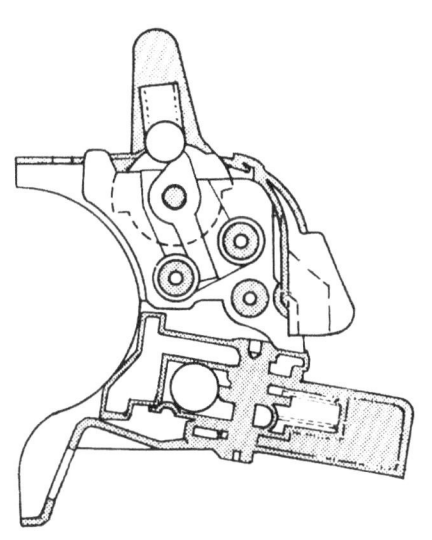

Change Over Switch

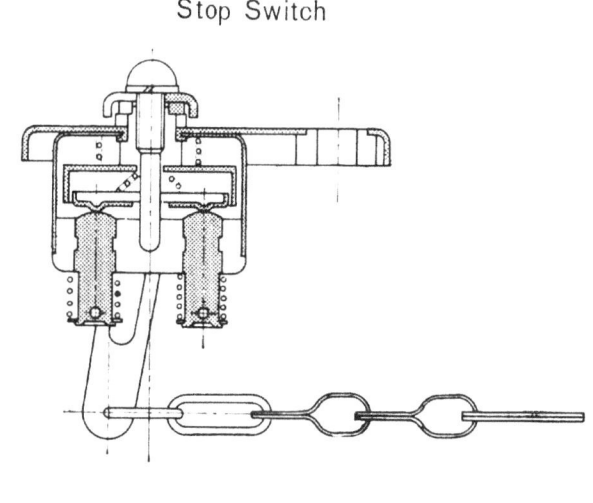

Stop Switch

## 3) Stop light switch

The stop switch makes and breakes the brake lamp circuit in gear with the brake lever. This switch is same as for YA—3 except the lever and the attaching plate. When the lever is turnd over 8°, two terminals are connected with each other.

## 4) Neutral switch

The neutral switch lights the pilot lamp in the speedometer only when the change gear being in neutral position. When the shifter cam is put into neutral the switch makes contact with the earthing rivet of the cam.

The normal stroke of the neutral switch is 1.0 m/m. After measuring the depth from the attached surface to the contact point of the shifter cam, the stroke should be adjusted to be 1.0 m/m by the fiber packing.

**Inspection standard**

| Name of Parts | Inspection standard | Inspection time |
|---|---|---|
| Head Light | 12—16V  35/25W | |
| Tail Light | ″       20/10W | |
| Meter Light | ″        2W | |
| Flasher Light | 12~16V  8W×4 | |
| Stop Light | ″       20/5W | |
| Charge Pilot Light | ″        2W | |
| Neutral Light | ″        2W | |
| Flasher Light | ″        2W | |
| Horn | 10~16 V  1.2 A and below | |
| Flasher Relay | 12 V 18 W at load. 80 times/min. ±20 times | Every 12,000 km |
| Speedometer | 60 km/H/1400 rpm | |
| Meter Cable | Apply grease thinly to inner cable. | Evry 3,000 km |
| Gear Unit | Supply oil. | Every 6,000 km |

## D. Battery

The battery supplies the electric power to the starting and the ignition systems in time of starting. In addition, it works instead of the dynamo when slowing down the cycle at a crossing, for example. During drive, it is charged by the dynamo.

### Care in using for the first time

Preparation: Dilute sulphuric acid (specific gravity of 1.28) 700 cc.

First, cut off the exhaust tube at 30 mm distance from its end. (see diagram below). Second, remove the six fluid plugs, and fill with dilute sulphuric acid to the maximum level line. Third, charge the battery with about 1A current for 4-5 hours.

Neutral Switch

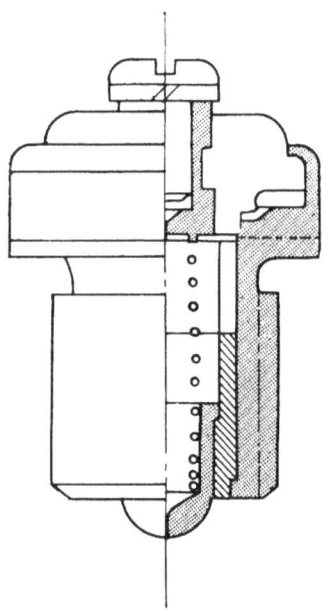

After the charging is over, float the foam by tipping the battery right and left. Then, once again, fill with dilute sulphuric acid or distilled water to the full level. After plugging up, wash the battery by pouring water on it, especially the plug section. Lastly, attach it to the body. After wiring, apply grease to the terminals.

## Periodical inspection

The battery should be inspected every month. The battery fluid should at all the times be above the mean of the maximum and minimum levels. If not, supply distilled water. On this occasion, dilute sulphuric acid or city water should not be used.

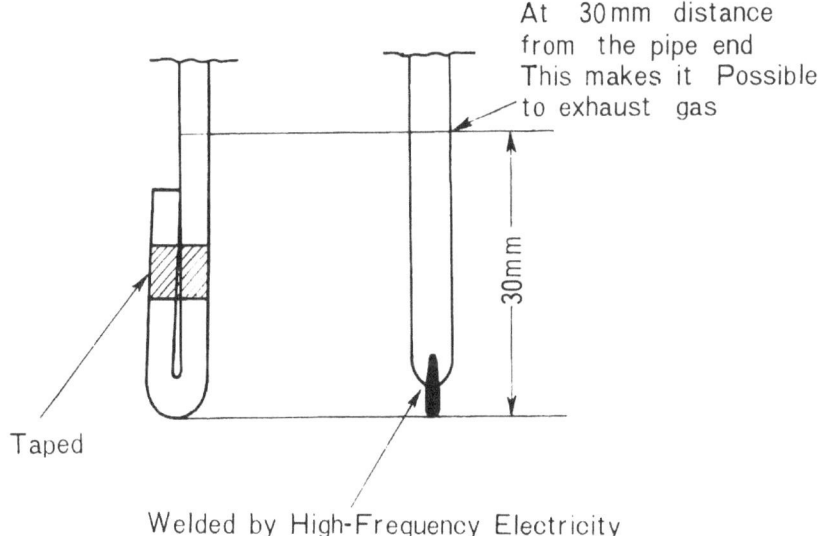

How To cut off Exhaust Pipe

## Note for Snowy Country

In the country where the cycle is out of use in winter, it is advisable to detach the battery and ask a battery service shop to preserve it.

Our dealer having a charger should preserve it as follows.
1) After detaching the battery from the cycle, charge it additionally.
2) After applying grease to the terminal section, keep it in the place where the temperature does not fall below zero.

3) Charge it once a month.
4) Charge it additionally before use in spring.

**Inspection standard**

| Inspection item | | Inspecton standard | Inspection time |
|---|---|---|---|
| Battery | Electrolyte | Specific gravity 1.28 (20°C) whole quantity about 700cc | In time of new cycle |
| | First charge | By means of 1 A current for 4~5h. | 〃 |
| | Supplementary fluid | Supply distilled water up to maximum level. | After 1 month |
| | Supplementary charge | By means of 1 A current for 13h. | In time of failure to start. |
| | Terminal section | Apply grease. | Every 6,000 km |
| | Terminal screws | Screw diameter 5; pitch 0.9 | |
| | Exhaust pipe | Length 250 mm | |
| | External dimensions. | Height 145 mm; Length 135 mm; Width 90 mm. | |

# CHAPTER 5.
# PERIODICAL INSPECTION & MAINTENANCE

Regular inspection and maintenance help to keep your cycle in good condition. In addition, this kind of care is the most important for the preservation of its life and the prevention of troubles. Do not wait until something goes wrong.

## 5—1 ASSEMBLY, CLEANING AND ADJUSTMENT OF CARBURETOR

The carburetor should be assembled and cleaned every 6,000 km (or every six months), besides adjusted, if necessary.

### How to disassemble and clean

a. Remove the carburetor cover.
b. Remove the air cleaner, the fuel pipe and the throttle wire.
c. Detach the carburetor.
   After dividing it into the following parts, disassemble each part.
   1). Float chamber
   2). Starter section
   3). Mixing body
   4). Throttle valve
d. Wash separate parts in gasoline, and blow air to every nozzle.
e. After cleaning, assemble them.

### How to adjust

a. When disassembling, make sure every part is a standard YAMAHA one. If not, replace it.
b. Adjust the idling revolution by means of the throttle stop screw, and control the density of mixture gas by means of the pilot air screw. The latter should be reversed 1 3/4 turns under normal conditions.
c. After the adjustment at low speed is over, make a trial run, and check whether the cycle accelerates according to opening of the grip. If not normal, change the position of the jet needle, or replace the main jet.

## 5—2 CLEANING OF AIR CLEANER

The air cleaner should be disassembled and cleaned every 1500 km. If used while dirty, it can lead to excessive fuel consumption and irregular functioning of the engine. After removing dirt from the air cleaner with gasoline, apply a small quantity of mobile oil.

## 5—3 IGNITION TIMING

In the case of 2 cycle engine, irregular firing has a harmful effect on the performance of the machine. The ignition timing should be checked every 3000~5000 km.

The point in adjustment of ignition timing is described under the head of "Attaching Dynamo" in the chapter 2.

## 5—4 INSPECTION OF SPARK PLUGS

If the spark plugs are dirty or damaged, or if the worn-out electorodes enlarge the spark plug gaps, the plugs throw little sparks and explode mixture gas poorly.

**Inspection**

If the ignition points of the plugs are burnt light brown, the plugs are normal.
a. Sputtering plugs.
    1). Driving with starter on.
    2). Air-gasoline mixture too rich.
    3). Incorrect gaps in plugs.
    4). Ignition timing too slow.
    5). Dirty or worn-out contact points.

After correcting the above points if still sputtering, replace the plug by the B-6H or the M45W type one.
b. Overburning.
    1). Loose plugs and insufficient gasket.
    2). Air-gasoline mixture too lean.
    3). Advance of ignition.

After correcting the above points, if still overburning, replace the plug by the cool type one.

As the spark plugs depend on the riding conditions of the user, it is desirable to select and recomend the plugs which meet user's requirements.

## 5—5 INSPECTION AND ADJUSTMENT OF CONTACT POINTS

If used while the contact breaker points are in bad contact, it can hasten their wear and tear.

The contact points should be adjusted so that the contact surfaces of the traveling and the fixed contacts run parallel with each other, besides the center lines of both surfaces coincide with each other.

If dirty or damaged, the contact surfaces should be filed by sand-paper.

## 5—6 INSPECTION OF BATTERY

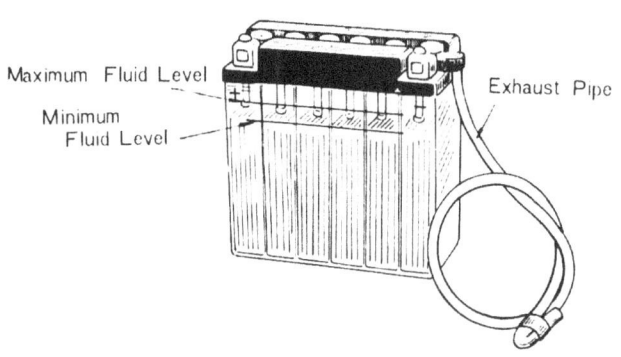

The battery fulfils its important function which acts as the power source for ignition, starting and lighting. Accordingly, it should be periodically inspected.

### How to inspect battery fluid

Regardless of whether the cycle is used or not, the battery is self-charged and its performance inclines gradually. As water in electrolyte escapes in vapour, the fluid level goes down.

Battery fluid should be above the minimum level line. When adding fluid, distilled water should be supplied (but not dilute sulphuric acid).

### How to measure specific gravity

The battery power is proportioned to the specific gravity of electrolyte. Therefore, the decrease of the specific gravity means the discharge of the battery or decrease of battery power.

1) **How to measure.**

   (a) Use a areometer (See diagram);
   
   (b) Insert its glass tube vertically into the battery;
   
   (c) Suck up electrolyte slowly;
   
   (d) And read the areometer. Note that your eyes should be kept on a level with the fluid surface.

2) Determination of charge rate by means of areometer. As the specific gravity of electrolyte decreases in proportion to the discharged quantity of electricity, the charge rate may be shown by it. The relationship between

the specific gravity of electrolyte and the charge rate is shown below.

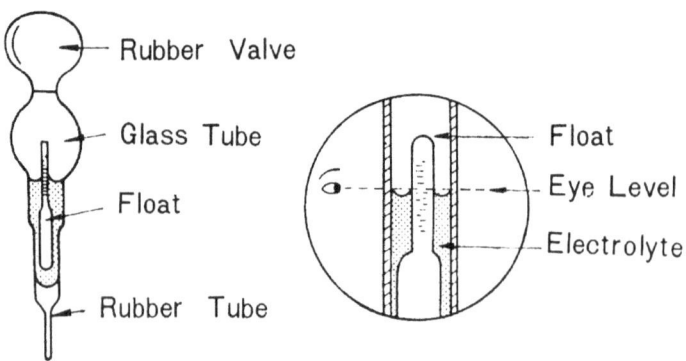

| Specific Gravity | Rate of Charged quantity of electricity |
|---|---|
| below 1.180 | 0% |
| 1.230~1.240 | 50% |
| 1.280 | 100% |

3) The specific gravity depends on the temperature.

The above values of the specific gravity of electrolyte and the charge rate are the standard ones obtained at 20°C.

Except at 20°C, they should be converted by the following expression.

Specific gravity at 20°C =
(Actual specific gravity at t°C) $+0.0007(t°C-20°)$

## 5—7 CARBON BRUSH

The worn-out carbon brush makes bad contact with the commutator. The more worn-out one weakens the contact pressure, and emits sparks, and burns out the commutator, and decreases the performance of the dynamo.

As the carbon brush is expendable, its length should be measured every 3000 km. If it reaches nearly the utility limit of 11.5 mm (the new carbon brush is 20 mm in length), replace it.

## 5—8 FRONT FORK

The function of the front fork depends remarkably on its oil. After first 5,000 km, be sure to change the oil, then every 5,000 km.

The proper quanity of oil is 170cc per one side of the fork.

The mixture of mobile oil　　No. 30.
　　　　　 and spindle oil　　 No. 60
in the ratio of half to half should be used.

### Hint on changing oil

Drainage : Remove the oil drain bolt from the lower end of the fork and the oil maybe drained.

Supply　 : Remove the dressed bolt from the upper end of the fork, and supply oil. The proper oil level is about 340 mm in height from the inner tube upper end when the fork being extended.

## 5—9  REMOVING CARBON

Carbon accumulates on the cylinder head, the piston head, the cylinder exhaust port and the muffler exhaust pipe, and has a harmful effect on them. It should be removed every 3,000 km.

The excessive accumulation of carbon is caused by the follwing points.

1) Isn't the gasoline-air mixture ratio too rich?
   Isn't the bad fuel or oil in use?
2) Isn't the the ignition timing too slow?

## 5—10  LUBRICATION

Lubrication is necessary for diminishing friction in the rotating and the sliding sections. Without lubricating, not only will they be damaged, but the cycle will be unable to fulfil its function. Be sure to apply grease and oil for the lubrication. The wheres and whens applied are listed below.

### Y A 5 OIL SUPPLY

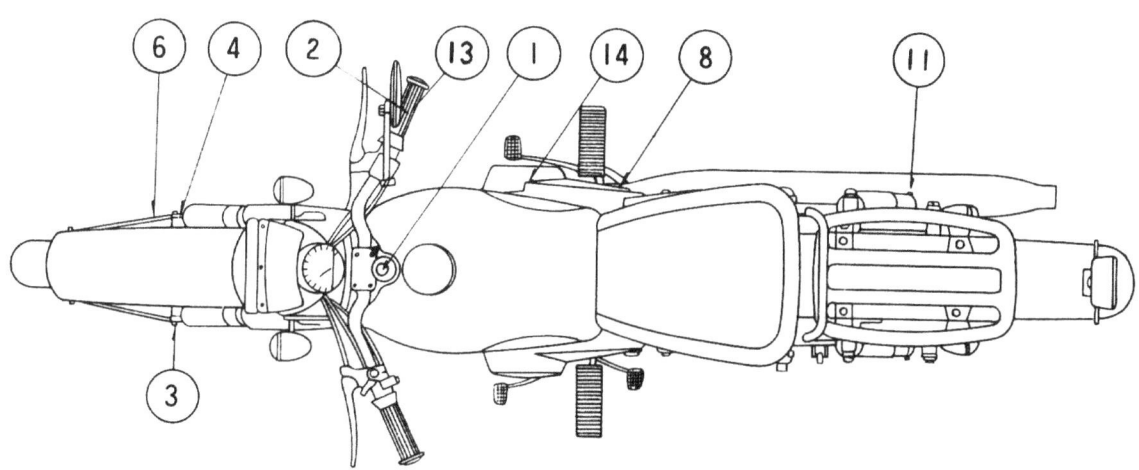

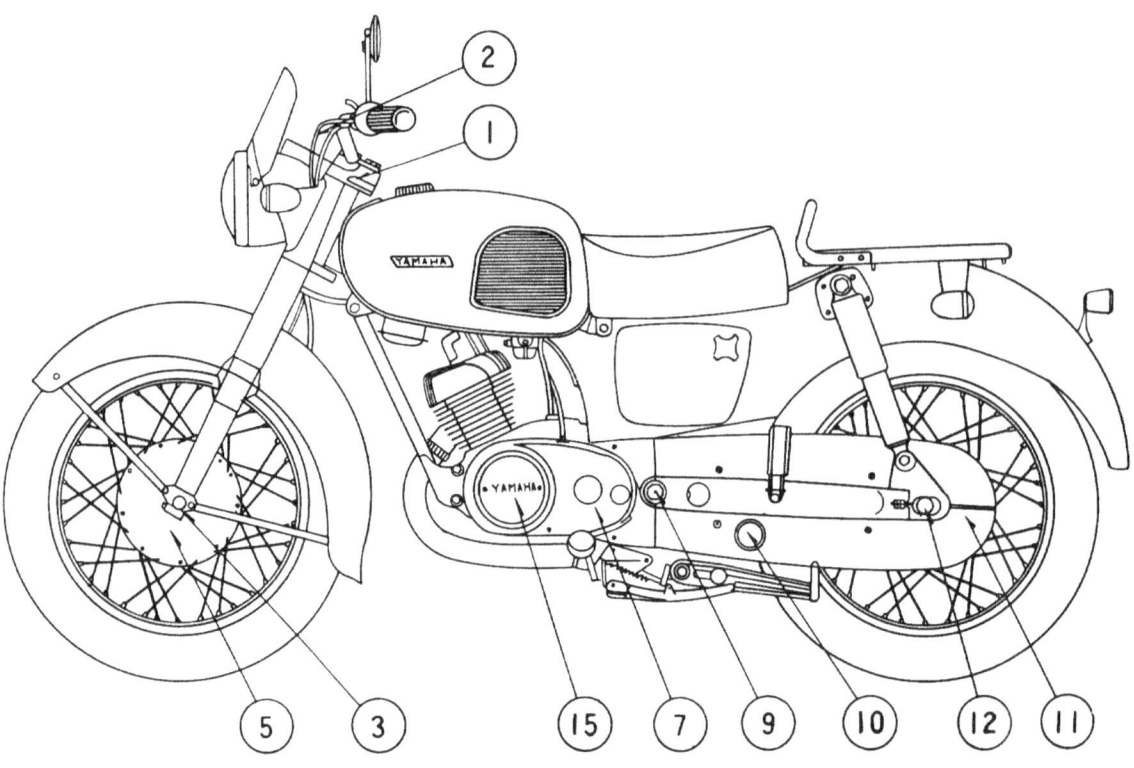

| No. | Where Supplied | Supplied Oil | Primary Oil Suply | Secondary Oil Supply |
|---|---|---|---|---|
| 1 | Steering Ball Race | Cap Grease | When disassembling or repairing | |
| 2 | Brake Clutch Wires | Cap Grease & Mobile Oil | 1500 km | every 3000 km |
| 3 | Meter Unit | Cap Grease | 6000 km | every 6000 km |
| 4 | Front Brake cam | Cap Grease | 1500 km | every 3000 km |
| 5 | Front Hub Bearing | Cap Grease | 6000 km | every 6000 km |
| 6 | Front Shoe Plate | Cap Grease | 6000 km | every 6000 km |
| 7 | Clutch Push Screw | Cap Grease | 1500 km | every 3000 km |
| 8 | Brake Pedal | Cap Grease | 1500 km | every 3000 km |
| 9 | Rear Arm Shaft | Cap Grease | 1500 km | every 3000 km |
| 10 | Secondary Chain | Mobile oil | 500 km | every 1500 km |
| 11 | Rear Brake Cam | Cap Grease | 1500 km | every 3000 km |
| 12 | Rear Hub Bearing | Cap Grease | 6000 km | every 6000 km |
| 13 | Handle Acceleration Grip | Cap Grease | 6000 km | every 6000 km |
| 14 | Mission Oil | Gear Oil #80 | 500 km | every 1500 km |
| 15 | Felt on Point Heel Section | Mobile Oil of a few drop | 1500 km | every 6000 km |

The mission oil should be supplied as follows:
Gear oil     #80 (SAF)
or Mobile Oil     #30 (MS class)
of 1000 cc or so.

# CHAPTER 6. TROUBLE SHOOTING

It is not too much to say that, if only a true trouble-source is found, the repairs will have been brought nearly to an end. Accordingly, to know how to trace the trouble-source, is the most important key to the successful repairs.

This chapter covers various trouble shooting with the adequate instruction for repairs.

## 6—1 FAILURE TO START

If the engine does not start when turning the starter lever according to the instruction, check whether the battery is well charged or there is sufficient fuel in the tank.

Then, trace the trouble-source in the following order.

|   | Inspection | Trouble-source | Remedy |
|---|---|---|---|
| 1 | Check whether gasoline is filled up to carburetor (float chamber). | If not, check the following points.<br>a. Clogged gasoline pipe.<br>b. Clogged gasoline cock.<br>c. Faulty or clogged float valve.<br>d. Clogged tank cap port. | Blow air.<br>Or, remove and clean. |
| 2 | Remove plugs, and attach them to cap, and earth them.<br>Then turn stater lever. See if there is spark. | If not, check the following points.<br>a. Dirty or damaged or wet plugs.<br>b. Dirty contact points. Incorrect gaps.<br>c. Bad condenser.<br>d. Faulty high-tension cord (puncture or disconnection)<br>e. Faulty ignition coil (disconnection or short circuit)<br>f. Bad main switch<br>g. Irregular firing. | See Chapter 4.<br>a. Clean or replace it.<br>b. File contact points. Adjust gaps.<br>c. Inspect it by means of tester. If bad, replace it.<br>d. Inspect it.<br>e. Inspect by means of tester. If faulty, replace it.<br>f. Inspect its continuity by means of tester. If faulty, replace it<br>g. Inspect it by means of timing light. |

| 3 | Check whether there is compression by turning starter lever (or by kicking). On this occasion, kick gear slip should not be taken account of. | If not, inspect the following point.<br>a. Incorrect valve seat angle.<br>b. Worn-out cylinder, piston or ring.<br>c. Leakage in head gasket.<br>d. Breakage in piston.<br>e. Leakage in crank case. | a. Inlet port should be opened when piston reaches upper dead point, and closed when it does lower one.<br>b. Replace it.<br>c. Renew packing.<br>d. Replace it.<br>e. Repair or replace it. |
|---|---|---|---|

If the above point get through the inspection, start the engine again according to the instructions.

| 4 | Check whether there are signs of explosioin. | If not, inspect the following points.<br>a. Mixture gas (of gasoline and air) too thin; Reversing carburetor air scerw too much; Passage of air through heat-proof packing.<br>b. Irregular firing. | a. Adjust carburetor. Apply "three Bond" to packing.<br>b. Correct ignition timing. |
|---|---|---|---|

## 6—2 SPEED IS SLOW, ENGINE POWER IS LOWER THAN USUAL

a)   Is the tire pressure adequate?

b)   Is the brake off?

c)   Are the wheel bearings good?

d)   Isn't the secondary chain tightened too much?

Then, trace the trouble-source in the following order.

|   | Inspection | Trouble source | Remedy |
|---|---|---|---|
| 1 | See if revolutions of engine increases. | If it increases, check the following points.<br>a. Slipping clutch. Set up main stand, and start engine, and put change gear, and lastly, blow engine with brake on. At this time, if engine does not stop to run, the cause lies in slipping clutch. | a. Adjust clutch, or replace friction disks. |

|   |   |   |   |
|---|---|---|---|
|   |   | b. Incorrect thermal value of plugs. | b. Replace it by plugs having correct thermal value. |
|   |   | If not, check the following points.<br>a. Bad starter plunger<br>b. Dirty air cleaner.<br>c. Insufficient gasoline flow. (clogged gasoline pipe).<br>d. Clogged tank cap port.<br>e. Clogged muffler or exhaust pipe. | a. Inspect starter wire drawing.<br>b. Clean it.<br>c. Clean carburetor, fuel pipe and cock.<br>d. Replace tank cap.<br>e. Clean it. |

When the above points are all right, make a trial run on a paved level road. If the engine power is still low, inspect the following points.

|   |   |   |   |
|---|---|---|---|
| 2 | Check whether ignition timing is correct. | Ignition timing should be inspected by timing light. | If incorrect, adjust it. |
| 3 | See if there is compression.<br><br>(Compression gauge should be used). | If not, check the following points.<br>a. Burned piston (no-ring tension).<br>b. Worn-out or damaged piston or cylinder.<br>c. Leakage in head gasket<br>d. Leakage in case.<br>e. Bad oil seal in crank chamber. | a. Replace piston ring.<br>b. Repair or replace it.<br>c. Replace it.<br>d. Repair or renew it.<br>e. Replace it. |
| 4 | Check every adjusting parts and whether carburetor is clogged. |   |   |
| 5 | See if engine overheats. | If engine overheats, check the following points.<br>a. Accumulation of carbon in combustion chamber.<br>b. Incorrect fuel mixture.<br>c. Slipping clutch. | a. Clean it.<br><br>b. Correct it. |

| 6 | | a. Passage of air through heat-proof packing or oil seal housing. | a. Apply "three Bond". Or replace it. |

## 6—3 ENGINE OVERHEATS

After the preliminary running (on the new machine or after engine overhaul) is over, if the engine overheats at high speed, check the following points:

a) Is the brake off?
b) Is the flow of fuel regular?
c) Is the cylinder fin clean?
d) Isn't the mission oil too much?

Then, trace the trouble-source in the following order.

| | Inspection | Trouble source | Remedy |
|---|---|---|---|
| 1 | Check whether compression is too high. | If compression is too high, it is caused by the following points.<br>a. Accumulation of carbon in combustion chamber.<br>b. Cylinder head packing too thin. | a. Clean it.<br>b. Replace it. |
| 2 | Check whether back pressure of muffler is sufficient. | If not, carbon is accumulated in exhaust pipe, muffler or cylinder exhaust outlet. | Clean it. |
| 3 | Inspect piston ring, then its action. | If piston ring does not work well, the reason lies in carbon accumulation. | Clean piston ring groove. |
| 4 | See if gasoline-air mixture gas is not excessively lean. | The reasons why mixture gas is too lean, lie in the points below.<br>a. Breakage in packings.<br>b. Damaged oil seal or loose housing. | a. Replace them.<br>b. Replace oil seal. Apply "Three Bond" to housing, then secure it. |

| | Inspection | Trouble source | Remedy |
|---|---|---|---|
| 5 | Check whether fuel ratio is correct. | Use higher octane fuel, and adjust fuel ratio correctly, or octane rating will decreases and carbon will accumulate. | Adjust fuel ratio correctly. |
| 6 | See if clutch works well. | Slipping clutch results in engine overheat. | Adjust it correctly. |
| 7 | See if ignition system functions effectively. | Ignition system should be inspected in the folloing order.<br>a. Condenser.<br><br>b. Wear and heat value of plugs.<br>c. Ignition coil<br><br>d. Ignition timing.<br>e. High-tension cord.<br>f. Contact points.<br><br>g. Spring of arm. | a. Inspect it by means of tester. If bad, replace it.<br>b. Replace it, and adjust electrodes.<br>c. Examine it with tester. If bad, replace it.<br>d. Correct it.<br>e. Renew it.<br>f. File contact points, and adjust gaps.<br>g. Replace arm. |

## 6—4 CLUTCH DOES NOT WORK WELL

There are two cases:

1). Sliding clutch;

2). No-breaking clutch.

| | Inspection | Trouble source | Remedy |
|---|---|---|---|
| 1 | Slipping clutch<br>(Set up main stand, and start engine, and put change gear, and finally blow engine with brake on. At this time, if engine does not stop to run, clutch is slipping.) | Slipping is caused by the following points<br>a. Weak clutch spring.<br>b. Worn-out or distorted pressure plates.<br>c. Deformed clutch housing.<br>d. Bad clutch plate spline. | a. Replace it.<br>b. Mend or renew it.<br>c. Repair or replace it.<br>d. Replace clutch plate. |
| 2 | No-breaking clutch. | No-breaking is caused by the following points.<br>a. Inadequate viscosity of oil. | a. Use specified viscosity oil. |

|  |  | b. Clutch boss too tightened.<br>c. Ineffective action of clutch plate.<br>d. Clutch spring tensions unbalanced.<br>e. Weak spring. | b. Correct or replace it.<br>c. Replace it.<br>d. Replace it.<br>e. Replace it. |
|---|---|---|---|

## 6—5 SPEED CHANGE IS INADEQUATE

After making sure the clutch action is smooth and the viscosity and quantity of mission oil is appropiate, the another inspection should be conducted in the following order.

Speed change troubles are divided into three cases.

|  | Inspection | Trouble source | Remedy |
|---|---|---|---|
| 1 | Speed change does not work well. | a. Bad shifter pawl holder.<br>b. Incorrect gap between shifter pawl and segment.<br>c. Burned mission gear.<br>d. Broken shifters A or B.<br>e. Burned shifters A or B. | a. Replace shifter pawl and spring.<br>b. Adjust it.<br>c. Replace it.<br>d. Replace it.<br>e. Replace shifter assembly. |
| 2 | Change pedal does not return. | a. Breakage in change lever spring.<br>b. Change shaft competes with crank case and case cover. | a. Replace it.<br>b. Repair bent change shaft or replace it. |
| 3 | Speed change slips out of position. | a. Worn-out or bent shifter A or B.<br>b. Worn-out or damaged dog clutch.<br>c. Broken or weak shifter cam stopper pin. | a. Replace it.<br>b. Repair or replace mission gear.<br>c. Replace it. |

## 6—6 ENGINE MAKES NOISE

The high speed running of the engine causes vibration and noise to its working parts to a certain degree. However, when the strange sounds are heard, there exist some troubles with the engine.

— 98 —

As the trouble source must be traced by hearing its sound, at times even an expert service man makes an error in judgment.

## 1. Intermittent sound

| | Diagnosis | Cause | Cure |
|---|---|---|---|
| 1 | Intermittent sound is heard at sharp acceleration. | a. Large clearance between piston ring and its groove.<br>b. Piston ring clogged with carbon.<br>c. Large clearance between connecting rod small end bush and piston pin.<br>d. Large clearance at connecting rod big end.<br>The above mentioned sound is metallic as a rule.<br>e. Knocking due to advance igniton. | a. Replace ring or piston.<br>b. Remove carbon<br>c. Inspect bush and piston pin. If faulty, replace it.<br>d. Repair crank.<br><br><br><br><br>e. Adjust ignition timing. |
| 2 | Intermittent sound is heard at low revolutions. | a. Somewhat large piston clearance (In this case, the sound is absorbed by openning throttle).<br>b. Piston is in bad contact. (When ring land is in contact, returning grip causes vibration to head). | a. Adjustment.<br><br><br><br><br>b. File ring land with sand paper. |

## 2. Sound which changes with time

| | Diagnosis | Cause | Cure |
|---|---|---|---|
| 1 | Sound at start | a. Large piston clearance. (when engine becomes warm, the sound is not heard).<br>b. Piston is in bad contact, (when ring land is in contact, returning grip causes vibration to head). | a. Replace piston.<br><br><br>b. File ring land with sand-paper. |

| 2 | Sound at high temperature. | a. Piston clearance is larger than 1-a.<br>b. Bent connecting rod. | a. Replace piston or repair cylinder.<br>b. Repair crank. |

## 3. Sound at ordinary times

| | Diagnosis | Cause | Cure |
|---|---|---|---|
| 1 | Off-set crank. | Crank touches crank chamber due to little clearance between crank and crank chamber. | Add adequate washer. |
| 2 | Bad bearing. | Sound is caused by bearing which is damaged, or clogged with carbon, or rusty. | Replace it. |
| 3 | Broken ring. | In case of broken ring, crackle is heard. | Replace it. |
| 4 | Sound of clutch. | a. Large play between friction disk and housing spline. (Even if clutch is broken, sound does not change).<br>b. Large play between clutch disk and boss spline. (If clutch is broken, sound will not be heard, or become lower).<br>c. Primary chain is excessively loose. Or it is not tightend evenly. | Replace friction disk.<br><br>Replace clutch disk.<br><br><br><br>Replace it. (If sound is still heard, replace sprocket.) |

## 6—7 HANDLE IS UNSATISFACTORY

After making sure the air pressure in tires is adequate, check the following points.

|   | Diagnosis | Cause | Cure |
|---|---|---|---|
| 1 | Steering is unsatisfactory. | a. Excessively tightened steering nut<br>b. Breakage in steel balls.<br>c. Bent steering shaft. | a. Adjustment.<br>b. Replace all the balls.<br>c. Replace underbracket. |
| 2 | Steering is unstable. | a. Ill-balanced fork.<br>b. Bent inner tube.<br>c. Bent rear arm.<br>d. Incorrect position of front and rear wheels. | a. Change oil.<br>b. Repair it.<br>c. Repair or replace it.<br>d. Correct it. |
| 3 | Front or rear wheel is in contact with frame. | a. Worn-out wheel bearing.<br>b. Deformed lim.<br>c. Loose spoke.<br>d. Worn-out rear arm bush.<br>e. Incorrect adjustment of secondary chain.<br>f. Distorted frame. | a. Replace it.<br>b. Replace it.<br>c. Tighten it.<br>d. Replace it.<br>e. Adjust it.<br>f. Replace it. |

## 6—8  BAD CUSHION

After making sure the air pressure in tires is adequate, check the following points.

|   | Diagnosis | Cause | Cure |
|---|---|---|---|
| 1 | Cushion is too soft. | a. Weak spring.<br>b. Leakage of oil. | a. Replace it.<br>b. Replace oil seal. |
| 2 | Cushion is too hard. | a. Excessive quantity of oil.<br>b. Bent inner tube. | a. Adjustment.<br>b. Repair it. |
| 3 | Cushion makes a noise. | a. Bad contact of spring with outer sleeve.<br>b. Leakage or too little quantity of oil.<br>c. Bad contact of inner sleeve with outer one due to bent shaft. | a. Apply grease to spring. Replace fiber packing.<br>b. Supply oil, or replace oil seal<br>c. Replace cushion unit. |

## 6—9 BRAKE DOES NOT WORK WELL

After adjusting a play of the brake, check the following point.

|   | Diagnosis | Cause | Cure |
|---|---|---|---|
| 1 | Brake refuses to work. | a. Ineffective front brake wire.<br>b. Play of brake pedal bearing.<br>c. Bad contact of brake linning.<br>d. Permeation of dirt or water into brake drum.<br>e. Dirty linning. | a. Replace it.<br>b. Replace it.<br>c. Correct or replace it.<br>d. Clean it.<br>e. Clean it. |
| 2 | Brake makes a noise. | a. Worn-out linning.<br>b. Dirty linning.<br>c. Rough contact surface of dram.<br>d. Insufficient grease in cam section. | a. Replace it.<br>b. Clean it.<br>c. Repair it.<br>d. Apply grease. |
| 3 | No adjusting clearance. | a. Worn-out linning.<br>b. Worn-out brake shoe pin.<br>c. Worn-out brake cam. | a. Replace it.<br>b. Replace brake shoe.<br>c. Change position of cam, or replace it. |

## 6—10 CHARGE IS INSUFFICIENT

The YAMAHA motorcycle has adopted the constant-voltage type as charge system. Accordingly, as the charging goes on and the battery becomes saturated, the charging current becomes reduced. Do not confuse this phenomenon with the insufficient charge. The electrical equipment should be inspected by measuring the voltage of the battery. The data obtained by the measurement of current are necessary only for reference.

|   | Diagnosis | Cause | Cure |
|---|---|---|---|
| 1 | Bad regulator | a. Dirty contact points.<br>b. Short circuit of cord.<br>c. Lower functioning. | a. File contact points with sand-paper #00~000.<br>b. Repair it.<br>c. Adjustment. |

| | | | |
|---|---|---|---|
| 2 | Bad wiring | a. Bad connection.<br>b. Damaged covering of cord.<br>c. Faulty cord end. | a. Correct it.<br>b. Replace or mend it with vinyl tape.<br>c. Mend it. |
| 3 | Bad dynamo | a. Dirty or damaged armature (commutator).<br>b. Ineffective armature. When there is continuity between commutator and shaft, and voltage of 7-9V is not caused by 1000 rpm at bad terminals A and E, armature is bad.<br>c. Ineffective dynamo. When there is no continuity between terminals D, F and E, it is bad. When there is continuity between terminal E and yoke, it is bad.<br>d. Fault in attaching dynamo. (Short circuit between locating knock and field)<br>e. Worn-out or damaged brushes. | a. File it with sandpaper and inspect brush spring.<br>b. Replace armature.<br><br>c. Replace yoke.<br><br><br><br>Insulate and repair them.<br><br>d. Drive knock in.<br><br><br><br>e. Replace them. |

## 6—11 SELF-STARTER DOES NOT TURN

Of course, the battery has the most serious effect on the self-starter. There are, however, other various causes for its troubles.

Assuming that the battery is fully charged, the following points are explained.

| | Diagnosis | Cause | Cure |
|---|---|---|---|
| 1 | Sound of "click" which shows action of starter switch is not heard even by pressing button. | a. Disconnection of use.<br><br>b. Looseness or disconnection of starting switch circuit. (blue-white spiral) | a. Replace it.<br><br>b. Measure continuity, and mend it. |

— 103 —

| | | | |
|---|---|---|---|
| | | c. Disconnection between S-E of starting switches. | c. Replace switch. |
| 2 | Sound of "click" is heard by pressing button, but self-starter does not turn. (Neutral lamp does not change its light.) | a. Looseness of starting switch terminals B-M, and of starter dynamo terminal M. b. Bad contact of carbon brush. | a. When voltage between starter dynamo terminals M-E is below 7V, tighten it. b. When spring pressure of brush is weak, replace it. |
| 3 | Sound of "click" is heard by pressing button, but self-starter does not turn. (Neutral lamp is about to go out) | a. Looseness of wires (+)-(−) of battery. b. Short circuit of circuit M (green). | a. When voltage between B-E of starting switch is below 8V, tighten it. b. Examine continuity between M-E, and mend cord, if necessary. |
| 4 | Self-starter turns, but revolution is slow. (below 100rpm at 5°C and less) | a. Increase of viscosity of mission oil. b. Reduction of battery performance due to low temperature. | |
| 5 | Self-starter turns, but revolution is slow. (below 100 rpm at normal temperature of 0°~40°C) | a. Burned engine. b. Bad contact of armature core. | a. Repair it. b. If there is no continuity between commutator and core, file contact surface of armature core. |

The troubles of the electrical equipment, especially charging system, depend on the driving condition of a user.

The charging performance of YA-5 has been designed so that its characteristics become excellent at low speed. Accordingly, the starter dynamo reaches its full power near 42 km/H (1,600rpm) at top speed. It is advisable to drive at the speed equivalent to 1,600 rpm for the user who frequently uses the self-starter or rides at low speed.

# YAMAHA YA5

# ILLUSTRATED PARTS LIST

**Specification of YAMAHA 125 Model YA5**

| | |
|---|---|
| Overall Length | 1,885mm |
| Overall Width | 680mm |
| Overall Height | 955mm |
| Wheel base | 1,250mm |
| Road clearance | 130mm |
| Dry weight | 120kg |
| Tank capacity | 8.5*l* |
| Mixing ratio | 20:1 |
| Maximum speed | Over 100km/h |
| Fuel consumption | 48km/*l* |
| Climbing ability | Sin 20° |
| Engine | Air cooling 2 stroke engine single cylinder |
| Cylinder capacity | 123c.c. |
| Bore and stroke | 56×50mm |
| Compression ratio | 6.75:1 |
| Maximum power | 10ps/6500rpm |
| Starter sysem | Electric starter |
| Ignition system | Battery ignition |
| Primary transmission | Chain |
| Secondary transmission | Chain |
| Clutch | Multi-plate clutch |
| Transmission | Foot operated 4 speed |
| Reduction ratio | |
| Low | 2.966 (22.575) |
| Second | 1.794 (13.654) |
| Third | 1.219 ( 9.826) |
| Top | 1.000 ( 7.611) |
| Brake | Front Drum type hand brake Rear Drum type foot brake |
| Suspension | Front Telescopic fork Rear Swing arm |
| Buffer Equipment | Coil spring and oil damper |
| Caster | 63° |
| Trail | 90mm |
| Tyre Front | 3.00-16-2pr |
| Rear | 3.00-16-4pr |

# YAMAHA MOTOR CO., LTD.

# MEMO

# CONTENTS

I  Engine Section
- AA  Cyinder., crank .................................................. 4
- AB  Carburetor (I) .................................................. 6
- AC  Muffler .................................................. 7
- AD  Clutch .................................................. 8
- AE  Mission .................................................. 10
- AF  Shifter .................................................. 11
- AG  Kickstarter .................................................. 13
- AH  Crankcase .................................................. 14
- AI  Carburetor (II) .................................................. 16

II  Frame Section
- AJ  Frame .................................................. 18
- AK  Foot-rest. Stand .................................................. 20
- AL  Chain case. Rear arm. Cushion .................................................. 22
- AM  Front fork .................................................. 24
- AN  Fuel tank .................................................. 26
- AO  Saddle. Carrier .................................................. 27
- AP  Front hub .................................................. 28
- AQ  Tyre. Rim .................................................. 29
- AR  Rear hub .................................................. 30
- AS  Handlebar .................................................. 32
- AT  Service tool .................................................. 34
- AU  Leg-shield .................................................. 35

III  Electric Section
- AV  Dyname .................................................. 36
- AW  Electrical eguipment .................................................. 38

IX  Old type
- AX  Engine. Electrical equipment .................................................. 40
- AY  Frame .................................................. 41

116

# ENGINE SECTION

## AA  Cylinder. Crank

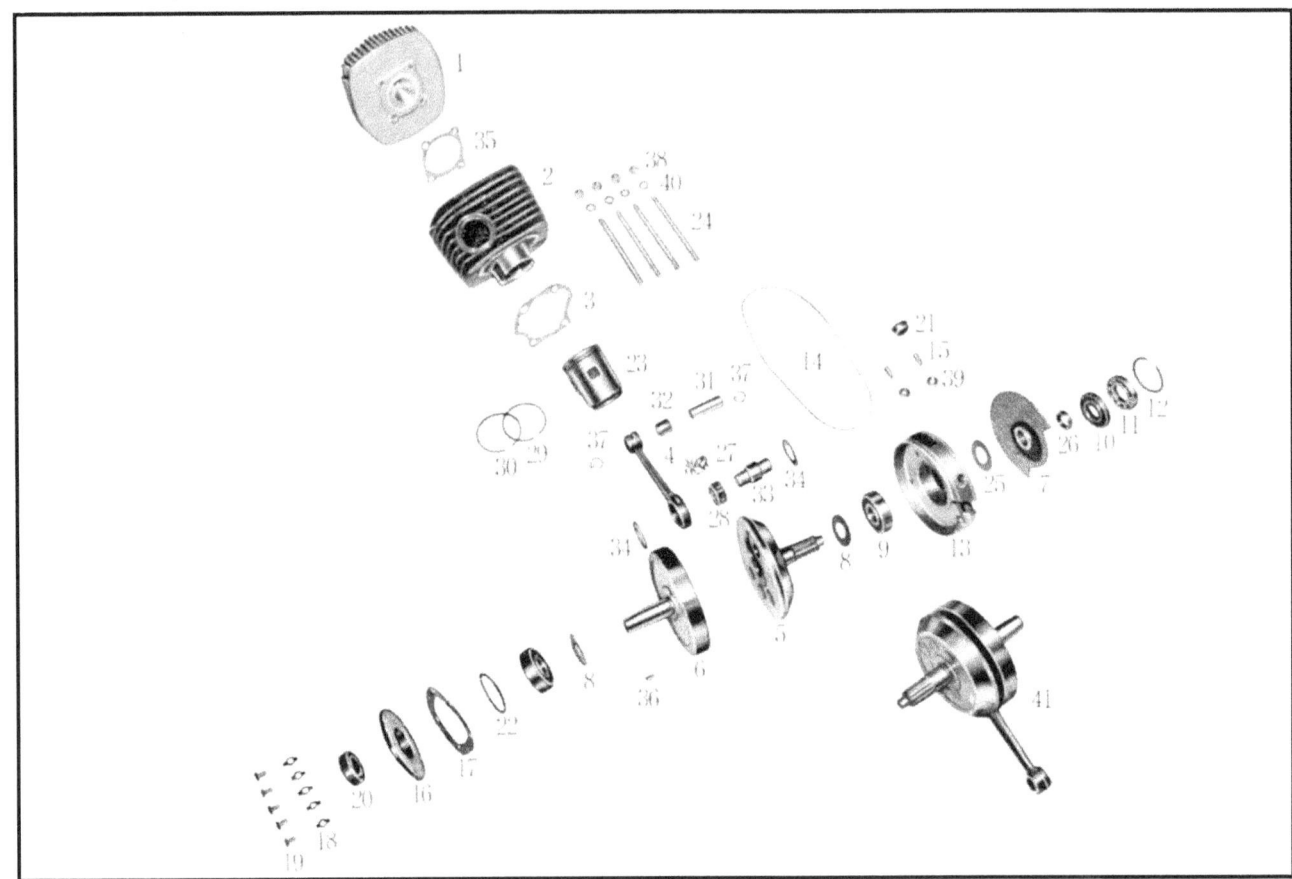

| Illustration No. | Stock No. | Name of items | Quantity required per one machine | Size | Unit price | Improved machine | Models for which inter-changeable | Remarks |
|---|---|---|---|---|---|---|---|---|
| AA01 | 150101-2 | Cylinder head B | 1 | | 1000 | 75001 | | |
| AA02 | 150102-2 | Cylinder B | 1 | | 2700 | 75001 | | |
| AA03 | 150103-1 | Cylinder packing | 1 | Thickness 0.2 | 10 | 38224 | | |
| AA04 | 150104 | Connecting rod assembly | 1 | | 1000 | | | |
| ※AA05 | 150105-1 | Crank, right A | 1 | | 2200 | 75001 | | |
| AA06 | 150106 | Crank, left | 1 | | 2200 | | | |
| ※AA07 | 150107-3 | Valve assembly C | 1 | | 930 | 75001 | | |
| AA08 | 150108 | Crank shaft cover | 2 | | 6 | 21527 | | |
| AA09 | 150109 | Bearing | 2 | #6304C₃ | The Current price | | | |
| AA10 | 150111 | Oil seal | 1 | SW25 × 47 × 8 | 100 | | | |
| AA11 | 150112 | Bearing | 1 | #16005 | The Current price | | | |
| AA12 | 150113 | Clip for bearing | 1 | | 40 | | | |
| AA13 | 150115 | Valve cover | 1 | | 620 | | | |
| AA14 | 150116 | O ring | 1 | | 60 | | | |
| AA15 | 150117 | Fitting bolt for valve cover | 2 | | 10 | | | |
| AA16 | 150118 | Oil seal housing | 1 | | 110 | | | |
| AA17 | 150119 | Packing | 1 | | 10 | | | |
| AA18 | 150120 | Washer | 5 | | 3 | | | |
| AA19 | 150121 | Bolt | 5 | | 5 | | | |
| AA20 | 150122 | Oil seal | 1 | SW20 × 36 × 10 | 130 | | | |

| Illustration No. | Stock No. | Name of items | Quantity required per one machine | Size | Unit price | Improved machine | Models for which inter-changeable | | Remarks |
|---|---|---|---|---|---|---|---|---|---|
| AA21 | 150123-1 | Plug for valve cover fitting bolt | 1 | | 20 | 23078 | | | |
| AA22 | 150124 | Bearing cover | 1 | | 7 | | | | |
| AA23 | 150125 | Piston | 1 | | 800 | | | | |
| AA24 | 150128-1 | Bolt | 4 | | 40 | 39885 | | | |
| AA25 | 150130 | Spacer | 1 | | 6 | 10927 | | | |
| AA26 | 150133 | Spacer | 1 | | 70 | 75001 | | | |
| AA27 | 150136 | Needle roller | 15 | | 5 | 72002 | YD 3 | | |
| AA28 | 150135 | Roller retainer | 1 | | 350 | 72002 | YD 3 | | |
| AA29 | 01101-1 | Piston ring, top | 1 | | 100 | 71213 | YDS 2 | YDS 1 | |
| AA30 | 01102 | Piston ring, second | 1 | | 50 | | YDS 2 | YDS 1 | |
| AA31 | 01107 | Gudgeon pin | 1 | | 300 | | YDS 2 | YDS 1 | |
| AA32 | 01112 | Connecting rod bush | 1 | | 130 | | YDS 2 | YDS 1 | |
| AA33 | 01115 | Crank pin | 1 | | 200 | | YDS 2 | YDS 1 | |
| AA34 | 01143 | Spacer for crank pin | 3 | | 50 | | YDS 2 YD 3 | YDS 1 YD 2 | |
| AA35 | 01202 | Cylinder head packing | 1 | | 10 | | YDS 2 | YDS 1 | |
| AA36 | 421141 | Crank shaft key | 1 | | 10 | | YD 3 | YD 2 | |
| AA37 | 411106 | Gudgeon pin clip | 2 | | 5 | | YDS 2 YD 3 | YDS 1 YD 2 | |
| AA38 | 301207 | Nut | 4 | | 5 | | YD 3 | YD 2 | |
| AA39 | YS 04-8 | Nut | 1 | | 5 | | | | |
| AA40 | YS 06-8 | Washer | 4 | | 1 | 100001 | | | |
| ※AA41 | | Crank assembly | 1 | | 7000 | | | | |

# M E M O

## AB Carburator

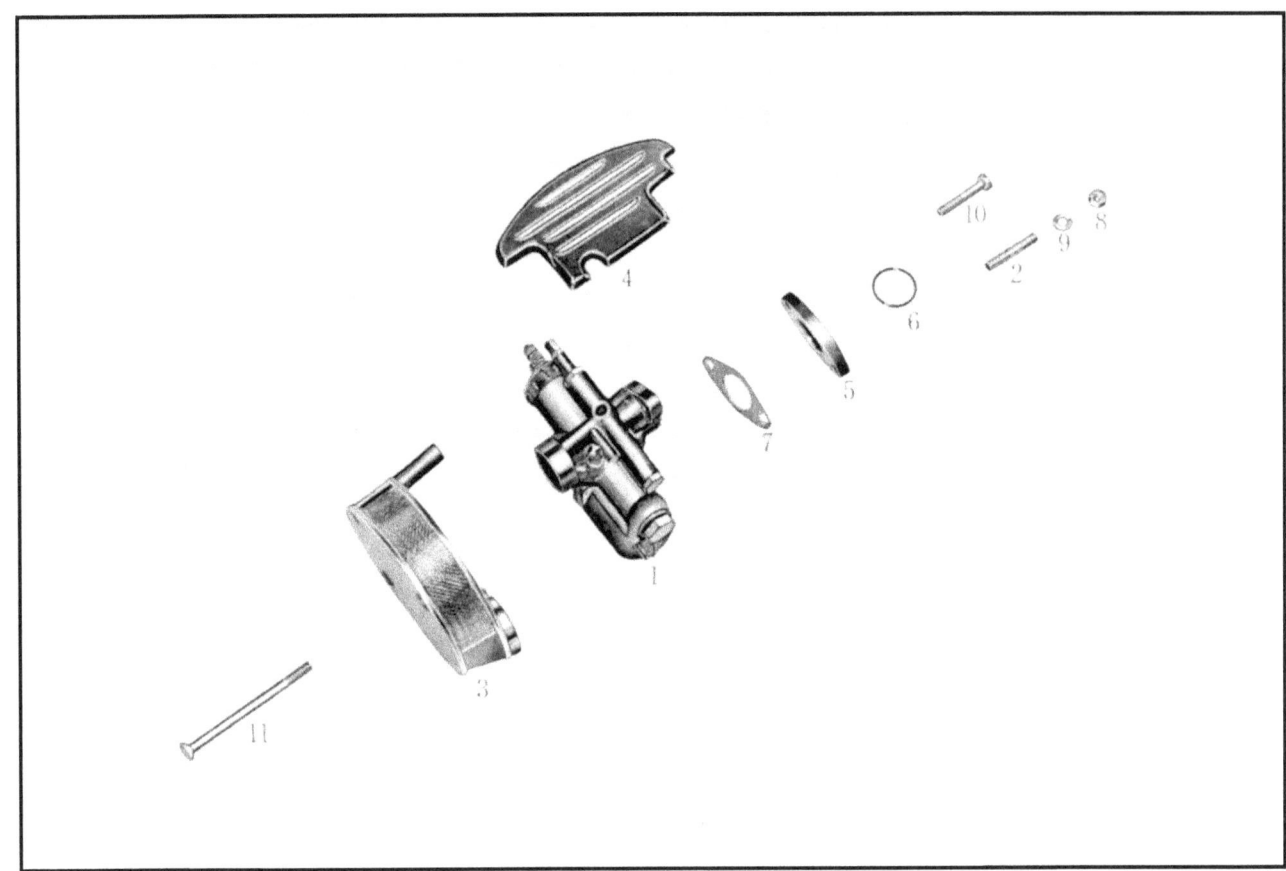

| Illustration No. | Stock No. | Name of items | Quantity required per one machine | Size | Unit price | Improved machine | Models for which inter-changeable | Remarks |
|---|---|---|---|---|---|---|---|---|
| AB01 | 150201-1 | Carburetor assembly | 1 | | 3100 | | | |
| AB02 | 150203 | Bolt A | 1 | | 10 | | | |
| AB03 | 150205 | Air cleaner | 1 | | 320 | | | |
| AB04 | 150207-1 | Air filter | 1 | | 150 | | | |
| AB05 | 150208 | Carburator joint | 1 | | 55 | 38224 | | |
| AB06 | 150209 | Carburator joint O ring | 1 | | 12 | 38224 | | |
| AB07 | 150210 | Carburator joint packing | 1 | | 8 | 38224 | | |
| AB08 | YS 02-6 | Nut | 2 | | 2 | | | |
| AB09 | YS 05-6 | Spring washer | 2 | | 1 | | | |
| AB10 | YS12-6.32-17 | Bolt (B) | 1 | | 5 | | | |
| AB11 | YS15-6.70-10 | Bolt | 1 | | 5 | | | |

AC Muffler

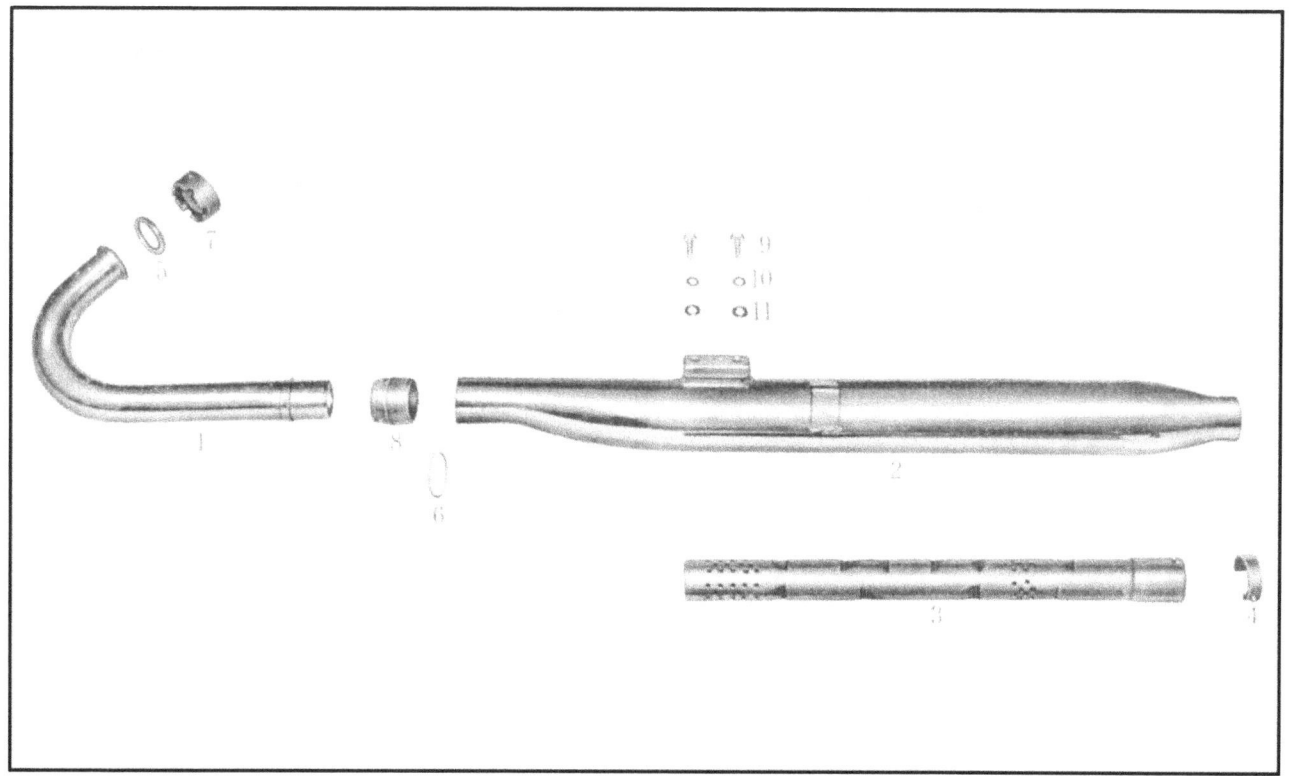

| Illustration No. | Stock No. | Name of items | Quantity required per one machine | Size | Unit price | Improved machine | Models for which inter-changeable | Remarks |
|---|---|---|---|---|---|---|---|---|
| AC01 | 150301 | Exhaust pipe | 1 | | 700 | | | |
| | 150301-1 | Exhaust pipe A | 1 | | 700 | | | |
| AC02 | 150302-2 | Mnffler B | 1 | | 1300 | 75001 | | |
| | 150302-3 | Muffler C | 1 | | 1300 | | | |
| AC03 | 150302-1 | Muffler inner cylinder | 1 | | 500 | 67473 | YD 3 | YA 3 YD 2 |
| AC04 | 150302-B | Fitting band for inner cylinder | 1 | | 50 | | YD 3 | YA 3 YD 2 |
| AC05 | 150306 | Gasket | 1 | | 40 | | | |
| | 020301 | Gasket | 1 | | | | YDS2 | |
| AC06 | 150307 | Stop ring | 1 | | 10 | | | |
| | 150309 | Joint ring (A) | 1 | | | | | |
| | 150311 | Joint gasket | 1 | | | | | |
| AC07 | 421801 | Ring nut | 1 | | 150 | | YD 3 | YA 3 YD 2 |
| | 01801 | Exhaust pipe ring nut | 1 | | | | YDS2 | |
| AC08 | 121704 | Joint rubber | 1 | | 100 | | YD 3 | YA 3 YD 2 |
| AC09 | YS01-8.23-11 | Bolt | 2 | | 8 | | | |
| AC10 | YS 05-8 | Spring washer | 2 | | 1 | | | |
| AC11 | YS 06-8 | Washer | 2 | | 1 | | | |

## AD Clutch

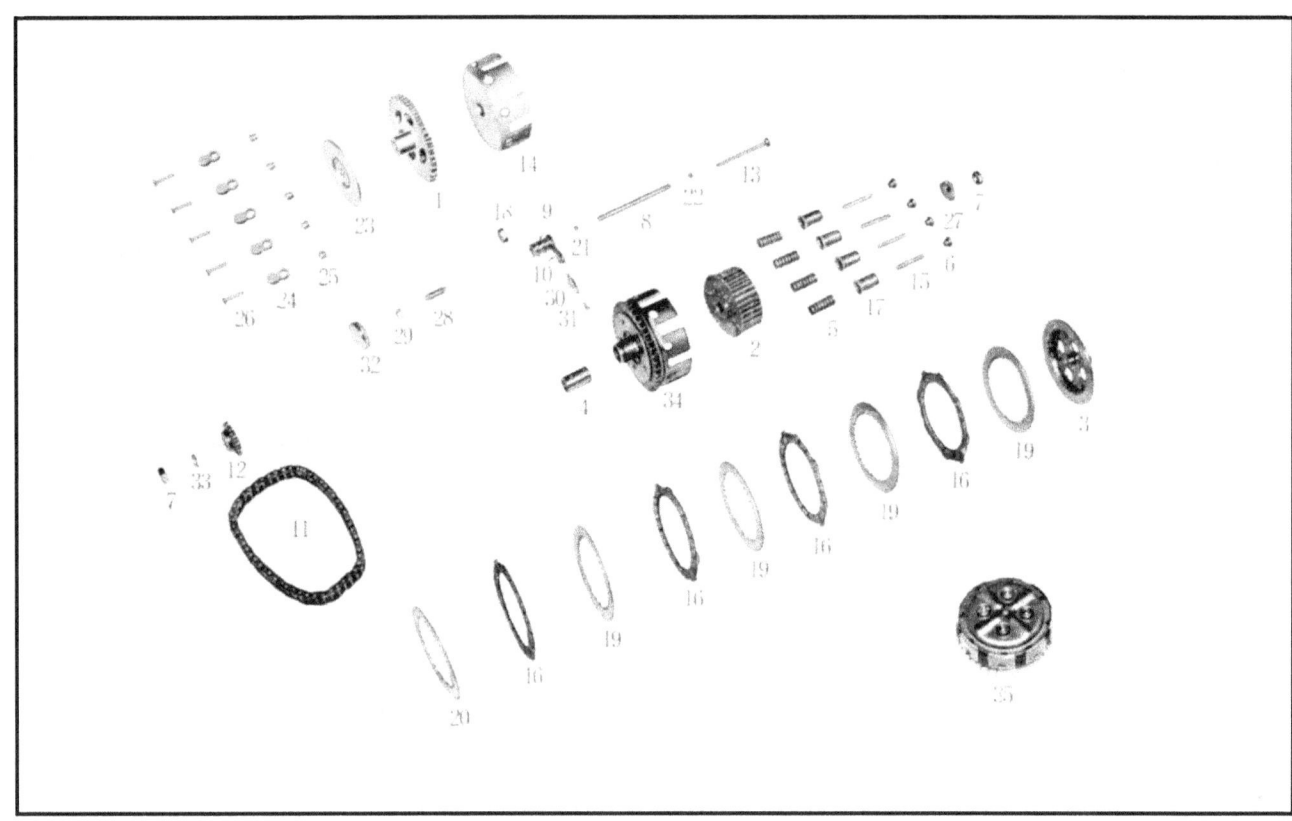

| Illustration No. | Stock No. | Name of items | Quantity required per one machine | Size | Unit price | Improved machine | Models for which inter-changeable | Remarks |
|---|---|---|---|---|---|---|---|---|
| AD01 | 150401-1 | Primary driven gear | 1 | 39 teeth | 850 | | | |
| AD02 | 150402 | Clutch boss | 1 | | 900 | | | |
| AD03 | 150403 | Pressure plate | 1 | | 90 | | | |
| AD04 | 150404 | Spacer | 1 | | 150 | | | |
| AD05 | 150405 | Clutch spring | 4 | | 30 | | | |
| AD06 | 150406 | Spring stopper | 4 | | 20 | | | |
| AD07 | 150407 | Clumping nut | 2 | | 15 | | | |
| AD08 | 150408 | Push rod | 1 | | 45 | | | |
| AD09 | 150409 | Clutch push screw | 1 | | 130 | | | |
| AD10 | 150411 | Clutch lever | 1 | | 30 | | | |
| AD11 | 150412-1 | Primery chain | 1 | DK 325 | 530 | 71445 | | |
| AD12 | 150413-1 | Primery drive sprocket | 1 | 14 teeth | 330 | | | |
| AD13 | 150414 | Push rod with button | 1 | | 140 | | | |
| AD14 | 150415 | Clutch housing | 1 | | 450 | | | |
| AD15 | 150416 | Fitting bolt for clutch spring | 4 | | 20 | | | |
| AD16 | 150417 | Clutch friction plate | 4 | | 210 | | | |
| AD17 | 150420 | Barrel for clutch spring | 4 | | 25 | | | |
| AD18 | 150421 | Dust seal | 1 | | 30 | | | |
| AD19 | 411414 | Clutch plate (A) | 4 | | 160 | | YD 1 | |
| AD20 | 411432 | Clutch plate (B) | 1 | | 180 | | YD 1 | |
| AD21 | 301437 | Push rod ball | 3 | | 3 | | YC 1 | |
| AD22 | 301435 | Ball | 5 | | 5 | | YC 1 | |

| Illustration No. | Stock No. | Name of items | Quantity required per one machine | Size | Unit price | Improved machine | Models for which inter-changeable | | Remarks |
|---|---|---|---|---|---|---|---|---|---|
| AD23 | 301407 | Transmission plate for kick starter | 1 | | 120 | | YC 1 | | |
| AD24 | 301409 | Yielding rubber | 5 | | 25 | | YC 1 | | |
| AD25 | 341410 | Yielding rubber bush | 5 | | 5 | | YC 1 | | |
| AD26 | 341411 | Rivet (A) | 5 | | 3 | | YC 1 | | |
| AD27 | 301414 | Washer | 1 | | 5 | | YC 1 | | |
| AD28 | 301428 | Clutch adjust screw | 1 | | 15 | | YC 1 | | |
| AD29 | 301427 | Clutch adjust screw nut | 1 | | 5 | | YC 1 | | |
| AD30 | 301433 | Clutch lever spring | 1 | | 10 | | YC 1 | | |
| AD31 | 111602 | Spring clutch | 1 | | 10 | | YD 3 YDS2 | YD 2 YA 3 | |
| AD32 | 111627 | Clutch adjust screw cover | 1 | | 50 | | YA 3 | | |
| AD33 | YS05-12 | Spring washer | 1 | | 3 | | | | |
| AD34 | | Clutch housing assembly | 1 | | 1700 | | | | |
| AD35 | | Clutch assembly | 1 | | 5000 | | | | |
| AD36 | | Push screw assembly | 1 | | 400 | | | | |

# M E M O

## AE Mission

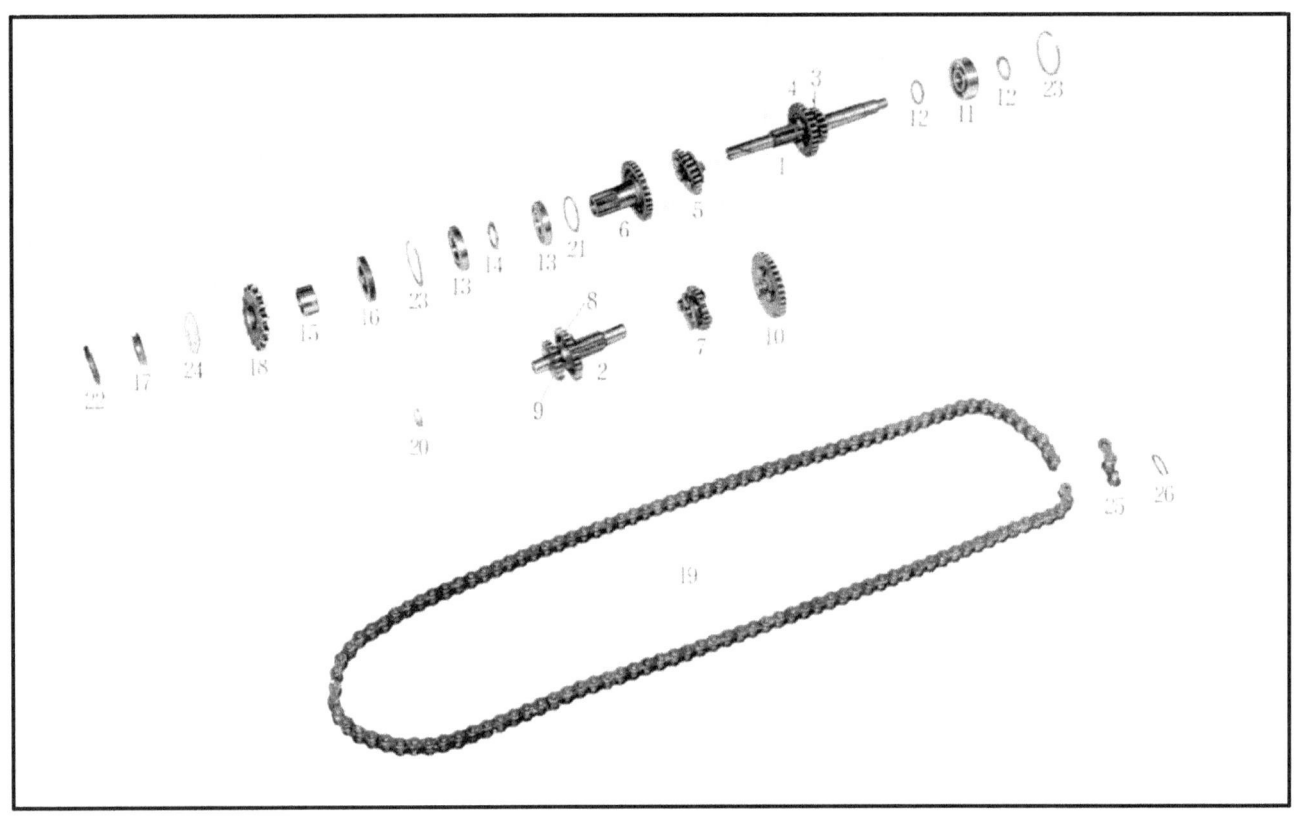

| Illustration No. | Stock No. | Name of items | Quantity required per one machine | Size | Unit price | Improved machine | Models for which inter-changeable | Remarks |
|---|---|---|---|---|---|---|---|---|
| AE01 | 150501 | Main shaft | 1 | | 1000 | | | |
| AE02 | 150502 | Counter shaft | 1 | | 700 | | | |
| AE03 | 150503 | Fixed gear (A) | 1 | 18 teeth | 400 | | | |
| AE04 | 150504 | Travelling gear (A) | 1 | 28 teeth | 640 | | | |
| AE05 | 150505 | Sliding gear (A) | 1 | 24 teeth | 700 | | | |
| AE06 | 150506 | Driving gear | 1 | 31 teeth | 1300 | | | |
| AE07 | 150507 | Sliding gear (B) | 1 | 21 teeth | 680 | | | |
| AE08 | 150508 | Travelling gear (C) | 1 | 25 teeth | 620 | | | |
| AE09 | 150509 | Fixed gear (B) | 1 | 18 teeth | 400 | | | |
| AE10 | 150510 | Travelling gear (B) | 1 | 31 teeth | 670 | | | |
| AE11 | 150511 | Bearing | 1 | #6303 | The current price | | | |
| AE12 | 150513 | Adjusting plate | 2 | | 20 | | | |
| AE13 | 150514 | Bearing | 2 | #6005 | The current price | | | |
| AE14 | 150515 | Spacer | 1 | | 25 | | | |
| AE15 | 150516 | Spacer | 1 | | 150 | | | |
| AE16 | 150517 | Oil seal | 1 | SD30×47×7 | 75 | | | |
| AE17 | 150518 | Sprocket lock nut | 1 | | 50 | | | |
| AE18 | 150519 | Drive sprocket | 1 | 15 teeth | 400 | | | |
| AE19 | 150520 | Chain | 1 | DK 428 | 1000 | | | |
| AE20 | 150522-1 | Cap for bearing | 1 | | 5 | 38224 | | |
| AE21 | 150523 | Adjusting plate | 1 | | 30 | 11640 | | |
| AE22 | 301315 | Push rod packing | 1 | | 10 | | YC 1 | |
| AE23 | 111221 | Clip for ball bearing | 2 | | 30 | | YA 3 | |
| AE24 | 111423 | Lock washer | 1 | | 10 | | YA 1 | |
| | | Main shaft assembly | 1 | | 2200 | | | |
| | | Courter shaft assembly | 1 | | 1900 | | | |
| AE25 | | Chain conecting link | 1 | | 50 | | | |
| AE26 | | Chain conecting clip | 1 | | 10 | | | |

AF Shifter

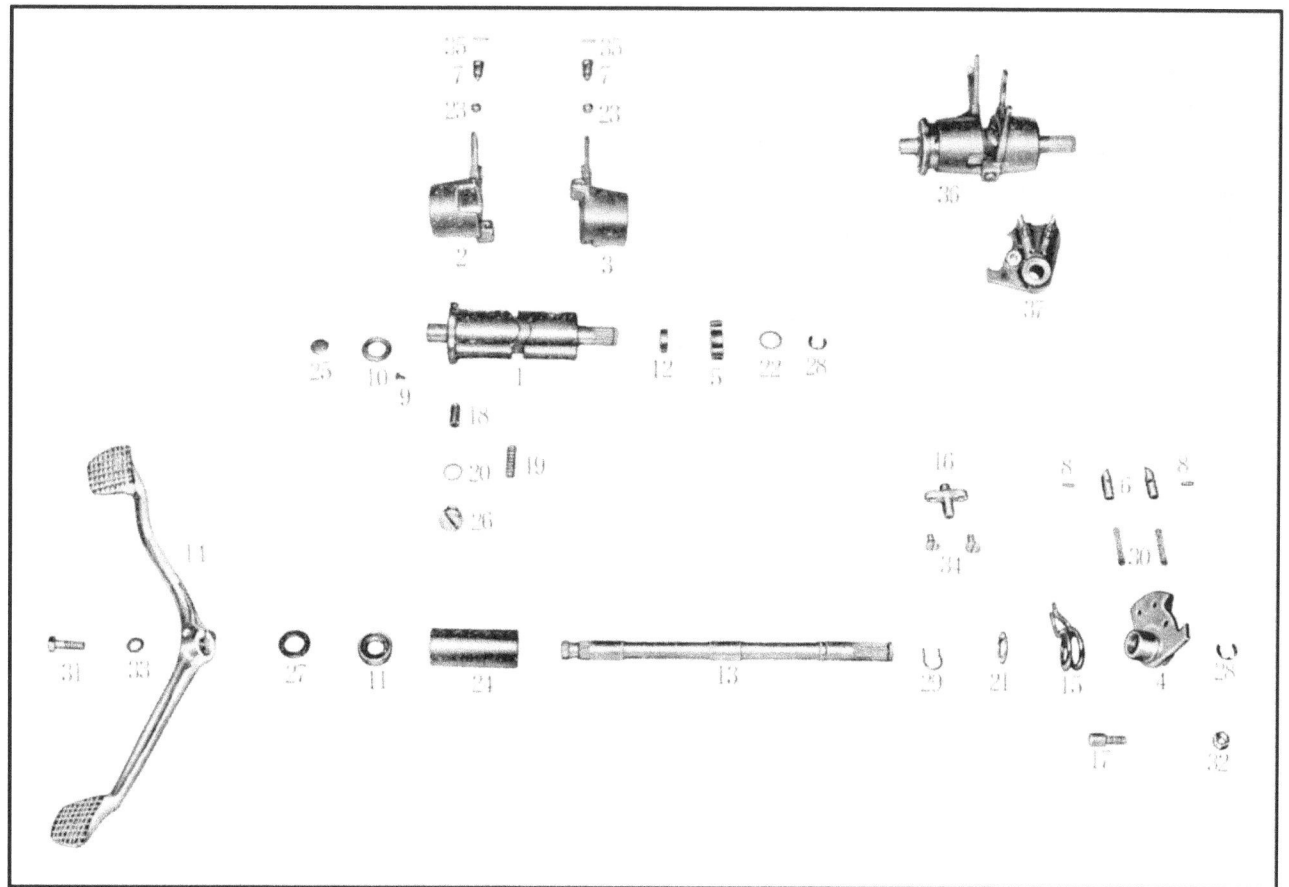

| Illustration No. | Stock No. | Name of items | Quantity required per one machine | Size | Unit price | Improved machine | Models for which inter-changeable | Remarks |
|---|---|---|---|---|---|---|---|---|
| AF01 | 150601 | Shifter cam | 1 | | 810 | | | |
| AF02 | 150602 | Shifter (A) | 1 | | 700 | | | |
| AF03 | 150603 | Shifter (B) | 1 | | 700 | | | |
| AF04 | 150604 | Shifter pawl retainer plate | 1 | | 430 | | | |
| AF05 | 150605 | Shifter segment | 1 | | 500 | | | |
| AF06 | 150606 | Shifter pawl | 2 | | 130 | | | |
| AF07 | 150607-1 | Shifter guide pin | 2 | | 130 | 21758 | | |
| AF08 | 150609 | Stopper pin | 2 | | 5 | | | |
| AF09 | 150610 | Neutral swicth point | 1 | | 10 | | | |
| AF10 | 150612 | Adjusting spacer | 1 | | 5 | | | |
| AF11 | 150613 | Oil seal | 1 | S22×12×7 | 35 | | | |
| AF12 | 150614 | Shifter cam shaft spacer | 1 | | 30 | | | |
| AF13 | 150616 | Change shaft | 1 | | 290 | | | |
| AF14 | 150617-1 | Change arm | 1 | | 460 | 11634 | | |
| AF15 | 150618 | Change lever spring | 1 | | 30 | | | |
| AF16 | 150619 | Spring stopper pin | 1 | | 150 | | | |
| AF17 | 150620 | Spring stopper screw | 1 | | 20 | | | |
| AF18 | 150622 | Shifter cam stopper pin | 1 | | 15 | | | |
| AF19 | 150623 | Stopper pin spring | 1 | | 7 | | | |
| AF20 | 150624 | Cam stepper fitting screw packing | 1 | | 8 | | | |
| AF21 | 150626 | Chang shaft spacer | 1 | | 5 | | | |
| AF22 | 150627 | Shifter segment spacer | 1 | | 3 | | | |

124

## AF Shifter

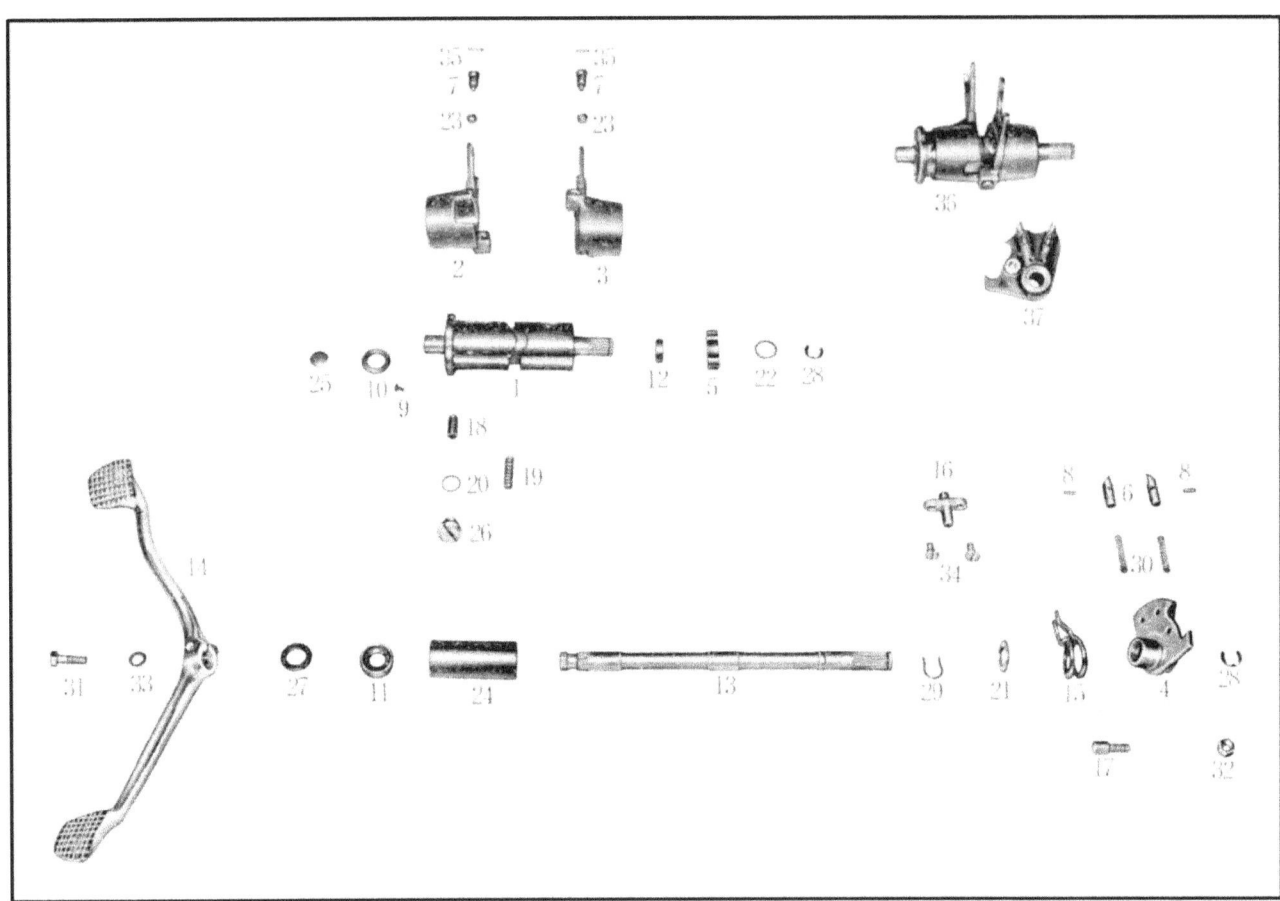

| Illustration No. | Stock No. | Name of items | Quantity required per one machine | Size | Unit price | Improved machine | Models for which inter-changeable | | Remarks |
|---|---|---|---|---|---|---|---|---|---|
| AF23 | 150628 | Shifter guide pin roller | 2 | | 40 | | | | |
| AF24 | 150629-1 | Oil seal cover | 1 | | 40 | 38224 | | | |
| AF25 | 150630 | Shifter cam shaft plug | 1 | 13φ | 10 | 17721 | | | |
| AF26 | 150632 | Fitting screw for shifter cam stoper | 1 | | 10 | 27063 | | | |
| AF27 | 150634 | Dust seal | 1 | | 30 | 38224 | | | |
| AF28 | 012632 | Change shaft clip | 2 | | 20 | | YDS 2 | YDS 1 | |
| AF29 | 421708 | Change shaft clip, outer | 1 | | 25 | | YD 3 | YD 2 | |
| AF30 | 111538 | Shifter pawl spring | 2 | | 5 | | YD 3 | YA 3 YD 2 | |
| AF31 | YS01-6.20-10 | Bolt | 1 | | 4 | | | | |
| AF32 | YS02-6 | Nut | 1 | | 2 | | | | |
| AF33 | YS05-6 | Spring washer | 1 | | 1 | | | | |
| AF34 | YS08-5.10-8 | Bolt | 2 | | 6 | | | | |
| AF35 | YS20-2-15 | Shifter guide pin stopper | 2 | | 5 | | | | |
| AF36 | | Shifter assembly | 1 | | 2800 | | | | |
| AF37 | | Shifter pawl retainer assembly | 1 | | 700 | | | | |

## AG Kickstarter

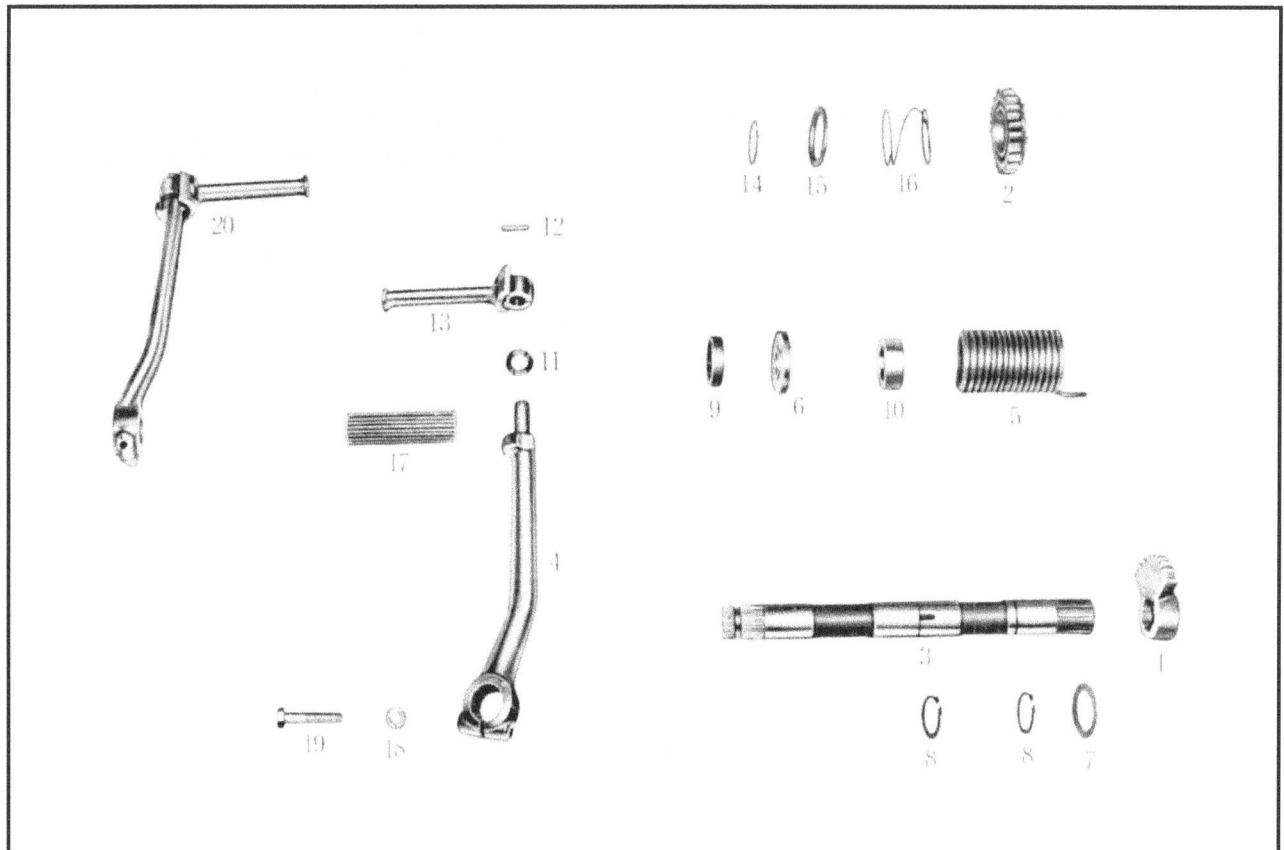

| Illustration No. | Stock No. | Name of items | Quantity required per one machine | Size | Unit price | Improved machine | Models for which inter-changeable | Remarks |
|---|---|---|---|---|---|---|---|---|
| AG01 | 150701 | Kickstarter gear | 1 | 6 teeth | 400 | | | |
| AG02 | 150702 | Kickstarter pinion | 1 | 23 teeth | 460 | | | |
| AG03 | 150703 | Kickstarter shaft | 1 | | 530 | | | |
| AG04 | 150704 | Kickstarter crank | 1 | | 700 | | | |
| AG05 | 150705 | Kickstarter spring | 1 | | 80 | | | |
| AG06 | 150706-1 | Kickstarter spring step | 1 | | 20 | 100001 | | |
| AG07 | 150707 | Spacer for kickstarter shaft | 1 | | 8 | | | |
| AG08 | 150708 | Clip for kickstarter shaft | 2 | | 20 | | | |
| AG09 | 150709 | Oil seal | 1 | S30×20×7 | 50 | | | |
| AG10 | 150714-1 | Inner cylinder for kickstarter spring | 1 | | 40 | 18373 | | |
| AG11 | 301510 | Spring washer | 1 | | 10 | | YD 3  YC 1 | |
| AG12 | 301512 | Knock pin | 1 | | 25 | | YD 3  YC 1 | |
| AG13 | 301511 | Kickstarter lever | 1 | | 100 | | YD 3  YC 1 | |
| AG14 | 301403 | Snap ring | 1 | | 5 | | YC 1 | |
| AG15 | 301404 | Step for kick pinion spring | 1 | | 5 | | YC 1 | |
| AG16 | 401405 | Kick pinion spring | 1 | | 15 | | YC 1 | |
| AG17 | 301513 | Kick starter | 1 | | 20 | | YD 3  YC 1 | |
| AG18 | YS05-12 | Washer | 1 | | 3 | | | |
| AG19 | 300107 | Bolt | 1 | | 20 | | | |
| AG20 | | Kickstarter crank assembly | 1 | | 1200 | | | |

## AH Crank case

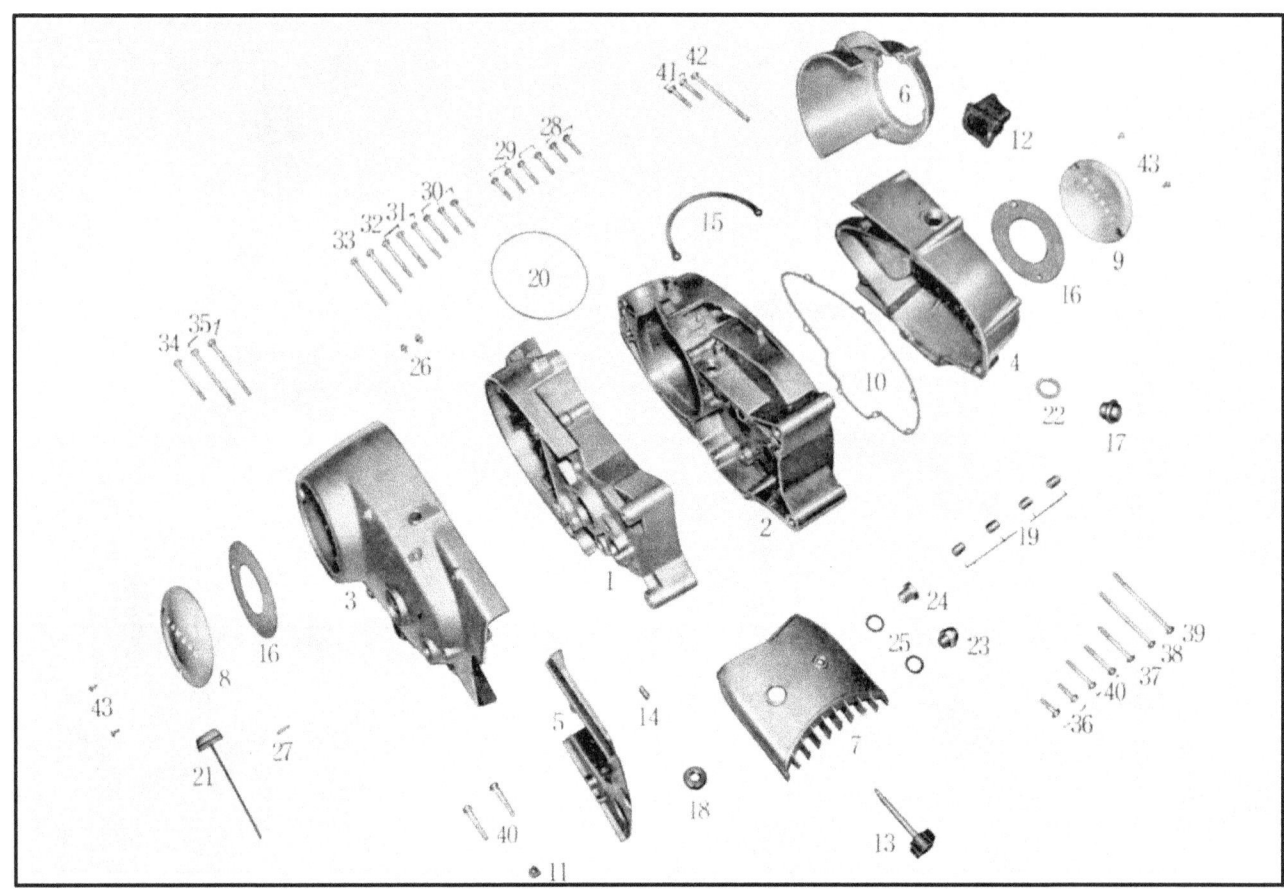

| Illustration No. | Stock No. | Name of items | Quantity required per one machine | Size | Unit price | Improved machine | Models for which inter-changeable | Remarks |
|---|---|---|---|---|---|---|---|---|
| ※AH01 | 150801-2 | Crankcase, left B | 1 |  | 4600 | 38224 |  |  |
| ※AH02 | 150802-4 | Crankcase, right C | 1 |  | 4300 | 100001 |  |  |
| ※AH03 | 150803-3 | Crankcase cover, left C | 1 |  | 1500 | 100001 |  |  |
| ※AH04 | 150804-2 | Crankcase cover, right B | 1 |  | 1100 | 38229 |  |  |
| AH05 | 150805 | Center cover | 1 |  | 200 |  |  |  |
| AH06 | 150806-2 | Carbureter cover B | 1 |  | 430 | 100001 |  |  |
| AH07 | 150807 | Air inlet cover | 1 |  | 350 |  |  |  |
| AH08 | 150810L | Crank case cover cap L | 1 | 107φ | 100 |  |  |  |
| AH09 | 150810R | Crank case cover cap R | 1 | 107φ | 100 |  |  |  |
| AH10 | 150813-1 | Crank case cover (R) packing | 1 |  | 50 | 38224 |  |  |
| AH11 | 150814 | Grommet | 1 |  | 10 |  |  |  |
| AH12 | 150815-1 | Carburetor cover cap A | 1 |  | 45 | 100001 |  |  |
| AH13 | 150816 | Bolt | 1 |  | 60 |  |  |  |
| AH14 | 150817 | Knock pin | 1 |  | 15 |  |  |  |
| AH15 | 150820 | Carburetor cover packing | 1 |  | 15 |  |  |  |
| AH16 | 150821 | Crankcase cover cap packing | 2 |  | 25 | 100001 |  |  |
| AH17 | 150822-1 | Oil level plug | 1 |  | 30 |  |  |  |
| AH18 | 150823 | Air inlet pipe grommet | 1 |  | 15 |  |  |  |
| AH19 | 150824 | Crankcase knock pin | 4 |  | 10 |  |  |  |
| AH20 | 150825 | O ring | 1 |  | 80 |  |  |  |
| AH21 | 150826 | Oil level gauge | 1 |  | 30 | 38224 |  |  |
| AH22 | 150827 | Packing for oil level plug | 1 |  | 5 | 38224 |  |  |

| Illustration No. | Stock No. | Name of items | Quantity required per one machine | Size | Unit price | Improved machine | Models for which inter-changeable | Remarks |
|---|---|---|---|---|---|---|---|---|
| AH23 | 121310 | Set screw for gas vent hole | 1 | | 60 | | YD 3 / YA 2 / YD 2 | |
| AH24 | 111306 | Set screw for oil extractor | 1 | | 20 | | YD 3 / YD 2 / YA 2 | |
| AH25 | 111307 | Gasket for oil extrator | 2 | | 3 | | YD 3 / YA 1 / YD 2 | |
| AH26 | 111326 | Grease nipple | 2 | | 10 | | | |
| AH27 | 110176 | Knock pin | 1 | | 10 | | | |
| AH28 | YS12-6.30-20 | Bolt | 2 | | 4 | | | |
| AH29 | YS12-6.44-15 | Bolt | 4 | | 6 | | | |
| AH30 | YS12-6.47-15 | Bolt | 3 | | 6 | | | |
| AH31 | YS12-6.60-15 | Bolt | 3 | | 8 | | | |
| AH32 | YS12-6.63-15 | Bolt | 1 | | 8 | | | |
| AH33 | YS12-6.76-13 | Bolt | 1 | | 12 | | | |
| AH34 | YS12-6.62-15 | Bolt | 1 | | 8 | | | |
| AH35 | YS12-6.90-15 | Bolt | 2 | | 20 | | | |
| AH36 | YS12-6.20-15 | Bolt | 2 | | 4 | | | |
| AH37 | YS12-6.44-15 | Bolt | 1 | | 6 | | | |
| AH38 | YS12-6.72-15 | Bolt | 1 | | 10 | | | |
| AH39 | YS12-6.80-15 | Bolt | 1 | | 13 | | | |
| AH40 | YS12-6.35-15 | Bolt | 4 | | 5 | | | |
| AH41 | YS12-6.40-20 | Bolt | 2 | | 6 | | | |
| AH42 | YS12-6.112-15 | Bolt | 1 | | 15 | | | |
| AH43 | YS12-4.7-6 | Bolt | 4 | | 2 | | | |

## MEMO

## A1 Carburefor

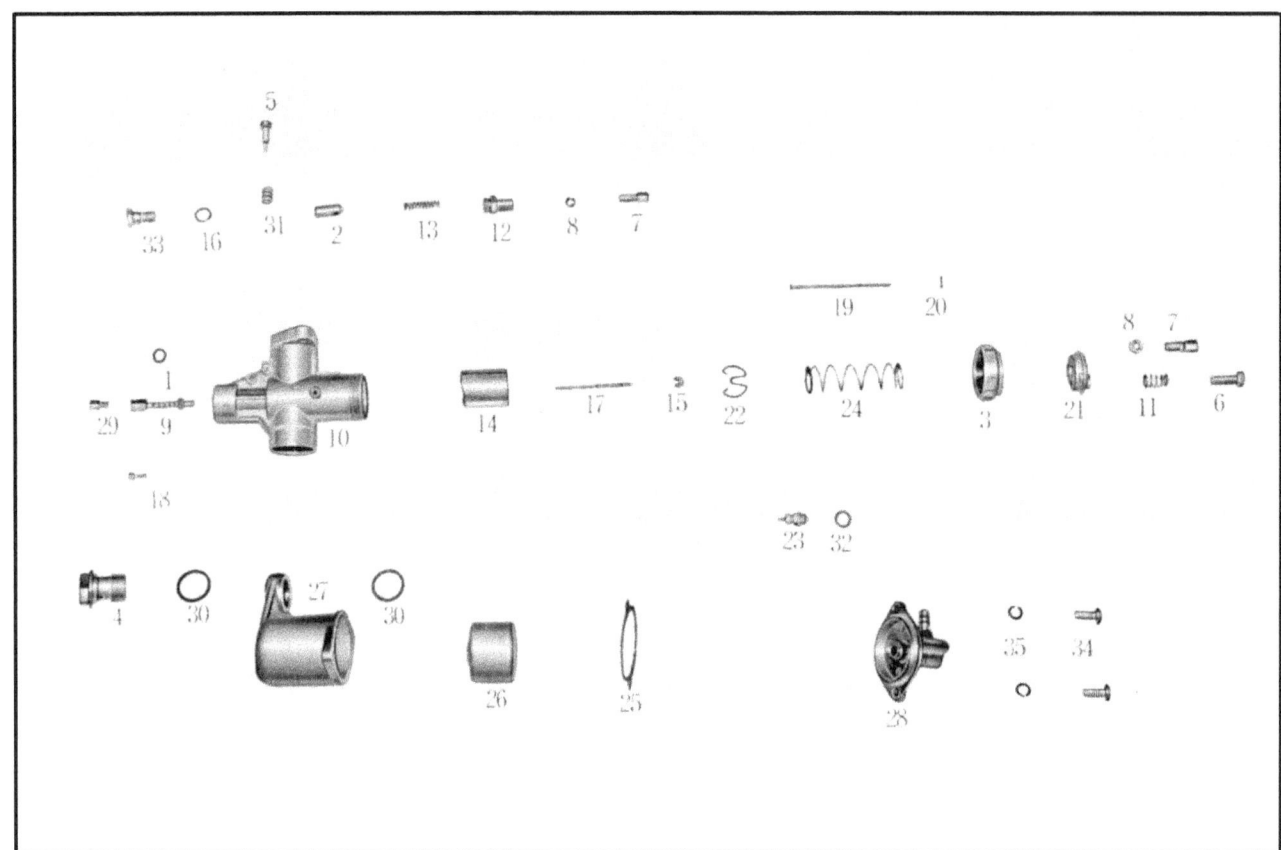

| Illustration No. | Stock No. | Name of items | Quantity required per one machine | Size | Unit price | Improved machine | Models for which inter-changeable | | Remarks |
|---|---|---|---|---|---|---|---|---|---|
| A1 01 | M21/05 | Needle washer | 1 | | 10 | | | | |
| A1 02 | M21/06 | Starter plunger complete | 1 | | 90 | | YD 3 | | |
| A1 03 | M21/10 | Mixing chamber cap | 1 | | 100 | | | | |
| A1 04 | M21/11 | Holding bolt | 1 | | 180 | | | | |
| A1 05 | M21/12 | Pilot air screw | 1 | | 70 | | | | |
| A1 06 | M21/13 | Throttle adjuster | 1 | | 40 | | YD 3 | YDS2 | |
| A1 07 | M21/14 | Cable adjuster | 2 | | 30 | | YD 3 | YDS2 | |
| A1 08 | M21/15 | Cable adjuster lock nut | 1 | | 10 | | YD 3 | YDS2 | |
| A1 09 | M21/16 | Needle jet | 1 | | 160 | | | | |
| A1 10 | M2S11/01 | Mixing chamber body | 1 | | 1400 | | | | |
| A1 11 | M20/11 | Throttle adjuster spring | 1 | | 15 | | YD 3 | YDS2 | |
| A1 12 | M20/64 | Spring guide | 1 | | 70 | | YD 3 | | |
| A1 13 | M20/65 | Starter plunger spring | 1 | | 20 | | MF.J.2 | YD 3 | |
| A1 14 | M20/69-1 | Throttle valve | 1 | | 400 | 89036 | YDS2 | | |
| A1 15 | M10/08 | Needle clip | 1 | | 20 | | MF.J.2 YDS2 | YD 3 | |
| A1 16 | M10/17 | Washer | 1 | | 2 | | | | |
| A1 17 | VM22/88 | Jet needle | 1 | | 100 | | | | |
| A1 18 | VM22/140-1 | Pilot jet | 1 | | 70 | 89036 | MF.J.2 | YDS2 | |
| A1 19 | VM21/08 | Throttle stop rod | 1 | | 20 | | | | |
| A1 20 | VM21/13 | Split cutter pin | 1 | | 2 | | YD 3 | | |
| A1 21 | VM20/53 | Mixing champer top | 1 | | 90 | | YD 3 | | |

| Illustration No. | Stock No. | Name of items | Quantity required per one machine | Size | Unit price | Improved machine | Models for which inter-changeable | Remarks |
|---|---|---|---|---|---|---|---|---|
| AI 22 | VM20/56 | Circlip | 1 | | 40 | | YD 3  YDS2 | |
| AI 23 | VM20H1/200 | Valve seat complete | 1 | | 400 | | | |
| AI 24 | RM18C1/41 | Throttle valve spring | 1 | | 30 | | | |
| AI 25 | FT22/03 | Float chamber packing | 1 | | 10 | | | |
| AI 26 | FT22/04 | Float | 1 | | 100 | | | |
| AI 27 | FT20V/01 | Float chamber body | 1 | | 350 | | | |
| AI 28 | FT20V4/160 | Float chamber cover | 1 | | 500 | | | |
| AI 29 | 4/042 | Main jet | 1 | | 60 | | YD 3  YDS2 | |
| AI 30 | 4/053 | Washer | 2 | | 2 | | YD 3 | |
| AI 31 | 4/148 | Air adjusting spring | 1 | | 15 | | YD 3 | |
| AI 32 | B21/108 | Packing 10φ | 1 | | 2 | | | |
| AI 33 | 26BCI/38 | Starter jet | 1 | | 120 | | | |
| AI 34 | S2-05-12 | Screw | 2 | | 10 | | | |
| AI 35 | W4-05-0 | Spring washer | 2 | | 4 | | | |

M E M O

## II  FRAME SECTION

### AJ  Frame

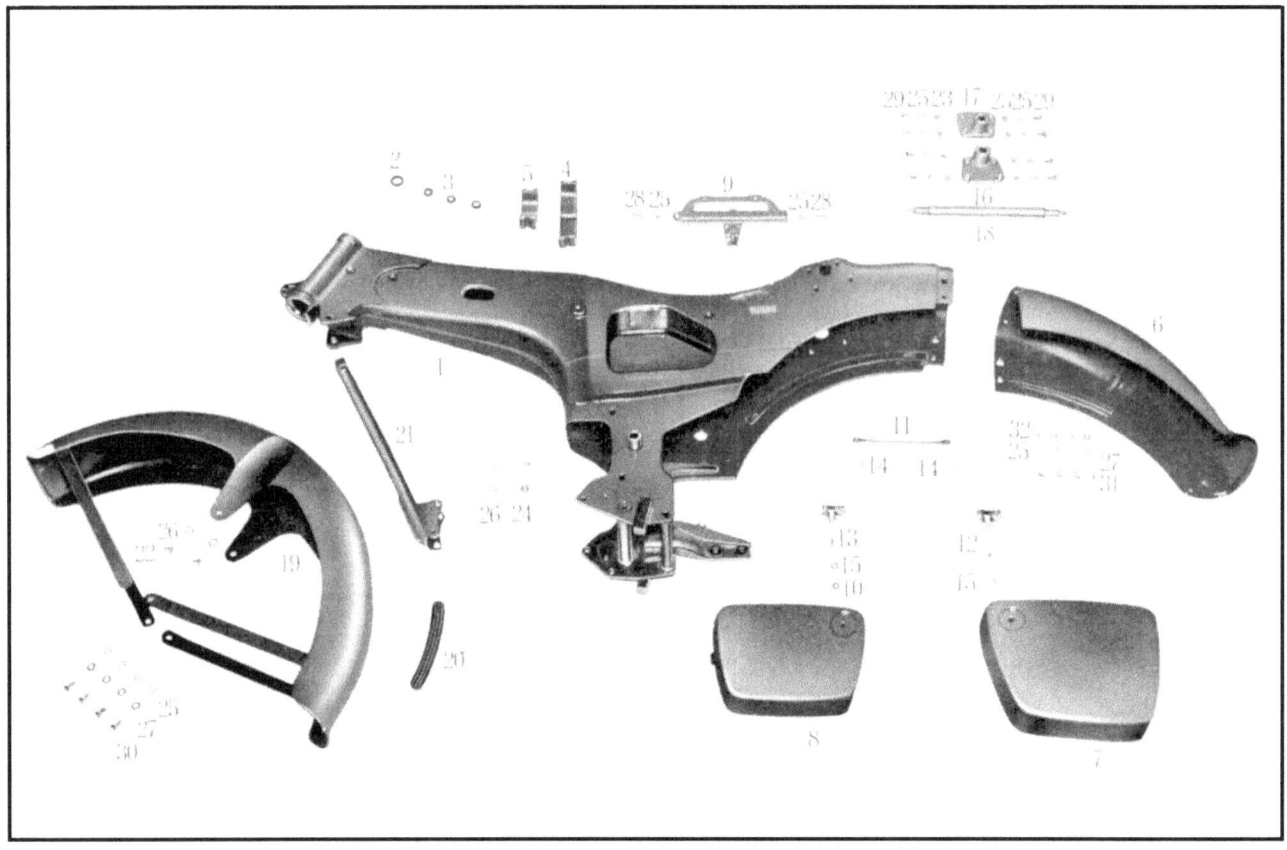

| Illustration No. | Stock No. | Name of items | Quantity required per one machine | Size | Unit price | Improved machine | Models for which inter-changeable | Remarks |
|---|---|---|---|---|---|---|---|---|
| AJ 01 | 151001-1 | Frame assembly | 1 | | 10000 | 71459 | | |
| AJ 02 | 151023 | Grommet 17φ | 1 | | 5 | | | |
| AJ 03 | 151024 | Grommet 10φ | 3 | | 5 | | | |
| AJ 04 | 151025 | Rubber | 1 | | 50 | | | |
| AJ 05 | 151035-1 | Yielding rubber for tank | 1 | | 40 | | | |
| ※AJ 06 | 151201-1 | Rear fender | 1 | | 1000 | 100001 | | |
| AJ 07 | 151301 | Side cover, right | 1 | | 500 | | | |
| AJ 08 | 151302-1 | Side cover, left | 1 | | 400 | | | |
| AJ 09 | 151307-1 | Battery band | 1 | | 150 | 10050 | | |
| AJ 10 | 151309 | Battery push rubber | 1 | | 5 | | | |
| AJ 11 | 151312 | Tool band | 1 | | 20 | | | |
| AJ 12 | 151314 | Clamping bolt for side cover R | 1 | | 90 | | | |
| AJ 13 | 151315 | Clamping bolt for side cover L | 1 | | 90 | | | |
| AJ 14 | 151316 | Ring | 2 | | 6 | | | |
| AJ 15 | 151356 | washer | 2 | | 5 | | | |
| AJ 16 | 151401L | Rear cushion step L | 1 | | 270 | | | |
| AJ 17 | 151401R | Rear cushion step R | 1 | | 270 | | | |
| AJ 18 | 151402 | Rear cushion fitting bolt upper | 1 | | 450 | | | |
| ※AJ 19 | 151501-1 | Front fender | 1 | | 2000 | | | |
| AJ 20 | 151552 | Rubber plate | 1 | | 15 | | | |
| AJ 21 | 151705 | Down tube | 1 | | 550 | | | |

| Illustration No. | Stock No. | Name of items | Quantity required per one machine | Size | Unit price | Improved machine | Models for which inter-changeable | Remarks |
|---|---|---|---|---|---|---|---|---|
| AJ 22 | YS01-8. 12-10 | Bolt | 2 | | 7 | | | |
| AJ 23 | YS02-6 | Nut | 8 | | 2 | | | |
| AJ 24 | YS02-8 | Nut | 2 | | 5 | | | |
| AJ 25 | YS05-6 | Spring washer | 18 | | 1 | | | |
| AJ 26 | YS05-8 | Spring washer | 4 | | 2 | | | |
| AJ 27 | YS06-6 | Washer | 8 | | 1 | | | |
| AJ 28 | YS11-6. 15-13 | Bolt | 2 | | 3 | | | |
| AJ 29 | YS13-6. 16-10 | Bolt | 8 | | 3 | | | |
| AJ 30 | YS01-6. 12-10 | Bolt | 4 | | 4 | | | |
| AJ 31 | YS01-6. 14-12 | Bolt | 4 | | 3 | | | |
| AJ 32 | YS03-6 | Nut | 4 | | 2 | | | |

MEMO

132

AK Foot-rest. Stand

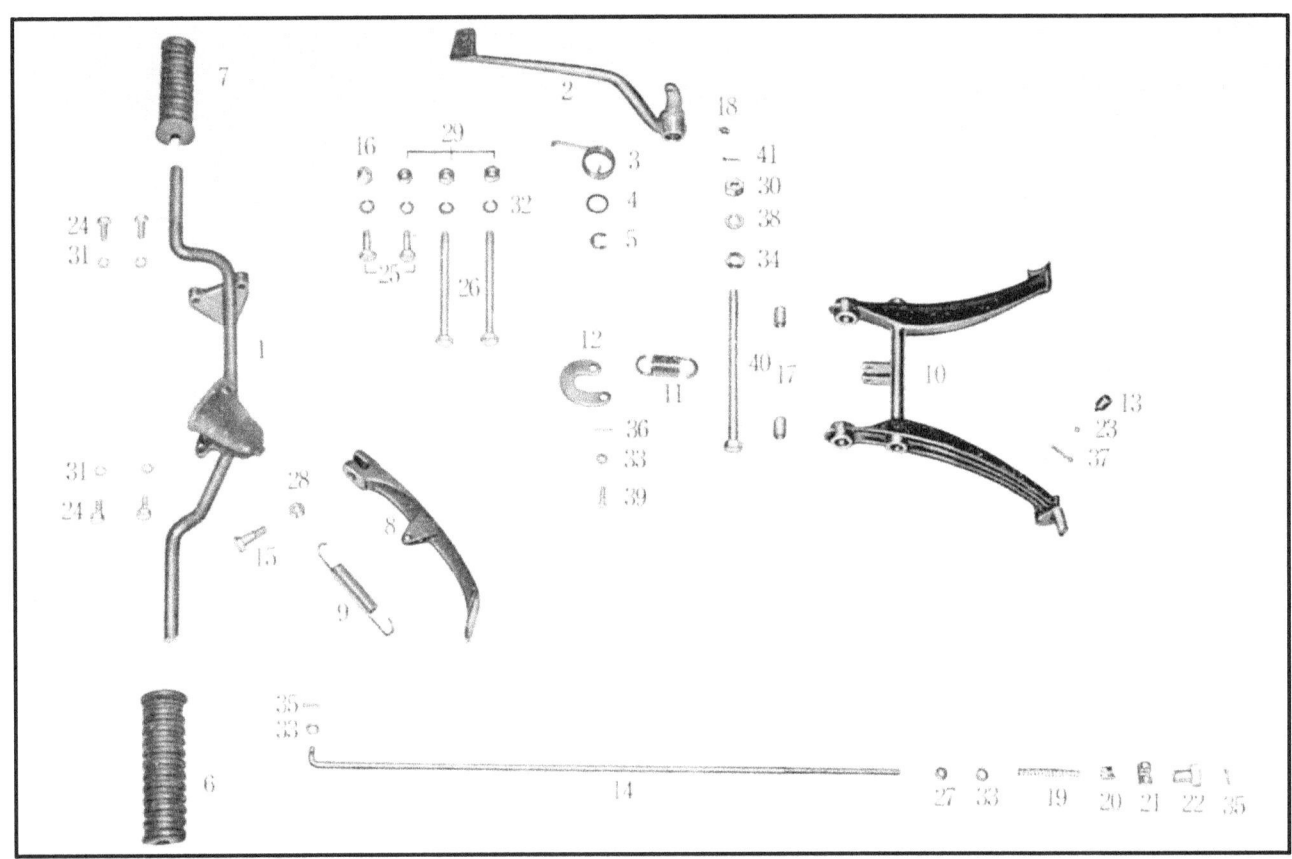

| Illustration No. | Stock No. | Name of items | Quantity required per one machine | Size | Unit price | Improved machine | Models for which inter-changeable | | Remarks |
|---|---|---|---|---|---|---|---|---|---|
| AK01 | 151709 | Foot-rest shaft assembly | 1 | | 700 | | | | |
| AK02 | 151711 | Brake pedal | 1 | | 650 | | | | |
| AK03 | 151712 | Brake spring | 1 | | 30 | | | | |
| AK04 | 151713 | Special washer | 1 | | 3 | | | | |
| AK05 | 151714 | E stop ring | 1 | | 15 | | | | |
| AK06 | 151722-1 | Foot-rest rubber, left | 1 | | 50 | 13871 | | | |
| AK07 | 151726-1 | Foot-rest rubber, right | 1 | | 50 | 13871 | | | |
| AK08 | 151731 | Side stand | 1 | | 450 | | | | |
| AK09 | 151732 | Side stand spring | 1 | | 40 | | | | |
| AK10 | 151741-1 | Main stand | 1 | | 900 | 32170 | | | |
| AK11 | 151744-1 | Main stand spring | 1 | | 40 | 27850 | | | |
| AK12 | 151745 | Main stand link | 1 | | 40 | | | | |
| AK13 | 151746 | Main stand stopper rubber | 1 | | 10 | | | | |
| AK14 | 157025-1 | Brake rod | 1 | | 60 | 17228 | | | |
| AK15 | 157043 | Bolt | 1 | | 20 | | | | |
| AK16 | 151403 | Bag nut | 1 | | 25 | | | | |
| AK17 | 422694 | Spacer | 2 | | 30 | | YD 3 | YD 2 | |
| AK18 | 422915 | Grease nipple | 1 | | 10 | | | | |
| AK19 | 422936 | Rod spring | 1 | | 10 | | YD 3 | YD 2 | |
| AK20 | 422939 | Rod washer | 1 | | 20 | | YD 3 | YD 2 | |
| AK21 | 422940 | Rod stopper metal | 1 | | 15 | | YD 3 | YD 2 | |
| AK22 | 422941 | Rod adjuster bolt | 1 | | 40 | | YD 3 | YD 2 | |

| Illustration No. | Stock No. | Name of items | Quantity required per one machine | Size | Unit price | Improved machine | Models for which inter-changeable | Remarks |
|---|---|---|---|---|---|---|---|---|
| AK23 | 422954 | Rubber washer | 1 | | 2 | | YD 2 | |
| AK24 | YS01-8.20-18 | Bolt | 4 | | 8 | | | |
| AK25 | YS01-10.48-12 | Bolt | 2 | | 15 | | | |
| AK26 | YS01-10.136-12 | Bolt | 2 | | 60 | | | |
| AK27 | YS02-6 | Nut | 1 | | 2 | | | |
| AK28 | YS02-8 | Nut | 1 | | 5 | | | |
| AK29 | YS02-10 | Nut | 3 | | 7 | | | |
| AK30 | YS23-10 | Nut | 1 | | 12 | | | |
| AK31 | YS05-8 | Spring washer | 4 | | 2 | | | |
| AK32 | YS05-10 | Spring washer | 4 | | 5 | | | |
| AK33 | YS06-6 | Washer | 3 | | 1 | | | |
| AK34 | YS06-10 | Washer | 1 | | 1 | | | |
| AK35 | YS20-1.2-15 | Split cutter pin | 2 | | 1 | | | |
| AK36 | YS20-1.6-15 | Split cutter pin | 1 | | 1 | | | |
| AK37 | YS20-2-20 | Split cutter pin | 1 | | 1 | | | |
| AK38 | YS05-10 | Spring washer | 1 | | 2 | | | |
| AK39 | YS21-6-22 | Pin | 1 | | 5 | | | |
| AK40 | YS22-10.178-2 | Bolt | 1 | | 80 | | | |
| AK41 | YS20-2-22 | Split cutter pin | 1 | | 1 | | | |

M E M O

## AL  Chain case, Rear arm, Cushion

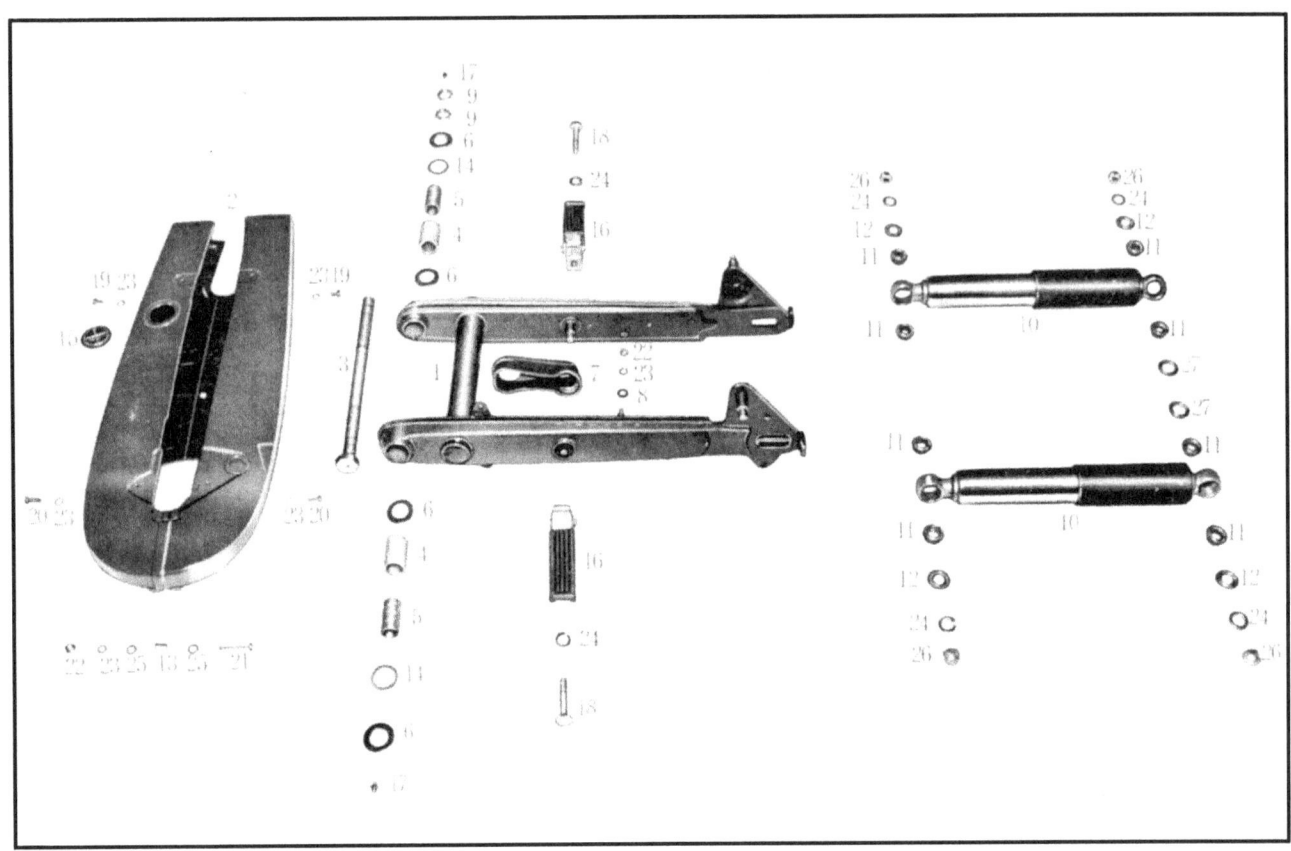

| Illustration No. | Stock No. | Name of items | Quantity required per one machine | Size | Unit price | Improved machine | Models for which inter-changeable | Remarks |
|---|---|---|---|---|---|---|---|---|
| ※AL01 | 152001-2 | Rear arm B | 1 | | 2500 | 29085 | | |
| AL02 | 152010-2 | Chain Case B | 1 | | 1400 | 29085 | | |
| AL03 | 152020-1 | Rear arm shaft | 1 | | 350 | | | |
| AL04 | 152021 | Bush, large | 2 | | 120 | | | |
| AL05 | 152022 | Bush, small | 2 | | 100 | | | |
| AL06 | 152023 | Thrust cover, small | 4 | | 15 | | | |
| AL07 | 152028 | Vibration-proof rubber | 1 | | 30 | | | |
| AL08 | 152029 | Plain washer | 1 | | 2 | | | |
| AL09 | 152030 | Arm shaft nut | 2 | | 20 | | | |
| AL10 | 152130 | Rear cushion unit | 2 | | 2200 | | | |
| AL11 | 152131 | Cushion rubber | 8 | | 50 | | | |
| AL12 | 152132 | Plain washer | 4 | | 8 | | | |
| AL13 | 152133 | Spacer | 1 | | 5 | | | |
| AL14 | 422931 | Adjusting washar | 2 | | 45 | | | |
| AL15 | 422965 | Testing-hole cap | 1 | | 15 | | YD 3   YD 2 | |
| AL16 | 422976 | Spare foot-rest | 2 | | 200 | | YD 3   YD 2 | |
| AL17 | 122304 | Grease nipple | 2 | | 10 | | | |
| AL18 | YS01-10.48-18 | Bolt | 2 | | 15 | | | |
| AL19 | YS12-6.10-8 | Bolt | 2 | | 3 | | | |
| AL20 | YS12-6.16-10 | Bolt | 2 | | 3 | | | |
| AL21 | YS12-6.43-10 | Bolt | 1 | | 6 | | | |
| AL22 | YS02-6 | Nut | 2 | | 2 | | | |

| Illustration No. | Stock No. | Name of items | Quantity required per one machine | Size | Unit price | Improved machine | Models for which inter-changeable | Remarks |
|---|---|---|---|---|---|---|---|---|
| AL23 | YS05-6 | Spring washer | 6 | | 1 | | | |
| AL24 | YS05-10 | Spring washer | 6 | | 2 | | | |
| AL25 | YS06-6 | Washer | 2 | | 1 | | | |
| AL26 | 151403 | Bag nut | 4 | | 25 | | | |
| AL27 | 122327 | Washer | 2 | | 8 | | | |

# M E M O

136

## AM Front fork

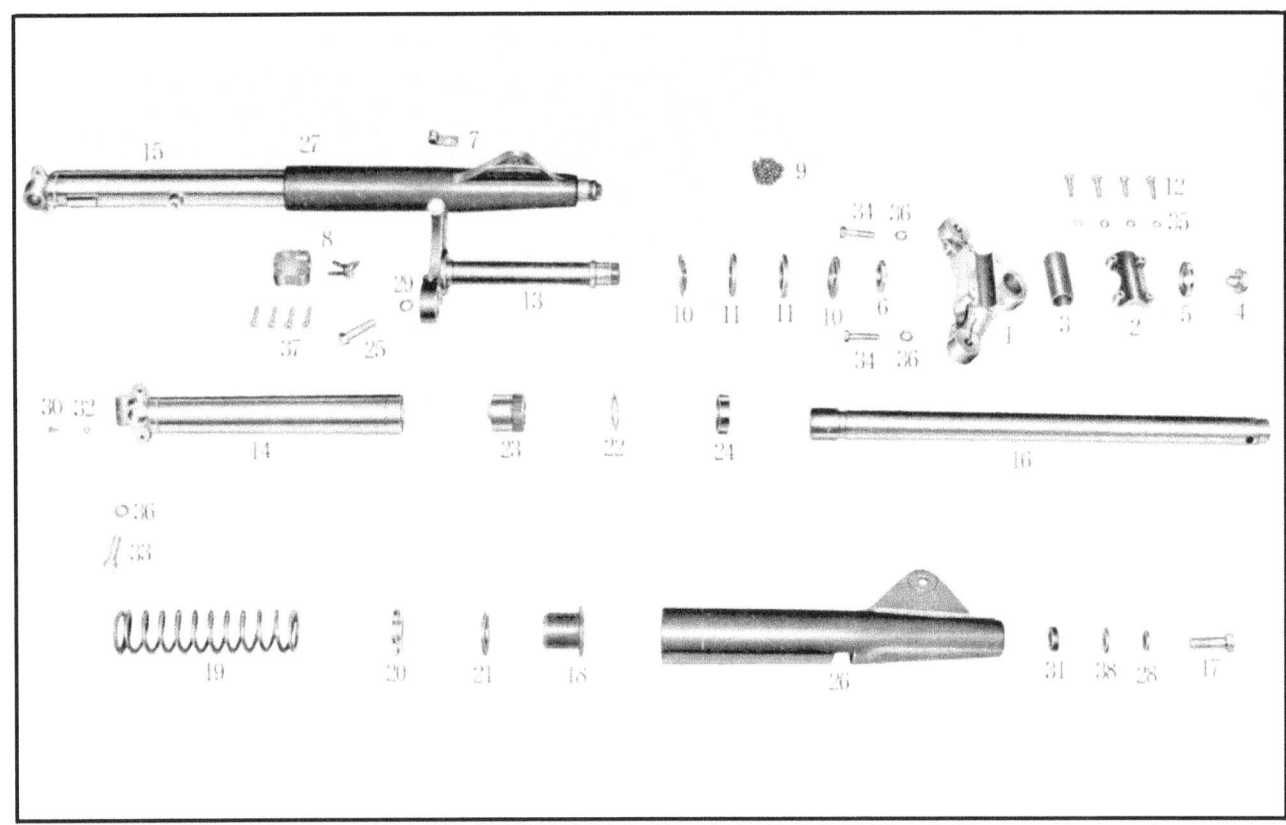

| Illustration No. | Stock No. | Name of items | Quantity required per one machine | Size | Unit price | Improved machine | Models for which inter-changeable | Remarks |
|---|---|---|---|---|---|---|---|---|
| AM01 | 153003 | Handle crawn | 1 | | 1300 | | | |
| AM02 | 153004 | Handle holder | 1 | | 220 | | | |
| AM03 | 153005 | Handle damper rubber | 1 | | 20 | | | |
| AM04 | 153006-1 | Bolt | 1 | | 70 | 27785 | | |
| AM05 | 153007 | Cover | 1 | | 10 | | | |
| AM06 | 153009-1 | Nut | 1 | | 40 | 27785 | | |
| AM07 | 1530105 | Brake wire holder | 1 | | 6 | | | |
| AM08 | 153200 | Handle lock | 1 | | 500 | | | |
| AM09 | 422312 | Ball | 38 | 6.35φ | 3 | | MF 2  YD 1 / YD 3  YD 2 | |
| AM10 | 422314 | Ball race (A) | 2 | | 130 | | MF 2  YD 1 / YD 3  YD 2 | |
| AM11 | 422315 | Ball race (B) | 2 | | 130 | | MF 2  YD 1 / YD 3  YD 2 | |
| AM12 | 422803 | Bolt | 4 | | 20 | YD 3 | YD 1  YD 2 | |
| AM13 | SA20500-1A | Under bracket A | 1 | | 2000 | 27785 | | |
| AM14 | SA20500-2L | Outer tube, left | 1 | | 1600 | | | |
| AM15 | SA20500-2R | Outer tube, right | 1 | | 1700 | | | |
| AM16 | SA20500-3-1 | Inner tube | 2 | | 1400 | 38140 | | |
| AM17 | S20500-38 | Bolt | 2 | | 100 | | | |
| AM18 | SA20500-40 | Cover guide | 2 | | 40 | | | |
| AM19 | SA20500-39 | Fork spring | 2 | | 240 | 75001 | | |
| AM20 | SA20500-13 | Spring guide | 2 | | 30 | | | |

| Illustration No. | Stock No. | Name of items | Quantity required per one machine | Size | Unit price | Improved machine | Models for which inter-changeable | Remarks |
|---|---|---|---|---|---|---|---|---|
| AM21 | SA20500-14 | Washer A | 2 | | 15 | | | |
| AM22 | SA20500-15 | Washer B | 2 | | 8 | | | |
| ※AM23 | SA20500-44 | Slide metal | 2 | | 220 | 38140 | | |
| AM24 | SA20500-21 | Oil seal | 2 | | 160 | | | |
| AM25 | SA20500-23 | Bolt 10φ | 2 | | 50 | | | |
| AM26 | SA20500-35L | Fork cover, left | 1 | | 750 | | | |
| AM27 | SA20500-35R | Fork cover, right | 1 | | 750 | | | |
| AM28 | SA20500-6 | Washer | 2 | | 40 | | | |
| AM29 | SA20200-33 | Spring washer 10φ | 2 | | 3 | | | |
| AM30 | SA30100-22 | Bolt | 2 | | 3 | | | |
| AM31 | SA20500-36 | O ring | 2 | | 35 | | | |
| AM32 | 2674-8 | Packing | 2 | | 5 | | | |
| AM33 | YS01-8.30-20 | Bolt | 1 | | 10 | | | |
| AM34 | YS01-8.36-18 | Bolt | 2 | | 20 | | | |
| AM35 | YS05-6 | Spring washer | 4 | | 1 | | | |
| AM36 | YS05-8 | Spring washer | 3 | | 1 | | | |
| AM37 | YS13-6.28-16 | Bolt | 4 | | 5 | | | |
| AM38 | SA20500-37 | Washer | 2 | | 10 | | | |
| | 153100 | Front fork assembly | 1 | | 12000 | | | |

## MEMO

138

AN  Fuel Tank

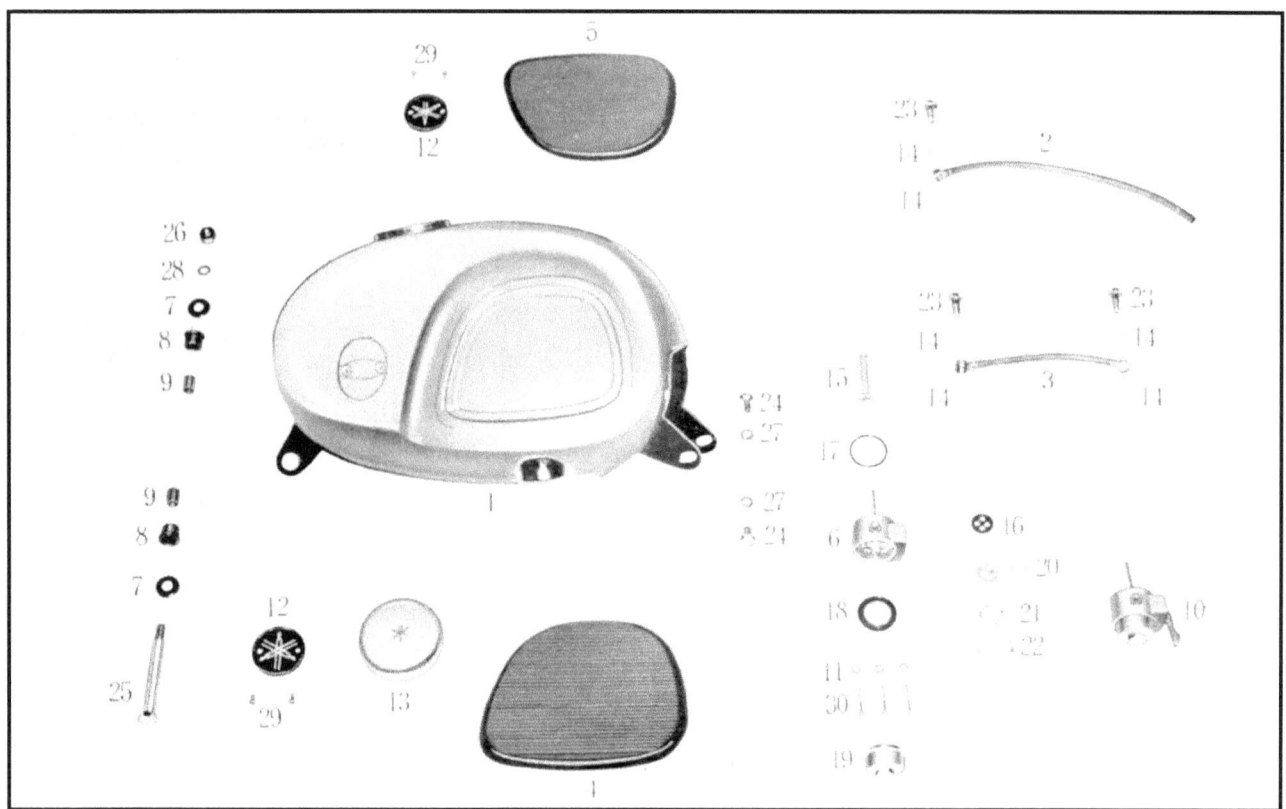

| Illustration No. | Stock No. | Name of items | Quantity required per one machine | Size | Unit price | Improved machine | Models for which inter-changeable | | Remarks |
|---|---|---|---|---|---|---|---|---|---|
| ※AN01 | 154000-1 | Fuel tank A | 1 | | 4000 | 100001 | | | |
| AN02 | 154001 | Fuel pipe | 1 | | 130 | | | | |
| AN03 | 154002 | Level pipe | 1 | | 90 | | | | |
| ※AN04 | 154006L-1 | Knee grip, left A | 1 | | 200 | 100001 | | | |
| ※AN05 | 154006R-1 | Knee grip, right A | 1 | | 200 | 100001 | | | |
| AN06 | 154010 | Cock body | 1 | | 300 | | YD 3 | | |
| AN07 | 154031 | Washer | 2 | | 6 | | | | |
| AN08 | 154032 | Grommet | 2 | | 10 | | | | |
| AN09 | 154033 | Distance piece | 2 | | 30 | | | | |
| AN10 | 154040 | Cock assembly | 1 | | 500 | | YD 3 | | |
| AN11 | 154041 | Lead packing | 3 | | 10 | | | | |
| ※AN12 | 434004 | Tank mark | 2 | | 100 | 100001 | YD 3 | | |
| AN13 | 422411 | Tank cap assembly | 1 | | 180 | | YD 3 | YD 2 | |
| AN14 | 422412 | Pipe packing | 6 | | 5 | | YD 3 | YD 2 | |
| AN15 | 422425 | Filter net | 1 | | 50 | | YD 3 | YD 2 | |
| AN16 | 422427 | Packing | 1 | | 20 | | YD 3 | YD 2 | |
| AN17 | 422429 | O ring | 1 | | 25 | | YD 3 | YD 2 | |
| AN18 | 422425 | Packing | 1 | | 5 | | YD 3 | YD 2 | |
| AN19 | 422423 | Filter cup | 1 | | 100 | | YD 3 | YD 2 | |
| AN20 | 422424 | Cock lever | 1 | | 35 | | YD 3 | YD 2 | |
| AN21 | 422428 | Lever stopper | 1 | | 20 | | YD 3 | YD 2 | |
| AN22 | 422426 | Bolt | 1 | | 5 | | YD 3 | YD 2 | |
| AN23 | 422414 | Bolt | 1 | | 25 | | YD 3 | YA 1 YD 2 | |
| AN24 | YS01-8.14-10 | Bolt | 2 | | 6 | | | | |
| AN25 | YS01-10.100-16 | Bolt | 1 | | 50 | | | | |
| AN26 | YS02-10 | Nut | 1 | | 7 | | | | |
| AN27 | YS05-8 | Spring washer | 2 | | 2 | | | | |
| AN28 | YS05-10 | Spring washer | 1 | | 2 | | | | |
| AN29 | YS11-4.8-8 | Bolt | 4 | | 1 | | | | |
| AN30 | YS15-5.32-15 | Bolt | 3 | | 5 | | | | |

AO  Saddle, Carrier

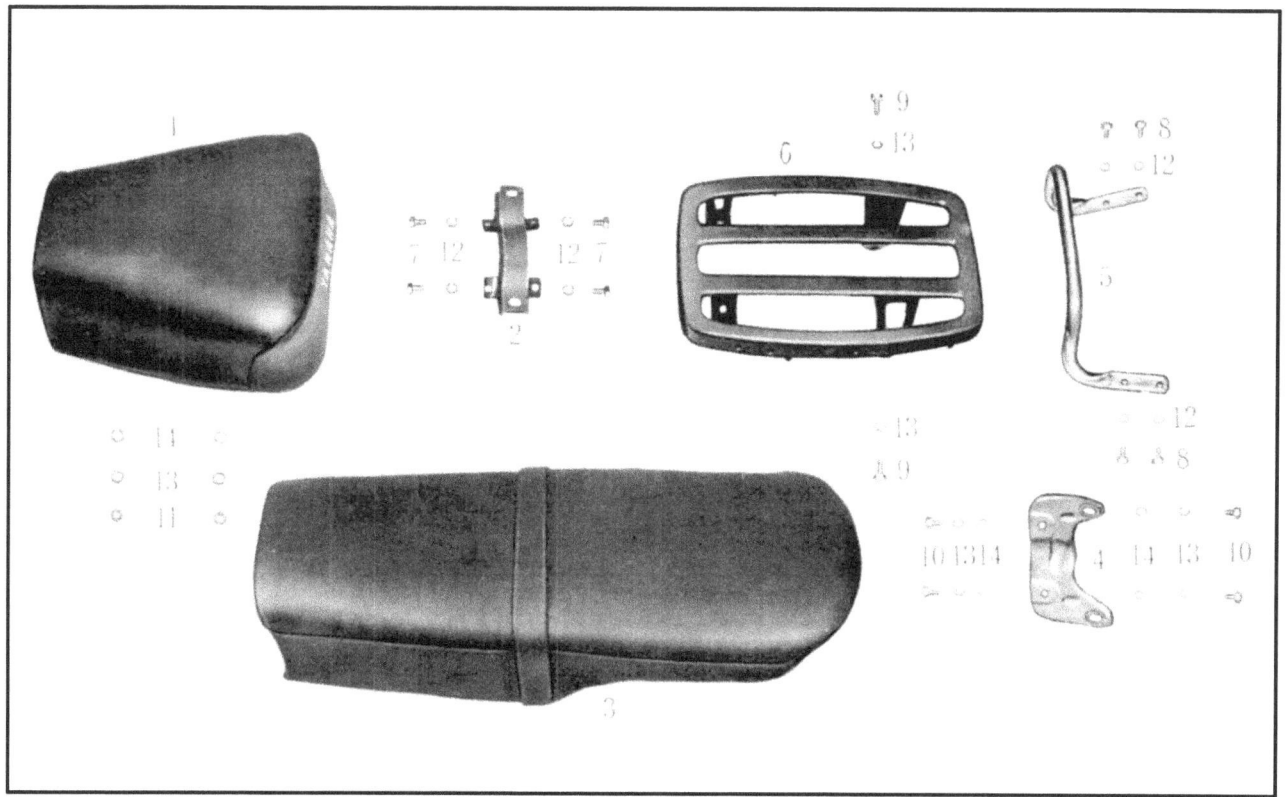

| Illustration No. | Stock No. | Name of items | Quantity required per one machine | Size | Unit price | Improved machine | Models for which inter-changeable | Remarks |
|---|---|---|---|---|---|---|---|---|
| AO01 | 154501-1 | Saddle A | 1 | | 2000 | 100001 | | |
| AO02 | 154502 | Fitting plate for saddle | 1 | | 120 | | | |
| AO03 | 154551-1 | Double seat A | 1 | | 3900 | | | |
| AO04 | 154552 | Double seat stay | 1 | | 250 | 100001 | | |
| AO05 | 154800 | Carrier knob | 1 | | 250 | | | |
| AO06 | 154801 | Carrier | 1 | | 850 | | | |
| AO07 | YS01-6.11-9 | Bolt | 4 | | 4 | | | |
| AO08 | YS01-6.12-10 | Bolt | 4 | | 4 | | | |
| AO09 | YS01-8.13-10 | Bolt | 2 | | 7 | | | |
| AO10 | YS01-8.16-12 | Bolt | 4 | | 8 | | | |
| AO11 | YS02-8 | Nut | 2 | | 5 | | | |
| AO12 | YS05-6 | Spring washer | 8 | | 1 | | | |
| AO13 | YS05-8 | Spring washer | 8 | | 2 | | | |
| AO14 | YS06-8 | Washer | 6 | | 1 | | | |

AP Front hub

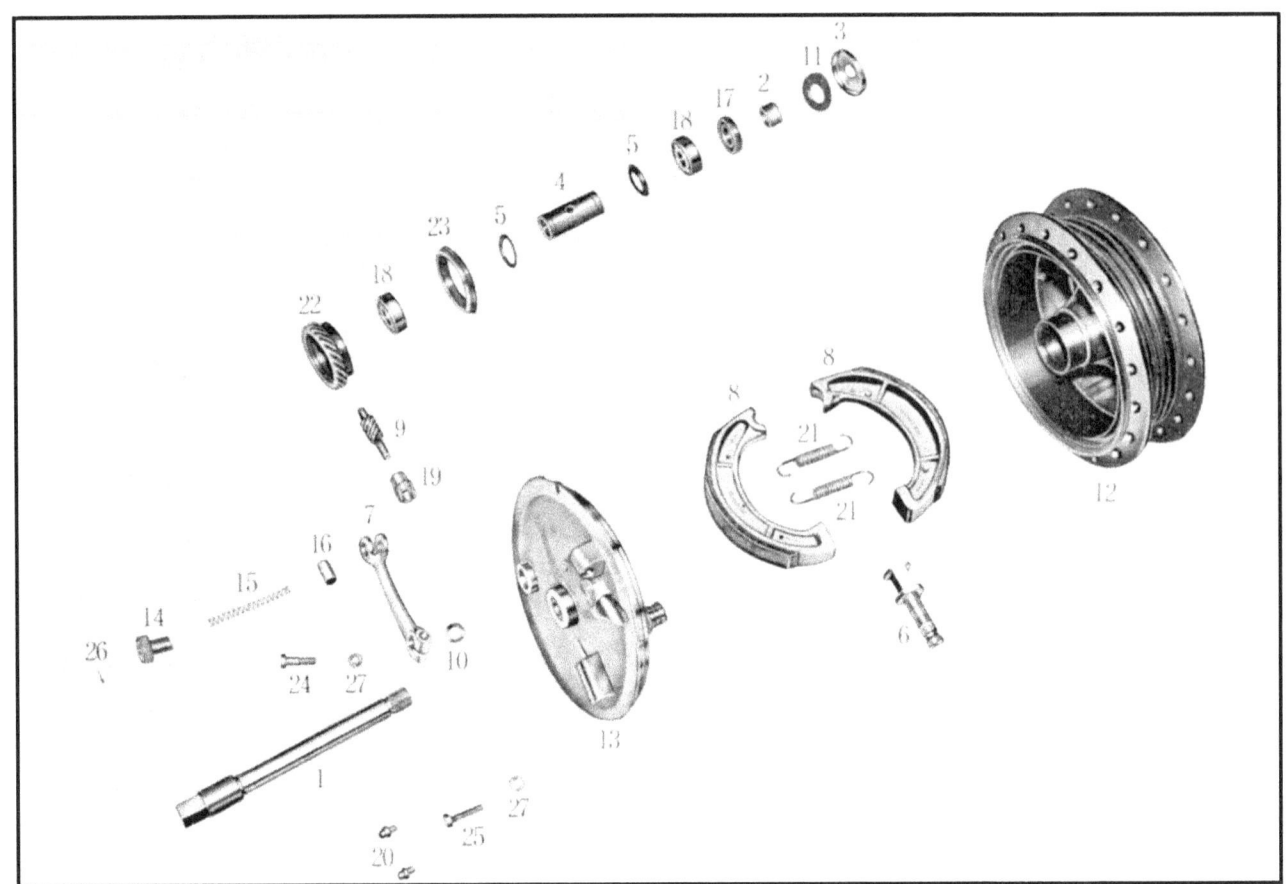

| Illustration No. | Stock No. | Name of items | Quantity required per one machine | Size | Unit price | Improved machine | Models for which inter-changeable | | Remarks |
|---|---|---|---|---|---|---|---|---|---|
| AP01 | 155001 | Front axle | 1 | | 400 | | | | |
| AP02 | 155002 | Collar | 1 | | 30 | | | | |
| AP03 | 155003 | Dust seal cover | 1 | | 20 | | | | |
| AP04 | 155004 | Spacer | 1 | | 100 | | | | |
| AP05 | 155005 | Center ring 30φ | 2 | | 5 | | | | |
| AP06 | 155007 | Brake cam, front | 1 | | 200 | | | | |
| AP07 | 155008 | Brake cam lever, front | 1 | | 110 | | | | |
| AP08 | 155009 | Brake shoe assembly | 2 | | 200 | | | | |
| AP09 | 155011 | Warm | 1 | 9 teeth | 200 | | | | |
| AP10 | 155012 | Ring 12φ | 1 | | 15 | | | | |
| AP11 | 155014 | Dust seal | 1 | | 10 | | | | |
| AP12 | 155015 | Front hub | 1 | | 1800 | | | | |
| AP13 | 155017-1 | Front shoe plate | 1 | | 800 | | | | |
| AP14 | 155022 | Adjusting nut | 1 | | 30 | 28850 | | | |
| AP15 | 155023 | Adjusting spring | 1 | | 10 | | | | |
| AP16 | 155024 | Stopper metal | 1 | | 30 | | | | |
| AP17 | 155030 | Oil seal | 1 | SD20×30×7 | 60 | | | | |
| AP18 | 155031 | Bearing | 2 | #6202 | The current price | | | | |
| AP19 | 155035 | Bush | 1 | | 100 | | | | |
| AP20 | 122710 | Grease nipple | 2 | | 10 | | YA 3 | YD 2 | |
| AP21 | 122718 | Brake shoe spring | 2 | | 15 | | YA 3 | | |
| AP22 | 122725 | Helical gear | 1 | 22 teeth | 400 | | YA 3 | YD 2 | |
| AP23 | 122732 | Oil seal | 1 | OS47×56×7 | 95 | | YA 3 | | |
| AP24 | YS01-6.24-12 | Bolt | 1 | | 5 | | | | |
| AP25 | YS01-6.25-18 | Bolt | 1 | | 5 | | | | |
| AP26 | YS20-1.2-10 | Split cutter pin | 1 | | 1 | | | | |
| AP27 | YS05-6 | Spring washer | 2 | | 1 | | | | |

AQ  Tyre, Rim

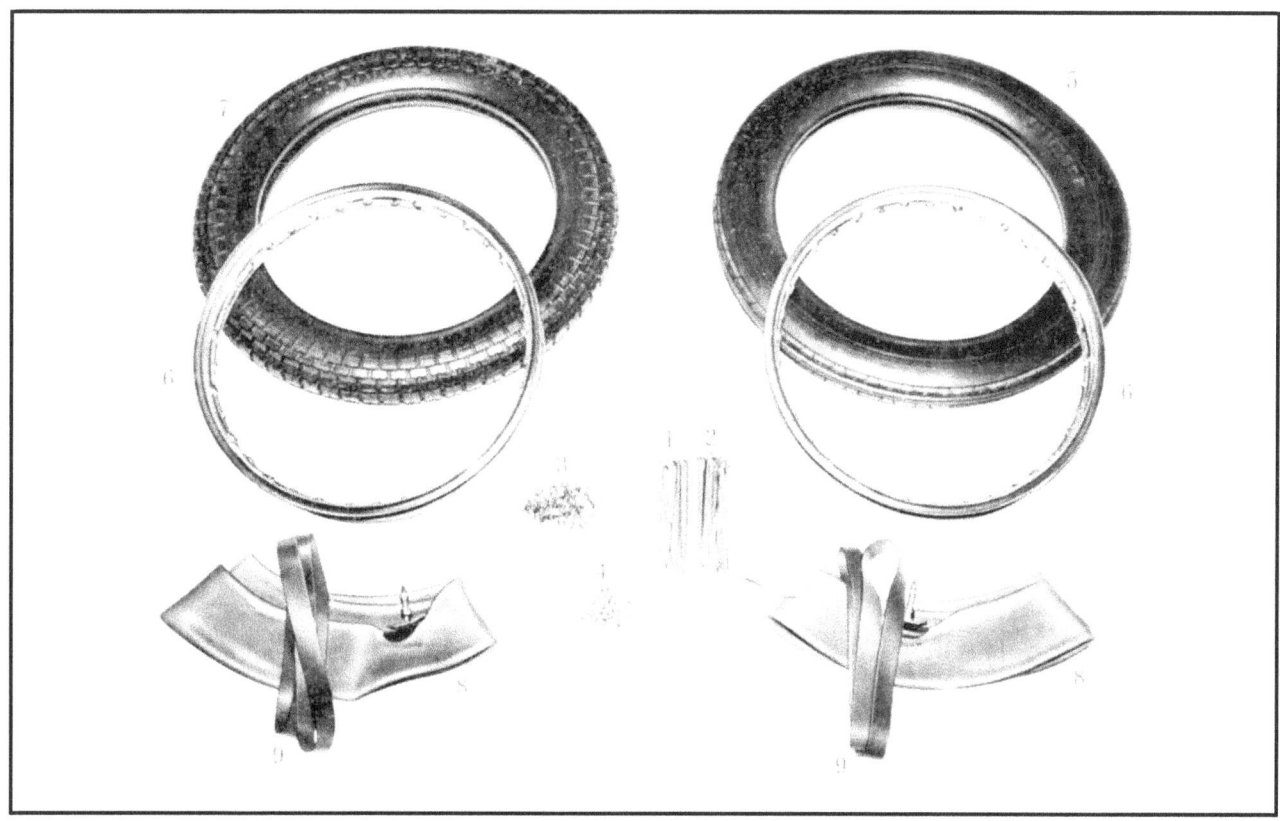

| Illustration No. | Stock No. | Name of items | Quantity required per one machine | Size | Unit price | Improved machine | Models for which inter-changeable | Remarks |
|---|---|---|---|---|---|---|---|---|
| AQ01 | 155025 | Spoke A | 36 | | The currnt price | | | |
| AQ02 | 155026 | Spoke B | 36 | 1 Set | The currnt price | | | |
| AQ03 | 155027S | Spoke nipple | 72 | | | | | |
| AQ04 | 155027N | Nipple washer | 72 | | | | | |
| AQ05 | 155028 | Front tyre | 1 | 3.00-16-2P | The currnt price | | | |
| AQ06 | 155029 | Rim | 2 | 160A-16 | The currnt price | | | |
| AQ07 | 155535 | Rear tyre | 1 | 3.00-16-4P | The currnt price | | | |
| AQ08 | 122507 | Tube | 2 | 3.00-16 | The currnt price | | | |
| AQ09 | 122508 | Rim band | 2 | 3.00-16 | The currnt price | | | |

## AR  Rear hub

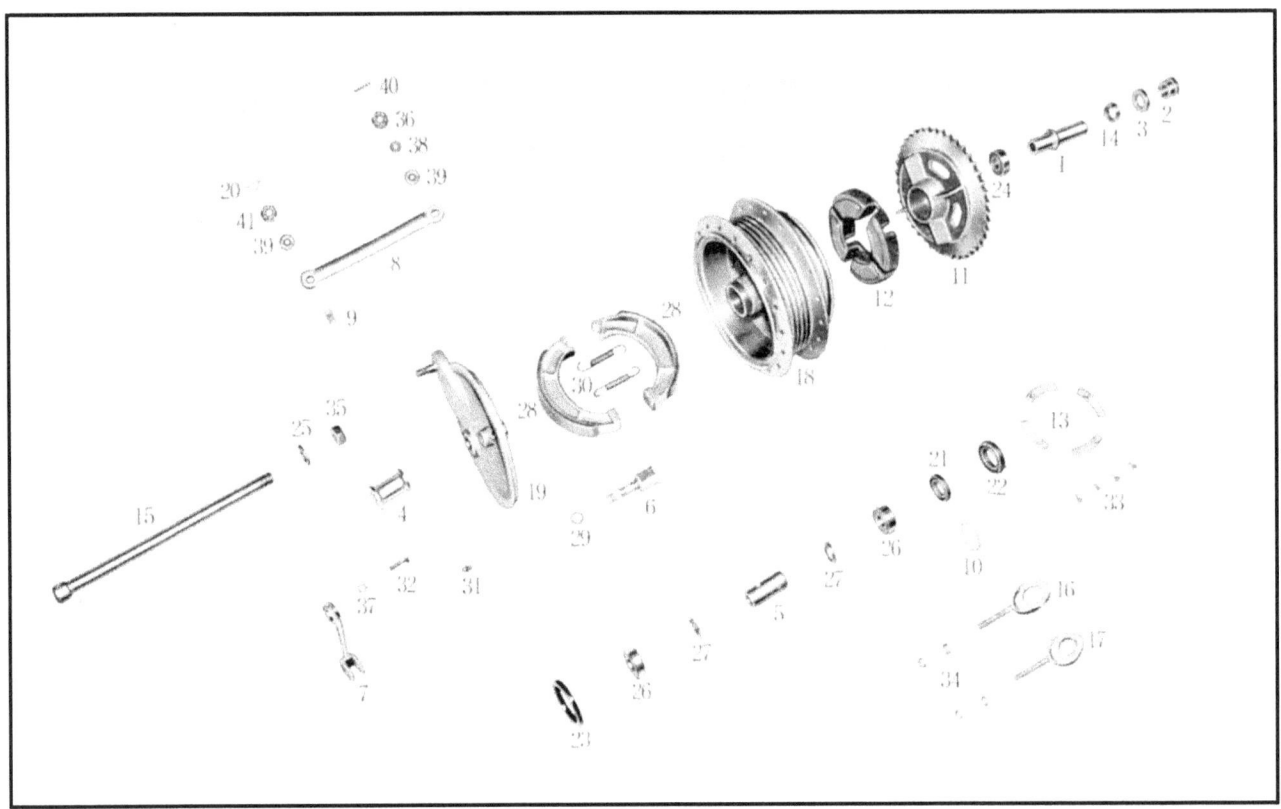

| Illustration No. | Stock No. | Name of items | Quantity required per one machine | Size | Unit price | Improved machine | Models for which inter-changeable | Remarks |
|---|---|---|---|---|---|---|---|---|
| AR01 | 155505 | Sprocket shaft | 1 | | 250 | | | |
| AR02 | 155506 | Sprocket shaft nut | 1 | | 110 | | | |
| AR03 | 155507 | Sprocket shaft collar | 1 | | 60 | | | |
| AR04 | 155509 | Distance piece | 1 | | 170 | | | |
| AR05 | 155510 | Spacer | 1 | | 100 | | | |
| AR06 | 155512 | Brake cam, rear | 1 | | 200 | | | |
| AR07 | 155513 | Brake cam lever, rear | 1 | | 150 | | | |
| AR08 | 155515 | Tension bar | 1 | | 130 | | | |
| AR09 | 155516 | Tension bar spring | 1 | | 5 | | | |
| AR10 | 155518 | O ring | 1 | | 20 | | | |
| AR11 | 155519 | Sprocket wheel | 1 | 41 teeth | 1400 | | | |
| AR12 | 155520 | Damper rubber | 1 | | 330 | | | |
| AR13 | 155521 | Damper rubber stopper | 4 | | 10 | | | |
| AR14 | 155523 | Plate for sprocket coller | 1 | | 35 | | | |
| AR15 | 155524 | Rear axle | 1 | | 470 | 29085 | | |
| ※AR16 | 155525-1 | Chain adjusting metal, left B | 1 | | 80 | 29085 | | |
| ※AR17 | 155526-1 | Chain adjusting metal, right B | 1 | | 80 | | | |
| AR18 | 155527 | Rear hub | 1 | | 2300 | | | |
| AR19 | 155528 | Rear shoe plate | 1 | | 750 | | | |
| AR20 | 155529 | Clip | 1 | | 6 | | | |
| AR21 | 155530 | Oil seal | 1 | S20×35×7 | 60 | | | |
| AR22 | 155531 | Oil seal | 1 | S26×42×8 | 60 | | YA 3 | |

| Illustration No. | Stock No. | Name of items | Quantity required per one machine | Size | Unit price | Improved machine | Models for which inter-changeable | Remarks |
|---|---|---|---|---|---|---|---|---|
| AR23 | 155532 | Oil seal | 1 | S42×56×6 | 80 | | | |
| AR24 | 155534 | Bearing | 1 | #6004 | The current price | | | |
| AR25 | 155537 | Rear shaft binding washer | 1 | | 15 | | | |
| AR26 | 155538 | Bearing | 2 | ≠6002 | The current price | | | |
| AR27 | 155005 | Center ring 30φ | 2 | | 5 | | | |
| AR28 | 155009 | Brake shoe assembly | 2 | | 200 | | | |
| AR29 | 155011 | O ring 12φ | 1 | | 15 | | | |
| AR30 | 422728 | Brake shoe spring | 2 | | 15 | | YD 2 | |
| AR31 | 122812 | Grease nipple | 1 | | 10 | YA 3 | YD 2 | |
| AR32 | YS01-6.24-12 | Bolt | 1 | | 5 | | | |
| AR33 | YS08-4.10-8 | Danper rubber pushing bolt | 4 | | 5 | | | |
| AR34 | YS03-6 | Nut | 4 | | 5 | | | |
| AR35 | YS03-14 | Nut | 1 | | 20 | | | |
| AR36 | YS04-10 | Nut | 1 | | 7 | | | |
| AR37 | YS05-6 | Brake cam lever fitting spring washer | 1 | | 1 | | | |
| AR38 | YS05-12 | Stopper torque for spring washer | 1 | | 3 | | | |
| AR39 | YS06-10 | Stopper torque for washer | 2 | | 2 | | | |
| AR40 | YS20-2ū20 | Split pin | 1 | | 1 | | | |
| AR41 | YS23-10 | Nut | 1 | | 20 | | | |

# MEMO

## AS Handle bar

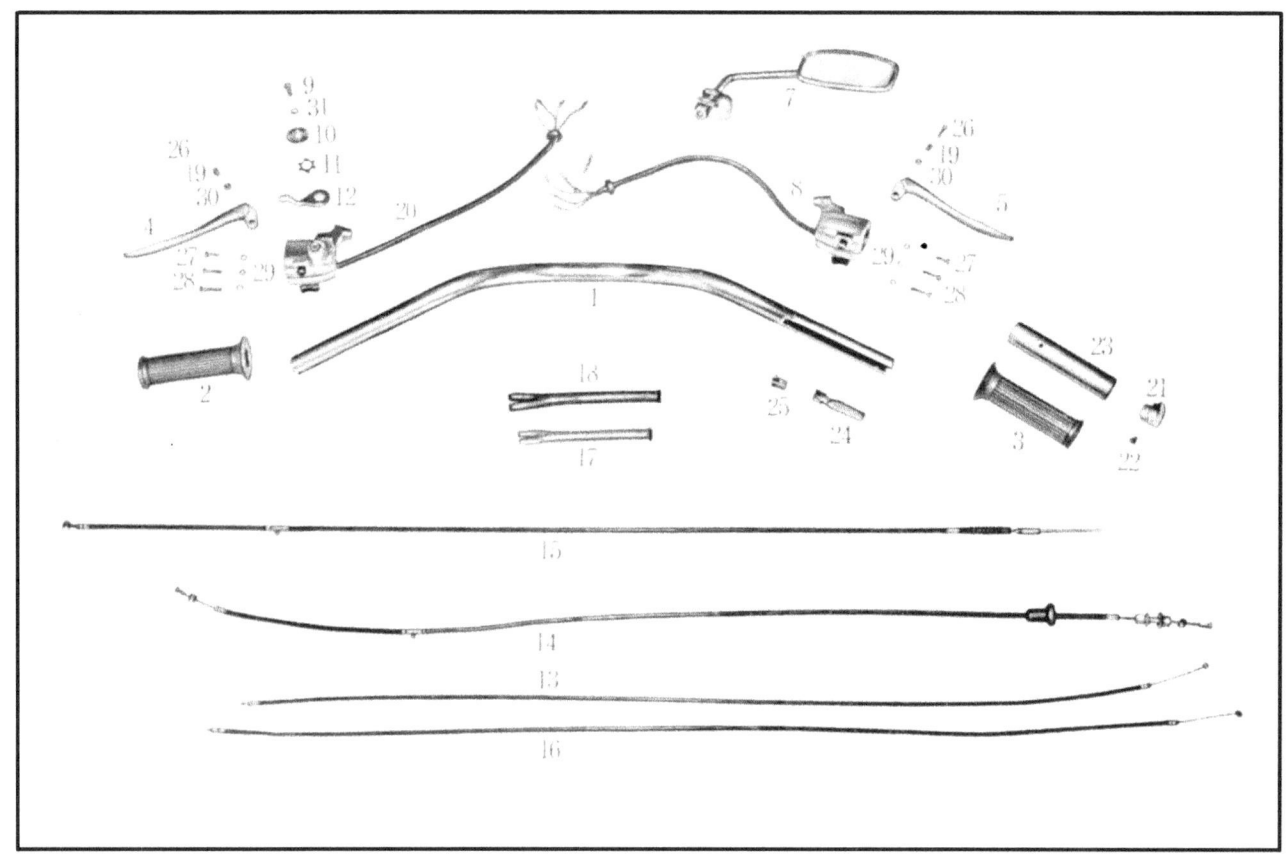

| Illustration No. | Stock No. | Name of items | Quantity required per one machine | Size | Unit price | Improved machine | Models for which inter-changeable | Remarks |
|---|---|---|---|---|---|---|---|---|
| AS01 | 156001 | Steering handle | 1 | | 530 | | | |
| AS02 | 156002 | Grip (left) | 1 | | 90 | | YD 3 | |
| AS03 | 156003 | Grip (right) | 1 | | 50 | | YD 3 | |
| AS04 | 156005L | Handle lever (left) | 1 | | 200 | | YD 3 | |
| AS05 | 156005R | Handle lever (right) | 1 | | 200 | | YD 3 | |
| AS06 | 156007 | Handle lever set bolt | 2 | | 10 | | YD 3 | |
| AS07 | 156008 | Back mirror assembly | 1 | | 350 | | YD 3 | |
| ※AS08 | 156100-1 | Handle lever holder (right) | 1 | | 650 | 70937 | | |
| AS09 | 156201 | Screw for start lever | 1 | | 15 | | MF 2 YD 3 | |
| AS10 | 156202 | Start lever cover | 1 | | 25 | | MF 2 YD 3 | |
| AS11 | 156204-1 | Pushing metal for start lever B | 1 | | 15 | 86020 | MF 2 YD 3 | |
| AS12 | 156205-1 | Start lever | 1 | | 100 | 86020 | MF 2 YD 3 | |
| AS13 | 156300 | Throttle cable | 1 | | 60 | | | |
| AS14 | 156400 | Clutch cable | 1 | | 140 | | | |
| AS15 | 156500-1 | Front brake cable | 1 | | 200 | | | |
| AS16 | 156600 | Starter cable | 1 | | 60 | | YD 3 | |
| AS17 | 156700 | Wire guide (right) | 1 | | 30 | | | |
| AS18 | 156800 | Wire guide (left) | 1 | | 30 | | | |
| AS19 | 156999 | Handle lever set collar | 1 | | 20 | | | |
| ※AS20 | 430019 | Handle lever holder (left) | 1 | | 650 | 70937 | YD 3 | |

| Illustration No. | Stock No. | Name of items | Quantity required per one machine | Size | Unit price | Improved machine | Models for which inter-changeable | Remarks |
|---|---|---|---|---|---|---|---|---|
| AS21 | 122912 | Grip end | 1 | | 60 | | YD 3 | YA 3 / YD 2 |
| AS22 | 122913 | Screw for grip end | 1 | | 5 | | YD 3 | YA 3 / YD 2 |
| AS23 | 122915 | Grip tube | 1 | | 100 | | | YA 3 |
| AS24 | 122918 | Sliding core for throttle grip | 1 | | 25 | | YD 3 | YD 3 / YA 3 |
| AS25 | 122919 | Throttle cable stopper | 1 | | 5 | | YD 3 | YA 3 / YD 2 |
| AS26 | YS12-5.18-18 | Bolt | 2 | | 4 | | | |
| AS27 | YS11-5.20-20 | Bolt | 2 | | 4 | | | |
| AS28 | YS12-5.22-22 | Bolt | 4 | | 4 | | | |
| AS29 | YS05-5 | Spring washer | 6 | | 1 | | | |
| AS30 | YS04-5 | Nut | 2 | | 1 | | | |
| AS31 | YS16-6 | Washer | 1 | | 2 | | | |
| | 156900 | Up handle | 1 | | 680 | | | |
| | 156901 | Brake cable for up handle | 1 | | 220 | | | |
| | 156902 | Clutch cable for up handle | 1 | | 220 | | | |
| | 156903 | Throttle cable for up handle | 1 | | 70 | | | |
| | 156904 | Starter cable for up handle | 1 | | 70 | | | |

# M E M O

## AT Service Tool

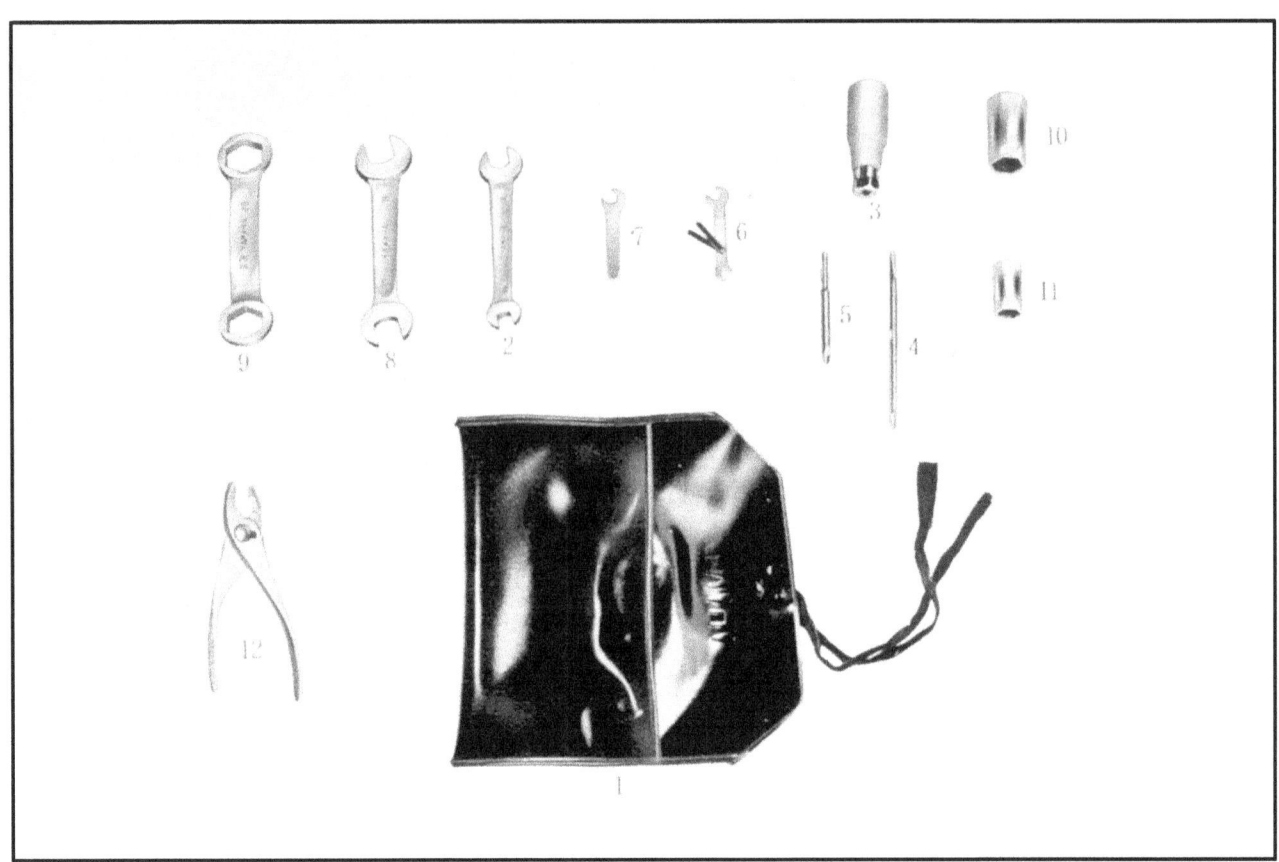

| Illustration No. | Stock No. | Name of items | Quantity required per one machine | Size | Unit price | Improved machine | Models for which inter-changeable | Remarks |
|---|---|---|---|---|---|---|---|---|
| AT01 | 158001 | Tool bag | 1 | | 70 | | | |
| AT02 | 158003 | Double-ended wrench | 1 | 10×14 | 100 | | | |
| AT03 | 158005 | Driver handle | 1 | | 40 | | | |
| AT04 | 158006 | Driver ⊕ ⊖ | 1 | | 60 | | | |
| AT05 | 158007 | Driver ⊕ | 1 | | 50 | | | |
| AT06 | 158000 | Dynamo spanner | 1 | 4×6 | 50 | | | |
| AT07 | 158009 | Dynamo spanner | 1 | 9 | 50 | | | |
| AT08 | 158010 | Double-ended spanner | 1 | 17×19 | 170 | | | |
| AT09 | 158012 | Hexagon spanner | 1 | 23×26 | 220 | | | |
| AT10 | 158013 | Spark plug box | 1 | 21×23 | 90 | | | |
| AT11 | 158015 | Box 14 m/m | 1 | | 80 | | | |
| AT12 | 158017 | Plier | 1 | | 220 | | | |
| | 158000 | Tool assembly | 1 | | 1200 | | | |

## AU  Leg shield

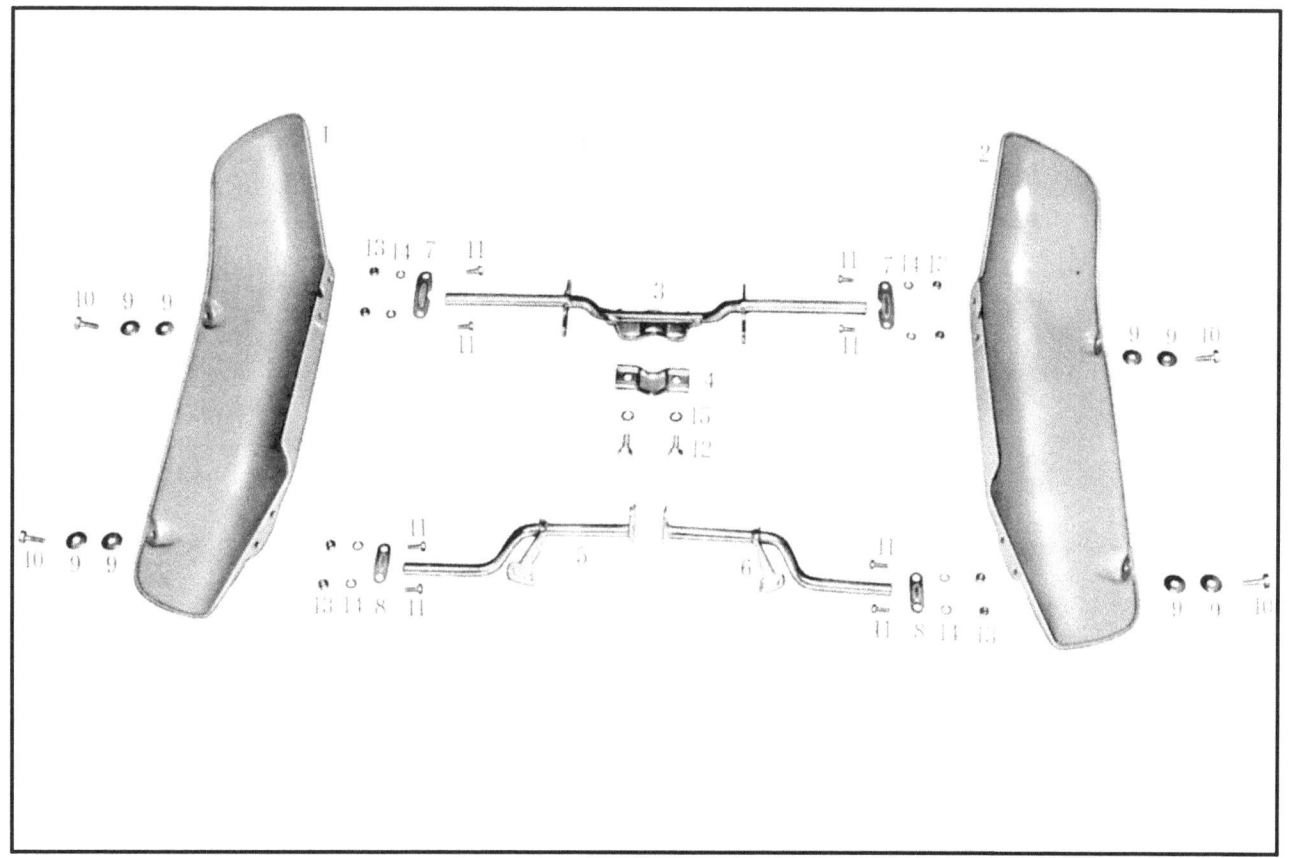

| Illustration No. | Stock No. | Name of items | Quantity required per one machine | Size | Unit price | Improved machine | Models for which inter-changeable | Remarks |
|---|---|---|---|---|---|---|---|---|
| AU01 | 159502 | Leg shield (left) | 1 | | 500 | | | |
| AU02 | 159503 | Leg shield (right) | 1 | | 500 | | | |
| AU03 | 159504 | Leg shield upper stay | 1 | | 550 | | | |
| AU04 | 159505 | Leg shield upper stay fitting plate | 1 | | 50 | | | |
| AU05 | 159506 | Leg shield lower stay (left) | 1 | | 250 | | | |
| AU06 | 159507 | Leg shield lower stay (right) | 1 | | 250 | | | |
| AU07 | 159509 | Leg Shield upper fitting plate | 2 | | 30 | | | |
| AU08 | 159510 | Leg shield lower fitting plate | 2 | | 20 | | | |
| AU09 | 159511 | Leg shield large washer | 8 | | 15 | | | |
| AU10 | 159512 | Bolt | 4 | | 20 | | | |
| AU11 | 159513 | Bolt | 8 | | 15 | | | |
| AU12 | YS01-8.24-16 | Bolt | 2 | | 15 | | | |
| AU13 | YS02-6 | Nut | 8 | | 2 | | | |
| AU14 | YS05-6 | Spring washer | 8 | | 1 | | | |
| AU15 | YS05-8 | Spring washer | 2 | | 1 | | | |
| | | Leg shield set | 1 | | 1000 | | | |
| | | Leg shield fitting metal set | 1 | | 1552 | | | |

## III  ELECTRICAL MECHANISM

### AV  Dynamo

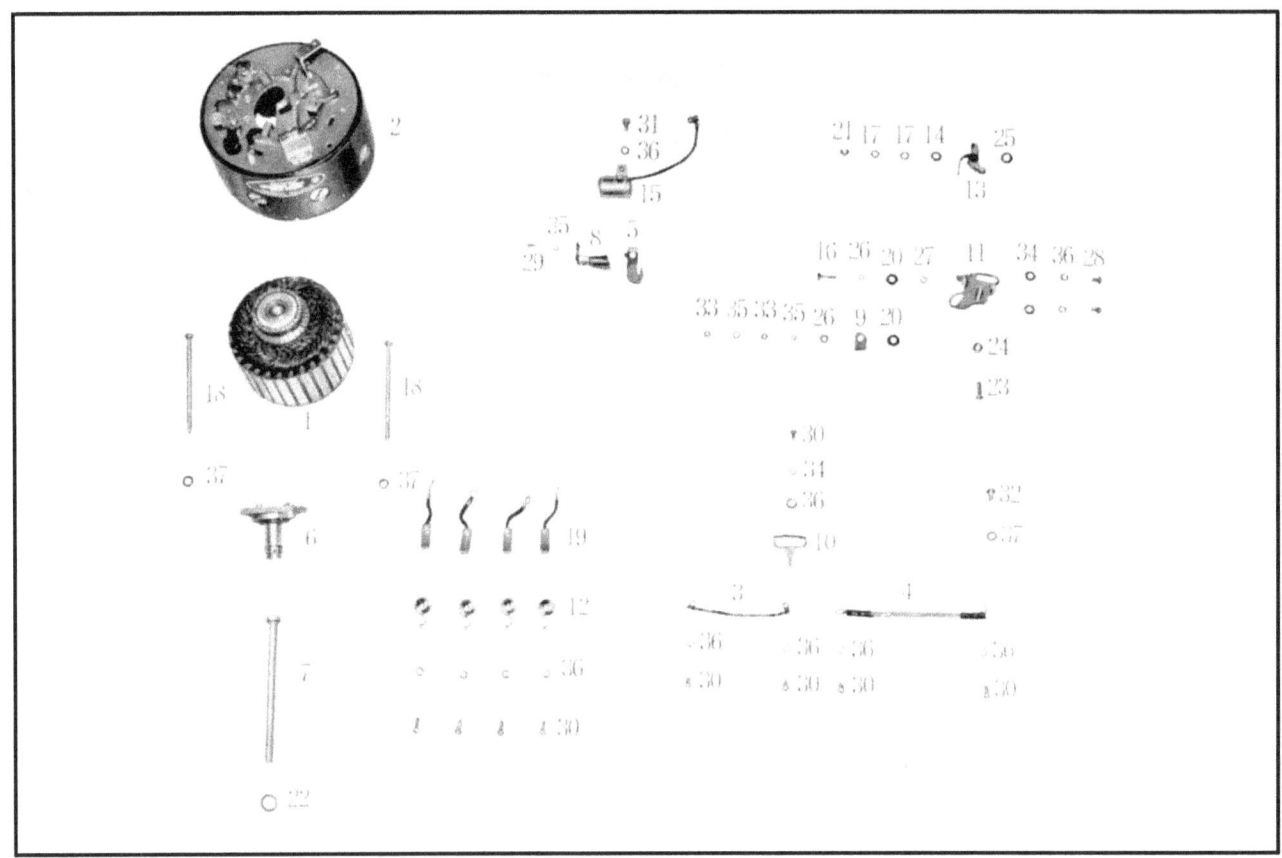

| Illustration No. | Stock No. | Name of items | Quantity required per one machine | Size | Unit price | Improved machine | Models for which inter-changeable | Remarks |
|---|---|---|---|---|---|---|---|---|
|  | GS113-01 | Dynamo assembly | 1 |  | 14000 |  |  |  |
| AV01 | 23113-1100 | Armature assemlby | 1 |  | 5200 |  |  |  |
| AV02 | 23113-1200 | York assembly | 1 |  | 5300 |  |  |  |
| AV03 | 23113-1211 | Lead wire assembly (1) | 1 |  | 20 |  |  |  |
| AV04 | 23113-1212 | Lead wire assembly (2) | 1 |  | 28 |  |  |  |
| AV05 | 23113-1215 | Lubricator fixture | 1 |  | 12 |  |  |  |
| AV06 | 23113-1650 | Covering assembly | 1 |  | 530 |  |  |  |
| AV07 | 23113-1804 | Bolt 7φ | 1 |  | 40 |  |  |  |
| AV08 | 23113-1818 | Lubricator assembly | 1 |  | 24 |  |  |  |
| AV09 | 23117-1608 | Insulater | 1 |  | 10 |  | MF, J2 YD 3 | MF 1 |
| AV10 | 23117-1620 | Timing plate | 1 |  | 14 |  |  |  |
|  | 23117-2600 | Contact breaker assembly | 1 |  | 290 |  |  |  |
| AV11 | 23117-2601 | Braker plate | 1 |  | 70 |  |  |  |
| AV12 | 23106-1303 | Brush spring | 1 |  | 30 |  | YD 3 |  |
| A 13 | 23106-1603 | Arm assembly | 1 |  | 104 |  |  |  |
| AV14 | 23106-1604 | Insulating washer 4φ | 1 |  | 8 |  | MF, J2 YD 3 | MF 1 |
| AV15 | 23106-1616 | Condenser | 1 |  | 150 |  | MF, J2 YD 3 |  |
| AV16 | 23106-1624 | Screw 3φ | 1 |  | 10 |  | MF, J2 YD 3 | MF 1 |
| AV17 | 2301-1619 | Washer | 1~3 |  | 10 |  | All Model |  |
| AV18 | 2301-1808 | York setting screw | 2 |  | 16 |  |  |  |

| Illustration No. | Stock No. | Name of items | Quantity required per one machine | Size | Unit price | Improved machine | Models for which inter-changeable | Remarks |
|---|---|---|---|---|---|---|---|---|
| AV19 | 2301-2301 | Brush | 4 | | 132 | | YD 3 | |
| AV20 | 3606-1607 | Insulating washer 3φ | 2 | | 8 | | MF, J2 YD 3 | MF 1 |
| AV21 | 3606-1613 | Clip | 1 | | 14 | | All Model | |
| AV22 | 3606-1803 | Lock washer 7φ | 1 | | 12 | | YD 3 | MF 1 |
| AV23 | 8322-1304 | Point | 1 | | 58 | | MF, J2 YD 3 | MF 1 |
| AV24 | 8322-1305 | Nut 5φ | 1 | | 12 | | MF, J2 YD 3 | MF 1 |
| AV25 | 2307-1605 | Insulating washer | 1 | | 8 | | MF, J2 YD 3 | MF 1 |
| AV26 | A1-158 | Washer 3φ | 2 | | 6 | | MF, J2 YD 3 | MF 1 |
| AV27 | E192749 | Insulating washer | 1 | | 6 | | MF, J2 YD 3 | MF 1 |
| AV28 | 7310408 | Screw 4φ | 2 | | 8 | | YD 3 | |
| AV29 | 7360306 | Screw 3φ | 2 | | 8 | | YD 3 | MF 1 |
| AV30 | 7360406 | Screw 4φ | 9 | | 8 | | MF, J2 YD 3 | MF 1 |
| AV31 | 7360408 | Screw 4φ | 2 | | 8 | | | |
| AV32 | 7360508 | Screw 5φ | 1 | | 8 | | MF, J2 YD 3 | MF 1 |
| AV33 | 7540300 | Nut 3φ | 2 | | 10 | | MF, J2 YD 3 | MF 1 |
| AV34 | 7630400 | Washer 4φ | 3 | | 8 | | YD 3 | |
| AV35 | 7660300 | Lock washer 3φ | 4 | | 8 | | YD 3 | |
| AV36 | 7660400 | Lock washer 4φ | 13 | | 8 | | YD 3 | |
| AV37 | 7660500 | Lock washer 5φ | 3 | | 8 | | YD 3 | |

*M E M O*

## AW  Electrical epripment

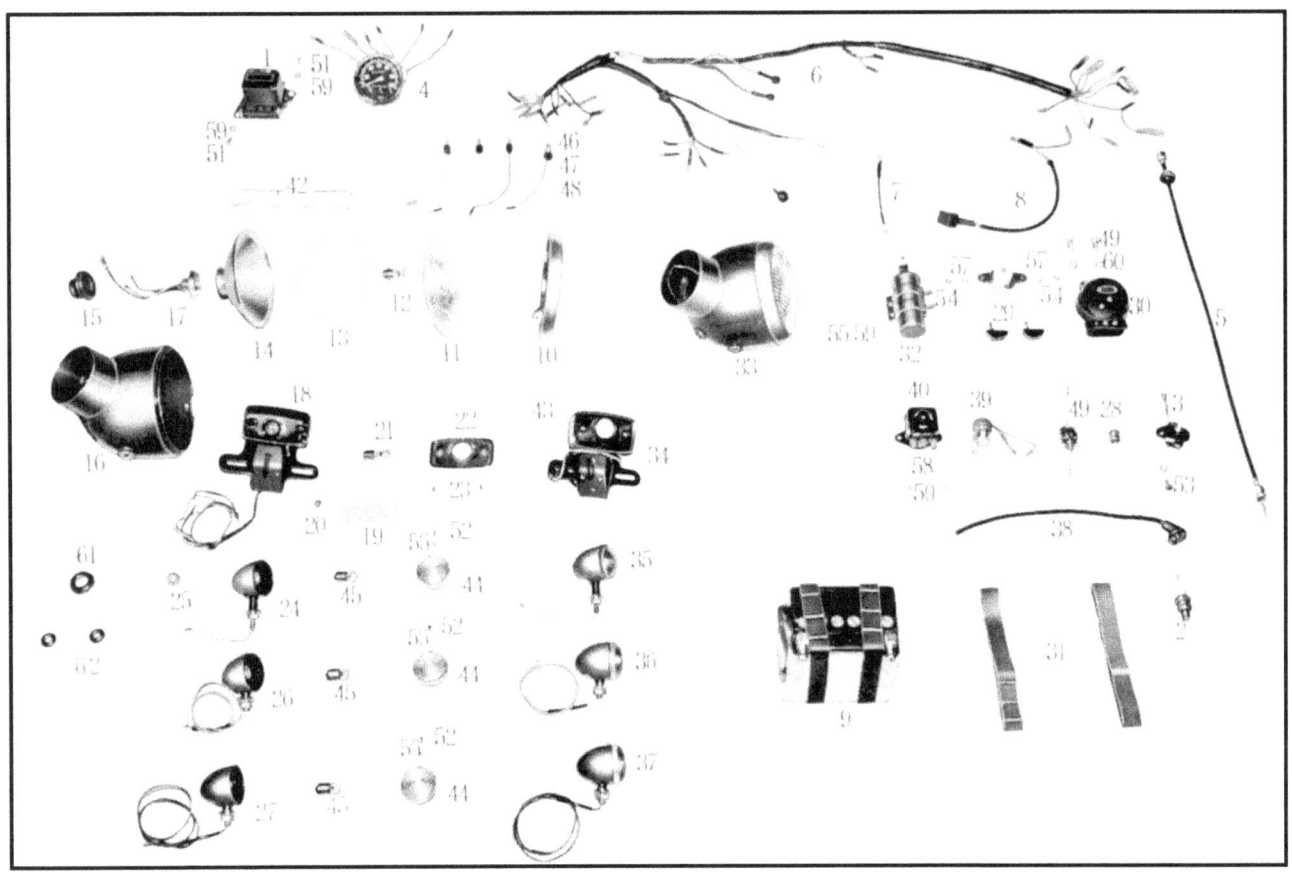

| Illustration No. | Stock No. | Name of items | Quantity required per one machine | Size | Unit price | Improved machine | Models for which inter-changeable | Remarks |
|---|---|---|---|---|---|---|---|---|
| AW01 | 150002 | Regulator | 1 | | 2200 | | | |
| AW02 | 150003 | Spark plug | 1 | B6-H | The current price | | | |
| AW03 | 150004 | Stop switch | 1 | | 150 | 23061 | | |
| AW04 | 150005-1 | Speedometer assembly | 1 | | 2200 | | | |
| AW05 | 150006 | Speedometer cable | 1 | | 180 | | | |
| AW06 | 150007 | Wire harness | 1 | | 1000 | | | |
| AW07 | 150008-1 | Battery wire | 1 | | 30 | 70937 | | |
| AW08 | 150009-1 | Battery lead wire | 1 | | 70 | 70937 | | |
| AW09 | 150011-1 | Battery | 1 | 12V10AH | The current price | 70937 | | |
| ※AW10 | 150012-Ⓐ | Head light rim | 1 | | 380 | 100001 | | |
| AW11 | 150012-Ⓑ | Head light lens | 1 | | 180 | | | |
| AW12 | 150012-Ⓒ | Head lamp | 1 | 12V35/25W | The current price | | | |
| AW13 | 150012-Ⓓ | Head light rubber paking | 1 | | 20 | | | |
| AW14 | 150012-Ⓔ | Head light reflecter | 1 | | 380 | | | |
| AW15 | 150012-Ⓕ | Head light rubber cover | 1 | | 30 | | | |
| ※AW16 | 150012-Ⓖ-1 | Head lignt body (A) | 1 | | 1200 | 100001 | | |
| AW17 | 150012-Ⓗ | Head lamp socket | 1 | | 130 | | | |
| AW18 | 150013-Ⓐ-1 | Tail light base | 1 | | 830 | 32556 | | |
| AW19 | 150013-Ⓑ | Licence lens | 1 | | 80 | | | |

| Illustration No. | Stock No. | Name of items | Quantity required per one machine | Size | Unit price | Improved machine | Models for which inter-changeable | Remarks |
|---|---|---|---|---|---|---|---|---|
| AW20 | 150013-C | Stop eyelt for licence lens | 3 | | 10 | | | |
| AW21 | 150013-E-1 | Tail lamp B | 1 | 12V20/18W | The current price | 32556 | | |
| AW22 | 150013-E | Tail lens | 1 | | 115 | | | |
| AW23 | 150013-F | Tail lens screw | 2 | | 10 | | | |
| AW24 | 150014-A | Front flasher | 2 | | 150 | | | |
| AW25 | 150014-B | Flasher light fitting washer | 4 | | 20 | | | |
| AW26 | 150015L-A | Rear flasher light base (left) | 1 | | 150 | | | |
| AW27 | 150015R-A | Rear flasher light base (right) | 1 | | 150 | | | |
| AW28 | 150016 | Neutral switch | 1 | | 150 | | | |
| AW29 | 150017 | Main switch | 1 | | 500 | | | |
| AW30 | 150018-1 | Horn | 1 | | 660 | 71459 | | |
| AW31 | 150023 | Battery rubber band | 1 | | 20 | | | |
| AW32 | 150024 | Ignition coil | 1 | | 900 | 100001 | YD 3 | |
| ※AW33 | 150012-1 | Head light assembly | 1 | | 2000 | 100001 | | |
| AW34 | 150013-1 | Tail light assembly | 1 | | 1100 | 32556 | | |
| AW35 | 150014 | Front washer light assembly | 2 | | 220 | | | |
| AW36 | 150015 L | Rear flasher light assembly (left) L | 1 | | 200 | | | |
| AW37 | 150015R | Rear flasher light assembly (right) R | 1 | | 200 | | | |
| AW38 | 430009 | High tension coil | 1 | | 210 | 100001 | YD 3 | |
| AW39 | 423403 | Flasher relay | 1 | | 280 | | YD 3  YD 2 | |
| AW40 | 423609 | Starting switch | 1 | | 1100 | | YD 3  YD 2 | |
| AW41 | 423910 | Fuse holder | 1 | 20A | 90 | | YD 3  YD 2 | |
| AW42 | 133202 | Reflector set spring | 4 | | 5 | | YA 3 | |
| AW43 | 133208 | Head light rim set bolt | 1 | | 35 | | YA 3 | |
| AW44 | 133404 | Flasher light lens | 4 | | 60 | | YA 3 | |
| AW45 | 133405 | Flasher lamp | 4 | 14V8W | The current price | | YA 3 | |
| AW46 | 133501 | Pilot lamp | 3 | 14V2W | The current price | | YA 3 | |
| AW47 | 133502 | Pilot lamp socket | 3 | | 50 | | YA 3 | |
| AW48 | 133506 | Pilot lamp rubber cover | 3 | | 30 | | YA 3 | |
| AW49 | YS01-8.16-12 | Bolt | 2 | | 8 | | | |
| AW50 | YS12-5.10-7 | Bolt | 2 | | 2 | | | |
| AW51 | YS12-6.10-8 | Bolt | 2 | | 3 | | | |
| AW52 | YS13-3.5-5 | Bolt | 4 | | 2 | | | |
| AW53 | YS14-6.13-9 | Bolt | 1 | | 3 | | | |
| AW54 | YS02-4 | Nut | 4 | | 2 | | | |
| AW55 | YS02-6 | Nut | 2 | | 2 | | | |
| AW56 | YS05-3 | Spring washer | 4 | | 1 | | | |
| AW57 | YS05-4 | Spring washer | 4 | | 1 | | | |
| AW58 | YS05-5 | Spring washer | 2 | | 1 | | | |
| AW59 | YS05-6 | Spring washer | 5 | | 1 | | | |
| AW60 | YS05-8 | Spring washer | 6 | | 1 | | | |
| AW61 | 150012-D | Grommet for head light shell (1) | 1 | | 15 | | | |
| AW62 | 150012-J | Grommnet for head light shell (2) | 2 | | 10 | | | |

## IV Old Model's Part

### AX  Engine & Electrical equipment

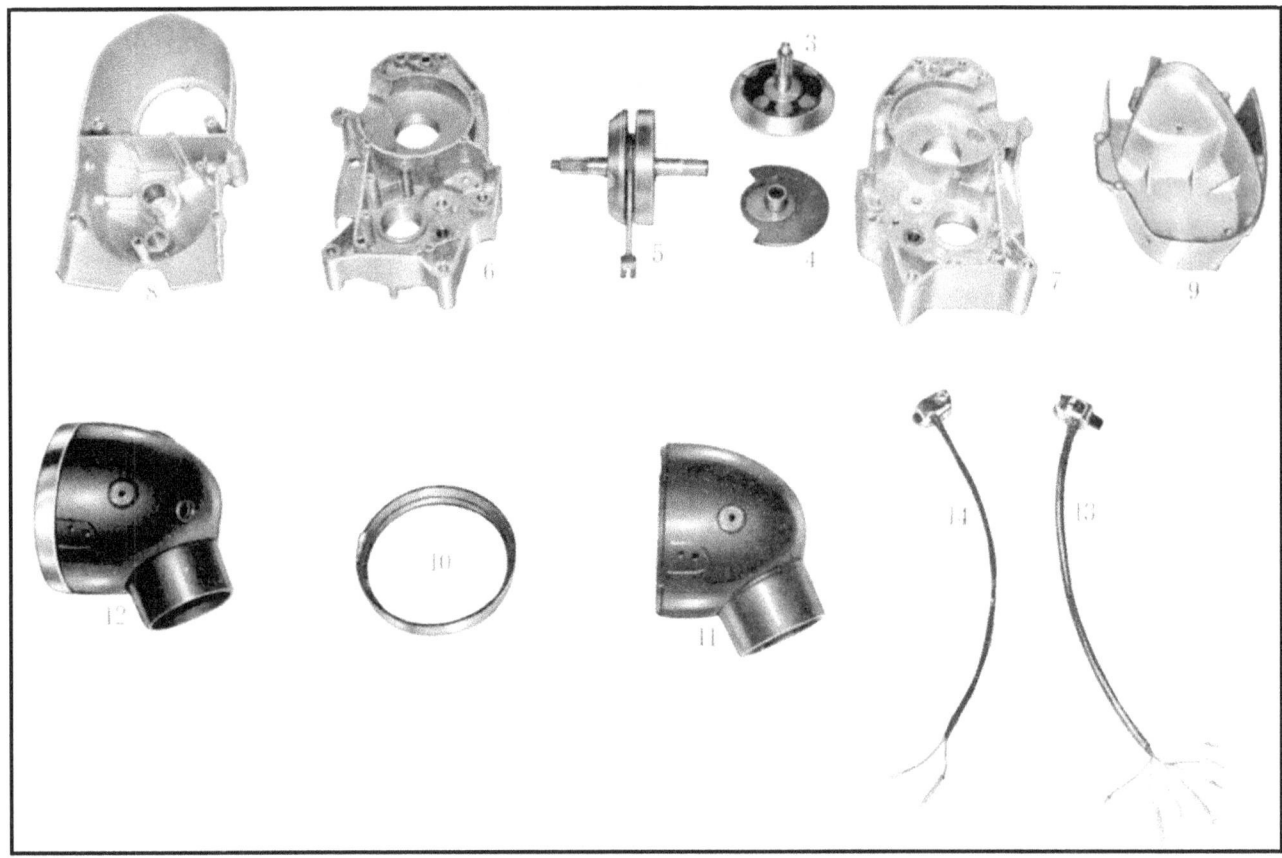

| Illustration No. | Stock No. | Name of items | Quantity required per one machine | Size | Unit price | Improved machine | Models for which inter-changeable | Remarks |
|---|---|---|---|---|---|---|---|---|
| AX01 | 150101-1 | Cylinder head A | 1 | | 960 | | | |
| AX02 | 150102-1 | Cylinder A | 1 | | 2300 | | | |
| AX03 | 150105 | Crank, right | 1 | | 2200 | | | |
| AX04 | 150107 | Valve assembly B | 1 | | 1000 | | | |
| AX05 | | Crank assembly | 1 | | 7000 | | | |
| AX06 | 150801-1 | Crank case, left A | 1 | | 4600 | | | |
| AX07 | 150802-2 | Crank case, right A | 1 | | 4300 | | | |
| AX08 | 150803-1 | Crank case, cover, left A | 1 | | 1500 | | | |
| AX09 | 150804-1 | Crank case cover, right A | 1 | | 1100 | | | |
| AX10 | 150012-Ⓐ | Head light rim | 1 | | 380 | | | |
| AX11 | 150012-Ⓑ | Head light shell | 1 | | 1200 | | | |
| AX12 | | Head light assembly | 1 | | 2000 | | | |
| AX13 | 150019 | Handle switch, left | 1 | | 400 | | | |
| AX14 | 150025 | Handle switch, right | 1 | | 160 | | | |

## AY Frame

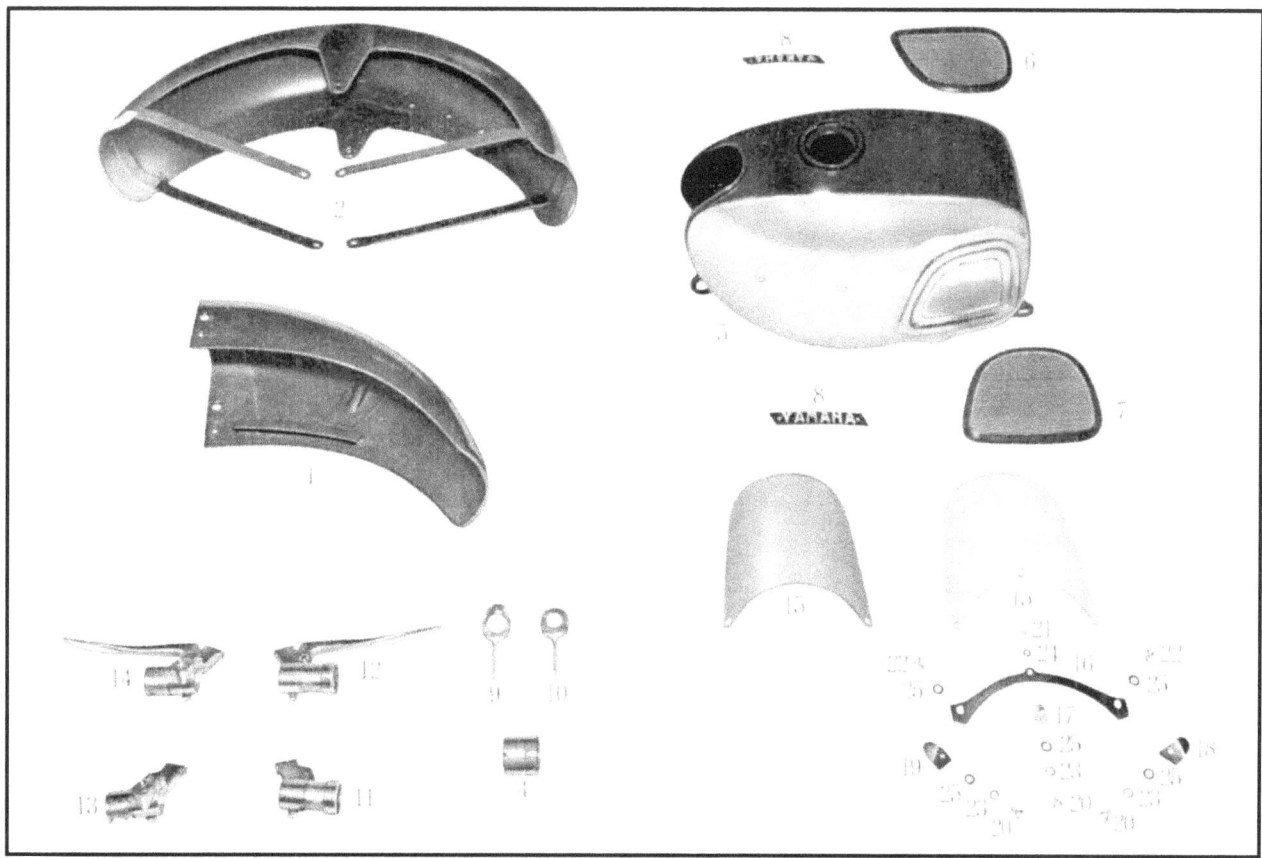

| Illustration No. | Stock No. | Name of items | Quantity required per one machine | Size | Unit price | Improved machine | Models for which inter changeable | Remarks |
|---|---|---|---|---|---|---|---|---|
| AY01 | 151201 | Rear fender | 1 | | 1000 | | | |
| AY02 | 150501 | Front fender | 1 | | 2000 | | | |
| AY03 | 152001-1 | Rear arm A | 1 | | 2500 | | | |
| AY04 | SA20500-16 | Slide metal | 2 | | 220 | | | |
| AY05 | 154000 | Fuel tank | 1 | | 4000 | | | |
| AY06 | 154006-R | Knee grip (left) | 1 | | 160 | | | |
| AY07 | 154006-L | Knee grip (right) | 1 | | 160 | | | |
| AY08 | 154034 | Tank mark | 2 | | 250 | | | |
| AY09 | 155525 | Adjusting metal for chain (left) | 1 | | 80 | | | |
| AY10 | 155526 | Adjusting metal for chain (right) | 1 | | 80 | | | |
| AY11 | 156100 | Lever holder right | 1 | | 250 | | | |
| AY12 | | Lever holder assembly (right) | 1 | | 450 | | | |
| AY13 | 156200 | Lever holder (left) | 1 | | 250 | | | |
| AY14 | | Lever holder assembly (left) | 1 | | 450 | | | |
| AY15 | 159001 | Wind shield | 1 | STD 240 DX 330 | | | | |
| AY16 | 159002 | Wind shield fitting cover | 1 | | 40 | | | |
| AY17 | 159003 | Wind shield fitting washer (A) | 1 | | 50 | | | |
| AY18 | 159004L | Wind shield fitting washer B (left) | 1 | | 80 | | | |
| AY19 | 159004R | Wind shield fitting washer B (right) | 1 | | 80 | | | |
| AY20 | YS01-6.10-8 | Bold | 3 | | 4 | | | |
| AY21 | YS12-4.6-5 | Bold | 1 | | 2 | | | |
| AY22 | YS12-6.10-8 | Bold | 2 | | 3 | | | |
| AY23 | YS05-6 | Spring washer | 3 | | 1 | | | |
| AY24 | YS06-4 | Washer | 1 | | 1 | | | |
| AY25 | YS06-6 | Washer | 5 | | 1 | | | |

Head patterns of standard parts are as under

Bolt

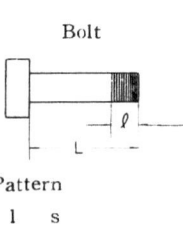

cf. Head Pattern
↓ d l s
YS 01 - 6 · 85 - 18

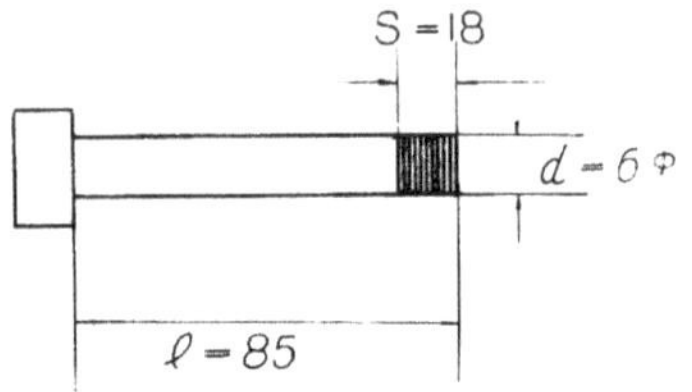

| YS 01 | YS 07 | YS 08 |
| YS 09 | YS 11 | YS 11 |
| YS 12 | YS 13 | YS 14 |

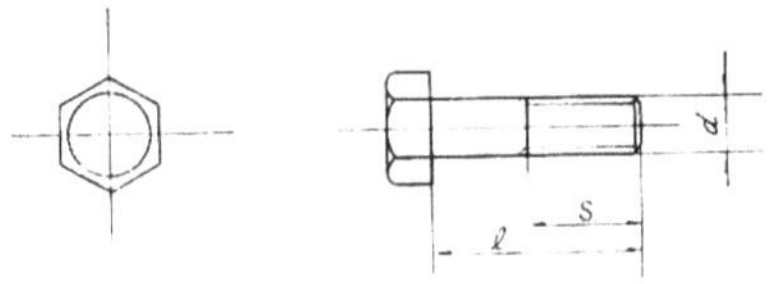

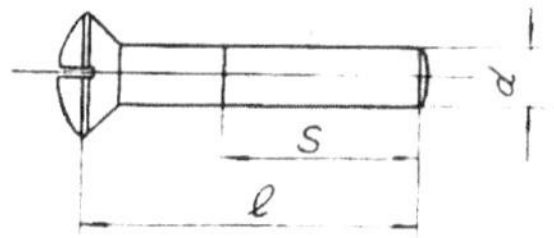

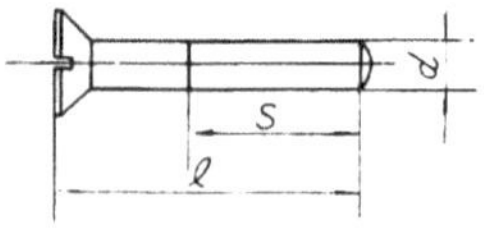

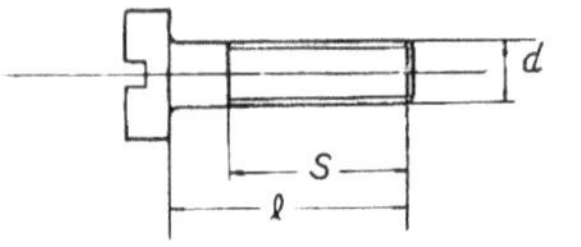

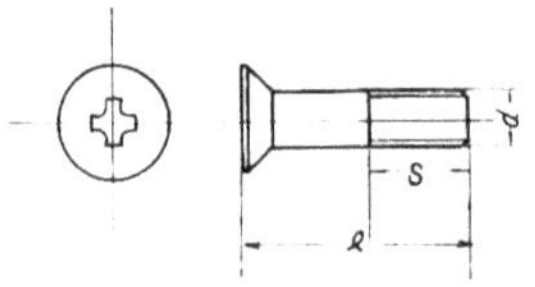

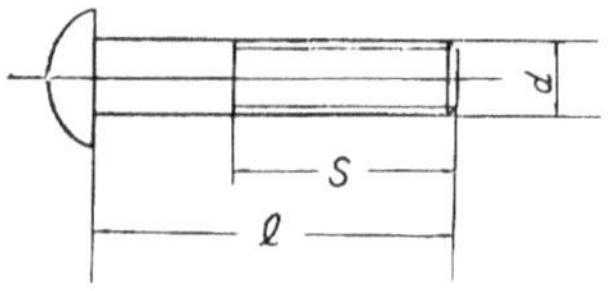

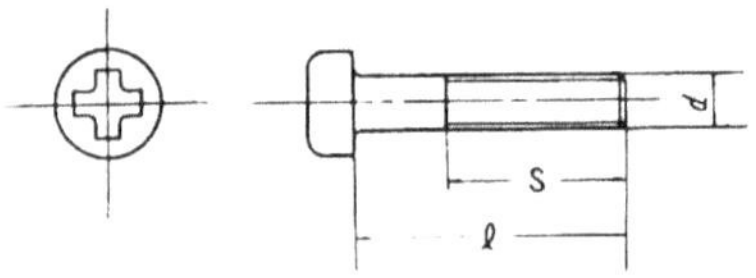

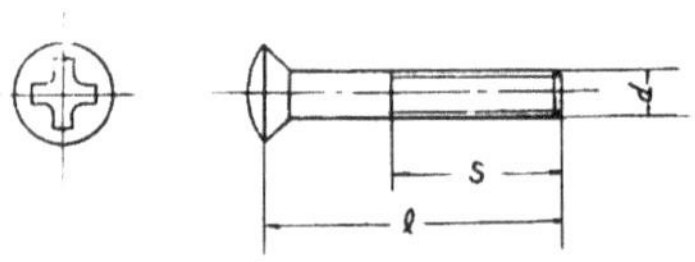

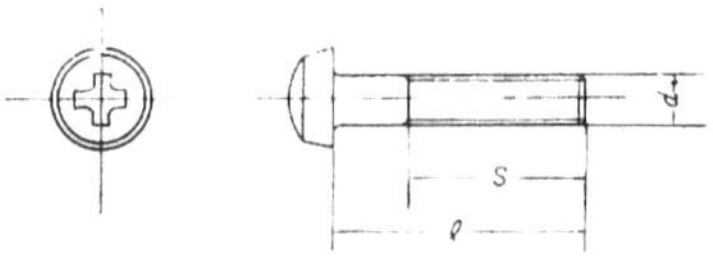

Nut

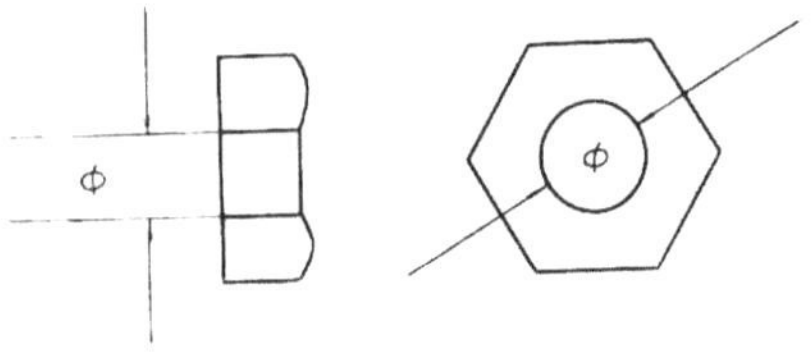

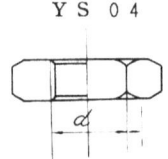

cf. Pattern
↓ d
YS 02 - 6

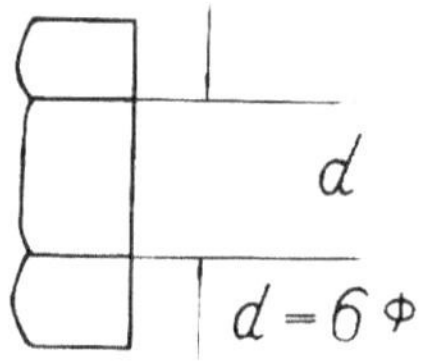

YS 03

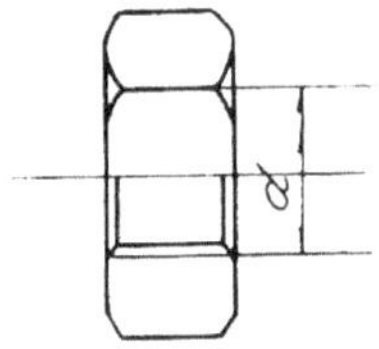

YS 04    YS 23

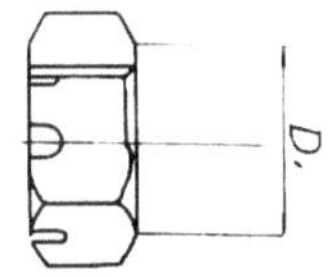

Washer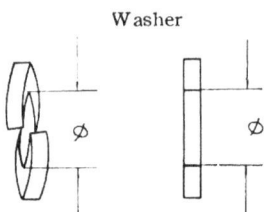

Spring Washer Pattern
↓ d
YS 05 - 6

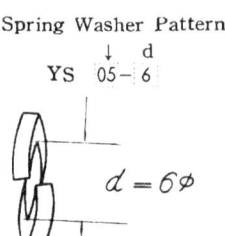   $d = 6\phi$

YS 06

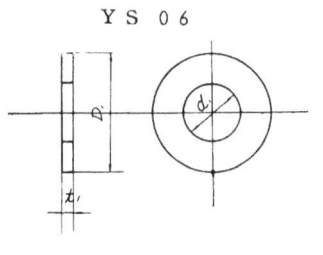

YS 16 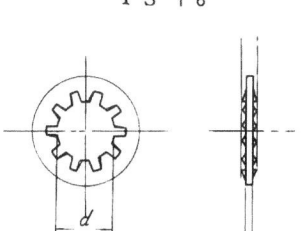  YS 17 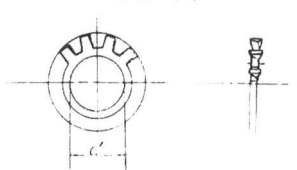  YS 19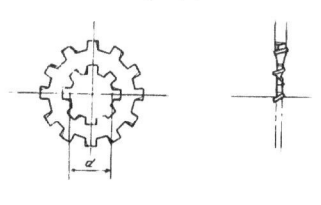

Spilit pin

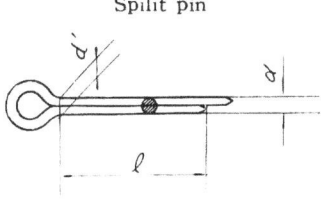

Spilit pin
　　　　b　l
YS 20　2 - 18

## APPENDIX

| Size | Name of Item | Unit price | Illustration No. | Quantity required per one machine |
|---|---|---|---|---|
| YS01-6.10-8 | Bolt | ¥ 4 | AY20 | 3 |
| YS01-6.11-9 | Bolt | 4 | A007 | 4 |
| YS01-6.12-10 | Bolt | 4 | A008, AJ30 | 8 |
| YS01-6.14-12 | Bolt | 3 | AJ31 | 4 |
| YS01-6.20-10 | Bolt | 4 | AF31 | 1 |
| YS01-6.24-12 | Bolt | 5 | AP24, AR32 | 2 |
| YS01-6.25-18 | Bolt | 5 | AP25 | 1 |
| YS01-8.12-10 | Bolt | 7 | AJ22 | 2 |
| YS01-8.13-10 | Bolt | 7 | A009 | 2 |
| YS01-8.14-10 | Bolt | 6 | AN24 | 2 |
| YS01-8.16-12 | Bolt | 8 | A010, AW49 | 6 |
| YS01-8.20-18 | Bolt | 8 | AK24 | 4 |
| YS01-8.23-11 | Bolt | 8 | AC09 | 2 |
| YS01-8.24-16 | Bolt | 15 | AU12 | 2 |
| YS01 8.30-20 | Bolt | 10 | AM33 | 1 |
| YS01 8 36-18 | Bolt | 20 | AM34 | 2 |
| YS01-10.48-12 | Bolt | 15 | AK25 | 2 |
| YS01-10.48-18 | Bolt | 15 | AL18 | 2 |
| YS01-10.100-16 | Bolt | 50 | AN25 | 1 |
| YS01-10.136-12 | Bolt | 60 | AK26 | 2 |
| YS02-4 | Nut | 2 | AW54 | 4 |
| YS02-6 | Nut | 2 | AB08, AF32, AJ23, AK27, AL22, AU13, AW55 | 24 |
| YS02-8 | Nut | 5 | AJ24, AK28, AO11 | 5 |
| YS02-10 | Nut | 7 | AK29, AN26 | 4 |
| YS03-6 | Nut | 5 | AJ32, AR34 | 8 |
| YS03-14 | Nut | 20 | AR35 | 1 |
| YS04-5 | Nut | 1 | AS30 | 2 |
| YS04-8 | Nut | 5 | AA39 | 1 |
| YS04-10 | Nut | 7 | AR36 | 1 |
| YS05-3 | Spring washer | 1 | AW56 | 4 |
| YS05-4 | Spring washer | 1 | AW57 | 4 |
| YS05-5 | Spring washer | 1 | AS29, AW58 | 8 |
| YS05-6 | Spring washer | 1 | AB09, AF33, AJ25, AL23, AM35, AO12, AP27, AR37, AU14, AW59, AY23 | 58 |
| YS05-8 | Spring washer | 2 | AC10, AJ26, AK31, AM36, AN27, AO13, AU15, AW60 | 31 |
| YS05-10 | Spring washer | 2 | AK32, AK38, AL24, AN28 | 12 |
| YS05-12 | Spring washer | 3 | AD33, AG18, AR38 | 3 |
| YS06-4 | Washer | 1 | AY24 | 1 |
| YS06-6 | Washer | 1 | AJ27, AK33, AL25, AY25 | 18 |
| YS06-8 | Washer | 1 | AA40, AC11, AO14 | 12 |
| YS06-10 | Washer | 2 | AK34, AR39 | 3 |
| YS08-4.10-8 | Bolt | 5 | AR33 | 4 |
| YS08-5.10-8 | Bolt | 6 | AF34 | 2 |

| Size | Name of Item | Unit price | Illustration No. | Quantity required per one machine |
|---|---|---|---|---|
| YS11-4.8-8 | Bolt | 1 | AN29 | 4 |
| YS11-5.20-20 | Bolt | 4 | AS27 | 2 |
| YS11-6.15-13 | Bolt | 3 | AJ28 | 2 |
| YS12-4.6-5 | Bolt | 2 | AY21 | 1 |
| YS12-4.7-6 | Bolt | 2 | AH43 | 4 |
| YS12-5.10-7 | Bolt | 2 | AW50 | 2 |
| YS12-5.18-10 | Bolt | 4 | AS26 | 2 |
| YS12-5.22-22 | Bolt | 4 | AS28 | 4 |
| YS12-6.10-8 | Bolt | 3 | AL19, AW51, AY22 | 6 |
| YS12-6.16-10 | Bolt | 3 | AL20 | 2 |
| YS12-6.20-15 | Bolt | 4 | AH36 | 2 |
| YS12-6.30-20 | Bolt | 4 | AH28 | 2 |
| YS12-6.32-17 | Bolt | 5 | AB10 | 1 |
| YS12-6.35-15 | Bolt | 5 | AH40 | 4 |
| YS12-6.40-20 | Bolt | 6 | AH41 | 2 |
| YS12-6.43-10 | Bolt | 6 | AL21 | 1 |
| YS12-6.44-15 | Bolt | 6 | AH29, AH37 | 5 |
| YS12-6.47-15 | Bolt | 6 | AH30 | 3 |
| YS12-6.60-15 | Bolt | 8 | AH31 | 3 |
| YS12-6.62-15 | Bolt | 8 | AH34 | 1 |
| YS12-6.63-15 | Bolt | 8 | AH32 | 1 |
| YS12-6.72-15 | Bolt | 10 | AH38 | 1 |
| YS12-6.76-13 | Bolt | 12 | AH33 | 1 |
| YS12-6.80-15 | Bolt | 13 | AH39 | 1 |
| YS12-6.90-15 | Bolt | 20 | AH35 | 2 |
| YS12-6.112-15 | Bolt | 15 | AH42 | 1 |
| YS13-3.5-5 | Bolt | 2 | AW52 | 4 |
| YS13-6.16-10 | Bolt | 3 | AJ29 | 8 |
| YS13-6.28-16 | Bolt | 5 | AM37 | 4 |
| YS14-6.13-9 | Bolt | 3 | AW53 | 1 |
| YS15-5.32-15 | Bolt | 5 | AN30 | 3 |
| YS15-6.70-10 | Bolt | 5 | AB11 | 1 |
| YS16-6 | Washer | 2 | AS31 | 1 |
| YS20-1.2-10 | Split cotter pin | 1 | AP26 | 1 |
| YS20-1.2-15 | Split cotter pin | 1 | AK35 | 2 |
| YS20-1.6-15 | Split cotter pin | 1 | AK36 | 1 |
| YS20-2-15 | Split cotter pin | 5 | AF35 | 2 |
| YS20-2-20 | Split cotter pin | 1 | AR40, AK37 | 2 |
| YS20-2-22 | Split cotter pin | 1 | AK41 | 1 |
| YS21-6-22 | Pin | 5 | AK39 | 1 |
| YS22-10.178-12 | Bolt | 80 | AK40 | 1 |
| YS23-10 | Grooved nut | 20 | AK30, AR41 | 2 |

## Oil Seal

| Parts No. | Size | Unit price |
|---|---|---|
| 150111 | SW25 × 47 × 8 | ¥ 100 |
| 150122 | SW20 × 36 × 10 | 130 |
| 150517 | SD30 × 47 × 7 | 75 |
| 150613 | S22 × 12 × 7 | 35 |
| 150709 | S30 × 20 × 7 | 50 |
| 155030 | SD20 × 35 × 7 | 60 |
| 122732 | OS47 × 56 × 7 | 95 |
| 155530 | S20 × 35 × 7 | 60 |
| 155531 | S26 × 42 × 8 | 60 |
| 155532 | S42 × 56 × 6 | 80 |

## Bearing & Roller

| Parts No. | Name of items | Size |
|---|---|---|
| 150109 | Ball bearing | $6304C_3$ |
| 150112 | Ball bearing | 16005 |
| 150511 | Ball bearing | 6303 |
| 150514 | Ball bearing | 6005 |
| 155031 & 155538 | Ball bearing | 6202 |
| 155534 | Ball bearing | 6004 |
| 150136 | Needle roller | |

# MEMO

YA5  125 c.c.   PARTS LIST

Third edition, March '63

# YAMAHA MOTOR CO., LTD.

HAMAMATSU JAPAN

# YAMAHA YA6

# WORKSHOP MANUAL

We are very proud to present the new Yamaha 125 YA6 that possesses the world-famous 2-cycle rotary valve engine plus the Yamaha Autolube.

The Yamaha Autolube, the entirely new lubricating device developped by the Yamaha Technical Research Laboratory has completely solved all the long-pending problems of the 2-cycle engines, such as excessive oil, carbon accumulation, use of gasoline-oil mixture etc.

This service manual covers all the steps necessary for inspecting and repairing the Yamaha 125 YA6. We hope this booklet will be a help to you.

**YAMAHA MOTOR CO., LTD.**

# YAMAHA YA6 SERVICE MANUAL

## CONTENTS

**CHAPTER 1　YAMAHA YA6 FEATURES AND SPECIFICATIONS** ............ 1

   1-1　YA6 FEATURES ............ 1
   1-2　YA6 SPECIFICATIONS ............ 2
   1-3　YA6 PERFORMANCE CURVES ............ 3

**CHAPTER 2　YAMAHA AUTOLUBE** ............ 4

   2-1　WHAT IS THE YAMAHA AUTOLUBE? ............ 4
   2-2　AUTOLUBE FEATURES ............ 5
   2-3　CONSTRUCTION ............ 6
      2-3-1　PUMP FEATURES ............ 6
      2-3-2　PUMP ASSEMBLY ............ 6
   2-4　PUMP MECHANISM ............ 8
      2-4-1　PUMP MECHANISM ............ 8
      2-4-2　MAIN PARTS AND THEIR FUNCTION ............ 8
      2-4-3　DISTRIBUTOR-PLUNGER MECHANISM ............ 11
   2-5　PERFORMANCE ............ 12
      2-5-1　CONTROL OF THE AMOUNT OF OIL ............ 12
      2-5-2　RELATION BETWEEN PLUNGER STROKE ............ 12
      2-5-3　OIL CONSUMPTION ............ 13
      2-5-4　GASOLINE-TO-OIL RATIO ............ 14
   2-6　INSPECTION AND MAINTENANCE ............ 14
      2-6-1　PUMP SETTING ............ 15
      2-6-2　LETTING AIR OUT OF THE PUMP ............ 15
      2-6-3　WHEN DISASSEMBLING AND ASSEMBLING ............ 16
   2-7　OIL FOR YAMAHA AUTOLUBE ............ 17

# CHAPTER 3　ENGINE ...18

3-1　GENERAL DESCRIPTION ...18

3-2　DISASSEMBLING AND ASSEMBLING THE ENGINE ...18

  3-2-1　DISASSEMBLING ...18

  3-2-2　ASSEMBLING ...20

3-3　INSPECTION AND REPAIR OF THE PART OF ENGINE ...21

  3-3-1　CYLINDER, PISTON AND PISTON HEAD ...21

  3-3-2　CRANK ASSEMBLY ...23

  3-3-3　ROTARY VALVE AND VALVE COVER ...24

  3-3-4　PRIMARY REDUCTION AND CLUTCH ...25

  3-3-5　TRNSMISSION, SHIFTER AND KICK CRANK ...27

  3-3-6　CRANKCASE ...31

  3-3-7　AIR CLEANER AND CARBURETOR ...32

# CHAPTER 4　FRAME ...35

4-1　YA6 FRAME FEATURES ...35

4-2　INSPECTION AND REPAIRING THE MAIN PARTS ...35

  4-2-1　FRAME ...35

  4-2-2　STEERING HANDLES AND WIRES ...36

  4-2-3　FRONT FORK ...36

  4-2-4　REAR CUSHION UNIT ...38

  4-2-5　FUEL TANK AND SADDLE ...38

  4-2-6　OTHER IMPROVEMENTS ...39

# CHAPTER 5　ELECTRICAL SYSTEM ...40

5-1　ELECTRICAL PARTS ...40

5-2　STARTER DYNAMO ...41

5-3　REGULATOR ...43

5-4　IGNITON COIL ...44

| | | |
|---|---|---|
| 5-5 | SPARK PLUG | 45 |
| 5-6 | BATTERY | 45 |

## CHAPTER 6    INSPECTION AND MAINTENANCE ............47

| | | |
|---|---|---|
| 6-1 | PERIODICAL INSPECTION | 47 |
| 6-2 | PERIODICAL INSPECTION CHART | 47 |
| 6-3 | INSPECTION AND MAINTENANCE OF THE MAIN PARTS | 47 |
| 6-3-1 | ENGINE | 47 |
| 6-3-2 | FRAME | 49 |
| 6-3-3 | ELECTRICAL SYSTEM | 50 |
| 6-4 | NECESSARY TOOLS AND TESTERS FOR INSPECTION AND MAINTENANCE | 51 |

# CHAPTER 1 YAMAHA YA6 FEATURES AND SPECIFICATIONS

## 1-1 YA6 FEATURES

(1) **YAMAHA AUTO LUBE**

The Auto Lube, depending on the engine RPM and load, controls and force the oil to the engine by means of the precision-machined pump. It has greatly improved the 2-cycle engine in performance.

(2) **HIGH-PERFORMANCE ROTARY VALVE ENGINE**

Yamaha's famous 2-cycle rotary valve engine plus the Auto Lube develops more than 70 MPH with fast pick-up. In addition, it keeps RPM steady when going up hills or at slowest speed.

(3) **4-SPEED ROTARY TRANSMISSION**

Yamaha's rotary gear always runs smoothly without any nock or noise at any speed.

(4) **SELF-STARTER DYNAMO AND CARBURETOR WITH BUILT-IN STARTER**

Yamaha's exclusive carburetor with built-in starter plus the powerful electric-starter dynamo start the engine easily in cold weather.

(5) **RELIABLE BRAKES**

The dust and water-proof brake drums proven all Yamaha models assure of having effectively working brakes even on rainy days or on dusty roads.

(6) **FINE DRIVING COMFORT**

The riding position based on years scientific researches keeps balance and steering perfect all the times even on bad roads or sharp curves. Driving is always smooth and never tiring on rough roads.
The frame is of a pressed steel monocoque construction that excels in strength and rigidity.

(7) **UNIQUE STYLING**

Smart styling, beautiful finish and trouble-free performance are suited for work, commutation, long distance touring etc.

## 1-2 YA6 SPECIFICATIONS

| NAME | | | YAMAHA | |
|---|---|---|---|---|
| MODEL | | | YA6 | |
| DIMENSIONS | Overall length | | 1920mm | (6'—5") |
| | Overall width | | 725mm | (2'—5") |
| | Overall height | | 1045mm | (3'—5") |
| | Wheelbase | | 1245mm | (4'—2") |
| | Minimum road clearance | | 135mm | ( —5") |
| WEIGHT | Bare weight | | 120kg | (264 lbs.) |
| | Seating capacity | | 2 persons | |
| | All-up weight | | 220kg | |
| | weight distr. without lord | front | 56kg | |
| | | rear | 64kg | |
| | weight distr. with load | front | 70kg | |
| | | rear | 160kg | |
| PERFORMANCE | Maximum speed | | 110km/h or over | (70mph) |
| | Fuel consmption | | 65km/ℓ at 35km/h | |
| | Climbing ability | | 20° | |
| | Braking distance | | 7.5m or less at 35km/h | (23ft/22mph) |
| | Minimum turning radius | | 1900mm | (5'—11") |
| ENGINE | Model | | 2-cycle, gasoline | |
| | Lubricating system | | Yamaha Auto Lube, automatic lubr. | |
| | Cooling system | | Air-cooled | |
| | Number of cylinder | | 1 | |
| | Displacement | | 123c.c. | |
| | Bore x stroke | | 56 × 50mm | |
| | Compression ratio | | 6.8 : 1 | |
| | Maximum torque | | 1.25kg-m/5000rpm | |
| | Min. fuel consumtion at full load | | 280g/ps/h/5000rpm | |
| | Gross weight | | 36.5kg (inclu. muffler) | |
| | Dimensions | Length | 525mm | |
| | | Width | 430mm | |
| | | Height | 325mm | |
| | Starting system | | Self-starter and kick starter | |
| IGNITION | Ignifion system | | Battery ignition | |
| | Ignition timing | | 2.5 to 2.6mm before upper dead point | |
| | Starting system | | Self-starter dynamo | |
| | Spark plug | | Hitachi M44, NGK B-7H, or A B-7HZ | |
| | Angular advance | | 19° | |
| | Point gap | | 0.3 to 0.35mm | |
| STARTER DYNAMO | Manufacturer | | Hitachi | |
| | Generator | | D.C. shunt | |
| | Output | | 90W/14V at 1600rpm | |
| | Model | | GS-113 | |
| | Voltage regulator | | "Tirr.ll" Type | |
| BATTERY | Manufacturer | | Furukawa, Yuasa or Nippon Denchi | |
| | Model | | SPΓ-12, MBH3-12 or MW3-12 | |
| | Capacity | | 1 OAH | |
| CARBURETOR | Manufacturer | | Mikuni | |
| | Model | | VM 22 SC | |
| AIR CLEANER | Dry, paper-filter | | | |
| TANK CAPACITY | Gasoline tank | | 9.0 liters | (2.4 gal) |
| | Oil tank | | 1.8 liters | (0.47 gal) |
| CLUTCH | Type | | Wet, multiple disk | |
| | Primary reduction | | Helical gear | |
| | Primary reduc. ratio | | 3.833 | |
| TRANSMISSION | Type | | Constant mesh, 4-speed | |
| | Gear ratio | Low | 2.533 | |
| | | Second | 1.524 | |
| | | Third | 1.120 | |
| | | Top | 0.828 | |

| FINAL DRIVE | Type | Chain |
|---|---|---|
| | Reduction ratio | 2.600 |
| FRAME | Backbone type monocoque | |
| SUSPENSIONS | Front | Telescopic fork |
| | Rear | Swinging arm |
| SHOCK ABSORBER | Front | Coil spring & oil damper |
| | Rear | Coil spring & oil damper |
| STEERING & WHEEL | Steering angle | 45° × 2 |
| | Caster | 64° |
| | Trail | 83mm |
| TIRE SIZE | Front | 3.0-16-4PR |
| | Rear | 3.0-16-4PR |
| BRAKE | Type | Internal expanding |
| | Front | Hand operated, wire |
| | Rear | Foot-opearted. rod, |
| BULBS | Headlight | 35W, 25W, 12 to 16V |
| | Taillight | (20W)/8W |
| | Stop light | 8W/(20W) |
| | Direction signal | 8W × 4 |
| | Pilot lamp | 3W |

## 1-3 YA6 PERFORMANCE CURVES

### (1) ENGINE PERFORMANCE CURVES

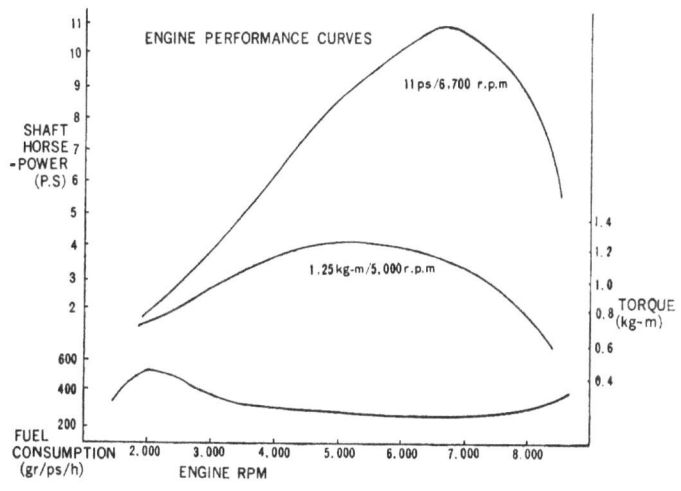

### (2) DRIVING PERFORMANCE CURVES

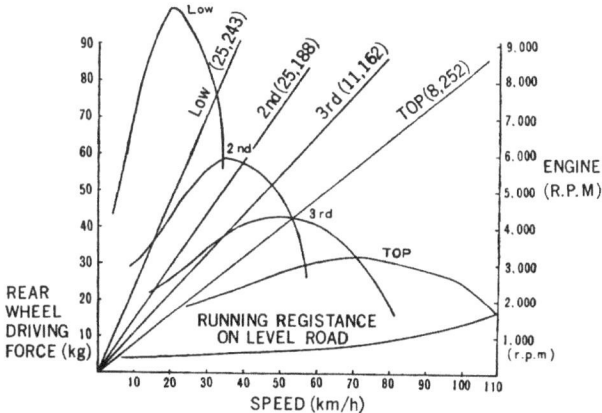

# YAMAHA 125 YA6

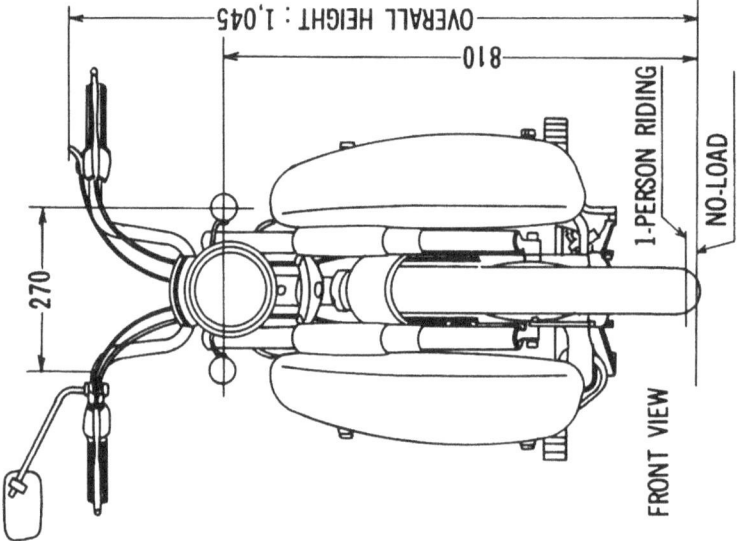

UNIT : m/m
SCALE : 1/10

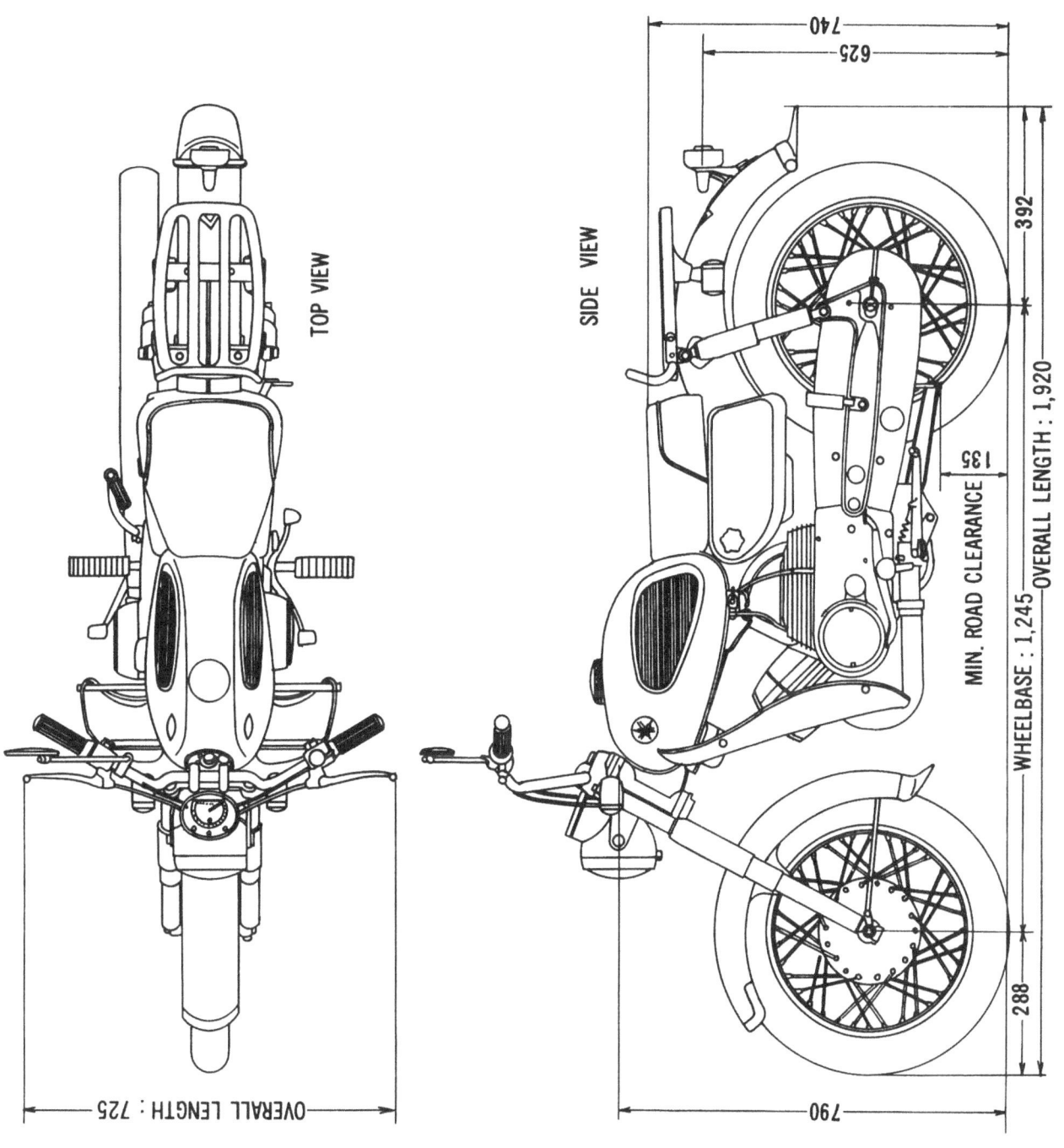

# CHAPTER 2   YAMAHA AUTOLUBE

## 2-1   WHAT IS THE YAMAHA AUTOLUBE ?

The Yamaha Auto Lube is an automatic lubricating device for 2-cycle engine newly developed by Yamaha Technical Research Institute.

It controls the amount of oil depending both on the engine RPM and on the load under any operating conditions and forces the proper amount of oil to the engine all the times by means of the precision-machined pump.

As a result, the new Yamaha 2-cycle engine does not use the gasoline-oil mixture that other makers' engines must do.    It is for the first time in the world that such a device was applied to the production model of 2-cycle engine.

The Yamaha Auto Lube is the best of the lubricating systems for 2-cycle engine.

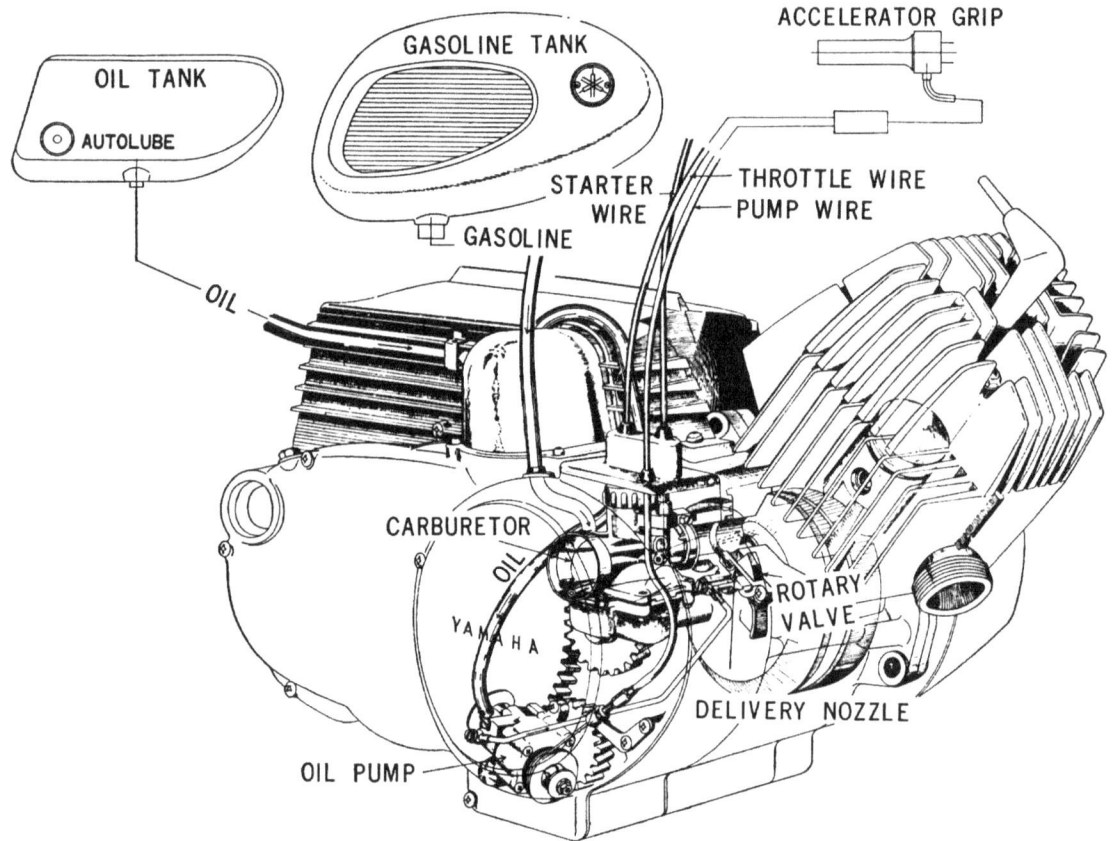

## 2-2   AUTOLUBE FEATURES

The conventional lubricating system uses the gasoline-oil mixture in the fixed ratio of 20:1.    This ratio was determined on the basis that it would not cause lack of oil at top speed and full throttle.

The operation test shows that the ratio of 60:1 to 80:1 is sufficient for driving 40 to 60 km/h with the throttle in ⅕ to ¼ open position and that even 120:1 is sufficient for idling at low RPM with throttle in ⅛ open position or closed. Therefore, if the gasoline-oil mixture is used in the fixed ratio of 20:1 regardless of the speed and the throttle, it leads to excessive oiling except when driving at full throttle.

Since the Auto Lube controls the amount of oil depending both on the engine RPM and on the load under any operating conditions and forces the proper amount of oil to the engine at any time. The engine gets freed from any troubles caused by excessive oiling. In addition, it has been improved in performance, because the new fresh oil is always applied to the lubrication surfaces.

It is superior to the circulating lubrication for 4-cycle engine.

## FEATURES AND ADVANTAGES

(1) **THE PROPER AMOUNT OF OIL IS ALWAYS APPLIED UNDER ANY OPERATING CONDITIONS**

    A  EXCELLENT LUBRICATION

       The fresh oil is always delivered from the oil tank to the engine (in 4-cycle engine, the oil is circulating) and there is less oil entering the combustion chamber because of larger particle.

    B  LESS CARBON ACCUMULATION

       The spark plug, piston, cylinder, ring, muffler and other parts are coated with less carbon. The engine has been greatly improved in performance and durability.

    C  ECONOMY OF OIL

       The Autolube gets about 3,000km (2,000 mile) per liter. The oil consumption is ⅓ or less of that of the conventional lubricating system that uses the gasoline-oil mixture.

    D  LESS EXHAUST GAS

       There is less oil entering the combustion chamber together with gasoline.

    E  IMPROVEMENT IN ENGINE PERFORMANCE

       The combustion efficiency has been heightened and the engine has been greatly improved in steadiness at the slowest speed and pickup.

(2) **SIMPLIFIED FUEL SUPPLY**

    It is not neccessary to mix with gasoline. Just fill the fuel tank with gasoline only.

    The tank and the carburetor have got freed from any troubles caused by the oil.

(3) **DEPENDABLE LUBRICATION**

    The user has no worry about the incorrect gasoline-to-oil ratio and the quality of oil.

## 2-3 CONSTRUCTION

### 2-3-1 PUMP FEATURES

The oil pump is a kind of engine-driven plunger pump used together with a cylindrical distributor.

(1) The amount of oil to be delivered is controlled depending on not only the engine RPM but also the carburetor throttle.
(2) The amount of oil to be delivered is adjustable micrometrically.
(3) The oil is delivered not only by the pump but also by hand.
(4) The air, if entered while piping the unit, can be completely removed.

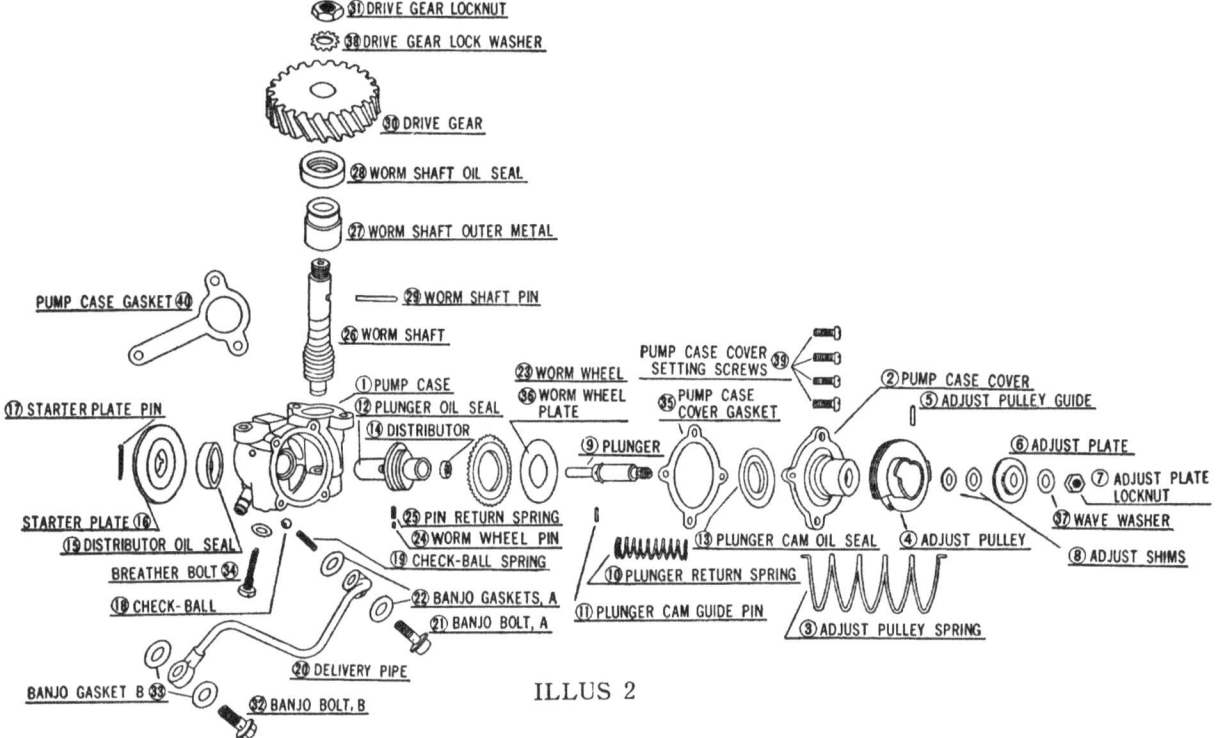

ILLUS 2

### 2-3-2 PUMP ASSEMBLY

(1) EXPLODED VIEW OF AUTOLUBE PUMP

(2) ASSEMBLY DRAWINGS

2a) SECTIONAL VIEW OF PUMP ASSEMBLY

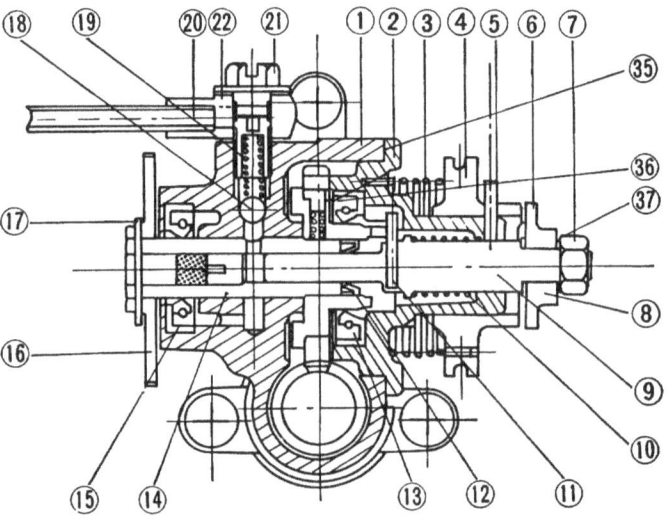

ILLUS 3

2b) SECTIONAL VIEW OF PUMP-DRIVING SECTION

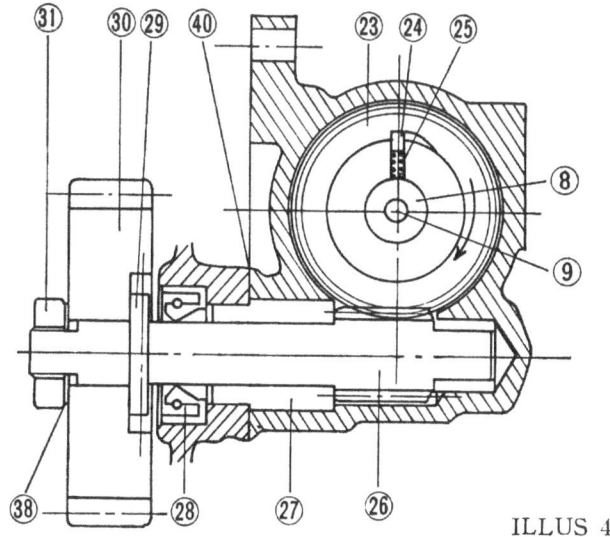

ILLUS 4

2c) SECTIONAL VIEW OF ALL-DELIVERING SECTION

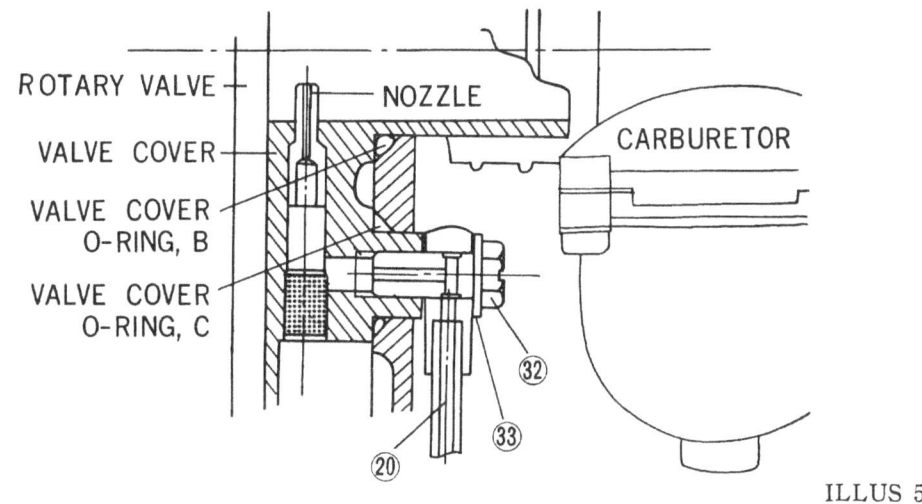

ILLUS 5

2d) PUMP FITTING

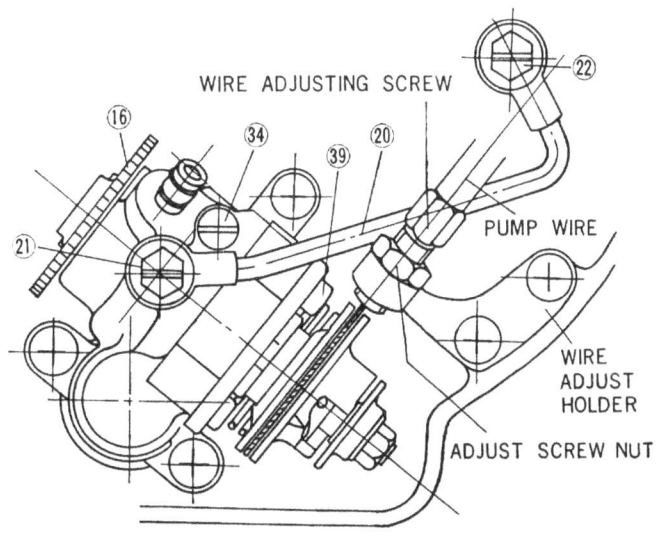

ILLUS 6

## 2-4 PUMP MECHANISM

### 2-4-1 PUMP MECHANISM

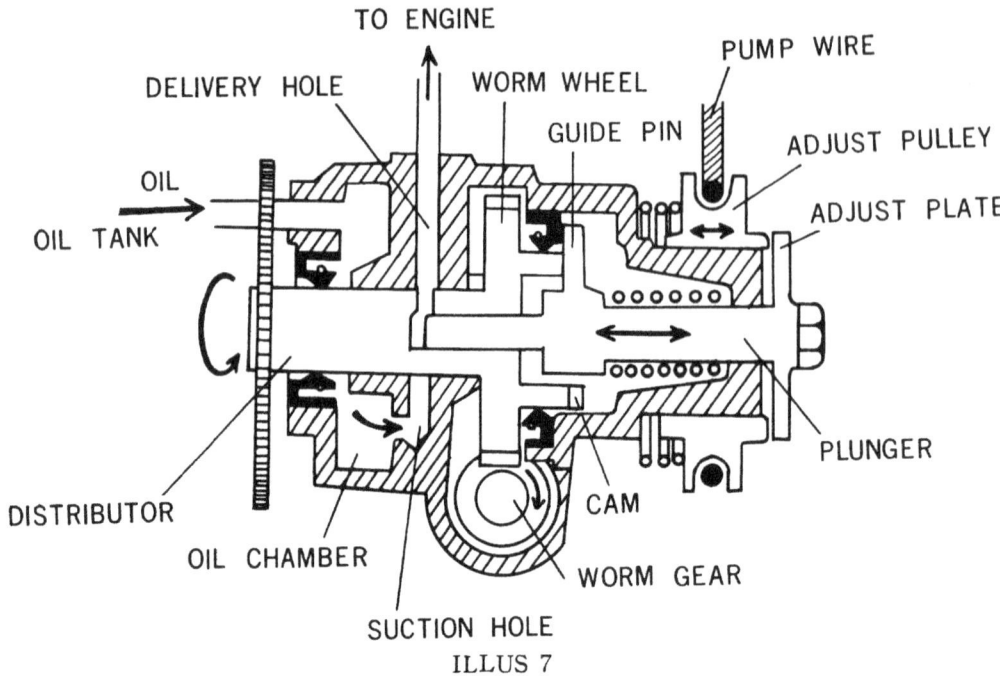

ILLUS 7

(1) The motive force is transmitted through reduction gears from the crank shaft of the engine to the worm gear, which rotates the worm wheel and the distributor as a unit.

$$\text{RPM OF DISTRIBUTOR} = \frac{\text{REDUCTION GEAR (18)}}{\text{DRIVE GEAR (23)}} \times \frac{\text{WORM GEAR (1)}}{\text{WORM WHEEL (36)}} = \frac{1}{46}$$

(2) An oil hole in the distributor opens or closes the suction hole and the delivery hole alternatively.

(3) In order to let oil in or out, the plunger moves alternatively back and forth along the cylinder cam, while the distributor rotates.

(4) The plunger stroke is regulated by means of the accelertor grip.

As describd above, the Auto Lube functions depending not only on the RPM of the engine but also on the turning of the accelerator grip so the oil is always delivered properly under any operating conditions:

DELIVERY OF OIL = (PLUNGER CAPACITY) × (PUMP RPM) × (PLUNGER STROKE)

$$Q = \frac{\pi d^2}{4} \times N \times \ell$$

### 2-4-2 MAIN PARTS AND THEIR FUNCTION

(1) OIL PASSAGE

An oil pipe carries oil from the oil tank into the oil chamber of the pump case and, by action of the plunger, the oil is brown into the oil chamber of the distributor through the suction hole in the pump case.

The oil, to which the pump pressure is applied, pushes up the check-ball and spring to enter the delivery pipe, which carries it to the nozzle in the rotary valve cover.

Lastly it is delivered to the suction passage through the nozzle.

(2) CHECK-BALL

The check-ball keeps the delivery pressure of pump constant regardless of the fluctuation of pressure in the suction passage and stabilizes the performance of the pump.

While the engine is not action, the check-ball prevents oil from leaking out of the clearance between the pump case and the distributor.

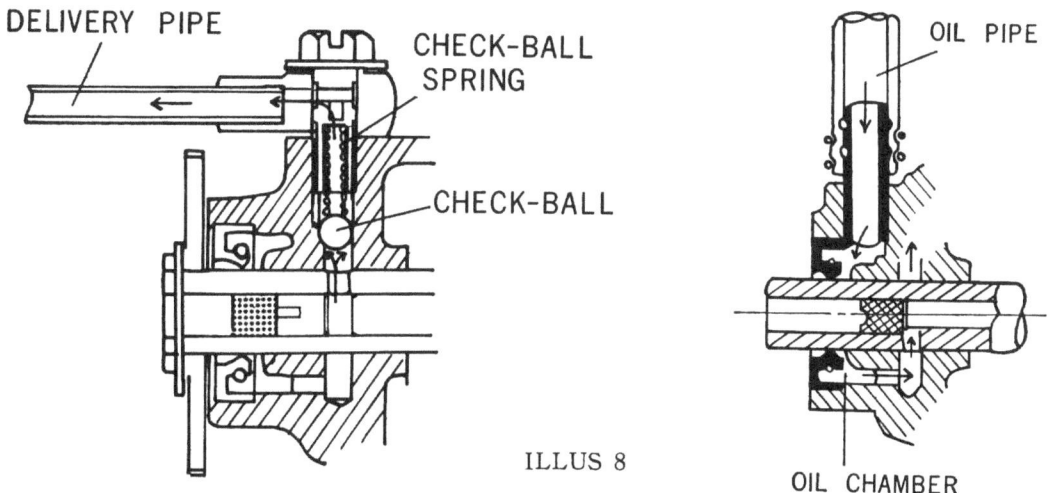

ILLUS 8

(3) DISTRIBUTER AND PLUNGER

The distributor is driven and rotated by the worm gear to open or close alternatively the suction hole and the delivery hole in the pump case.

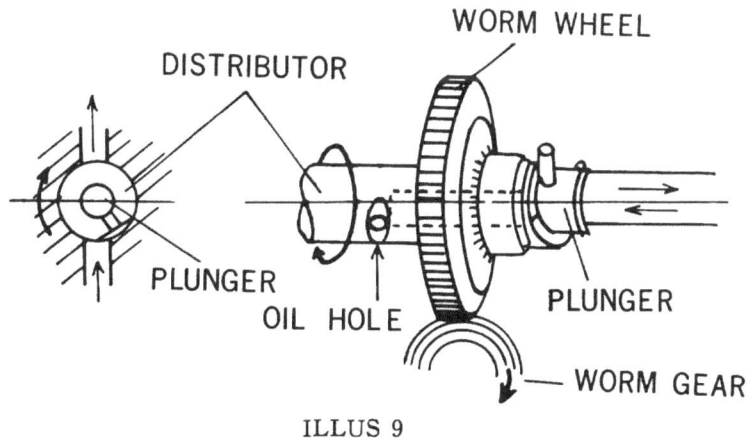

ILLUS 9

The plunger, whose guide pin is pressed against the plunger cam by the plunger return spring, moves alternatively back and forth according to the shape of the cam, with which the distributor rotates as a unit.

### (4) RELATION BETWEEN THE PLUNGER STROKE AND THE THROTTLE (ACCELERATER WIRE)

The amount of oil to be delivered is controlled in proportion to the engine RPM and, at the same time, the plunger stroke is regulated by turning the accelerator grip or by opening the carburetor throttle valve.

The plunger stroke is equal to the clearance between the adjust plate on the right side of the plunger and the adjust pulley fitted around the pump case. The clearance is controlled by means of the accelerator grip as:

a) The accelerator grip pulls the pump wire while turned;
b) The pump wire rotates the adjust pulley;
c) The plunger cam guide pin moves the pulley to the left by height of the plunger cam and the clearance is widened.

$L$, height of plunger cam.    2.0mm ($\ell = L = 2.0$mm at max. stroke and full throttle)

$\ell$, clearance between adjust plate and pulley:    Ⓐ $0.24 +^{0.02}$ ($0.18 +^{0.02}$) at min. stroke and less than 1/5 throttle.

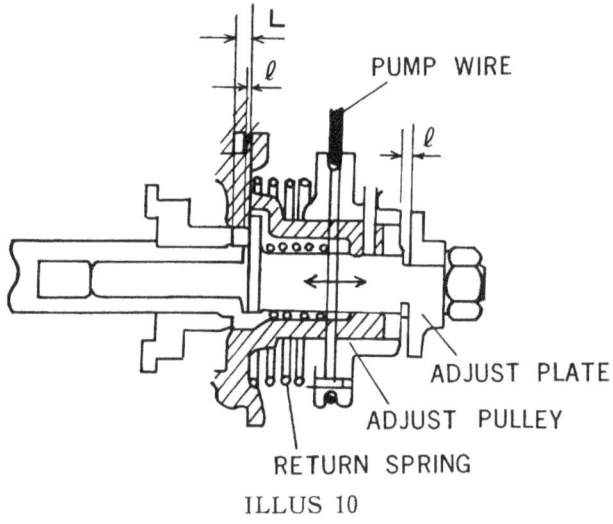

ILLUS 10

NOTE : The plunger cam guide pin is contact with the section $\ell$ but not with the section L (L - $\ell$) of the plunger cam.

### (5) BREATHER BOLT AND STARTER PLATE

The breather bolt (34) is used to let the air out of the pump. Remove the bolt and the oil flows from the oil chamber into the worm gear case through the oil hole at the top of the oil chamber and runs over through the breather bolt hole.

The starter plate (16) fitted around the distributor is used to drive the pump not by the engine but by hand.
Turn it in the specified direction by hand and the pump works.

## 2-4-3 DISTRIBUTOR - PLUNGER MECHANISM

NOTATION:  D : Distributor   P : Plunger   C : Cylindrical cam
O : Oil hole   S : Suction hole   D : Delivery hole

### SUCTION STROKE

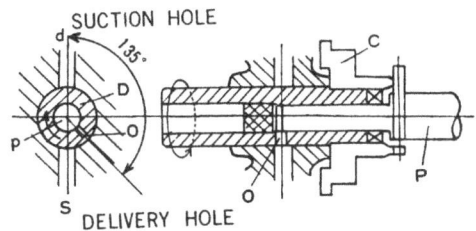

1 Plunger is not in action; Suction hole is going to be opened.

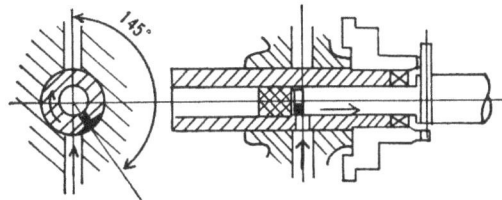

2 Plunger moves back or let oil in.

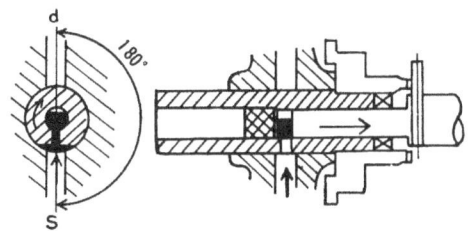

3 Plunger goes on moving back; Suction hole is fully opened.

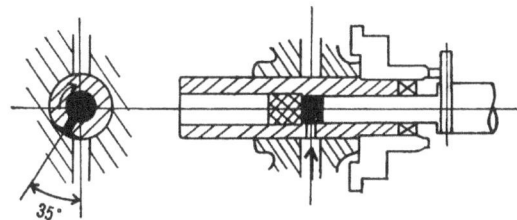

4 Plunger stops: Suction hole is still slightly opened

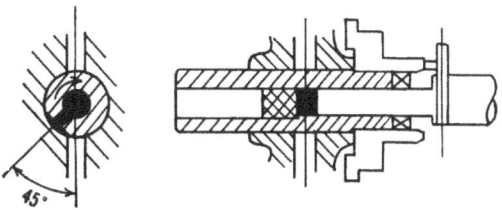

5 Plunger is not in action; Suction hole is closed.

### DELIVERY STROKE

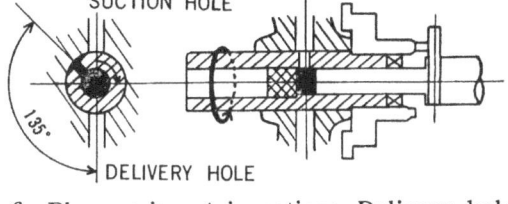

6 Plunger is not in action; Delivery hole is going to be opened.

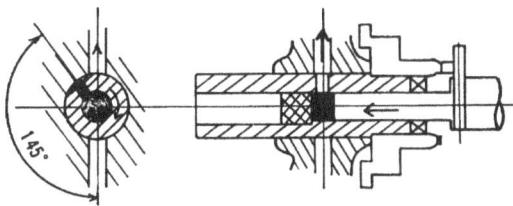

7 Plunger moves forth to let oil out.

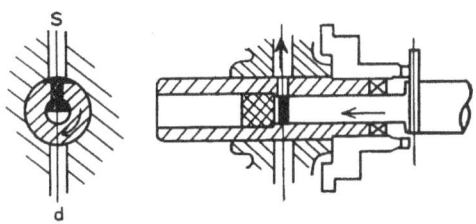

8 Plunger goes on moving forth.

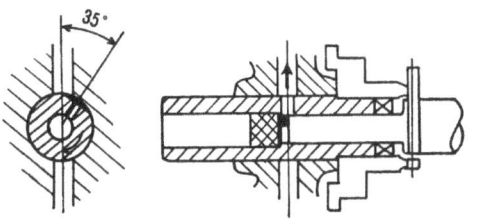

9 Plunger stops; Delivery hole is still slightly opened.

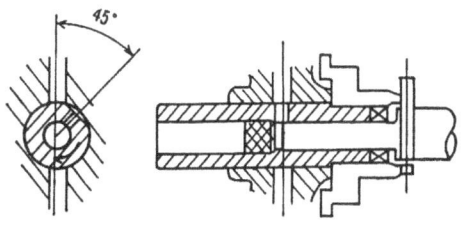

10 Plunger is not in action; Delivery hole is closed.

— 11 —

## 2-5 PERFORMANCE

### 2-5-1 CONTROL OF THE AMOUNT OF OIL

If the plunger stroke is fixed, the amount of oil delivered is in proportion to engine RPM:

$$Q, \text{cc/h} = \frac{\pi d^2}{4} N \quad \text{where} \quad d: \text{diameter of plunger;} \quad N: \text{engine RPM.}$$

As described above, if the plunger stroke is fixed, the amount of oil depends only on the engine RPM or speed rergardless of city driving, hill climbing and other various driving conditions. If the amount of oil is fixed on the basis of high-speed running, it will turn excessive for driving at slow speed. On the other hand, if it is fixed on the basis of high-speed running, it will lead to lack of oil or may cause the engine to scorch at top speed.

In order to prevent these troubles, the Auto Lube has been designed to control the amount of oil depending not only on the engine RPM but also on the plunger stroke. According as the throttle is opened more widely, the plunger stroke becomes larger:

$$Q, \text{cc/h} = \frac{\pi d^2}{4} N \times \ell \times \frac{60}{1.000}, \quad (N = \frac{n}{i})$$

where $\ell$: plunger stroke; $n$: crank RPM $\quad i$: total reduction ratio $= 46$

### 2-5-2 RELATION BETWEEN PLUNGR STROKE & THROTTLE

The relation *between the throttle, speed, engine RPM and stroke is given below:

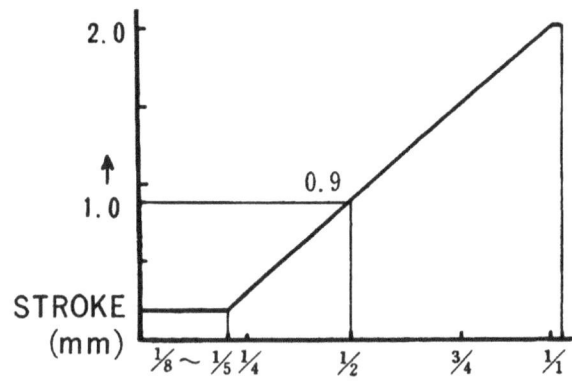

| THROTTLE | SPEED, km/h | ENGINE RPM | STROKE, mm |
|---|---|---|---|
| 1/6 | 52 | 3300 | 0.18 |
| 1/5 | 64 | 4300 | 0.18 |
| 1/4 | 47 | 5300 | 0.30 |
| 1/3 | 77 | 6100 | 0.50 |
| 1/2 | 88 | 7000 | 0.90 |
| 3/4 | 91 | 7200 | 1.52 |
| 1/1 | 93 or over | 7400 | 2.00 |

* Driving on paved level road with normal riding position and gear in TOP.

## 2-5-3 OIL CONSUMPTION

Fig. 3 is given by the expression $Q = \dfrac{\pi d^2}{4} \; N \times \ell \times \dfrac{60}{1000}$

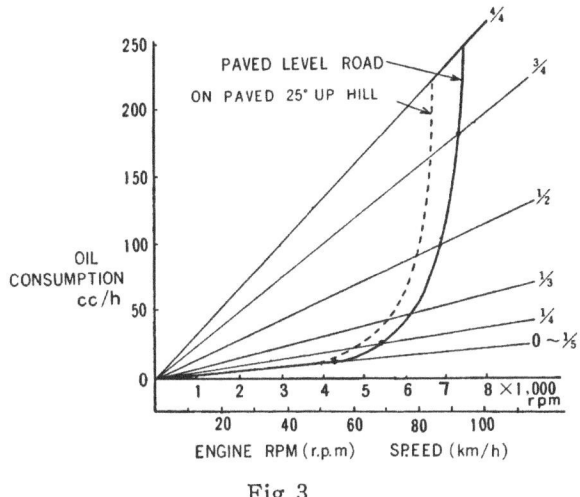

Fig 3

As shown in Fig. 3, the same speed does not always require the same amount of oil. The oil consumption for climbing a hill is much more than that for driving on a paved level road because of more opened throttle. Under the normal driving condition, the engine uses up 8 c.c./h at 40km/h. If the throttle is opned ⅓ for pick-up, the oil consumption reaches about 25c.c./h at the moment.

Since the engine RPM increases with acceleration, further amount of oil is necessary.

Other factors which affect the oil consumption are the gear, load, riding position, road conditions etc.

## 2-5-4 GASOLINE-TO-OIL RATIO

The gasoline-to-oil ratio fo driving on a paved level road with the gear in top varies as shown in Fig. 4:

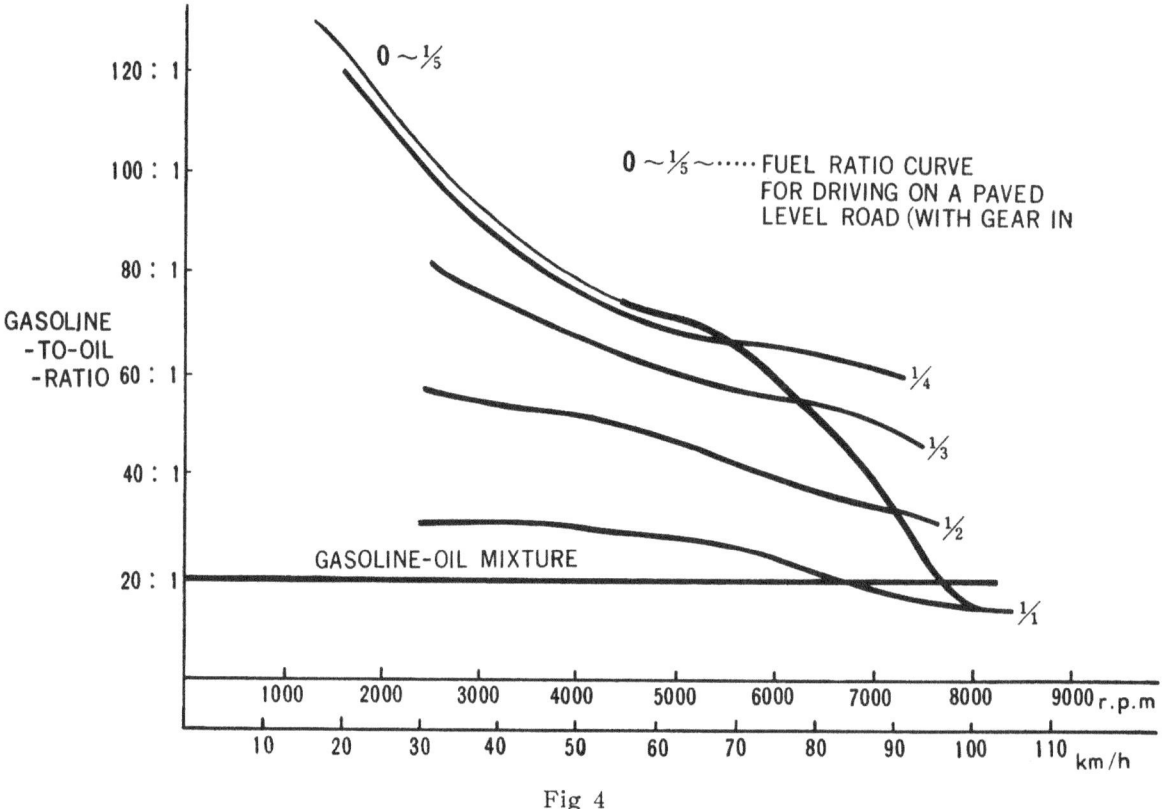

Fig 4

Fig. 4 shows that how excessive oil there is the mixture of gasoline and oil of the ratio of 20:1;

At top speed (more than 7700rpm), the fuel ratio is about 18:1 (Fig. 4). This prevents the engine from overheating or scorching. At less than 1/5 throttle, the pulunger stroke is fixed as shown in Fig. 2, even if the throttle is suddenly closed. This means there is no lack of oil, even if the engine brake is applied for a long time.

## 2-6 INSPECTION AND MAINTENANCE

The oil pump free from any troubles, if it is cared for properly.
The oil passage will not be clogged, if any brand of motor oil sold by major brand service station is used.
The unit should be removed, disassembled or assembled with a special care, because it consists of a number of precision-machined parts.
When mounting the engine, be sure to let air out of the pump and adjust the plunger stroke as described below:

## 2-6-1 PUMP SETTING

(1) The correct plungr stroke is Ⓐ $0.24 ^{+0.02}_{0}$ ($0.18 ^{+0.02}_{0}$) when the engine is idling or the adjust pulley in full open position.

After assembling, drive the pump by operating the starter plate by hand and adjust $\ell$ to be Ⓐ $0.24 ^{+0.02}_{0}$ ($0.18 ^{+0.02}_{0}$) by means of the adjust shim.

NOTE: Every pump assembly has been adjusted in Yamaha factory.

(2) At ½ throttle, a V-mark on the adjust pulley should be aligned to the adjust pulley guide pin as follows:

A) After mounting the pump on the engine, connect the pump wire;

B) Open the throttle fully by turning the accelerator grip;

C) As shown in the Illust. No. 12, set the adjusting mark on the throttle valve to the highest position of the main bore of the carburetor.

Then the throttle is just half opened.

Note: The YA6 of early production (Model No. To be uiformed later) has no mark on the throttle valve, and in order to set the valve at ½ position use the pump setting tool.

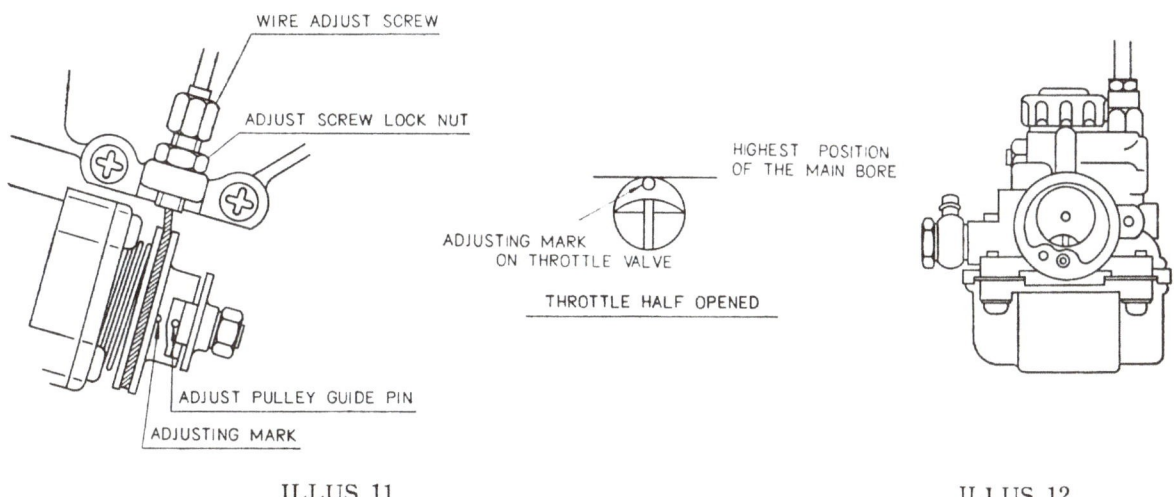

ILLUS 11                    ILLUS 12

## 2-6-2 LETTING AIR OUT OF THE PUMP

To let air out of the pump, remove the breather bolt and then turn the starter plate clockwise until oil runs over through the breather bolt hole or start the engine and let it run idle.

## 2-6-3 WHEN DISASSEMBLING AND ASSEMBLING

(1) When disassembling, be careful not to scratch the lip of each oil seal, case-to-distributor surfaces, distributor-to-plunger surfaces, plunger cam guide pin and is groove in the pump case cover.

(2) When assembling:

A) Be sure to apply grease to the lip of the oil seals.
   Attach them correctly:
   1. Distributor oil seal should not be out of the case end;
   2. Plunger oil seal should be inserted more than 3.2 mm from the plunger cam face;
   3. Plunger cam oil seal should be out of the pump case cover end.

B) Apply the Auto Lube oil between the distributor and the pump case. Make sure the distributor turns smoothly.

C) The wheel should be attached as illustrated right. Make sure the pin on it works normal.

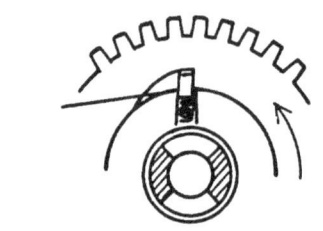

D) The plunger cam guide pin should be well fitted into the guide groove in the pump case cover.

E) Be careful not to tighten the adjust plate locknut excessively. Stop tightening as soon as the wave of the lock washer will be made flat.

F) After oiling the distributor and the plunger, apply the Yamaha Bond #3 to the packing between the pump cases.
   Tighten 4 bolts evenly.

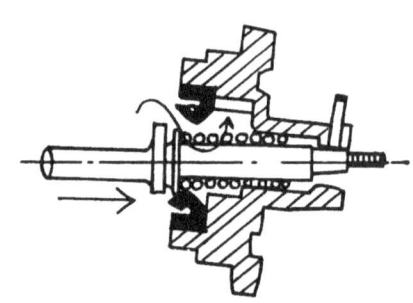

G) Check, by turning the starter plate, whether the plunger stroke is correct. The correct stroke is $0.24^{+0.02}_{0}$ ($0.18^{+0.02}_{0}$).

H) Clean and then attach the delivery pipe, banjo bolt, banjo gasket, check-ball and spring.

(3) When mounting the pump on the engine

A) Apply grease to the worm shaft oil seal.
B) Be careful not to scratch the teeth of the drive gear.
C) Apply Yamaha Bond #2 or Three-Bond to the pump case and gasket and then tighten 3 bolts evenly.
D) After connecting the pump wire and the oil pipe, let air out of the pump by removing the breather bolt.
E) Adjust the plunger stroke (See-2-6-1 "PUMP SETTING")

(4) After mounting, check the pump for oil leak.

## 2-6-4 CHECK POINTS AFTER MOUNTING

After mounting the pump on the engine, start the engine and check as follows:

(1) Check whether the starter plate rotates slowly and smoothly.
(2) Check, by turning the accelerator grip, whether the adjust plate moves back and forth.
(3) Check whether the oil tank is filled with Auto Lube oil.
   If the oil is below the level gauge, replenish with 1 liter oil. (0.2 gal)

## 2-7 OIL FOR YAMAHA AUTOLUBE

The lubricating oil must have the properties as:
1 Strong oil film (excellent oiliness);
2 Less remained carbon;
3 Excellent purification.

The oil used in the mixture for the conventional 2-cycle engines must have another property that is the solubility in gasoline.
It is for this purpose that it has lower viscosity, which affects the oiliness badly. Since such a property is not necessary for the Auto-Lube, it can use the oil selected on the basis of oiliness.

The oil for Auto Lube, however, must have another property, too:

4 Excellent fluidity in the lowest temperature,

because it uses oil separately from gasoline. To meet the above requirements, Yamaha has examined various brands oil in the market and found "SHELL 2T,, is one of the most suitable oil for Yamaha autolube.

NOTE: It is advisable to use motor oil of best brand in your market if "SHELL 2T" is not available.

# CHAPTER 3   ENGINE

## 3-1   GENERAL DESCRIPTION

The YA6 engine is the rotary valve engine that has won the high reputation as the best of the 2-cycle engines.   Since the Auto Lube has been newly applied to it, it has been greatly improved in performance and reliability.   In addition, every part of the engine has been improved to get more performance and relibility.

## 3-2   DISASSEMBLING AND ASSEMBLING THE ENGINE

### 3-2-1   DISASSEMBLING

A   REMOVING THE ENGINE
(1) Removing the parts from the right side of the frame
1a) Remove the ring nut connecting the exhaust pipe with the cylinder by means of the ring nut turning tool.
1b) Remove the foot rest fitting nut and then the foot rest.
1c) Remove the carburetor cover, carburetor and pump wire. Prevent oil and gasoline from flowing out of the fuel pipe and oil pipe respectively.
(2) Removing the parts from the left side of the frame
2a) Remove the shift pedal and then the left crankcase cover.
2b) Disconnect the wire harness for starter dynamo.
Be sure to do the neutral switch wire.   It is advisable to remove the dynamo and the armature this time.
Use the armature puller.
2c) Remove the chain case and then the chain.   To make it easier to remove the transmission gear on, remove the driving sprocket.
(3) Removing engine fitting parts.
3a) Remove the air cleaner cover and then air cleaner.
3b) Remove the engine fitting bolts (2 bolts) from the near section of the engine and a bolt from the mount stay in the central section while holding the engine.

And the engine is removed from the frame.   Be sure to drain the gear oil before removing the engine.

### B REMOVING THE PARTS FROM THE RIGHT SIDE OF THE ENGINE

(1) Remove the crank arm and the right crankcace cover.

(2) Remove the oil pump and the banjo bolt from the delivery pipe. (or remove pump as a unit before removing the crank case cover.)

(3) Remove clutch assembly and the primary pinion with the clutch holder and the primary pinion puller.

ILLUS 13

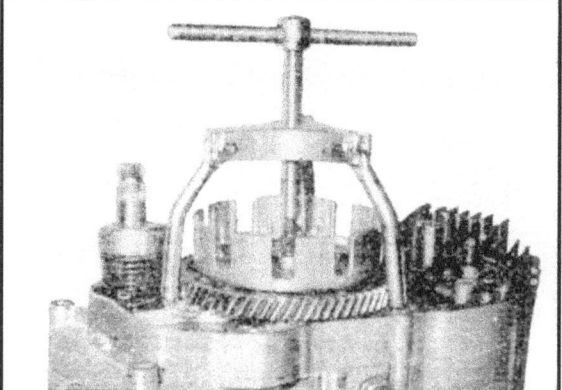
ILLUS 14

(4) Remove the valve unit collar, rotary valve knock pin.

(5) Remove the shift lever, and the shifter rachet wheel. (See p. 27)

NOTE: The engine is disassembed with the kick cranking device left in place. (See P. 28)

### C REMOVE THE CYLINDER HEAD AND THEN CYLINDER PISTON

### D DIVING THE CRANKCASE

(1) Remove the crankcase tightening bolts from the left side of the crankcase.

Be sure to loosen them alternatively in the crank section and the transmission section.

(2) Divide the crank-case by using the crank case disassembling tool as shown in Illus. 15. Be sure to divide the crank section and the transmission section even with a hammer.

ILLUS 15

E  REMOVING THE PARTS FROM THE LEFT CRANKCASE

(1) Remove the transmision assembly (main axle and drive axle) and the shifter assembly at the same time. See p. 30

(2) Remove the crank from the case by using the crankcase disassembling tool.

F  REMOVE THE KICK-CRANKING DEVICE FROM THE RIGHT CASE.

ILLUS 16

## 3-2-2  ASSEMBLING

Assmble the engine in the reverse order of disassembling.

(1) NOTES ON ASSMBLING

1a) Clean all the parts and check for wear.

1b) Check especially joint surfaces of the crankcase and the lip of each oil for wear or scratch with a special care.

1c) Apply grease to the lip of each oil seal; replace the O-ring, packings, gaskets etc.; and apply Yamaha Bond #5 to the joint surfaces of the crankcase and the O-rings and Yamaha Bond #5 to the joint surfaces of the crankcase and the O-ring and Yamaha Bond #2 to the packing.

(2) ASSEMBLING THE ENGINE

2a) Install the crank by using the crank fitting tool as shown in Illus. 17.

2b) Install the transmission assembly and the shifter assembly at the same time.

2c) Install the kick-cranking device.

2d) Joint the crankcases together.  Apply Yamaha Bond #5 to the joint surfaces.
After jointing, make sure the transmission, shifter and crank function normally.  Tighten the crankcace tightening bolts evenly and fully.

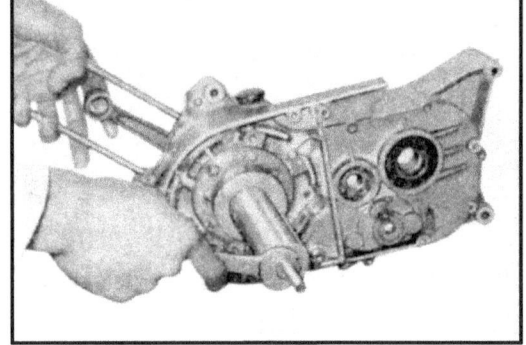

ILLUS 17

2e) Install the parts related to the valve, transmission, shifter and clutch on the outside of the right crankcase.

2f) Put the right crankcace cover on and install the pump.

2g) Install the piston, cylinder and cylinder head.

2h) Install the dynamo and adjust the ignition timing.

(3) MOUNTING THE ENGINE

Mount the engine on the body in the reverse order of removing. Before starting the engine, check and or adjust the following points:

3a) Adjust the plunger stroke of the oil pump.   (See p. 15)
3b) Let air out of the pump.   (See p. 15)
3c) Adjust the clutch.   (See p. 49)
3d) Apply gear oil to the transmission and the clutch.
   (See p. 32)
3e) Adjust the drive chain.

And then make a test run of the engine.

## 3-3   INSPECTION AND REPAIR OF THE PARTS OF ENGINE.

### 3-3-1   CYLINDER, PISTON AND PISTON HEAD

The cylinder and its head have been improved in the cooling fin for more cooling capacity. On the other hand, the piston has been improved in the skirt (lower section) for less deformation due to the heat expansion.

### CYLINDER

The third scavenging port that performs the important function in the rotary valve engine is the same not on YA5 but on YG and Moped. The mixture gas enters the combustion chamber through this port directly from the crankcase.

### PISTON

Since the cyinder has been improved as described above, the piston has no scavenging port. The piston skirt has been reinforced a rib for less deformation due to the heat expansion.

A   INSPECTING AND REPAIRING

(1) INSPECTING AND REPAIRING THE CYLINDER

Check the cylinder for wear by measuring its inner diameter with an inside micrometer or a cylinder gauge at the measuring points as shown in Illus. 18.

1a) If there is a difference of more than 0.05mm between the muximum and the minimum diameters, hone the cylinder.

1b) If there is a relatively big difference, rebore, and hone the cylinder.

1c) The finished size should be equal to the piston size (oversize) plus the clearace of 0.30 to 0.040mm (Ⓐ 0.042 to 0.047mm)

1d) The allowable error in the finished diameter should be within 0.01mm at each measuring point.

1e) Be sure to round the corner of each port as shown in Illus. 19.

CAUTION: The orignal factory size of the cylinder bore should not be changed more than 0.5mm.

(2) The correct clearance between the piston and the cylinder wall is 0.03 to 0.04mm (A 0.42 to 0.047mm).

2a) To get a correct par of the cylinder and the piston, measure the inner diameter of the piston at the measuring point D in Illus. 18 and the diameter of the piston 10mm up from the bottom of the skirt.

NOTE: The size of the cylinder is marked on the skirt and the size of the piston is on the head.

2b) The pistons for replacement are:

Standard size ......... 97, 98 and 99

Oversize ......... 56.00, 56.25 and 56.50

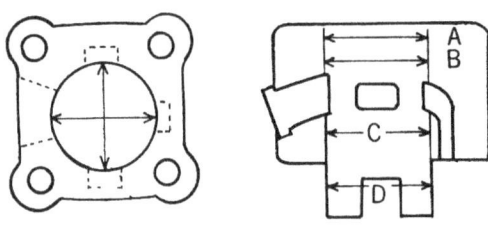

ILLUS 18

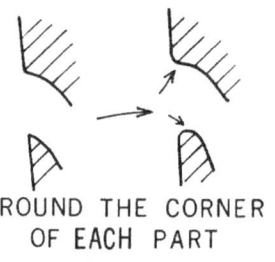

ROUND THE CORNER OF EACH PART
ILLUS 19

(3) The correct piston ring clearance.

0.15 to 0.30mm for the first ring*

0.10 to 0.20mm for the second ring.**

3a) To measure the clearance, fit the ring into the skirt of the cylinder horizontally and use a thickness gauge.

3b) The piston rings for replacement are:

Standerd size

Oversize ......... 0.25 and 0.50

*First ring ......... chrome-plated

**second ring ......... parkerized

B INSTALLING

(1) Install the second ring and then the first ring around the piston. Place the face marked with TP up.

(2) Fit the piston into the connecting rod with the arrow mark toward the front, and fit the pin and clip into the piston firmly.

(3) Make the knock pin and the ring clearance meet and install the cylinder.

## 3-3-2 CRANK ASSEMBLY

The crank and crank shaft function as a unit. The connecting rod is held between the right and left cranks connected together by means of the crank pin. At the connecting rod small end, a needle roller is used in place of a bush for longer life.

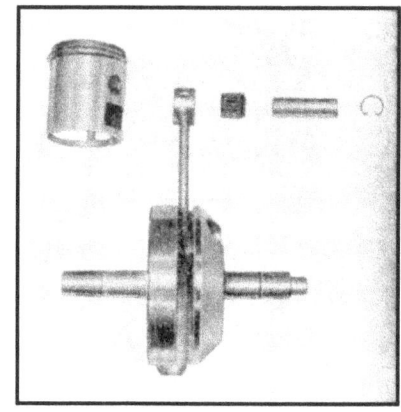

ILLUS 20

A INSPECTING AND REPAIRING

(1) Connecting rod

1a) Check to see there is a proper play between the piston pin and the needle roller at the connecting rod small end.
If there is too much play, replace the needle roller and the piston pin.

1b) Check the connecting rod big end for wear by trying to sway the small end at the upper dead point.
If it moves more than 3mm, replace the connecting rod, roller and crank pin. After replacement, there should be a sway of 0.8 to 1.0mm.

1c) The proper axial play of the connecting rod big end is 0.1 to 0.2mm.

(2) Crank assembly

2a) Check the crank pin for wear. If the wear is more than 0.05mm or there is any cranck in the running surface of the roller, replace the crank pin and the roller.

Standard diameter: $24 \phi \begin{array}{c} +0.04 \\ -0.05 \end{array}$

2b) Measure the crank assembly with a dial gauge:

| Measuring Point | Reading. mm |
|---|---|
| 1 * | 0.0 3 |
| 2 | 0.0 2 |
| 3 & 4 | 0.0 6 |
| 5 | within 0.0 2 |

* The figure is for the circled number in Illus. 22.

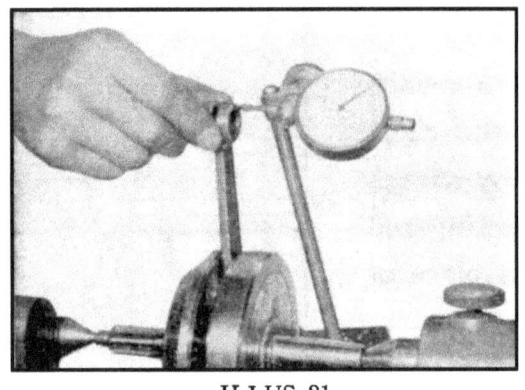
ILLUS 21

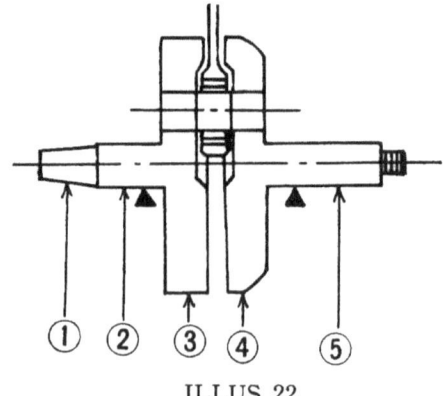
ILLUS 22

## CRANK ASSEMBLY SPECIFICATIONS

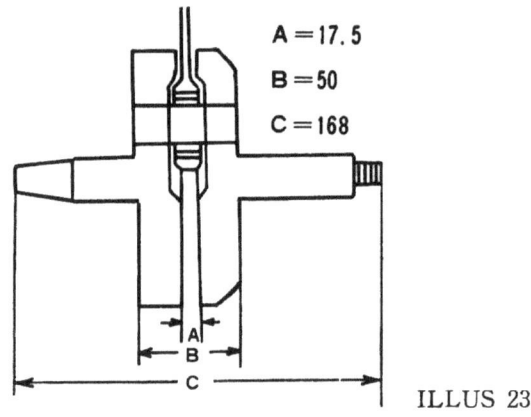

A = 17.5
B = 50
C = 168

ILLUS 23

### B  INSTALLING

After cleaning, install the crank as follows:

(1) Attach one bearing cover around each of the right and left crank shafts to make a proper clearance of 0.15 to 0.2mm between the crank and the crank case.

> NOTE: Usually the bearing cover is not replaced.   If the new one is necessary when the crank or the crankcase is replaced or reassembled its thickness should be determined by the expression:
>
> $$\text{Thickness of valve cover} = \frac{\text{Inner width of crankcase} - \text{width of crank assembly}}{2}$$
> $$- \text{Clearance } (0.15 \text{ to } 0.2\text{mm})$$

(2) Install the crank to the left crankcase by using the crank fitting tool as shown in Illus. 17.

(3) After installing, make sure the crank turns smoothly.

### 3-3-3  ROTARY VALVE AND VALVE COVER

The YA6 possesses a floating type rotary valve like YG and Moped.
On the YA5, both valve and valve cover were built into the crank case. On the YA6, however, these are on the outside of the crankcase for more performance and easier inspection.

### ROTARY VALVE

The rotary valve is made of asbestos cloth coated with phenolic resins to get freed from any troubles caused by heat and wear.   It is rotated by means of the valve knock pin and the valve unit collar.

A INSPECTING

Place the valve on a flat plate and check it for bend, on distortion, crack or wear.    If there is any trouble in it, replace.

Thickness of valve : 4mm $^{+0}_{-0.05}$    ; Repair limit : 0.4mm

CAUTION: Don't place the valve on a metal plate or in wet place, or it will be bent or distorted.    After washing in gasoline, be sure to apply oil to it.

## VALVE COVER

Under the valve cover there is the inlet pipe connected directly with the carburetor.    The delivery nozzle of the Auto Lube also is located here.

A INSPECTING AND INSTALLING

(1) Insert the crank shaft O-ring between the valve unit collar and the crank shaft.

NOTE: Replace the O-ring whenever the valve unit will be disassembled.

(2) Check the valve cover O-ring for wear and defect. If it is faulty, replace.

(3) To keep air tight, apply Yamaha Bond #5 to the O-ring before inserting.

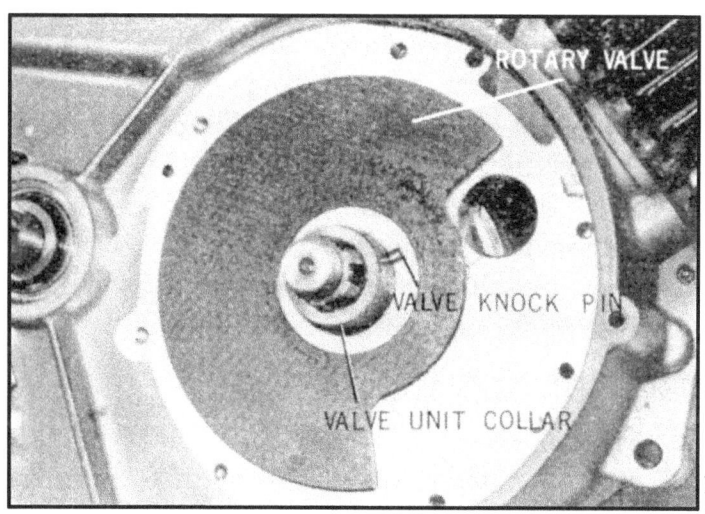

ILLUS 24

## 3-3-4    PRIMARY REDUCTION AND CLUTCH

The primary reduction has been improved in ratio and driving system from the chain to the gear.    Larger primary reduction ratio assures the perfect distribution of the gear ratio and the secondary reduction ratio.    The clutch has been improved as described below:

## CLUTCH ASSEMBLY

The clutch is of a multiple disk type and consists of the 4 friction plates and the 5 clutch plates.    The clutch and the primary gear are installed as a unit to the main shaft through the clutch boss.    The clutch mechanism for engaging and disengaging is of a inner push type.

The improvements of the clutch:

(1) The clutch housing has been enlarged for more performance;

(2) The clutch housing and boss have been reduced in weight;

(3) Two 6003 bearings have been used to the section where the primary gear and the main shaft are joined longer life and prevention of noise.

NOTE: To remove or install the clutch, use the clutch holder and the reduction gear puller.

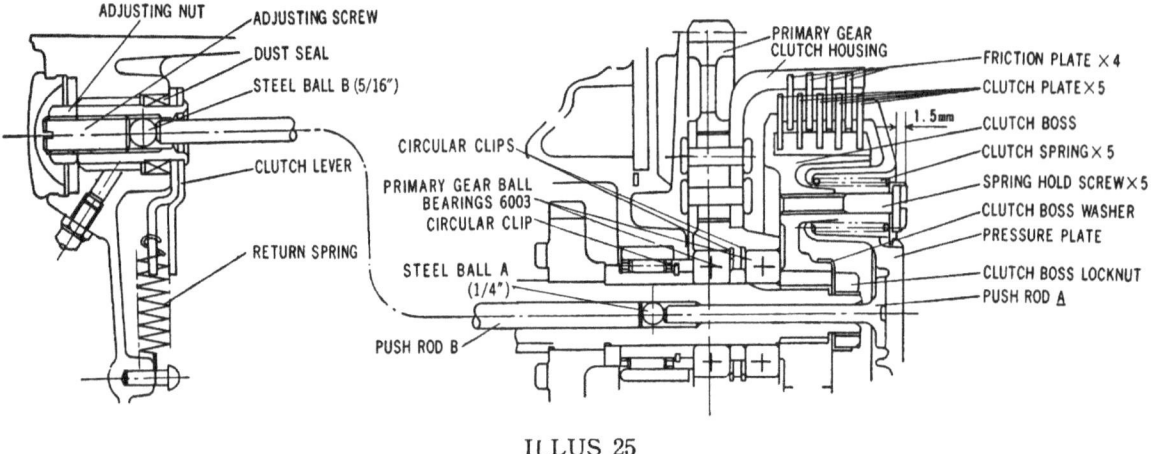

ILLUS 25

A ASSEMBLING

(1) Hammer the housing assembly into the main shaft by using a guide sleeve.
(2) When securing the clutch boss, be sure to bend a part of the clutch boss locknut washer and tighten the locknut.
(3) Install the clutch plates and then the friction plates.
(4) After inserting the push rod, cover it with the pressure plate.
(5) Insert the 5 clutch springs and then tighten the spring hold screws with washers as shown in Illus. 25.

B INSPECTING AND REPAIRING

(1) The correct thickness of the friction plate is 4.0mm.
   If it is reduced in thickness more than 0.3mm, replace.

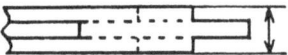

(2) The correct free length of the clutch spring is 31.5mm.
   If it is reduced in length more than 3mm, replace.

(3) The correct clearance between the clutch housing and the friction plate is 0.1mm. If clearance is more than 0.3mm, replace.

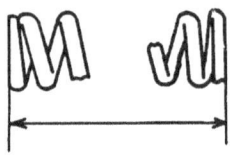

## 3-3-5 TRANSMISSION, SHIETER AND KICK CRANK

The YA6 is equipped with a 4-speed constant mesh see-saw transmission. The shitfer and kick-cranking device also have been greatly improved as described below.

### TRANSMISSION

Since the primary reduction has been improved in driving system from the chain to the gear as described above, the drive sprocket of the transmission has been attached around the drive axle.

The clutch side of the main shaft is in the needle roller bearing.

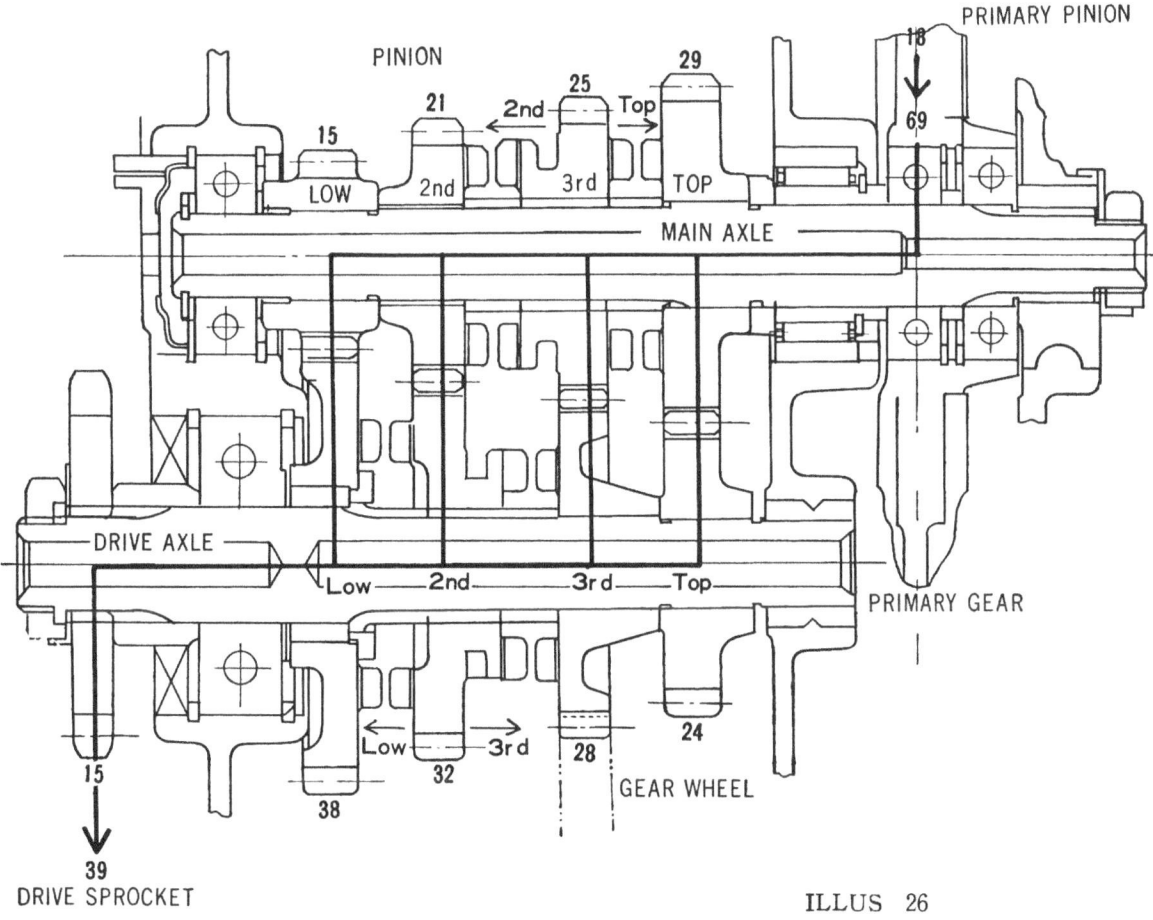

ILLUS 26

| Gear | Total Reduction Ratio * |
|---|---|
| Low | 3.833 × 2.533 × 2.600 - 25.243 |
| Second | 3.833 × 1.524 × 2.600 - 15.188 |
| Third | 3.833 × 1.120 × 2.600 - 11.162 |
| Top | 3.833 × 0.828 × 2.600 -  8.252 |

\* Primary reduction × Gear × Secondary reduction

## KICK - CRANKING DEVICE

(1) The kick gear is always mesh with the third gear.
(2) As soon as the kick shaft is turned, the kick ratchet wheel comes out of the wheel guide and engages with the kick gear under the pressure of the ratchet wheel spring.
(3) The kick gear drives the third gear and the power is tranmsitted as follows:
Thrid gear → Third pinion → Main axle → Clutch → Primary gear → Primary pinion → Crank.

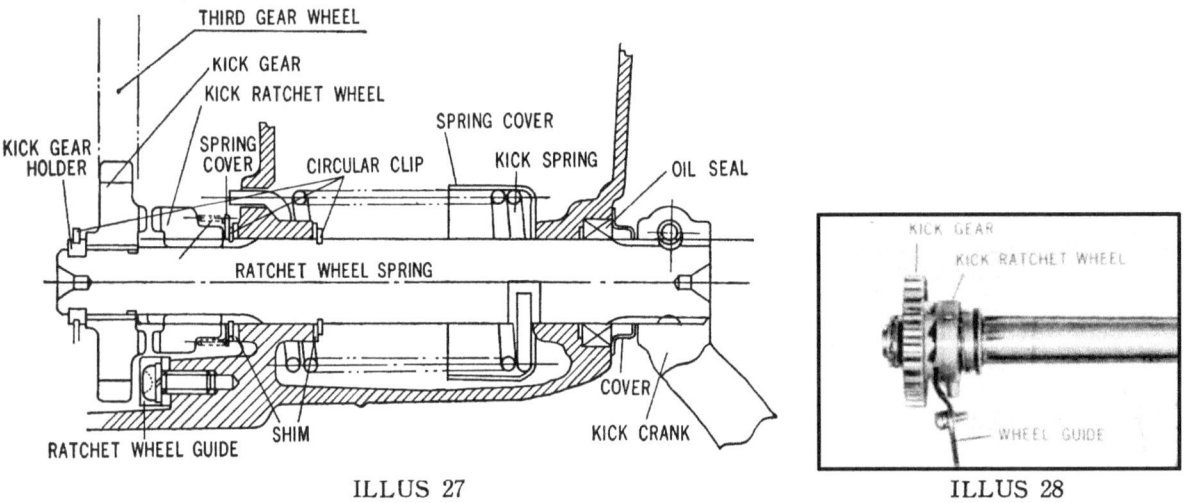

ILLUS 27          ILLUS 28

A  DISASSEMBLING
(1) Remove the spring cover and pull out the kick spring.
(2) Remove the circular clip from the starter axle and the starter axle can be removed.
(3) Remove the circular clip from the kick gear and the kick gear can be removed.
(4) Remove the circular clip from the kick ratchet wheel and the kick rachet wheel can be removed.
NOTE: The crankcase is disassembled with the kick-cranking device left in place.

B  ASSEMBLING
The kick-crank device is installed in the right crankcase.

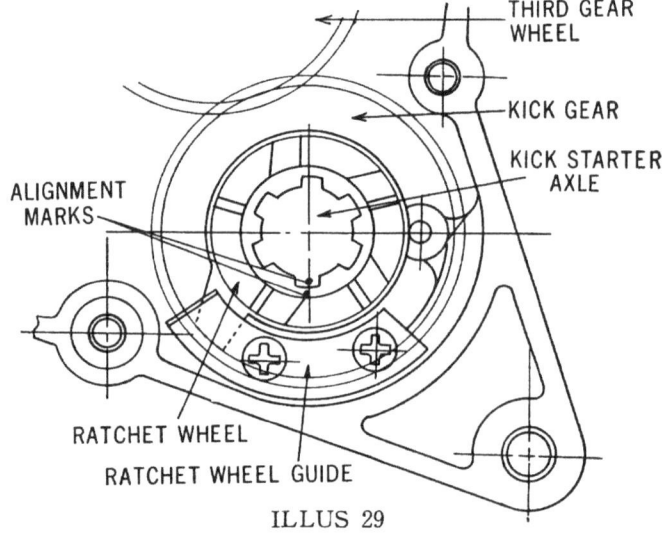

(1) To fit the ratchet wheel around the starter axle, make two marks meet as shown in Illus. 29.
(2) Fix one end of the kick spring in the crankcase; turn it 140°, and fix another end

ILLUS 29

in the axle.

NOTE: When jointing the right and left crankcases together, interlock the kick gear with the third gear.

## SHIFTER

The YA6 see-saw shifter is the same as on YA5 except the shifter cam driving mechanism.

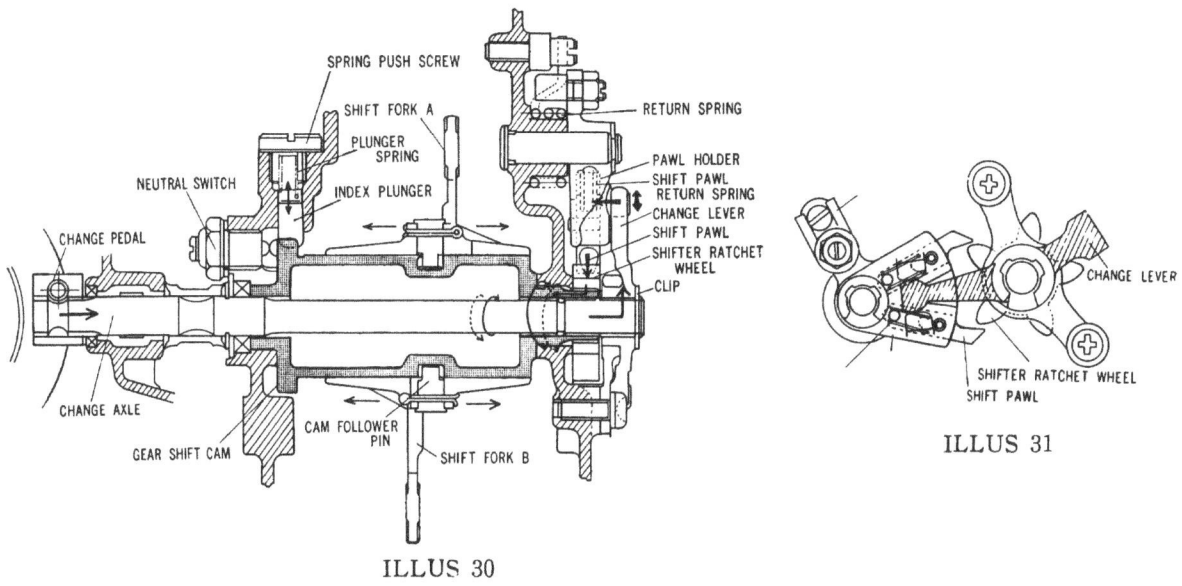

ILLUS 30

ILLUS 31

A   MECHANISM

The shifter mechanism consists of the gear shifter cam and the cam driving device.

(1) SHIFTER CAM DRIVING DEVICE

When the change pedal is stepped on, the change axle and the change lever function as a unit to transmit the power to the pawl holder, whose pawl pushes one of the teeth of the shifter ratchet wheel to rotate the gear shift cam.

(2) SHIFTER CAM

The shifter cam is for the purpose to drive the sliding gears (third pinion and second gear wheel) to shift gears.

2a) The rotary motion of the gear shift cam is changed to the axle motion of the shift fork through the cam follow pin.

2b) The gear shift cam is given $1/5$ (72°) turning by the shifter ratchet wheel and the rotary motion of the cam is stopped exactly in the predetermined position by the index plunger (stopped pin).

## B DISASSEMBLING AND ASSEMBLING THE TRANSMISSION AND THE SHIFTER

(1) DISASSEMBLING

Remove the transmission and the shifter at the same time.

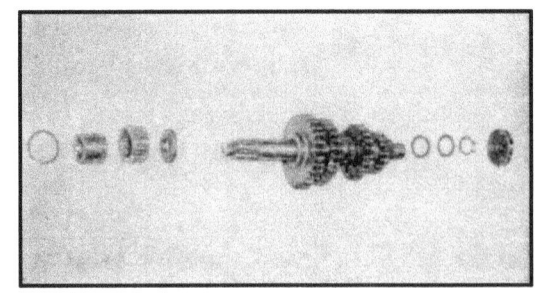

ILLUS 32

1a) Remove the main axle bearing cover and then the main axle circular clip on the outside of the left cra nkcase.

1b) Remove the drive sprocket from the drive axle.

1c) Remove the spring push screw from the bottom of the left crankcase, and then pull out the spring and the index plunger (stopper pin).

1d) Remove the drive axle together with the shifter and the main axle by tapping the drive axle with a soft hammer.

(2) ASSEMBLING

Install the main axle, drive axle and shifter assembly at the same time.

2a) Place the gear shift cam in neutral position and install the main axle, drive axle and shift fork into the left crankcase at the same time. Be sure to use the washer.

2b) After installing, attach the washer and clip around the main axle (left side) and put the rubber cap on.

2c) Install the stopper pin (index plunger and spring).

2d) Join the right and left crankcases together after interlocking with the kick gear; install the shifter cam driving device; and try to shift gears.

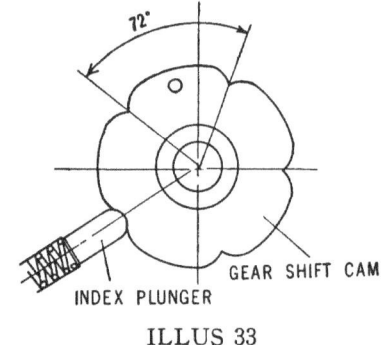

ILLUS 33

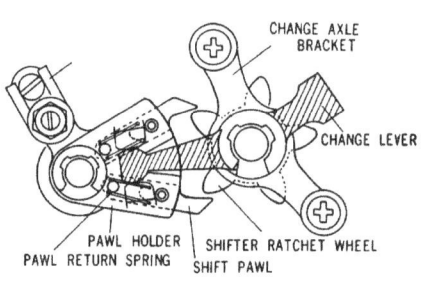

ILLUS 34

### 3-3-6 CRANKCASE

The crankcase is of die-cast aluminium alloy.    The right and left crankcase are joined together by Yamaha Bond #5 and 14 bolts.

A   ASSEMBLING

See p. 20.

NOTES :   1) Be sure to apply gear oil to the bearings and grease to the lip of each oil seal before assembling.
2) When replacing the bearing, heat the crankcase up to about 100°C and fit the bearing into it under pressure or hammer the bearing into it evenly by using a guide metal.

B   BEARING AND OIL SEALS OF CRANK AND TRANSMISSION

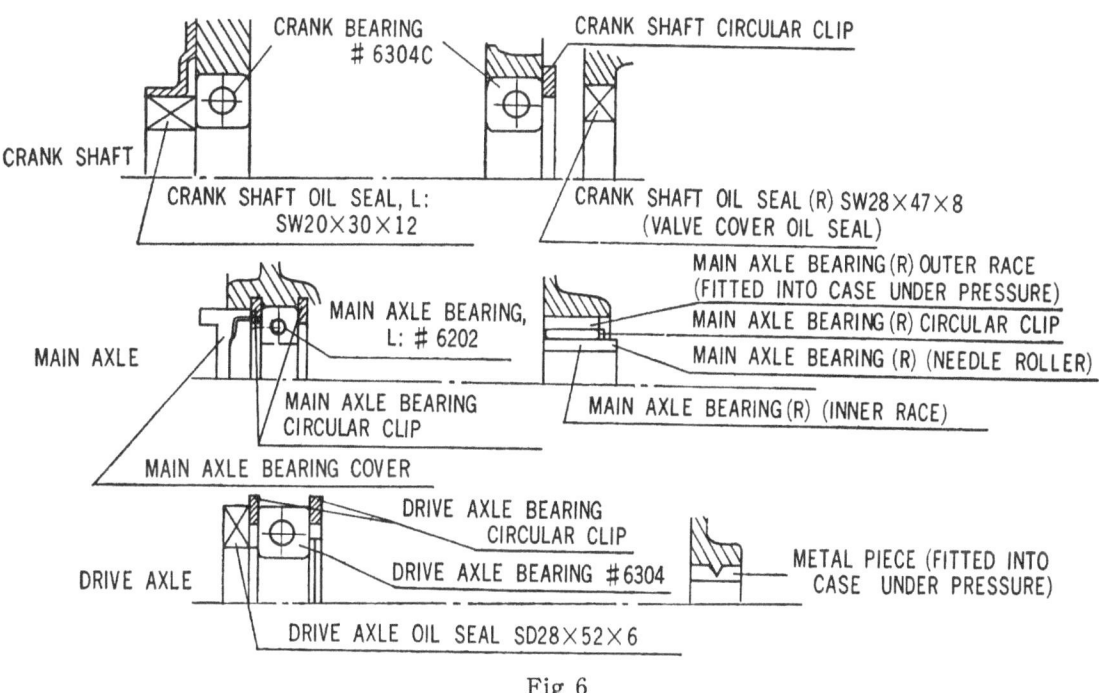

Fig 6

C   APPLYING GEAR OIL

Be sure to apply the specified amount of oil to the transmission and the clutch through the correct oil hole, because the proper oil level in the gear box is different from that in the clutch housing.
Use the level gauge as shown in ILLUS. 35.

Remove the left air cleaner cover and then the inlet plug from the left crankcase.    Pour oil through this hole as specified below.

Oil :   Yamaha Gear oil B ; Amount of oil : 1,300c.c. (1.3 liters)

## D DRAINING GEAR OIL

To drain gear oil, remove two drain plugs from the bottom of the crankcase cover.

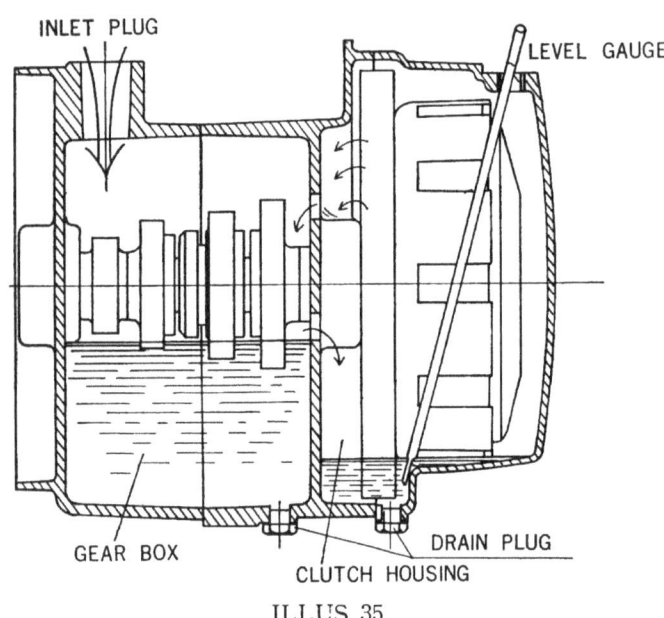

ILLUS 35

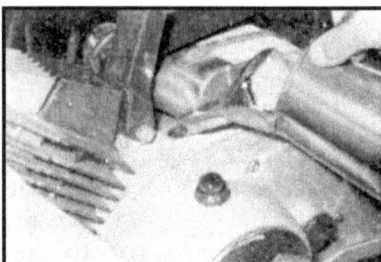

ILLUS 36

ILLUS 37

### 3-3-7  AIR CLEANER AND CARBURETOR

The air cleaner is located under the cleaner cover on the engine, but not attached directly to the carburetor.  The carbretor is connected with the inlet pipe under the valve cover between the right crankcase and the carburetor cover.

### AIR CLEANER

The air cleaner is of a large-sized paper filter type.   As shown in ILLUS. 38, it is located on the crankcase.   Air flows from the frame inlet port to into the cleaner through the air-tight frame.

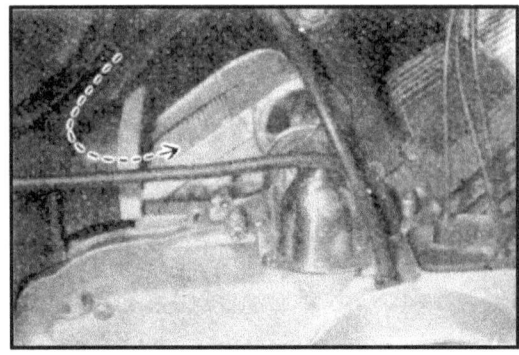

ILLUS 38

A  REMOVING AND INSTALLING

(1) To remove the air cleaner, remove 3 bolt from the carburetor cover.
(2) When installing, be sure to join the air cleaner and the air joint of the air duct together firmly by means of a clip.
(3) First, partly tighten the bolts A, B and then C.
Next. fully tighten the bolts A, B and C.

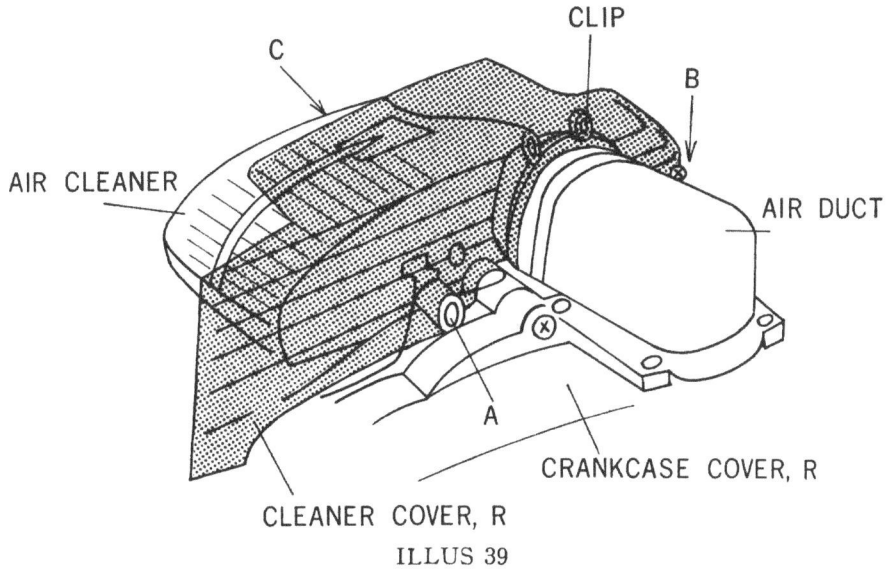

ILLUS 39

B  CLEANING

Blow air from the inside of the cleaner and remove dust by tapping carefully with fingers.

## CARBURETOR

When the starter lever on the handlebar is used, the starter plunger of the carburetor moves up to make richer mixture gas for easier starting of the engine in cold weather.

| CARBURETOR SETTING GUIDE - MODEL VM22SC | |
|---|---|
| Main jet | #190 |
| Air jet | 2.0 |
| Needle jet | 0-0 |
| Jet needle | 22M3 - 2 - way |
| Throttle valve cutaway | 2.5 |
| Pilot jet | #30 |
| Air screw loosening | 1 ¾ - ¼ turns |

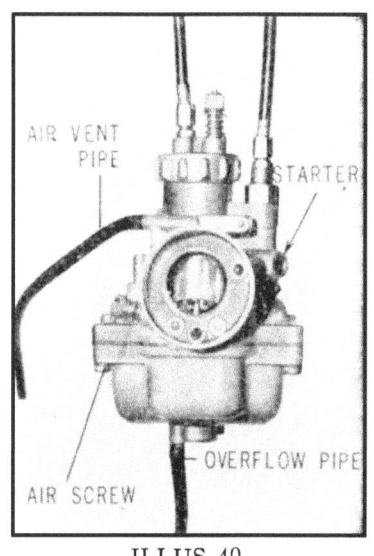

ILLUS 40

CAUTION : Be sure to put one end of the air vent pipe out of the carburetor. The pipe is for the purpose to always keep the oil level fixed regardless of the fluctuations of pressure in the craburetor.

A  INSTALLING

Since the carburetor is filled with clean air that passed through the air cleaner, it should be kept airtight. The pipes, grommets and gaskets related to the carburetor should be sealed with a special care.

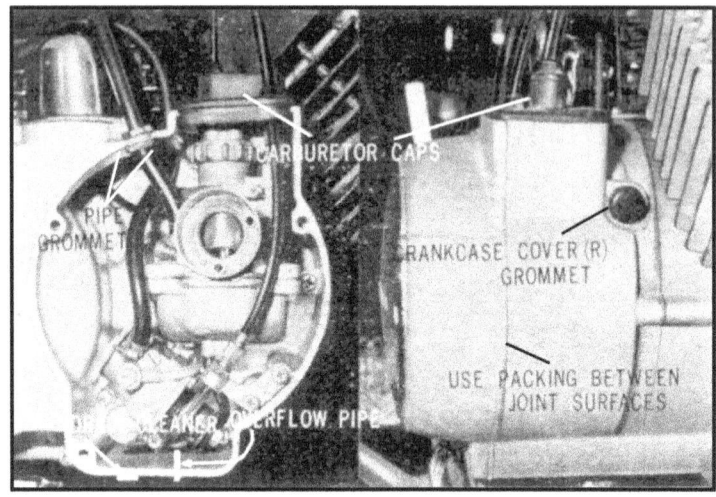

ILLUS 41

When installing the carburetor, check the following points:

(1) Put one end of the air vent pipe and the overflow pipe out of the carburetor.
(2) Seal the grommets of the gasoline pipe, oil pipe and case cover.
(3) Seal the screwdriver hole for installing the carburetor.
(4) Seal the carburetor cap.
(5) And then install the carburetor. cover.

NOTE : Wash the drain cleaner in gasoline from time to time.
After washing apply gear oil to it.

# CHAPTER 4    FRAME

The frame is of a dressed steel monocoque construction, lightweight yet strong.   It has been greatly improved, on the basis of the new Yamaha Auto Lube engine:

## 4-1    YA6 FRAME FEATURES

(1) New engine support for shorter wheelbase, smarter styling and more cooling effect.
(2) New oil tank for easier filling.
(3) Foam rubber seat and improved riding position for more driving comfort.
(4) Improved speedometer for easier reading.
(5) Plastic lamp frames and left side cover.
(6) Front and rear fenders with a flap to prevent mud from splashing about.
(7) The battery, regulator, service tools etc.    are all placed under the left side cover easier inspection.

## 4-2    INSPECTING AND REPAIRING THE PARTS

### 4-2-1    FRAME

A  INSPECTING

(1) Frame
The frame of the motorcycle that has a collision record should be inspected for any crack from the head pipe to the rear fender at regular intervals.    If a crack, is found replace, weld or repair properly.

(2) Head pipe
The head pipe, distorted or eccentric, affects the steering and balance during the operation.    If distorted remarkably, replace.

(3) Steel balls and races
Inspect the steel balls and rsces for wear and crack especially on the long used motorcycle to keep the steering always in the best conditions.    Even if one of them is defective, replace all.

Removing; Insert rod into the head pipe from the inside and tap around it.

Assembling: Never attempt to use the new balls together with the used balls with the new races. Even if one of them is defective, replace all. Before assembling, clean the races carefully and appllly grease to them. Even a particle of dust or sand will damage them.

| Part Name | Instructions | Description |
|---|---|---|
| Ball race A | Drive into frame head pipe. | Same as on YA 5 |
| Ball race B | Into handle crown under bracket section. | Same as on YA 5 |
| Balls, 6.35 φ | 19 balls each for races A and B | Same as on YA 5 |

## 4-2-2　STEERING HANDLES AND WIRES

The handlebars are made of pipe. There are the throttle grip and the front brake lever on the rignt side of the handlebars and the clutch lever and the starter lever on the left side. The wires except the throttle wire are distributed on the outside of the pipe. It is possible to grease up the front brake wire and clutch wire. The wire harnesses of the right and left handle holders are distributed through the pipe.

To install the handlebars, use a damper rubber and tighten 4 bolts. The position of the handlebars is freely adjustable.

INSPECTING AND REPAIRING

(1) If the insulator of the throttle wire, clutch wire, brake wire or starter is worn out or defective, repair with tape or replace.

(2) If the bent or broken outer wire of the above wires causes its inner one to work improperly, replace the wire assembly.

(3) Apply the sufficient amount of oil to the inner wires for smooth action.

(4) When instaling, apply grease to the accelerator shoe and grip metal part.

## 4-2-3　FRONT FORK

The telescopic front fork consists of the coil spring and the oil damper. Same as one YA 5.

The lower section of the steering shaft is connected with the inner tube by means of the under bracket and with the head pipe of the frame through the ball race.   The top of the shaft is connected with the handle crown through the ball race.   The handle crown is held by the inner tubes both sides.

A  DISASSEMBLING

When disassembling, the front fork should be held straight to prevent oil from flowing out of the inner tube:

(1) Remove the front wheel, front fender, headlamp and steering handle assembly.

(2) Remove the handle crown and then the locknut.   And remove the front fork as a unit.   Be careful not to damage the ball races and fork covers.
To remove either of the inner tubes, remove the ornamental bolt from the handle crown, loosen the bolt holding the under bracket, and use the fork attaching and detaching tool.

(3) Hold the axle fitting section of the tube with a vise and loosen the outer tube nut.   And the inner tube will be removed.

B  ASSEMBLING

After cleaning, every parts assemble the front fork:

(1) When inserting the oil seal, be careful not to damage its lip.

(2) The damping oil should be used as specified below:

| Oil | Kayaba #4 or mixture of motor oil #30 and spindle oil #60 in the ratio of 8:1 |
|---|---|
| Amount of oil | 165 to 175 C C each |

1. Outer tube
2. Slide metal
3. Outer tube nut
4. Rolling packing
5. Oil seal
6. Plate
7. Inner tube
8. Dust seal
9. Spring seat
10. Spring
11 Spring guide
12. Forkcover, lower
13. Cover guide
14. Packing
15. Cover guide
16. Fork cover, upper
17. Packing
18. Washer
19. Ornamental bolt
20. Under bracket assembly
21. Ball race A

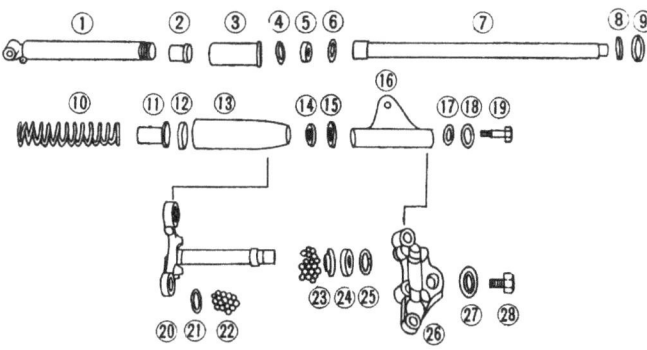

ILLUS 42

22. Balls
23. Ball race B
24. Bearing cover
25. Steering nut
26. Upper bracket
27. Washer
28. Steering bolt

C INSPECTING AND CHANGE OF OIL
(1) Inspect the outer tube nut and the drain plug for oil leaking. Oil leaking causes the front fork to work improperly and make a noise.
(2) Change the damping oil every 6,000km. 4,000mile   To remove the oil, remove the ornamental bolt of the handle crown.

## 4-2-4 REAR CUSHION UNIT

The rear cushion unit consists of the suspension spring and the shock absorber and is attached to the frame through the upper and lower rubber bushes that absorbs the sligtest vibration from the ground which the shock absorber cannot do.  The cushion rubber acts as a sub-spring when a big shock is given.

The shock absorber consists of the cylinder, piston, valve mechanism, piston rod, oil seal etc.

DISSEMBLING AND ASSEMBLING

The rear cushion is a non-disassembled unit.  However, if the inspection of the spring, cushion rubber etc. is necessary, do as follows:
(1) Remove the roll pin.
(2) Hold the under cover with a special care and remove the bracket by turning counterclock wise.
(3) Hold the end of the piston rod and turn the lower cover counter clock-wise.   And the spring cushion rubber etc.   will be removed.

CAUTION: Never attempt to disassemble the shock absorber including the piston rod and tube.   Once disassembled, it will never be reassembled.

(4) Assemble the rear cushion in the reverse order of disassembling.

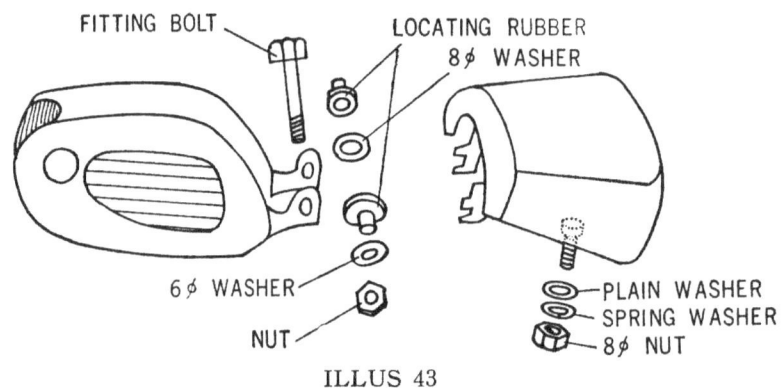

ILLUS 43

## 4-2-5 FUEL TANK AND SADDLE

The way of fitting the fuel tank and the saddle has been improved: the damper rubber is placed between the fuel tank and the frame; and the rear of the tank is bolted to the saddle.

The saddle has been improved in material from spring to foam rubber. It is secured to the frame with a 8φ bold.

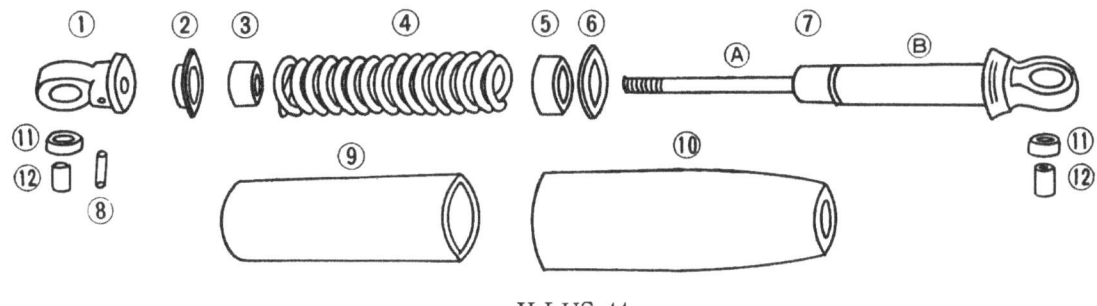

ILLUS 44

1. Under bracket
2. Stopper
3. Cushion rubber
4. Spring
5. Spacer
6. Washer
7. Oil damper:
7A Piston rod
7B Cylinder
8. Roll pin
9. Under cover
10. Upper cover
11. Rubber bush bush, 2×2
12. Bush collar, 2

## 4-2-6  OTHER IMPROVEMENTS

(1) Rear arm:
   1a) The metal bush has been changed to the rubber bush in the bearing of the pivot shaft;
   1b) The chain adjuster has been changed from the push type to the puller type;
   1c) The stop switch has been newly installed.

(2) Center stand
   2a) The center stand and the brake pedal have the same shaft.
   2b) The position of the center stand stopper rubber has been changed from the side stand to the muffler side.

(3) Drive chain:

| Model of Chain | D K 428 |
|---|---|
| Num. of links | 108 |

# CHAPTER 5  ELECTRICAL SYSTEM

The electrical system has been improved on the basis of the previous data collected from the three-years road tests of the former model YA5.

## 5-1 ELECTRICAL PARTS:

| Section | Part Name | Manufacturer | Model & Standard | Description |
|---|---|---|---|---|
| Engine | Starter dynamo | Hitachi | GS113, 14V 90W/1600rpm | Same as on YA5 and YAT1 |
| | Neutral switch | Asahi | YNS 5 | |
| | Spark plug | NGK Hitachi | B-7H; Ⓐ B-7 HZ M44 | |
| Frame | Battery | Furukawa | SPT-12, 12V10AH | Exhaust tube outlet has been reversed. |
| | | Yuasa | MBH3-12, 12V10AH | |
| | | GS | MW3-12, 12V10AH | |
| | Regulator | Hitachi | T107-52 | with built-in starter switch |
| | Ingition coil | Hitachi | C11-13 | Same as on YA5 & YAT |
| | Fuse holder | Taiko | 20A × 3 | Usable to all models |
| | Horn | Nikko | Y12 | |
| Front | Speedometer | Yasaki | BSG | |
| | Main switch | Asahi | YAM 6 | |
| | Head lamp | Koito | S9913 (bulb:35/25W) | |
| | Flasher relay | Toshin | 12T-1, 12V19W | Usable to all models |
| | Handlebar switch, right | Asahi | YG6R | |
| | Flasher lamp, front | Kinsen | FLF-YA6, 12V8W×2 | |
| Tail | Tail lamp, | Koito | S 88802, 12V20/9W | |
| | Flasher lamp, rear | Kinsen | FLR-YA6, 12V8W×2 | |
| Swinging arm | Stop switch | Asahi | YS 13 | |

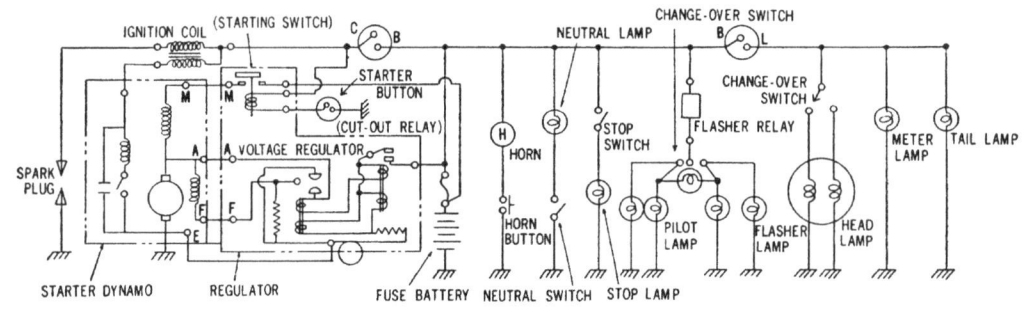

ILLUS 45

## 5-2 STARTER DYNAMO

The starter dynamo is the same as on YA5

### 1) PERFORMANCE OF THE STARTER DYNAMO

1a) At the compression pressure of 8kg/cm², the crank RPM is about 600 and the current is about 30A.

1b) The rated output of 90w is produced at more than 1.600 rpm or at 20km/h with gear in TOP.

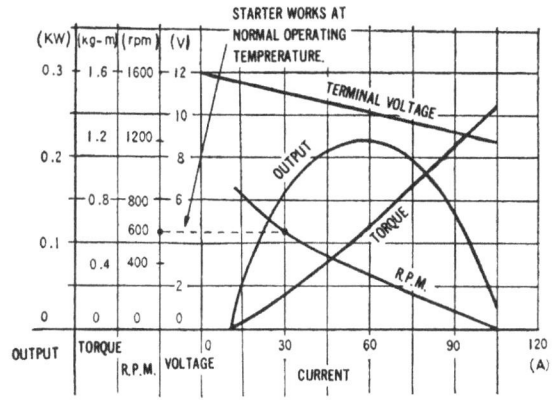
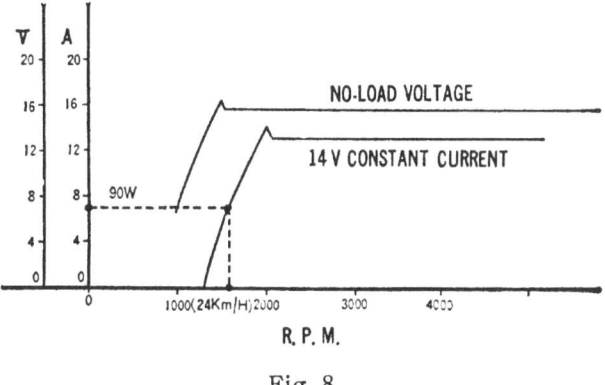

Fig 8

### 2) IGNITION CIRCUIT

The ignition circuit consists of the contact breaker, condenser, ignition coil and spark plug. Interrupting the flow of primary current causes a voltage surge to be generated in the secondary winding of the ignition coil  Each high-voltage surge jumps across the spark plug and ignites the compressed air-fuel mixture.

### ADJUSTING IGNITION TIMING

(1) File the ignition points with sand paper or oil stone and clean with waste.

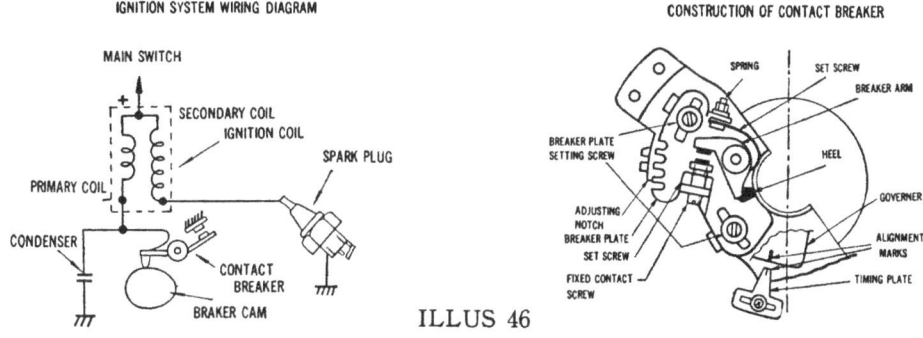

ILLUS 46

(2) Open the point gap fully by turning the cam and adjust it to 0.3 to 0.35mm with a point spanner.

(3) Install a dial gauge* on the cylinder head and then a tester (lamp)** for indicating the open and close of the points.

  * Use a dial gauge holder.
  ** Use Yamaha Electro-tester.

(4) With the governor in open position, move the piston down to 2.5 to 2.6mm before the upper dead point by means of the reading of the dial gauge.*

* Turn the crank in the reverse direction.

(5) Adjust the breaker plate so the contact points are opened and closed at 2.5 to 2.6mm.

NOTE: Without the dial gauge, adjsut so the points open and close when the alignment marks are in a line.

## INSPECTING

Start the engine and check the alignment marks by using a timing light.

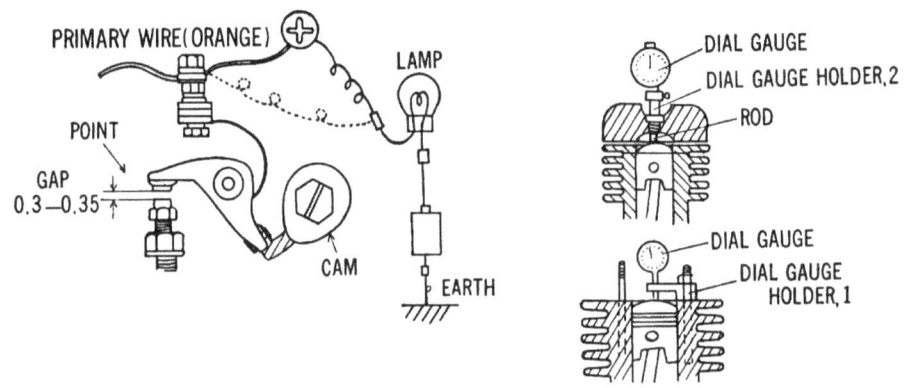

ILLUS 47

## STARTER DYNAMO ADJUSTING GUIDE

| Item | | Standard | Inspection |
|---|---|---|---|
| Field | Num. of pole | 6 | at abnormal voltage |
| | Resistance   shunt w. | 6.8Ω (20°C) | |
| |            series w | 0.0145Ω (20°C) | |
| Brush | Lengtn of Brush | 19.5mm | after 6,000km of driving |
| | Allowable Min. Length | 11.5mm | every 3,000km |
| | Force of Spring | 400 to 500g | |
| | Materials | MH33 | |
| | Num | 4 | |
| Commutator | Dia. of Commutator | 37.5 φ | every 3,000km |
| | Allowable Min Dia | 35.5 φ | |
| | Mica Cut | 0.5 to 0.8mm | |
| | Allowable Mica Cut | 0.2mm | |
| | Difference between Max. & Min Diameters | 0.05mm or less | |
| Breaker | Point gap | 0.3 to 0.35mm | every 3,000km |
| | Point Pressure | 500 to 700g | |
| | Condenser Capacity | 0.22μF ± 10% | |
| | Angle of Advance | 5° at 1200rpm | |
| | 〃 | 24° (2.6mm) at 1600rpm | |
| Others | Air gap | 0.35 | |
| | Armature taper | 20φ × ⅟₁₀ | |

## 5-3  REGULATOR

A cut-out relay and a starter switch have been built into the regulator. The flow of current in the shunt coil of the dynamo is controlled to keep the voltage constant by means of the constant-voltage relay of the regulator.

When the engine is not in motion or runs at **low RPM**, higher voltage in the battery causes reverse current. The cut-out relay prevents it.

The starter switch lets current flow from the battery directly to the starter coil as soon as the self-starter button is pushed.

MEASURING AND ADJUSTING THE VOLTAGE

The no-load voltage is measured by the voltmeter installed in place of the terminal B. However, the measurement of the ignition coil load voltage is easier as described below:

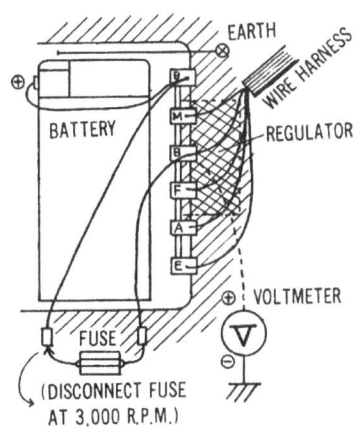

ILLUS 48

(1) MEASURING THE IGNITION COIL LOAD VOLTAGE
   1a) Connect the voltmeter (or Yamaha Electro-tester) as shown in Illus. 48.
   1b) Start the engine and keep the RPM at 3,000 with the engine-speed tester.
   1c) Disconnect the fuse and read the voltmeter. The correct voltage is 15.3 to 16.2v.

NOTE: If the machine is used for night driving only or if it runs little every day, for example, the voltage should be adjusted a little higher: 15.5 to 16.5V.

(2) ADJUSTING THE VOLTAGE
   If the voltage is not within the range specified above or if the battery is too low or too high in charge, the voltage should be adjusted by means of the adjusting of plate of the voltage relay.

| | | | |
|---|---|---|---|
| Voltage relay | No-load voltage | 15.8 to 16.5V at 1800rpm | Hold the unit horizontally.<br>When battery is bad in charge. |
| | Ignition coil load voltage | 15.3 to 16.2V at 3000rpm | |
| | Voltage coil resistance | 14.4Ω at 20°C | |
| | Field-coil resistance | 10Ω at 20°C | |
| | Compensation resistance | 12.5Ω | |
| Charging relay | Cut-in voltage | 12.5 to 13.5V | When battery is bad in charge. |
| | Voltage coil resistance | 14.4Ω at 20°C | |
| | Compensation resistance | 12.5Ω | |
| Starter switch Voltage-electro magnetic coil | Point resistance | 0.25V/100A or less | When engine does not start easily |
| | Coil resistance | 11.3Ω at 20°C | |

| Voltage relay | Core gap | 0.4 to 0.5 |
|---|---|---|
| | Yoke gap | 0.6 to 0.7 |
| | Point gap | 0.4 to 0.5 |
| Charging relay | Yoke gap 1 | 0.6 to 0.7 |
| | Yoke gap 2 | 1.0 to 1.1 |
| | Point gap | 0.6 to 0.7 |
| Starter switch | Point gap | 1.4 to 1.5 |
| | Core gap | 1.3 to 1.4 |

Table 10

## 5-4 IGNITION COIL

The ignition coil, of which primary coil and secondary coil are in the turn ratio about 50:1, is a kind of transformer. When the primary current is interrupted by the contact breaker, the self-inductance causes a voltage surge of 150 to 300V. Then the mutual inductance in the secondary coil causes, according to the turn ratio, a high-voltage surge of 7000 to 12000V, which the high-tension cord carries to the spark plug to ignite fuel mixture.

(1) INSPECTING THE IGNITION COIL

1a) Test the primary coil and the secondary coil and check them for breaking.

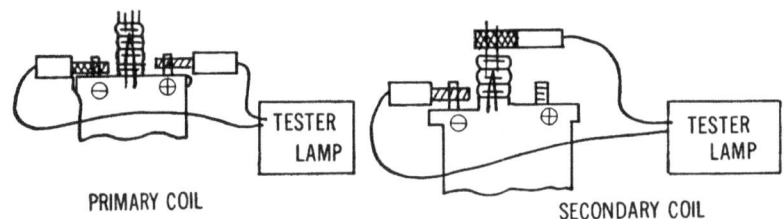

1b) Measure the resistance in the coils with the Yamaha Electro-tester:

| Primary coil resistance | 4.9Ω at 20°C |
|---|---|
| Secondary coil resistance | 5.5Ω at 20°C |

1c) Measure the spark with the Yamaha Electro-tester as shown in Illus. 49. If the tester reads more than 6mm spark, the ignition coil is good.

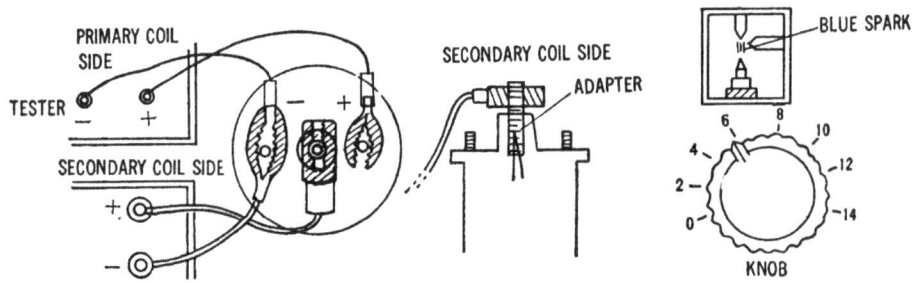

ILLUS 49

## 5-5  SPARK PLUG

　　　　Standad plug : NGK B-7H or A B-7HZ

The heat rang of the plug is determined on the basis of the average driving conditions.   Engines driven under severe operating conditions require cooler-runing spark plug than the engines at continuously low speeds.   Every periodical inspection, check the spark plug as described below:

(1) If the insulator is relatively clean and has a tan color, the heat range of the spark plug is correct.

(2) If the plug soots up with oil and carbon, hotter-running plug should be used.

(3) If the insulator is white and hot and the electrodes will be impaired in a relatively short time, cooler-running should be used.

NOTES : 1) The engine driven in the city at continuously low speed requires the plug B - 6 H or M45.
   2) For high-speed runnig or long-distance touring, use the plug M44.
   3) Replacing the plug every 3,000 or 6,000km is rather economical than using it until it will be defective.

### CLEANING AND ADJUSTING

Please tell the users that the spark plug should be cleaned every 1,000km (600 mile).   Remove carbon from the electrodes and adjust the gap to 0,6 or 0.7mm.

## 5-6  BATTERY

The battery furnishes a current not only to the starting and ignition system but also to the lamp and horn system when the engine runs at low RPM at the inter section, for example.

Usually the dynamo charges the battery.

(1) INITIAL CHARGING

The new empty battery should be charged by the battery service station, if possible.

1a) Prepare about 700c.c. electrolyte that is a solution of sulfuric acid and water; the acid being 1.28 times heavier than an equal volume of water.

1b) Cut off the tip of the exhaust tube as illustrated below.

1c) Remove six filler plugs and fill the cells with the electrolyte up to the maximum level line.

1d) Charge the battery with about 1A current for about 20 to 25 hours.

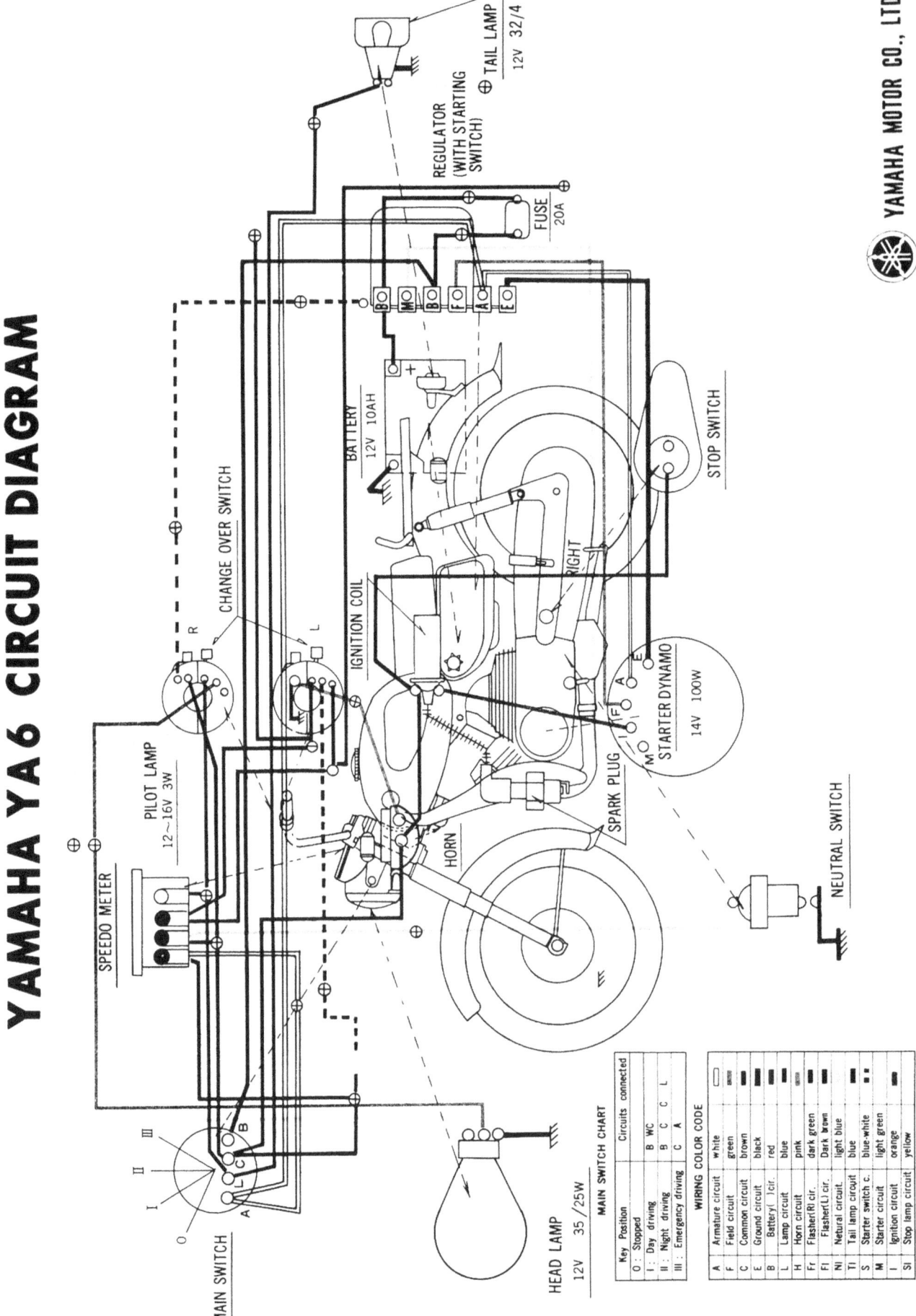

## YA6 Handle Switch Lead Wire Connections in the Head Lamp

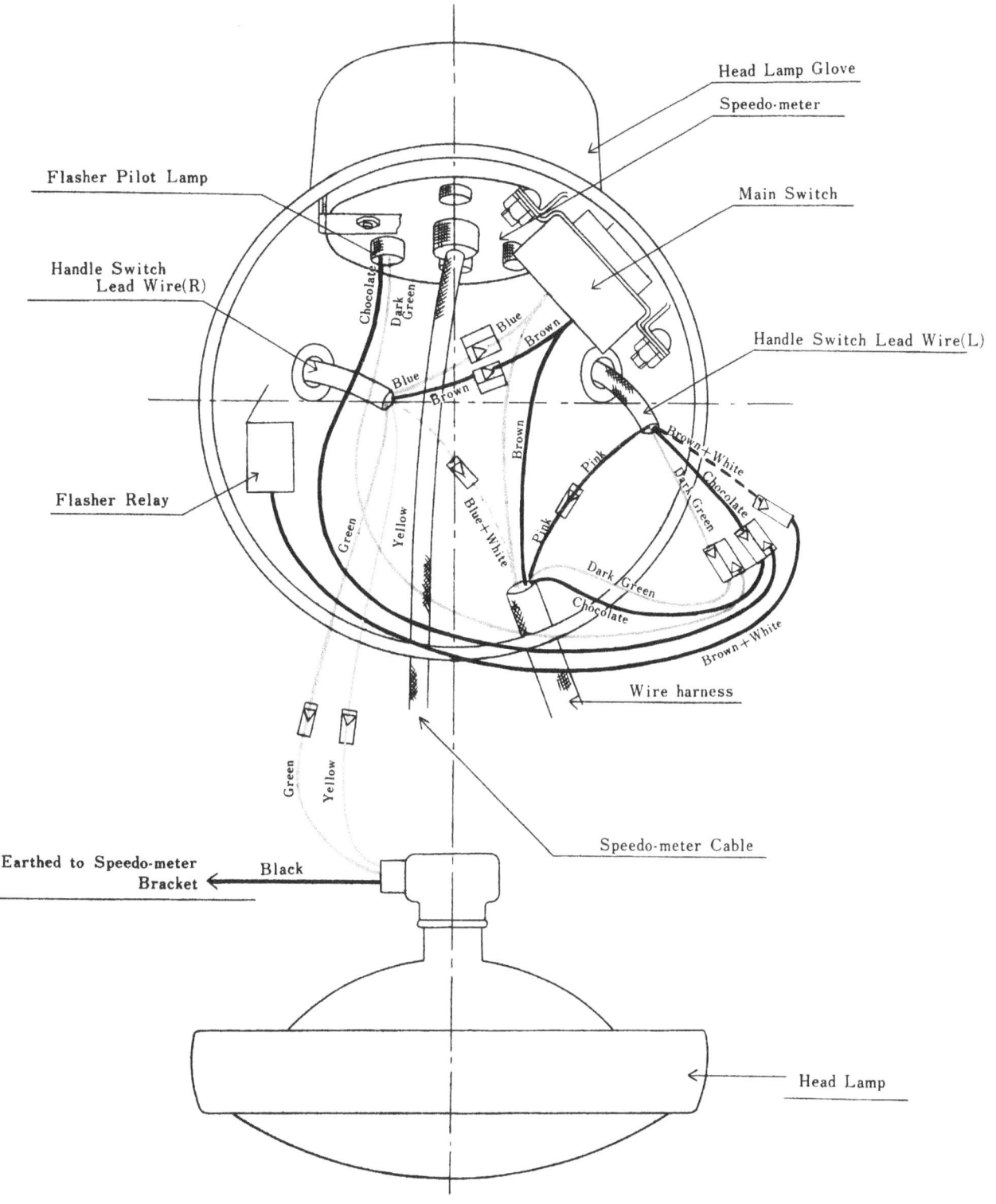

1e) After charging, let gas out of the cells by shaking.
1f) Add the dilute sulfuric acid or distilled water up to the maximum level line so the specific gravity becomes 1.28.
1g) Tighten the six plugs firmly and then wash the outside of the battery with water to remove acid especially from the terminals.
1h) After installing and wiring, apply grease to the terminals.

(2) PERIODICAL INSPECTION

Check the electrolyte level once a month. If the fluid level is below the middle of the maximum and the minimun level lines, add the distilled water.

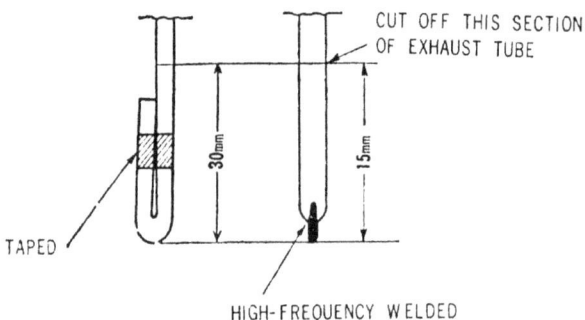

(3) STORING

If the battery is not used for a long time in winter or for other reasons, take it to the battery service station or, if you have a charger, store it as described below:
3a) Recharge the battery directly after demouting.
3b) Apply grease the terminals and place it in the place where the temperature is more than zero.
3c) Recharge the battery once a month.
3d) Recharge the battery before installing.

(4) MAINTENANCE GUIDE

| Item | Instructions | Inspection |
|---|---|---|
| Electrolyte | Specific gravity: 1.28 at 20°C<br>Amount of electrolyte: about 700cc | before first use<br>〃 |
| Inital charging | Charge with 1A current for 25 h. | 〃 |
| Replenishment | Add distilled water up to the max. level line. | every month |
| Recharging | 1A. 13 hours | When engine does not start at all. |
| Greasing | Apply grease to terminals | every 6,000km |
| Terminal screw | Dia : 5<br>Pitch : 0.9<br>Distance from head : 22 (Yuasa)<br>24 (GS)<br>Thread size : 22 (Yuasa)<br>16 (GS) | |
| Exhaust tube | Length : 400mm | |
| Dimensions | Height : 145mm<br>Length: 135mm<br>Width : 90mm | |

# CHAPTER 6 INSPECTION AND MAINTENANCE

## 6-1 PERIODICAL INSPECTION

The regular inspection and maintenance help always keep the machine in top conditions. They are preventive measures against troubles and rather time-saving for both user and dealers.

## 6-2 PERIODICAL INSPECTION CHART

| Check Point | At first 300km of driving | At first 3000km of driving | At first 6000km of driving | Every 400km |
|---|---|---|---|---|
| Adjustment of front & rear brakes | 0 | 0 | 0 | 0 |
| Adjustment of clutch | 0 | 0 | 0 | 0 |
| Change of gear oil | 0 | 0 | 0 | 0 |
| Greasing | | 0 | 0 | 0 |
| Replenishment of battery fluid | 0 | 0 | 0 | 0 |
| Cleaning of spark plug | 0 | 0 | 0 | 0 |
| Adjustment of ignition timing | | 0 | 0 | 0 |
| Adjustment of carburetor | | | | |
| Cleaning of carburetor | | 0 | 0 | 0 |
| Cleaning of air cleaner | | 0 | 0 | 0 |
| Cleaning of cyinder head & piston | | 0 | 0 | 0 |
| Cleaning of muffler | | 0 | 0 | 0 |
| Bolts, nuts and screws | 0 | 0 | 0 | 0 |
| Adjustment of drive chain | 0 | 0 | 0 | 0 |
| Auto lube oil | | | | |
| Auto lube pump | | See p. 14 | | |

## 6-3 INSPECTION AND MAINTENANCE OF THE MAIN PARTS

### 6-3-1 ENGINE

A) Removing carbon

The Yamaha Auto Lube engine features less carbon formation. Check to remove carbon from the following parts every 3,000km:
1) Cylinder head;
2) Piston head;
3) Cylinder exhaust port;
4) Exhaust pipe;
5) Muffler inner tube.

If these parts are coated with much more carbon than usual, check the setting of the Autolube pump and the throttle wire.    Refer to p. 14.

B) Cleaning the air cleaner

The air cleaner is just like a flu masks for the engine.

The mask must be clean at all times.    The dirty cleaner affects the life of the engine.

Demount the air cleaner; clear dust away with fingers; and blow air from the inside.

C) Carburetor

In addition to the periodical inspection, the carburetor should be disassembled and cleaned in case of hard starting, poor acceleration, excessive fuel consumption or other troubles.

After demounting the carburetor,

1) Wash in gasoline the float chamber, starter section, throttle valve, jet needle, main jet, pilot jet etc. and blow air into each nozzle of the mixing body,

2) After assembling (See "CARBURETOR SETTING GUIDE", p. 33) and installing, adjust the carburetor while the engine is idling.    Loosen the air screw by the specified turns and do the idle adjustment.    If it is still bad, adjust it within the range $+-\frac{1}{4}$.

3) Adjust the relation between the Autolube pump and the carburetor (See p. 14).

4) Clean the drain cleaner (See p. 33).

D) Spark plug

Check the electrodes for dirt and wear.

If the insulator has a tan color, the plug is correct.

If the insulator soots up with carbon and oil, use cooler-running plug:

| Maker | Standard Plug | Cooler-running Plug |
|---|---|---|
| NGK | B - 7 H | B - 6 H |
| Hitachi | M - 44 | M - 45 |

E) Clutch wire

Adjust, by turning the adjusting screw on the left crankcase cover, the clutch wire so that it has a play of 2 to 3mm.

F) Change of gear oil

Be sure to change the gear oil every 1,000km (600 mile) at least. Use Yamaha Gear Oil B of 1,300c.c. (See p. 32).

## 6-3-2  FRAME

A) Bolt, nuts and screws

Check the bolts, nuts and screws for looseness:
(1) Front and rear axle nuts;
(2) Swinging arm shaft nut;
(3) Steering handle tightening nut;
(4) Handle crown fitting bolt;
(5) Foot rest tightening bolt;
(6) Center stand tightening bolt;
(7) Side stand tightening bolt;
(8) Muffler fitting bolts and nuts;
(9) Engine fitting bolts;
(10) Other bolts, nuts and screws.

B) Front and rear brakes.

Check and, if necessary, adjust a play of the brake lever and the brake pedal.

Remove the wheels; clean the brake shoes; and apply grease the bearings every 6,000km (4,000 mile).

C) Drive chain

The drive chain is protected from dust under the chain case.

After driving for a long time, however, dust may cause lack of oil, or the loose chain may cause loss of power.

Check the chain for looseness and, if necessary, adjust a play of the chain at regular intervals.

Wash the chain in gasoline and apply oil to it every 3,000km (2,000 mile).

D) Oiling and greasing

| No.* | Where oiled or greased | Distance for 1st lubr, km | Lubrication interval, km | Type of lubricant |
|---|---|---|---|---|
| 1 | Rear brake cam shaft | 1,500 | 3,000 | cup grease |
| 2 | Rear wheel bearing | 3,000 | 3,000 | 〃 |
| 3 | Brake pedal shaft | 1,500 | 3,000 | 〃 |
| 4 | Gear box | 500 | 1,000 | Yamaha Gear oil B |
| 5 | Front brake cam shaft | 1,500 | 3,000 | cup grease |
| 6 | Steering head | 6,000 | 6,000 | fiber grease |
| 7 | Front brake wire | 1,500 | 3,000 | cup grease |
| 8 | Accelerator grip | 1,500 | 3,000 | 〃 |
| 9 | Meter gear unit | 6,000 | 6,000 | 〃 |
| 10 | Front wheel bearing | 3,000 | 3,000 | 〃 |
| 11 | Stand shaft | 1,500 | 3,000 | 〃 |
| 12 | Shift pedal shaft | 1,500 | 3,000 | 〃 |
| 13 | Drive chain | 300 | 1,000 | motor oil |
| 14 | Dynamo lubricator | 6,000 | 6,000 | Swallow M22 |
| 15 | Front fork oil | 10,000 | 10,000 | Kayaba #4 oil. 170cc |

No.* in this chart agrees with the circled number in the illustrations below.

## 6-3-3 ELECTRICAL SYSTEM

A) Ignition timing

The improper ignition timing causes poor performance, overheat, carbon accumulation, and other troubles.
Check the ignition timing with the timing light; clean the points; and check the point gap at regular intervals.

B) Battery

Check the electrolyte once a month at least.  If the level is too low, add distilled water up to the maximum level line. Never use city water, well water or dilute sulfuric acid.

The correct specific gravity of the electrolyte is 1.26 to 1.28.
If not, recharge the battery.

C) Carbon brush

The life of the carbon brush is equal to the driving distance of about 10,000km (6,000 mile). Check it, however, at about 6,000km (4,000 mile) of driving.
If the length of the brush is less than 100mm, replace it.

D) Regulator voltage

If the battery is discharged or the electrolyte level is reduced in shorter time than usual or if the bulb is burnt out, check the regulator voltage. If not within the specified range, take it to the nearest service station.
See p. 44.

## 6-4 NECESSARY TOOLS AND TESTERS FOR INSPECTION AND MEINTENANCE

A) Tools for YA6:

(1) Pump setting tool:

(2) Clutch holder.

B) Tools for YA6 and other models:

| No. | Tool Name | Model for which the tool is used. | Description |
|---|---|---|---|
| 1 | Crankcase disassembling tool | All models | Used for removing crank, too. |
| 2 | Crank fitting tool | Fitting pipe: All models<br>Nut : All models<br>Bolt: YG1, MF2, MF1, | |
| 3 | Reduction gear puller | All models | |
| 4 | Exhaust ring nut tool | All models | Used for turning muffler-exhaust pipe joint ring too. |
| 5 | Front fork mounting & dismounting tool | All models | Use attachments for YD2, YD3, YDS1 or YDS2. |
| 6 | Sprocket (flying wheel magneto) holder | All models | |
| 7 | Steering nut tightening tool | SC1 | |
| 8 | Armature pulling bolt | All models with no flying wheel magneto | |
| 9 | Dial gauge holder and 2 | 1 : All models<br>2 : All models except YA5 | |

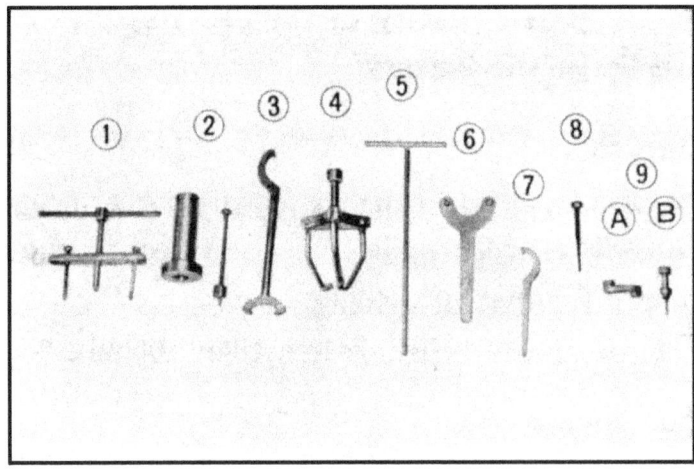

ILLUS 50

C) Testers*

| No. | Tester | Use |
|---|---|---|
| 1 | Electro-tester | All-round tester |
| 2 | Engine speed tester | Measurement of engine RPM |
| 3 | Dial gauge | Measurement of ignition timing. play of crank etc. |
| 4 | Hydrometer | Measurement of specific gravity of electrolyte |

* Used for all models.

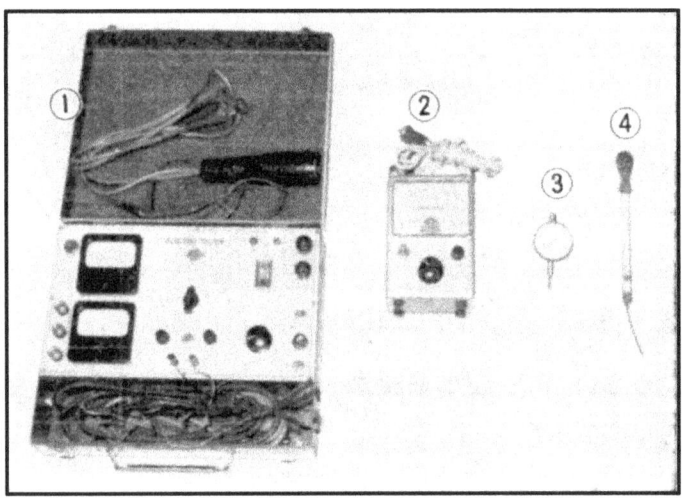

ILLUS 51

# YAMAHA YA6

# ILLUSTRATED PARTS LIST

**KEY TO SYMBOLS:**

    R.H. ....... Right hand side (Viewed from the rider's seat facing forward)

    L.H. ....... Left hand side (Viewed from the rider's seat facing forward)

    S.R. ....... Suggested retail price

    UR. ....... Use size (thickness) and/or numbers as required

    ⊙ ....... Painted parts

    ☆ ....... Government inspected parts

    △ ....... Not supplied as a single part

    S ....... Indicates "S" shaped circlip

    E ....... Indicates "E" shaped circlip

    R ....... Indicates "R" shaped circlip

    T ....... Number of teeth in a gear

    V ....... Voltage for light bulbs

    W ....... Wattage for light bulbs

    L ....... Length

    S ....... "S" type oil seal

    SD ....... "SD" type oil seal

    SO ....... "SO" type oil seal

    SW ....... "SW" type oil seal

**COMPONENT PARTS:** Component parts of an assembly are preceded by a dot (.) as follows:

    KICK CRANK ASS'Y

    . WASHER, spring    )

    . LEVER, kick    ) Component parts

    . PIN    )

Component parts which are mounted on either side of the m/c. are listed in the following sequence:

5a). - Parts to be mounted on "LEFT SIDE" are listed first. -

5b). - Parts to be mounted on "RIGHT SIDE" are listed second. -

5c). - Parts which can be mounted on "EITHER SIDE" are listed next to the above parts. -

# YAMAHA
## YA6

## SPECIFICATION

| | |
|---|---|
| Overall Length | 75.6in (1,920mm) |
| Overall Width | 28.5in (725mm) |
| Overall Height | 41.1in (1,045mm) |
| Wheel Base | 49.0in (1,245mm) |
| Road Clearance | 5.3in (135mm) |
| Net Weight | 264 lbs (120kg) |
| Bore and Stroke | 56×50 |
| Compression Ratio | 6.8 : 1 |
| Fuel Tank Capacity | 9.0 ℓ |
| Maximum Power | 11ps/6,700rpm |
| Maximum Torque | 1.25kgm/5,000rpm |
| Speed Range | 69m/h (140km/h) |
| Climbing Ability | 20° |
| Starting System | Electric and Kick |
| Front Tyre | 3.00-16-4PR |
| Rear Tyre | 3.00-16-4PR |

# CONTENTS

## ENGINE

| | | | |
|---|---|---|---|
| Fig. | 1 | Crank Case | 1 |
| Fig. | 2 | Crank Case Cover | 3 |
| Fig. | 3 | Crank and Piston | 7 |
| Fig. | 4 | Clutch | 9 |
| Fig. | 5 | Transmission | 11 |
| Fig. | 6 | Shifter (1) | 15 |
| Fig. | 7 | Shifter (2) | 17 |
| Fig. | 8 | Kick | 19 |
| Fig. | 9 | Carburetor | 21 |
| Fig. | 10 | Muffler and Air Cleaner | 25 |
| Fig. | 11 | Oil Pump | 27 |
| Fig. | 12 | Generator | 31 |

## CHASSIS

| | | | |
|---|---|---|---|
| Fig. | 13 | Frame | 35 |
| Fig. | 14 | Rear Arm and Chain Case | 37 |
| Fig. | 15 | Stand and Brake Pedal | 39 |
| Fig. | 16 | Handle and Front Fender | 41 |
| Fig. | 17 | Front Fork | 45 |
| Fig. | 18 | Tank | 49 |
| Fig. | 19 | Oil Tank | 51 |
| Fig. | 20 | Seat and Carrier | 53 |
| Fig. | 21 | Front Wheel | 55 |
| Fig. | 22 | Rear Wheel | 57 |
| Fig. | 23 | Head Lamp and Tail Lamp | 61 |
| Fig. | 24 | Electrical System | 63 |
| Fig. | 25 | Leg Shield and Tools | 65 |

# Fig. 1 CRANK CASE

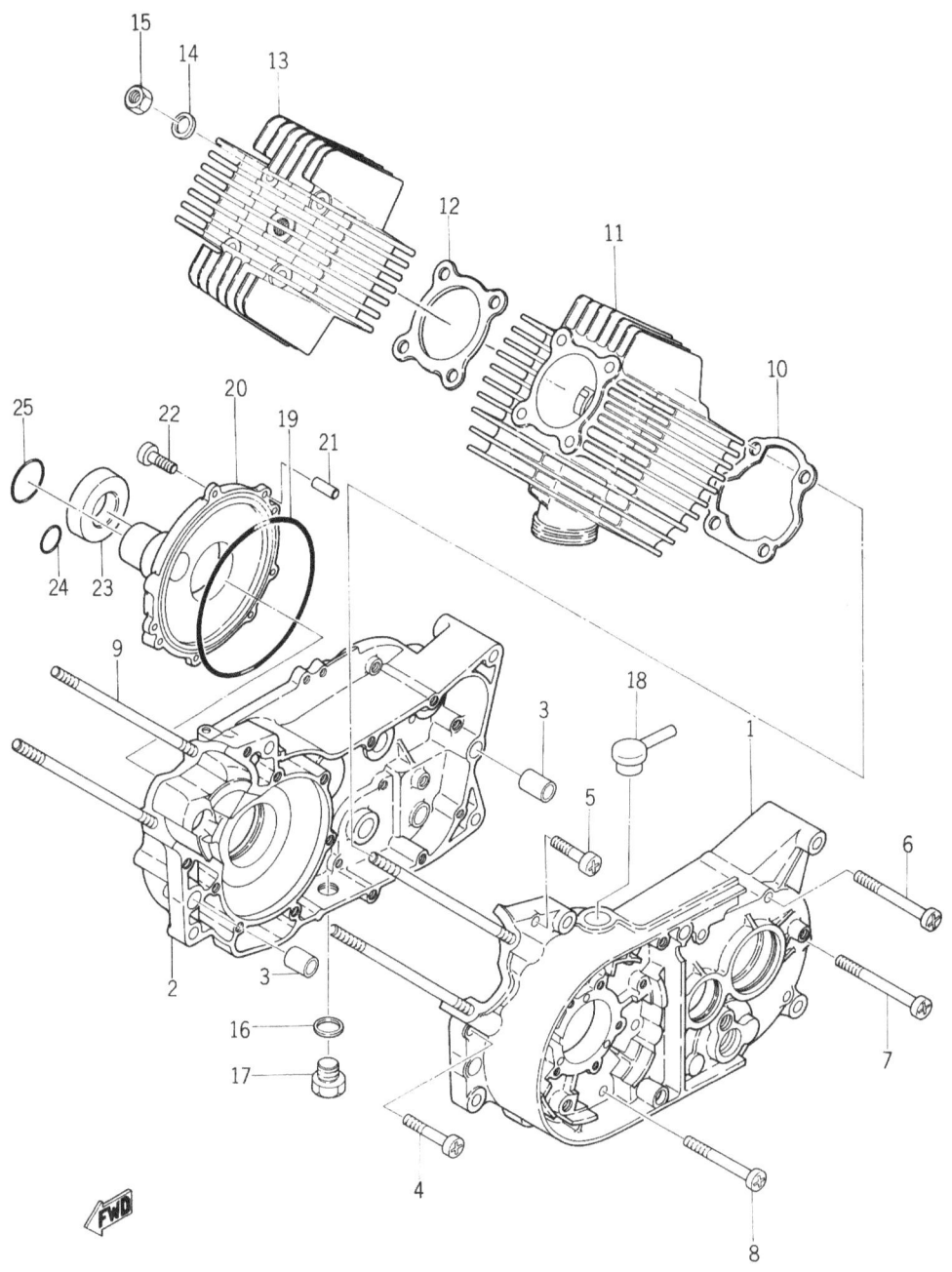

| Ref. No. | Part No. | Part Name | Description | Q'ty | S·R | Remarks |
|---|---|---|---|---|---|---|
| 1- 1 | 137-15111-00 | CASE, crank (L.H) | | 1 | 28.00 | |
| 1- 2 | 137-15121-01 | CASE, crank (R.H) | | 1 | 34.40 | |
| 1- 3 | 91810-08016 | PIN, dowel (1) | 8.4-12-16 | 2 | .12 | |
| 1- 4 | 92501-06035 | SCREW, pan head | | 2 | .06 | |
| 1- 5 | 92501-06025 | SCREW, pan head | | 1 | .06 | |
| 1- 6 | 92501-06070 | SCREW, pan head | | 5 | .16 | |
| 1- 7 | 92501-06090 | SCREW, pan head | | 1 | .20 | |
| 1- 8 | 92501-06040 | SCREW, pan head | | 6 | .10 | |
| 1- 9 | 137-11361-00 | BOLT, cylinder holding | | 4 | .40 | |
| 1-10 | 137-11351-00 | GASKET, cylinder | | 1 | .12 | |
| 1-11 | 137-11311-00 | CYLINDER | | 1 | 24.00 | |
| 1-12 | 137-11181-00 | GASKET, cylinder head | | 1 | .08 | |
| 1-13 | 137-11111-00 | HEAD, cylinder | | 1 | 9.60 | |
| 1-14 | 92901-08200 | WASHER, plain | | 4 | .01 | |
| 1-15 | 92801-08200 | NUT | | 4 | .04 | |
| 1-16 | 137-15353-00 | GASKET, drain plug | 14-21-1.5 | 1 | .02 | |
| 1-17 | 102-15351-00 | PLUG, drain | | 1 | .20 | |
| 1-18 | 137-15363-01 | PLUG, oil | | 1 | .40 | |
| 1-19 | 93211-19064 | O-RING | | 1 | .16 | |
| 1-20 | 137-13551-00 | COVER, valve | | 1 | 4.96 | |
| 1-21 | 93604-14012 | PIN, dowel | 4-13.8 | 2 | .04 | |
| 1-22 | 92501-06018 | SCREW, pan head | | 7 | .04 | |
| 1-23 | 93103-28012 | OIL SEAL | SW-28-47-8 | 1 | 1.40 | |
| 1-24 | 93210-12014 | O-RING | 2.4-11.8 | 1 | .16 | |
| 1-25 | 93210-26033 | O-RING | 3.2-26 | 1 | .16 | |

## Fig. 2 CRANK CASE COVER

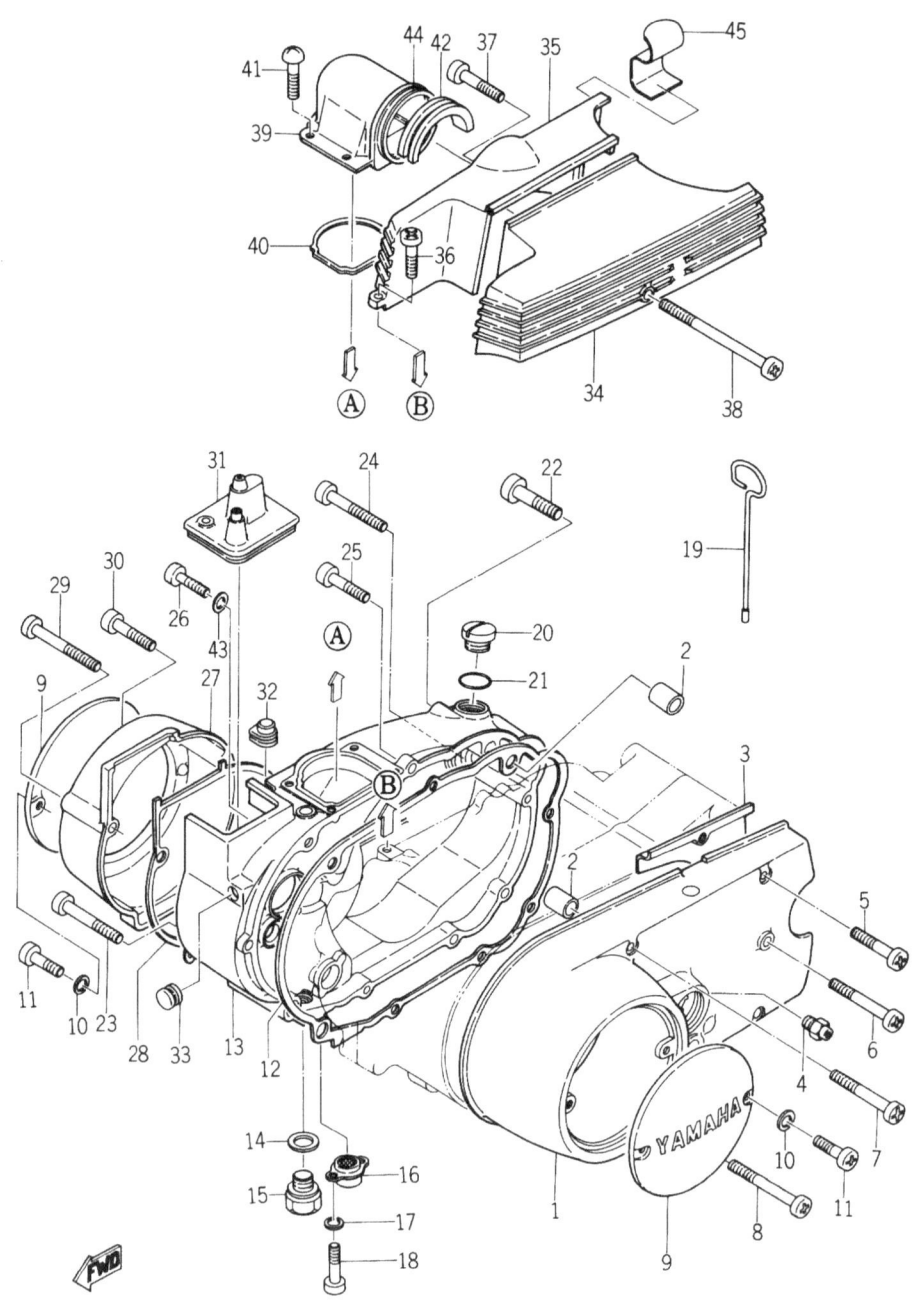

| Ref. No. | Part No. | Part Name | Description | Q'ty | S·R | Remarks |
|---|---|---|---|---|---|---|
| 2-1 | 137-15410-00 | CRANK CASE COVER ASS'Y (L.H) | | 1 | 13.60 | |
| 2-2 | 91810-03014 | PIN, dowel | 8.5-10-14 | 4 | .12 | |
| 2-3 | 137-15418-00 | COVER, chain case (1) | | 1 | 1.44 | |
| 2-4 | 93700-06001 | NIPPLE, grease | | 1 | .10 | |
| 2-5 | 92501-06040 | SCREW, pan head | | 2 | .10 | |
| 2-6 | 92501-06050 | SCREW, pan head | | 1 | .10 | |
| 2-7 | 92501-06045 | SCREW, pan head | | 1 | .10 | |
| 2-8 | 92501-06055 | SCREW, pan head | | 1 | .12 | |
| 2-9 | 141-15415-00 | COVER (1) | | 2 | .64 | |
| 2-10 | 92901-04100 | WASHER, spring | | 4 | .01 | |
| 2-11 | 92503-04012 | SCREW, pan head | | 4 | .04 | |
| 2-12 | 137-15451-00 | GASKET, crank case cover (R.H) | | 1 | .28 | |
| 2-13 | 137-15421-00 | COVER, crank case (R.H) | | 1 | 14.00 | |
| 2-14 | 137-15353-00 | GASKET, drain plug | 14-21-1.5 | 1 | .02 | |
| 2-15 | 102-15351-00 | PLUG, drain | | 1 | .20 | |
| 2-16 | 126-15433-00 | CLEANER, drain | | 1 | .80 | |
| 2-17 | 92901-04100 | WASHER, spring | | 2 | .01 | |
| 2-18 | 92501-04008 | SCREW, pan head | | 2 | .04 | |
| 2-19 | 137-15361-00 | GAUGE, level | | 1 | .12 | |
| 2-20 | 137-15363-00 | PLUG, oil level | | 1 | .44 | |
| 2-20-1 | 116-15363-00 | PLUG, oil | | 1 | .40 | |
| 2-21 | 93210-13016 | O-RING | 1.8-13 | 1 | .12 | |
| 2-21-1 | 93210-22028 | O-RING | 2-22 | 1 | .12 | |
| 2-22 | 92501-06075 | SCREW, pan head | | 1 | .16 | |
| 2-23 | 92501-06080 | SCREW, pan head | | 1 | .16 | |
| 2-24 | 92501-06060 | SCREW, pan head | | 1 | .12 | |
| 2-25 | 92501-06030 | SCREW, pan head | | 5 | .06 | |
| 2-26 | 92501-06035 | SCREW, pan head | | 1 | .06 | |
| 2-27 | 137-15413-00 | COVER, carburetor | | 1 | 3.60 | |
| 2-28 | 137-15453-00 | GASKET, carburetor cover | | 1 | .16 | |
| 2-29 | 92501-06050 | SCREW, pan head | | 2 | .10 | |
| 2-30 | 92501-06015 | SCREW, pan head | | 1 | .04 | |
| 2-31 | 137-14481-00 | COVER, carburetor | | 1 | .72 | |
| 2-32 | 137-15486-00 | GROMMET (1) | | 1 | .24 | |

## Fig. 2  CRANK CASE COVER

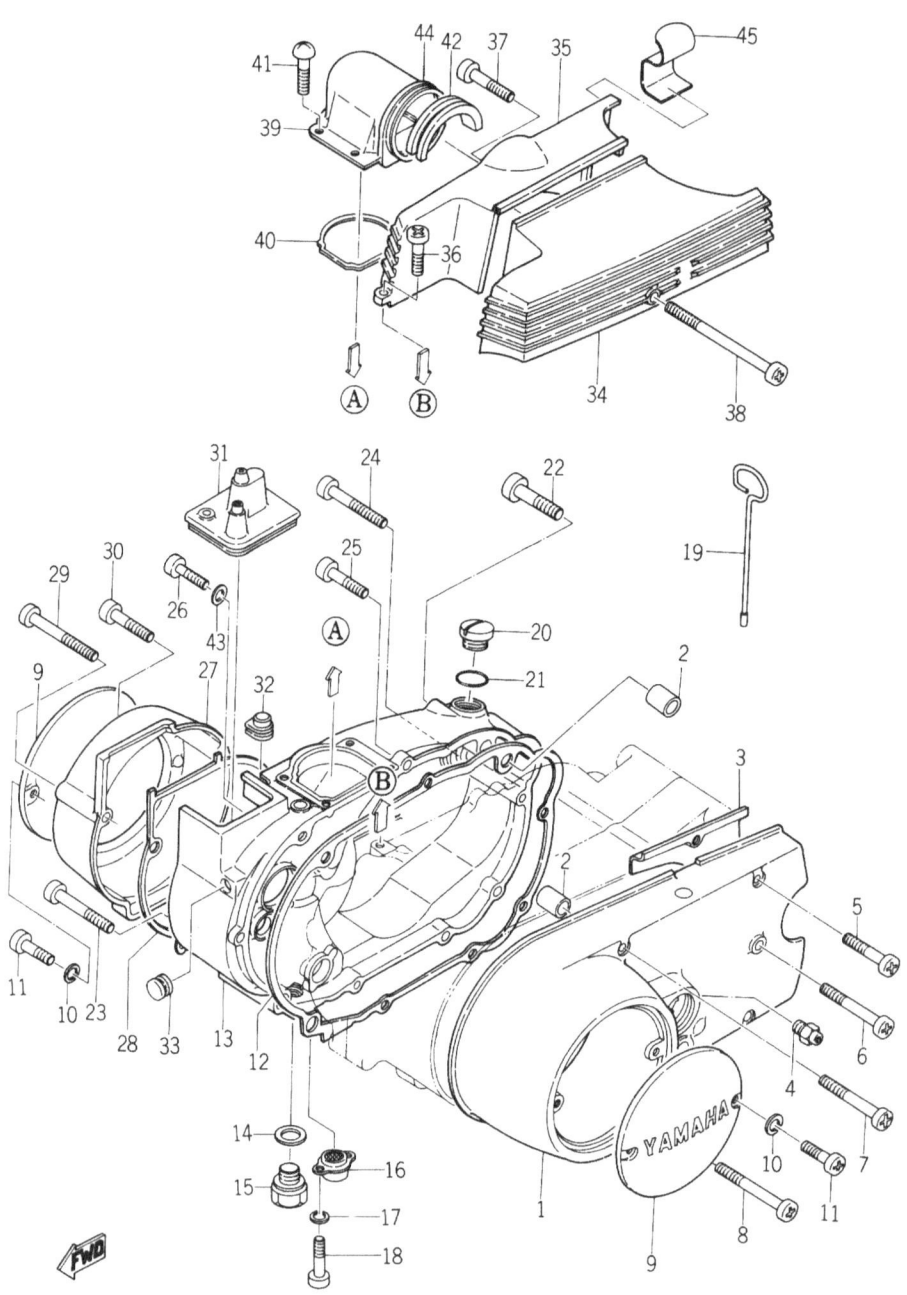

| Ref. No. | Part No. | Part Name | Description | Q'ty | S·R | Remarks |
|---|---|---|---|---|---|---|
| 2-33 | 122-15486-00 | GROMMET (1) | | 1 | .06 | |
| 2-34 | 137-15414-00 | COVER, air cleaner (L.H) | | 1 | 3.04 | ⊙ |
| 2-35 | 137-15424-00 | COVER, air cleaner (R.H) | | 1 | 3.04 | ⊙ |
| 2-36 | 137-15444-00 | SCREW, fitting | | 1 | .04 | |
| 2-37 | 92501-06018 | SCREW, pan head | | 1 | .04 | |
| 2-38 | 92501-06150 | SCREW, pan head | | 1 | .36 | |
| 2-39 | 137-15471-00 | DUCT, air | | 1 | 2.40 | |
| 2-40 | 137-15472-00 | SEAL, air duct | | 1 | .32 | |
| 2-41 | 92403-05008 | SCREW, round head | | 4 | .06 | |
| 2-42 | 137-15434-00 | SEAL, cleaner cover | | 1 | .20 | |
| 2-43 | 137-15384-00 | GASKET, screw | | 1 | .02 | |
| 2-44 | 137-14454-00 | JOINT, air | | 1 | .44 | |
| 2-45 | 137-15485-00 | CLAMP, oil pipe | | 1 | .12 | |

## Fig. 3  CRANK AND PISTON

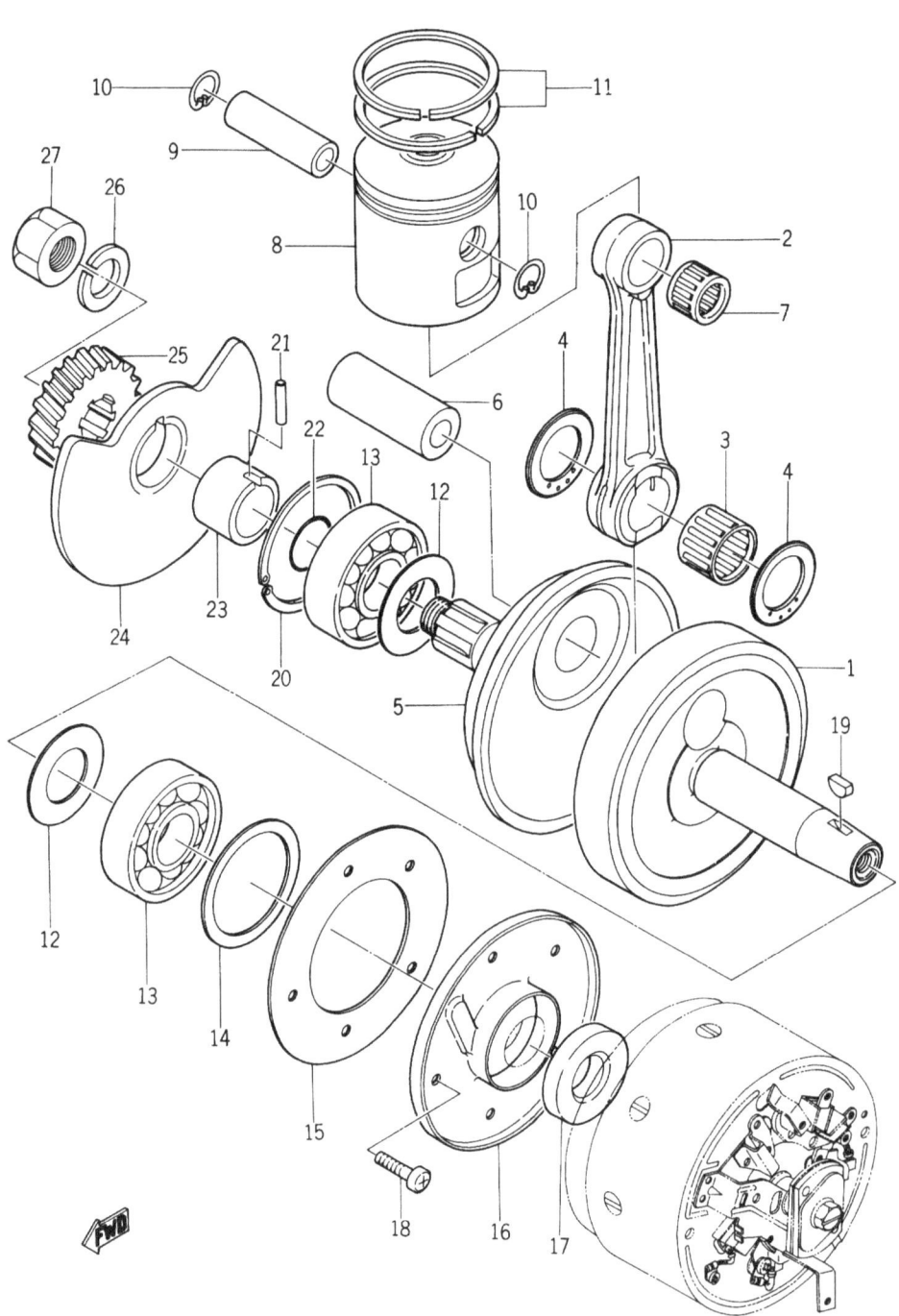

| Ref. No. | Part No. | Part Name | Description | Q'ty | S·R | Remarks |
|---|---|---|---|---|---|---|
| 3- 0-1 | 137-11400-00 | CRANK SHAFT ASS'Y | | 1 | 50.00 | |
| 3- 1 | 137-11412-00 | . CRANK (L.H) | | 1 | 17.60 | |
| 3- 2 | 137-11651-00 | . ROD, connecting | | 1 | 7.20 | |
| 3- 3 | 93310-42417 | . BEARING, connecting rod | 24-30-15 | 1 | 3.36 | ☆ |
| 3- 4 | 152-11685-00 | . WASHER, crank pin | | 2 | .40 | |
| 3- 5 | 137-11422-00 | . CRANK (R.H) | | 1 | 17.60 | |
| 3- 6 | 137-11681-00 | . PIN, crank | | 1 | 1.76 | |
| 3- 7 | 93310-21606 | BEARING, connecting rod | 16-20-16.8 | 1 | 2.16 | ☆ |
| 3- 8 | 137-11631-60 | PISTON | S.T.D | 1 | 6.40 | |
| 3- 8-1 | 137-11631-80 | PISTON | 0.25mm | 1 | 6.40 | |
| 3- 8-2 | 137-11631-90 | PISTON | 0.50mm | 1 | 6.40 | |
| 3- 9 | 137-11633-00 | PIN, piston | | 1 | 1.20 | |
| 3-10 | 137-11634-00 | CLIP, piston pin | | 2 | .08 | |
| 3-11 | 150-11601-00 | PISTON RING SET | S.T.D | 1s | 1.84 | |
| 3-11-1 | 150-11601-10 | PISTON RING SET | 0.25mm | 1s | 1.84 | |
| 3-11-2 | 150-11601-20 | PISTON RING SET | 0.50mm | 1s | 1.84 | |
| 3-12 | 136-11561-00 | SHIM, crank | | 2 | .05 | |
| 3-13 | 93306-30402 | BEARING | 6304C3 | 2 | 3.60 | ☆ |
| 3-14 | 136-11565-00 | WASHER, bearing cover | | 1 | .06 | |
| 3-15 | 137-15369-00 | GASKET, housing | | 1 | .08 | |
| 3-16 | 137-15359-00 | HOUSING, oil seal | | 1 | .96 | |
| 3-17 | 93103-20004 | OIL SEAL | SW-20-36-10 | 1 | 1.00 | |
| 3-18 | 92501-05008 | SCREW, pan head | | 5 | .04 | |
| 3-19 | 146-11545-00 | KEY, woodruff | | 1 | .10 | |
| 3-20 | 93450-52010 | CIRCLIP | 52⌀ | 1 | .48 | |
| 3-21 | 93604-14012 | PIN, dowel | 4-13.8 | 1 | .04 | |
| 3-22 | 93210-18023 | O-RING | 1.2-17.6 | 1 | .08 | |
| 3-23 | 137-13515-00 | COLLAR, valve | | 1 | 2.64 | |
| 3-24 | 137-13512-00 | VALVE | | 1 | 6.40 | |
| 3-25 | 137-16111-00 | GEAR, primary drive | | 1 | 3.20 | |
| 3-26 | 92901-14100 | WASHER, spring | | 1 | .04 | |
| 3-27 | 137-16134-00 | NUT, lock | | 1 | .24 | |

## Fig. 4  CLUTCH

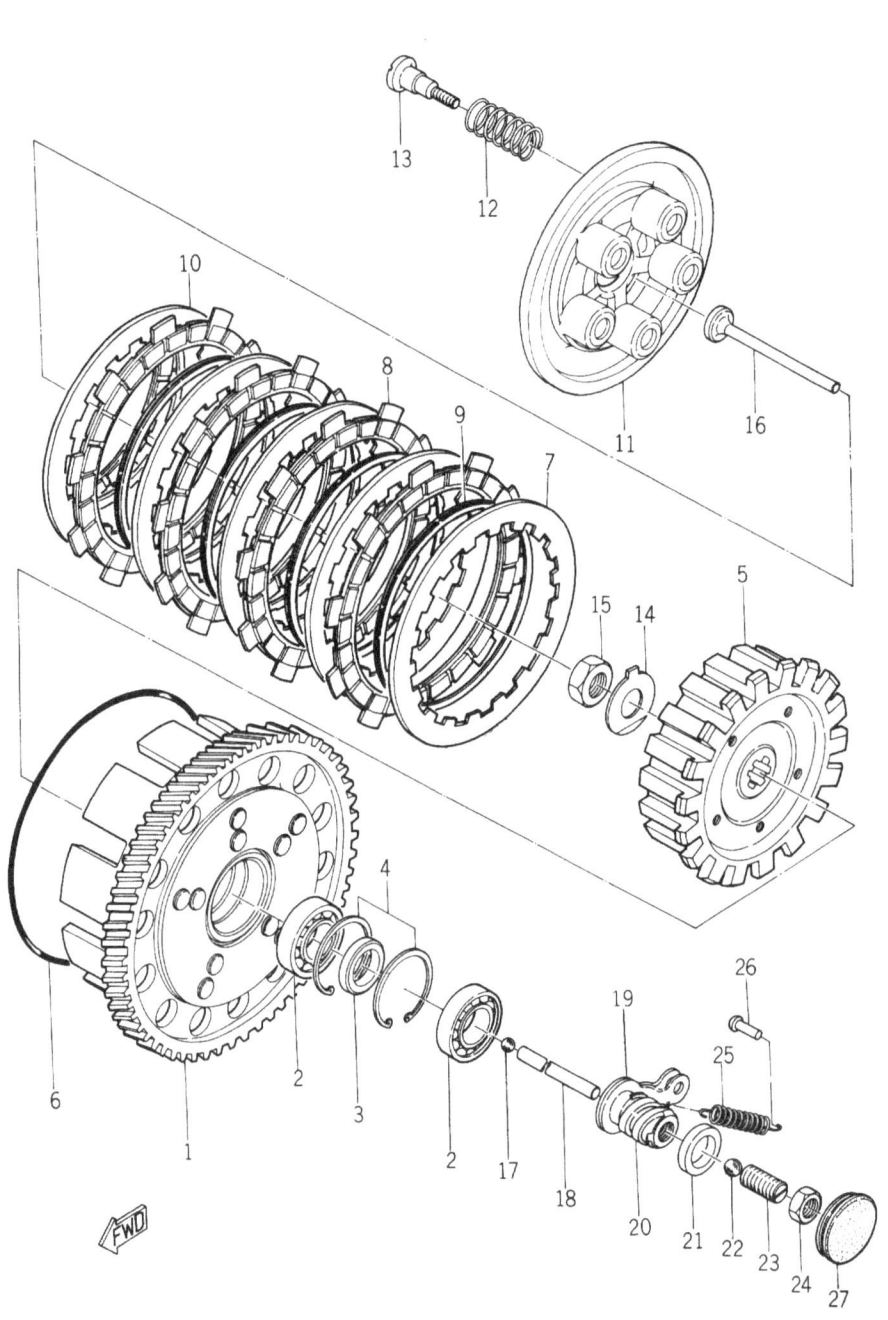

| Ref. No. | Part No. | Part Name | Description | Q'ty | S·R | Remarks |
|---|---|---|---|---|---|---|
| 4- 0-1 | 137-16301-00 | CLUTCH ASS'Y | | 1 | 40.00 | |
| 4- 1 | 137-16105-00 | . DRIVEN GEAR ASS'Y | | 1 | 20.80 | |
| 4- 2 | 93306-00301 | . BEARING | 6003 | 2 | 3.44 | ☆ |
| 4- 3 | 137-16181-00 | . SPACER | | 1 | .28 | |
| 4- 4 | 93420-35004 | . CIRCLIP | R-35 | 2 | .24 | |
| 4- 5 | 137-16371-00 | . BOSS, clutch | | 1 | 4.96 | |
| 4- 6 | 93211-08068 | . RING, friction (1) | 3.5-108 | 1 | .64 | |
| 4- 7 | 137-16325-00 | . PLATE, clutch (2) | | 1 | 1.30 | |
| 4- 8 | 132-16321-00 | . PLATE, friction | | 4 | 1.50 | |
| 4- 9 | 137-16367-00 | . RING, cushion | | 4 | .32 | |
| 4-10 | 137-16324-00 | . PLATE, clutch (1) | | 4 | 1.30 | |
| 4-11 | 137-16351-00 | . PLATE, pressure | | 1 | 1.60 | |
| 4-12 | 137-16333-60 | . SPRING, clutch | | 5 | .16 | |
| 4-13 | 137-16337-00 | . SCREW, spring | | 5 | .36 | |
| 4-14 | 137-16378-00 | WASHER, clutch boss | | 1 | .06 | |
| 4-15 | 137-16377-00 | NUT, clutch boss | | 1 | .16 | |
| 4-16 | 137-16356-00 | ROD, push (1) | | 1 | 1.12 | |
| 4-17 | 93501-04004 | BALL | 1/4" | 1 | .02 | ☆ |
| 4-18 | 137-16357-00 | ROD, push (2) | | 1 | .36 | |
| 4-19 | 137-16342-00 | LEVER, push | | 1 | .32 | |
| 4-20 | 137-16341-00 | SCREW, push | | 1 | 1.04 | |
| 4-21 | 136-16347-00 | SEAL, dust | | 1 | .26 | |
| 4-22 | 93505-16006 | BALL | 5/16" | 1 | .04 | ☆ |
| 4-23 | 137-16343-00 | SCREW, adjusting | | 1 | .12 | |
| 4-24 | 132-16344-00 | NUT, adjusting | | 1 | .04 | |
| 4-25 | 137-16345-00 | SPRING, lever return | | 1 | .08 | |
| 4-26 | 132-16346-00 | HOOK, spring | | 1 | .08 | |
| 4-27 | 137-15417-00 | COVER, cap | | 1 | .24 | |

## Fig. 5 TRANSMISSION

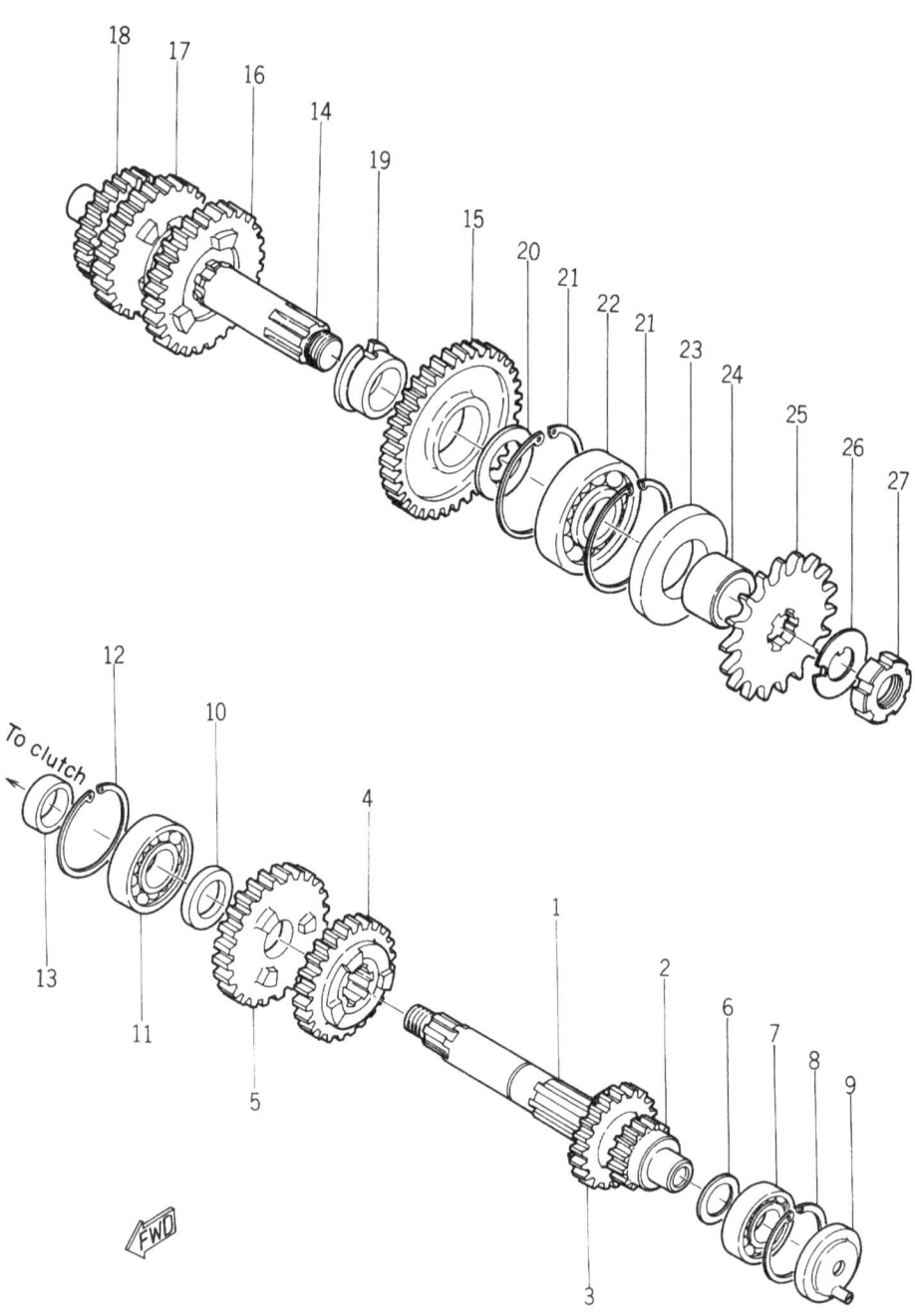

| Ref. No. | Part No. | Part Name | Description | Q'ty | S·R | Remarks |
|---|---|---|---|---|---|---|
| 5- 0-1 | 137-17401-01 | MAIN AXLE ASS'Y | | 1 | 21.52 | |
| 5- 1 | 137-17411-00 | . AXLE, main | | 1 | 7.52 | |
| 5- 2 | 137-17111-00 | . GEAR, 1st pinion | 15T | 1 | 2.72 | |
| 5- 3 | 137-17121-00 | . GEAR, 2nd pinion | 21T | 1 | 4.24 | ~ No. 166150 |
| 5- 3-1 | 140-17121-00 | . GEAR, 2nd pinion | 21T | 1 | 4.24 | No. 166151 ~ |
| 5- 4 | 137-17131-00 | . GEAR, 3rd pinion | 25T | 1 | 7.04 | ~ No. 166150 |
| 5- 4-1 | 140-17131-00 | . GEAR, 3rd pinion | 25T | 1 | 7.04 | No. 166151 ~ |
| 5- 5 | 137-17141-00 | . GEAR, 4th pinion | 29T | 1 | 3.60 | ~ No. 166150 |
| 5- 5-1 | 137-17141-01 | . GEAR, 4th pinion | 29T | 1 | 3.60 | No. 166151 ~ |
| 5- 6 | 137-17417-00 | SHIM, main axle | 15-22-0.5 | 1 | .08 | |
| 5- 7 | 93306-20201 | BEARING | 6202 | 1 | 1.76 | ☆ |
| 5- 8 | 93420-35003 | CIRCLIP | R-35 | 1 | .36 | |
| 5- 9 | 137-15389-00 | SEAL, push rod | | 1 | .68 | |
| 5-10 | 137-17158-00 | COLLAR, 4th pinion | | 1 | .72 | |
| 5-11 | 93313-41704 | BEARING | | 1 | 5.20 | ☆ ~ No. 149272 |
| 5-11-1 | 93306-20301 | BEARING | 6203 | 1 | 2.50 | ☆ No. 149273 |
| 5-12 | 93420-40005 | CIRCLIP | R-40 | 1 | .36 | No. 149273 ~ |
| 5-12-1 | 93420-37019 | CIRCLIP | | 1 | .36 | ~ No. 149272 |
| 5-13 | 137-17419-00 | SPACER, main axle | | 1 | .48 | No. 149273 ~ |
| 5- 0-2 | 137-17402-00 | DRIVE AXLE ASS'Y | | 1 | 24.40 | |
| 5-14 | 137-17421-00 | . AXLE, drive | | 1 | 8.00 | |
| 5-15 | 137-17211-00 | . GEAR, 1st wheel | 58T | 1 | 7.68 | |
| 5-16 | 137-17221-00 | . GEAR, 2nd wheel | 32T | 1 | 7.68 | ~ No. 166150 |
| 5-16-1 | 140-17221-00 | . GEAR, 2nd wheel | 32T | 1 | 7.68 | No. 166151 ~ |
| 5-17 | 137-17231-00 | . GEAR, 3rd wheel | 28T | 1 | 4.40 | ~ No. 166150 |
| 5-17-1 | 140-17231-00 | . GEAR, 3rd wheel | 28T | 1 | 4.40 | No. 166151 ~ |
| 5-18 | 137-17241-00 | . GEAR, 4th wheel | 24T | 1 | 4.32 | |
| 5-19 | 137-17258-00 | COLLAR, 1st wheel | 15-24-1 | 1 | 1.60 | |
| 5-20 | 137-17427-00 | SHIM, drive axle | 21-33-0.7 | 1 | .14 | |
| 5-21 | 93450-52010 | CIRCLIP | SM-52 | 2 | .48 | |
| 5-22 | 93306-30401 | BEARING | 6304 | 1 | 3.40 | ☆ |
| 5-23 | 93102-28023 | OIL SEAL | SD-28-52-6 | 1 | .72 | |
| 5-24 | 102-17462-00 | COLLAR, distance | | 1 | .80 | |
| 5-25 | 174-17461-50 | SPROCKET, drive | 15T | 1 | 3.20 | |
| 5-25-1 | 174-17461-40 | SPROCKET, drive | 14T | 1 | 3.20 | |

# Fig. 5 TRANSMISSION

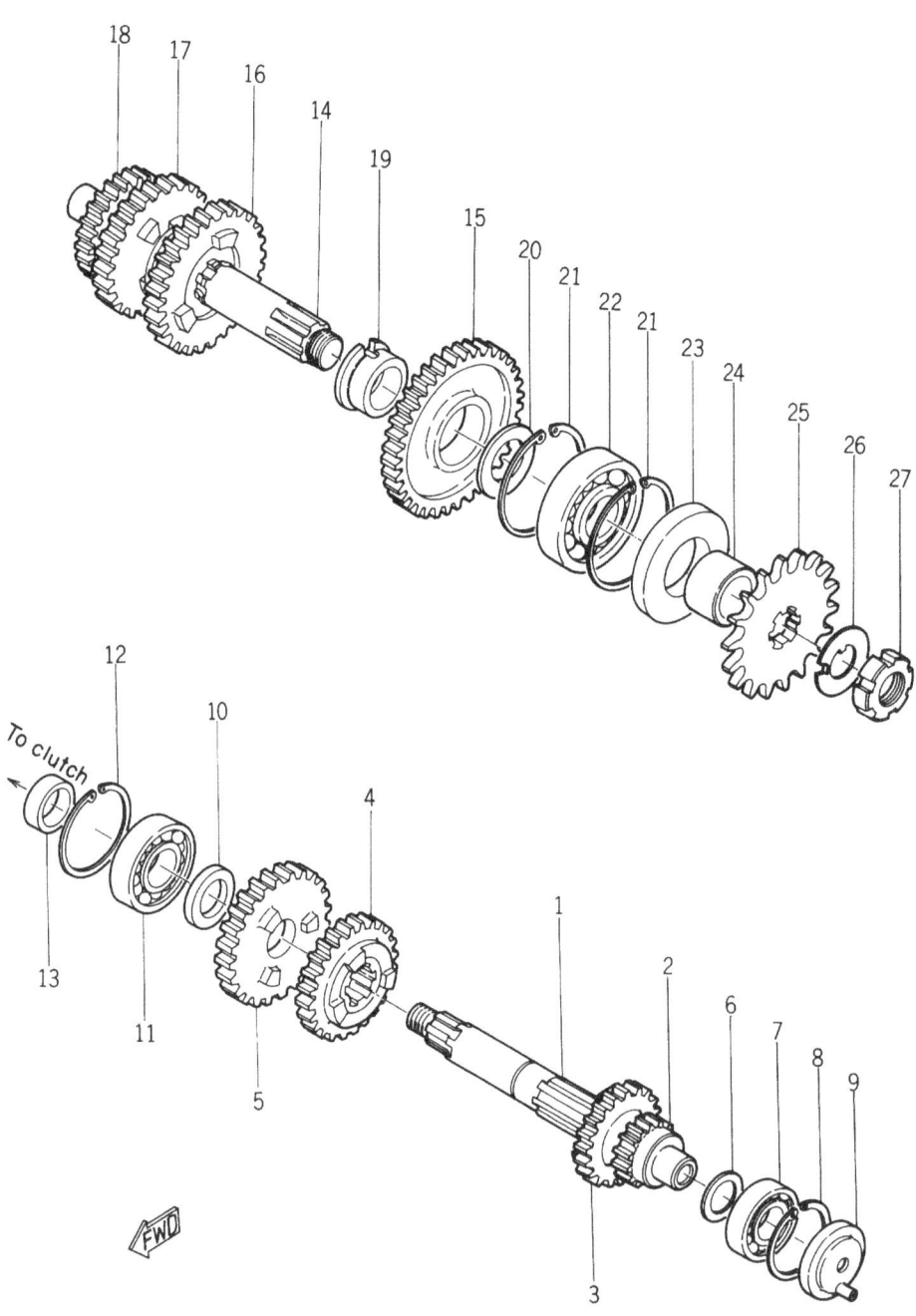

| Ref. No. | Part No. | Part Name | Description | Q'ty | S·R | Remarks |
|---|---|---|---|---|---|---|
| 5-25-2 | 174-17461-60 | SPROCKET, drive | 16T | 1 | 3.20 | |
| 5-26 | 102-17464-00 | WASHER, lock | | 1 | .03 | |
| 5-27 | 102-17463-00 | NUT, lock | | 1 | .20 | |

# Fig. 6 SHIFTER (1)

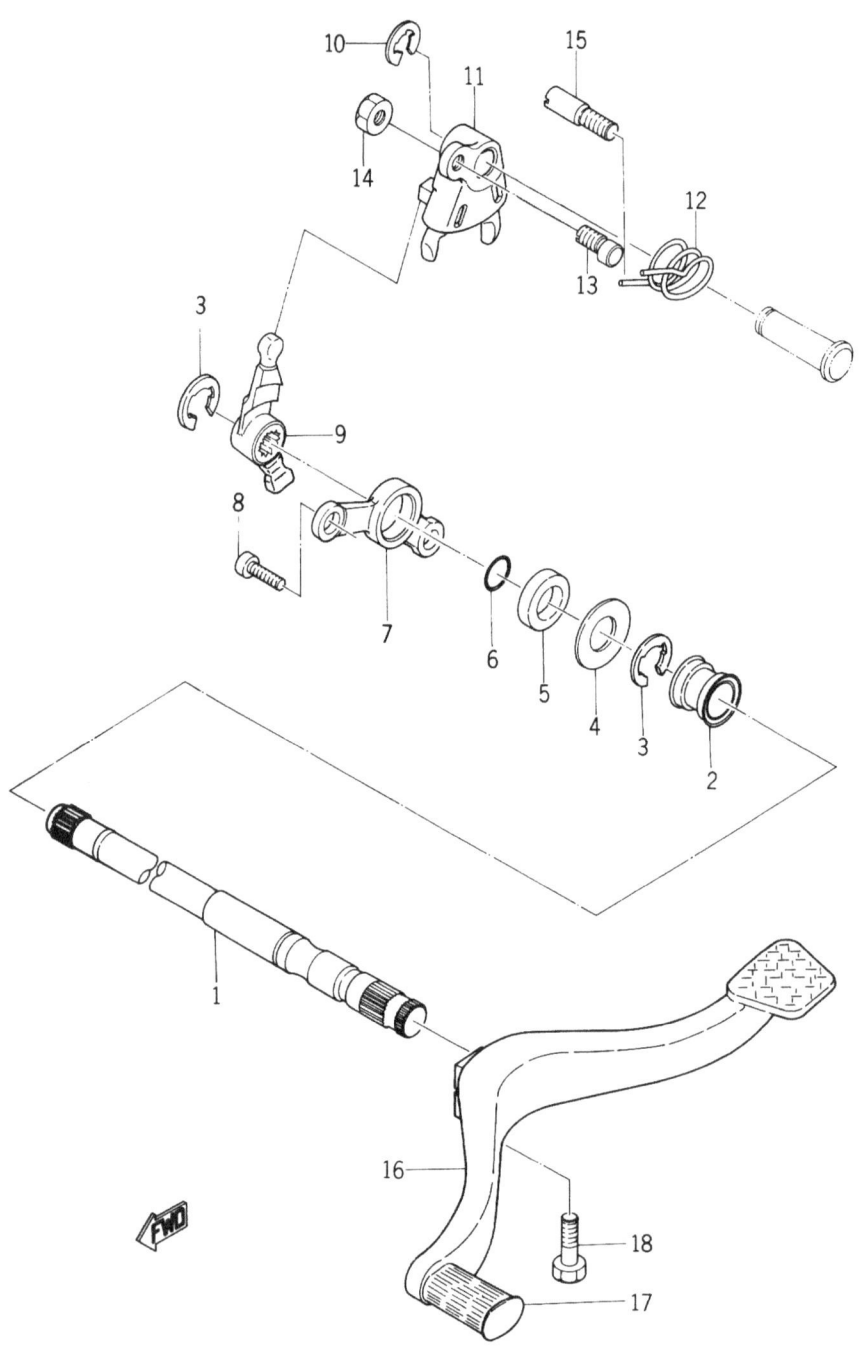

| Ref. No. | Part No. | Part Name | Description | Q'ty | S·R | Remarks |
|---|---|---|---|---|---|---|
| 6- 1 | 137-18125-00 | SHAFT, change | | 1 | 2.32 | |
| 6- 2 | 137-18131-00 | BOOT, sealing | | 1 | .16 | |
| 6- 3 | 93430-10015 | CIRCLIP | E-10 | 2 | .08 | |
| 6- 4 | 137-18137-00 | WASHER, change shaft | 12-25.5-1.5 | 1 | .08 | |
| 6- 5 | 93101-12004 | OIL SEAL | S-12-22-5 | 1 | .40 | |
| 6- 6 | 93210-09008 | O-RING | 1.6-8.6 | 1 | .12 | |
| 6- 7 | 137-18128-00 | BRACKET, change shaft | | 1 | 2.16 | |
| 6- 8 | 92501-06018 | SCREW, pan head | | 2 | .04 | |
| 6- 9 | 137-18121-01 | LEVER, change | | 1 | 3.84 | |
| 6-10 | 93430-08007 | CIRCLIP | E-8 | 1 | .06 | |
| 6-11 | 137-18180-01 | PAWL HOLDER ASS'Y | | 1 | 5.36 | |
| 6-12 | 137-18123-00 | SPRING, lever return | | 1 | .32 | |
| 6-13 | 136-18186-00 | SCREW, adjusting | | 1 | .16 | |
| 6-14 | 92801-06100 | NUT | | 1 | .01 | |
| 6-15 | 137-18127-00 | STOPPER, screw | | 1 | .28 | |
| 6-16 | 137-18111-60 | PEDAL, change | | 1 | 4.80 | |
| 6-17 | 132-18113-00 | COVER, change pedal | | 1 | .12 | |
| 6-18 | 91201-06020 | BOLT | | 1 | .04 | |

# Fig. 7 SHIFTER (2)

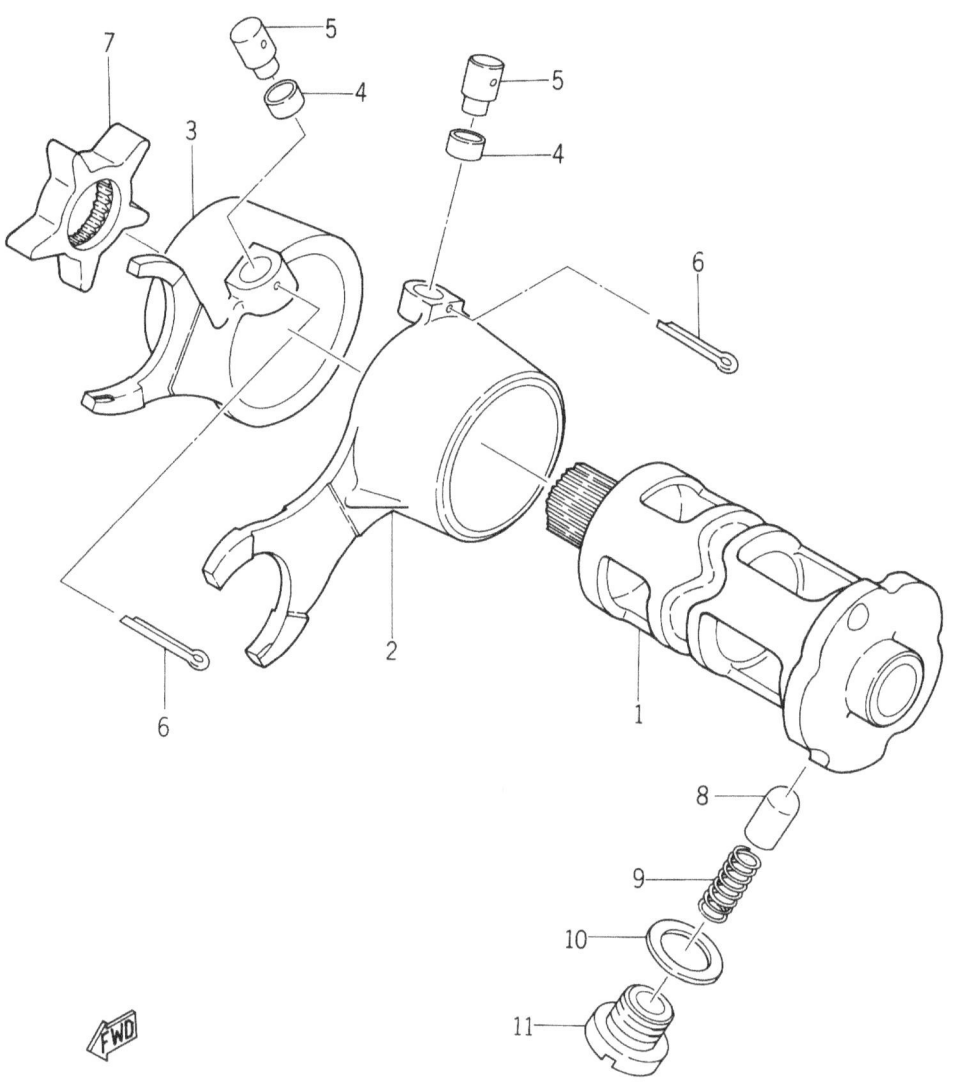

| Ref. No. | Part No. | Part Name | Description | Q'ty | S·R | Remarks |
|---|---|---|---|---|---|---|
| 7- 0-1 | 137-18500-60 | SHIFTER ASS'Y | | 1 | 22.40 | |
| 7- 1 | 137-18541-60 | . CAM, shift | | 1 | 6.48 | |
| 7- 2 | 140-18512-00 | . FORK, shift (2) | | 1 | 6.08 | |
| 7- 3 | 140-18511-00 | . FORK, shift (1) | | 1 | 6.08 | |
| 7- 4 | 136-18551-00 | . ROLLER, cam hollower | | 2 | .32 | |
| 7- 5 | 137-18552-00 | . PIN, cam hollower | | 2 | 1.04 | |
| 7- 6 | 91401-25018 | . PIN, cotter | | 2 | .01 | |
| 7- 7 | 137-18185-60 | SEGMENT | | 1 | 2.40 | |
| 7- 8 | 137-18547-00 | STOPPER, cam | | 1 | .12 | |
| 7- 9 | 137-18557-00 | SPRING, cam stopper | | 1 | .08 | |
| 7-10 | 137-18567-00 | GASKET, cam stopper | 12-20-1 | 1 | .04 | |
| 7-11 | 137-18577-00 | BOLT, stopper | | 1 | .12 | |

# Fig. 8 KICK

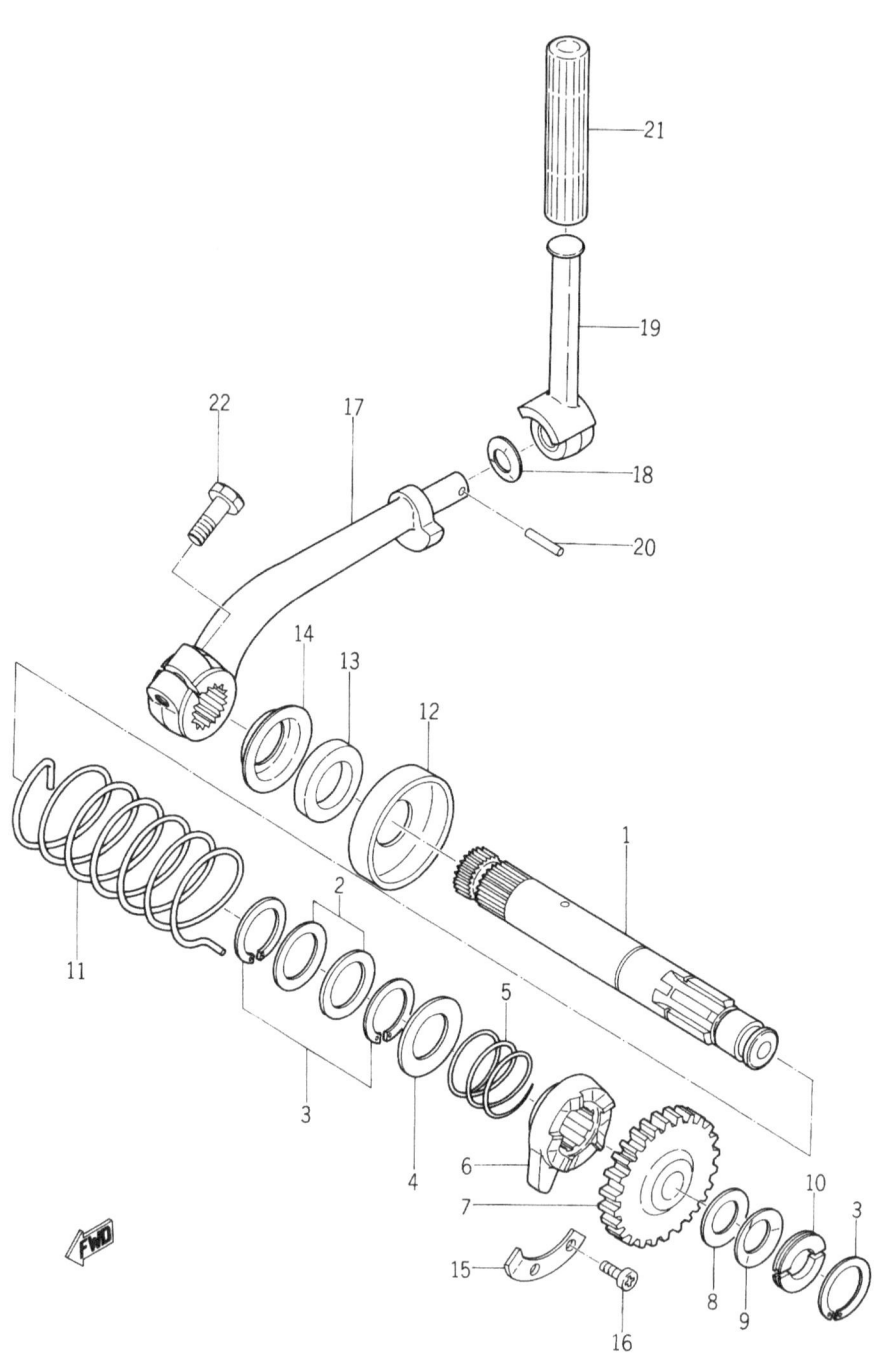

| Ref. No. | Part No. | Part Name | Description | Q'ty | S·R | Remarks |
|---|---|---|---|---|---|---|
| 8- 1 | 137-15661-00 | AXLE, kick | | 1 | 4.40 | |
| 8- 2 | 137-15669-00 | WASHER, kick axle | 20-28-1 | 2 | .06 | |
| 8- 3 | 93410-20009 | CIRCLIP | S20 | 3 | .16 | |
| 8- 4 | 137-15676-00 | COVER, spring | 20-30-1 | 1 | .06 | |
| 8- 5 | 137-15675-00 | SPRING, ratchet wheel | | 1 | .12 | |
| 8- 6 | 137-15671-00 | WHEEL, ratchet | | 1 | 2.80 | |
| 8- 7 | 137-15641-00 | GEAR, kick | 26T | 1 | 3.20 | |
| 8- 8 | 137-15644-00 | SHIM, kick gear | 15-23-0.5 | 1 | .12 | |
| 8- 9 | 137-15643-00 | WASHER, wave | | 1 | .16 | |
| 8-10 | 137-15654-00 | HOLDER, kick gear | | 2 | .64 | |
| 8-11 | 137-15665-00 | SPRING, kick | | 1 | .64 | |
| 8-12 | 137-15664-00 | GUIDE, spring | | 1 | .16 | |
| 8-13 | 93101-20008 | OIL SEAL | S-20-30-7 | 1 | .40 | |
| 8-14 | 146-15662-00 | COVER, kick axle | | 1 | .16 | |
| 8-15 | 137-15674-00 | GUIDE, ratchet wheel | | 1 | .44 | |
| 8-16 | 92501-05012 | SCREW, pan head | | 2 | .04 | |
| 8- 0-1 | 137-15610-00 | KICK CRANK ASS'Y | | 1 | 7.44 | |
| 8-17 | 137-15611-00 | . CRANK, kick | | 1 | N/A | △ |
| 8-18 | 132-15613-00 | . WASHER, spring | | 1 | .08 | |
| 8-19 | 137-15612-00 | . LEVER, kick | | 1 | 1.20 | |
| 8-20 | 93604-18017 | . PIN, dowel | | 1 | .20 | |
| 8-21 | 156-15618-01 | COVER, kick lever | | 1 | .18 | |
| 8-22 | 91201-06025 | BOLT | | 1 | .06 | |

## Fig. 9 CARBURETOR

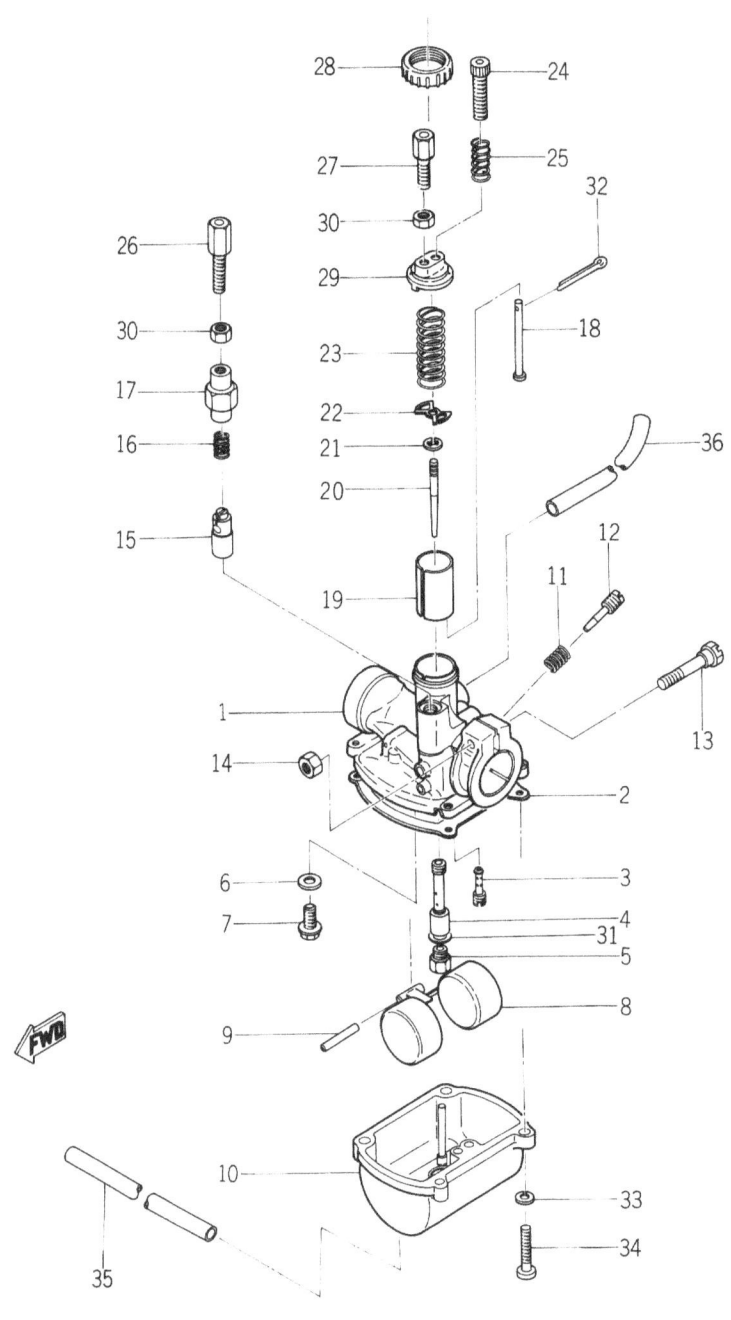

| Ref. No. | Part No. | Part Name | Description | Q'ty | S·R | Remarks |
|---|---|---|---|---|---|---|
| 9- 0-1 | 137-14101-60 | CARBURETOR ASS'Y | | 1 | 20.00 | |
| 9- 1 | | . BODY, mixing | | 1 | N/A | △ |
| 9- 2 | 137-14184-00 | . GASKET, float chamber | | 1 | .36 | |
| 9- 3 | 127-14142-30 | . JET, pilot | #30 | 1 | .62 | |
| 9- 4 | 137-14141-30 | . NOZZLE, main | O-0 | 1 | 2.18 | |
| 9- 5 | 137-14143-38 | . JET, main | #190 | 1 | .56 | |
| 9- 5-1 | 137-14143-40 | . JET, main | #200 | 1 | .56 | |
| 9- 5-2 | 137-14143-42 | . JET, main | #210 | 1 | .56 | |
| 9- 5-3 | 137-14143-44 | . JET, main | #220 | 1 | .56 | |
| 9- 5-4 | 137-14143-46 | . JET, main | #230 | 1 | .56 | |
| 9- 6 | 127-14195-00 | . WASHER, valve seat | | 1 | .02 | |
| 9- 7 | 137-14190-20 | . VALVE SEAT ASS'Y | #2.0 | 1 | 3.50 | |
| 9- 8 | 137-14185-00 | . FLOAT | | 1 | 1.58 | |
| 9- 9 | 137-14186-00 | . PIN, float | | 1 | .10 | |
| 9-10 | 137-14181-00 | . BODY, float chamber | | 1 | 4.10 | |
| 9-11 | 137-14134-00 | . SPRING, air adjusting | | 1 | .14 | |
| 9-12 | 137-14123-00 | . SCREW, air adjusting | | 1 | .62 | |
| 9-13 | 137-14125-00 | . SCREW, body fitting | | 1 | .16 | |
| 9-14 | 137-14164-00 | . NUT, holding | | 1 | .06 | |
| 9-15 | 127-14171-00 | . PLUNGER, starter | | 1 | .72 | |
| 9-16 | 137-14135-00 | . SPRING, plunger | | 1 | .14 | |
| 9-17 | 127-14174-00 | . CAP, plunger | | 1 | .40 | |
| 9-18 | 137-14114-00 | . BAR, throttle | | 1 | .24 | |
| 9-19 | 137-14112-25 | . VALVE, throttle | #2.5 | 1 | 3.48 | |
| 9-20 | 166-14116-06 | . NEEDLE | 4J6-3 | 1 | .88 | |
| 9-21 | 137-14137-00 | . CLIP | | 1 | .18 | |
| 9-22 | 137-14136-00 | . SEAT, spring | | 1 | .36 | |
| 9-23 | 137-14131-00 | . SPRING, throttle valve | | 1 | .26 | |
| 9-24 | 127-14121-00 | . SCREW, throttle | | 1 | .56 | |
| 9-25 | 137-14133-00 | . SPRING, throttle stop | | 1 | .12 | |
| 9-26 | 127-14124-20 | . SCREW, wire adjusting | 20L | 1 | .24 | |
| 9-27 | 127-14124-23 | . SCREW, wire adjusting | 23L | 1 | .24 | |
| 9-28 | 137-14168-00 | . CAP, mixing chamber | | 1 | .96 | |
| 9-29 | 137-14158-00 | . TOP, mixing chamber | | 1 | .96 | |

## Fig. 9  CARBURETOR

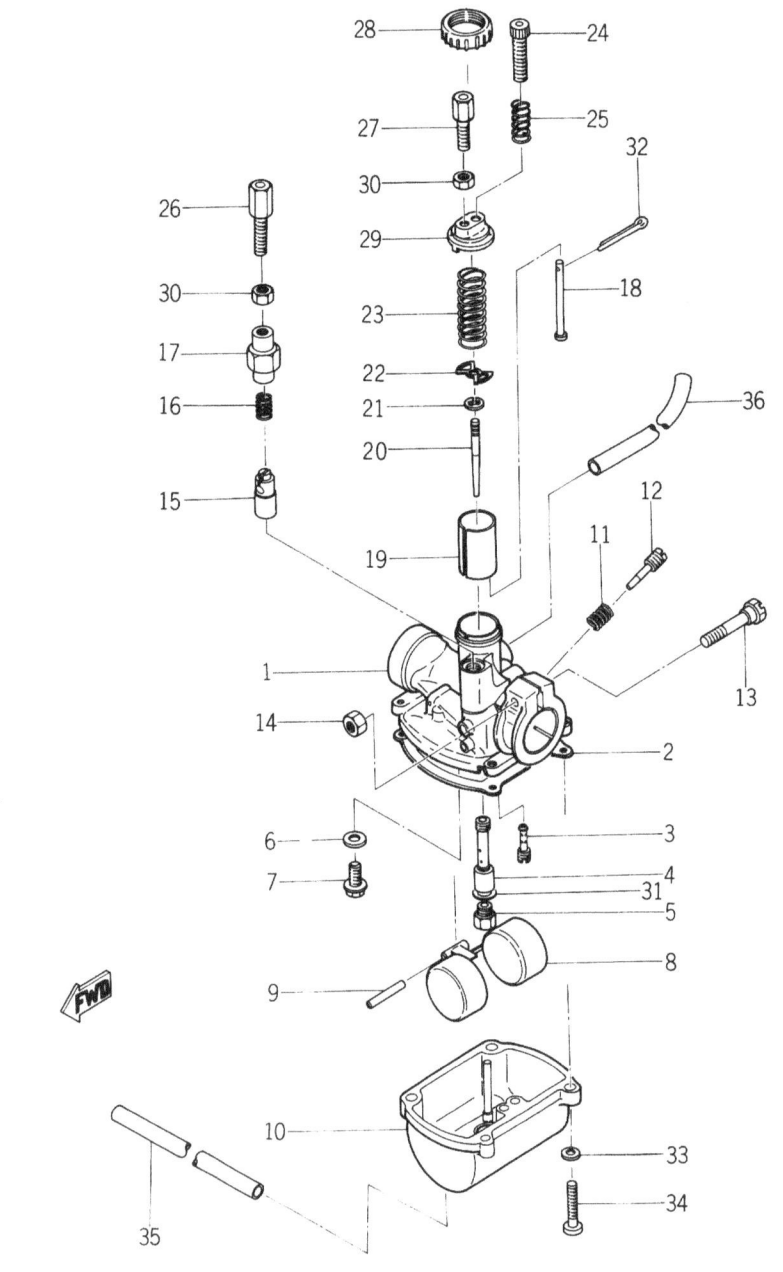

| Ref. No. | Part No. | Part Name | Description | Q'ty | S·R | Remarks |
|---|---|---|---|---|---|---|
| 9-30 | 127-14161-00 | .NUT, wire adjusting | | 2 | .08 | |
| 9-31 | 137-14153-00 | .WASHER, main jet | | 1 | .08 | |
| 9-32 | 91401-10010 | .PIN, cotter | | 1 | .01 | |
| 9-33 | 92901-04100 | .WASHER, spring | | 4 | .01 | |
| 9-34 | 92501-04015 | .SCREW, pan head | | 4 | .04 | |
| 9-35 | 137-14196-00 | PIPE, over flow | | 1 | .24 | |
| 9-36 | 137-14197-00 | PIPE, air vent | | 1 | .24 | |

# Fig. 10 MUFFLER AND AIR CLEANER

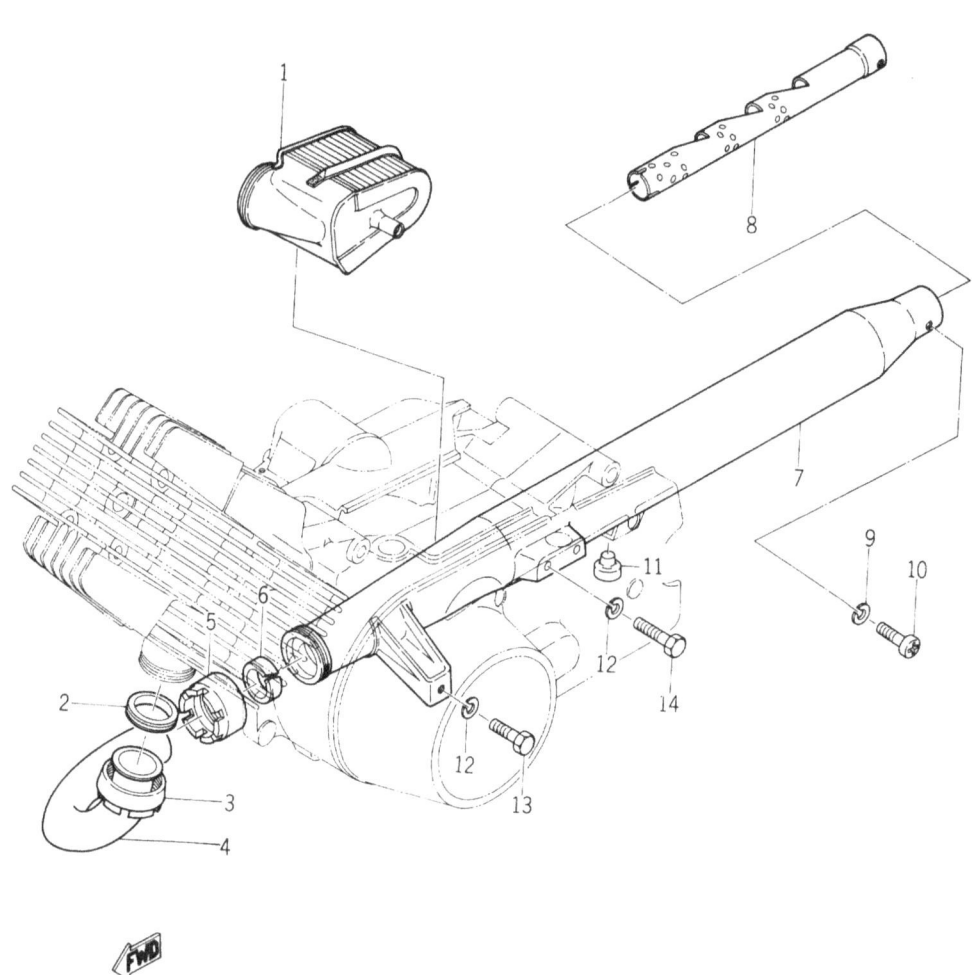

| Ref. No. | Part No. | Part Name | Description | Q'ty | S·R | Remarks |
|---|---|---|---|---|---|---|
| 10- 1 | 137-14451-00 | ELEMENT, air cleaner | | 1 | 3.20 | |
| 10- 2 | 152-14613-00 | GASKET, exhaust pipe | | 1 | .56 | |
| 10- 3 | 150-14612-00 | NUT, exhaust pipe | | 1 | 1.20 | |
| 10- 4 | 137-14611-00 | PIPE, exhaust | | 1 | 5.60 | |
| 10- 5 | 137-14713-00 | NUT, muffler joint | | 1 | 1.40 | |
| 10- 6 | 136-14714-60 | GASKET, muffler joint | | 1 | .70 | |
| 10- 7 | 137-14710-90 | MUFFLER ASS'Y | | 1 | 17.60 | ~No.173000 |
| 10- 7-1 | 137-14710-00 | MUFFLER ASS'Y | | 1 | 17.60 | No.173001~ |
| 10- 8 | 156-14753-00 | . SILENCER | | 1 | 3.00 | ~No.173000 |
| 10- 8-1 | 137-14753-00 | . SILENCER | | 1 | 2.40 | No.173001~ |
| 10- 9 | 92901-05100 | . WASHER, spring | | 1 | .01 | |
| 10-10 | 92501-05008 | . SCREW, pan head | | 1 | .04 | |
| 10-11 | 102-27114-00 | STOPPER, main stand | | 1 | .14 | |
| 10-12 | 92901-08100 | WASHER, spring | | 3 | .01 | |
| 10-13 | 91201-08018 | BOLT | | 1 | .10 | |
| 10-14 | 91201-08025 | BOLT | | 2 | .12 | |

## Fig.11 OIL PUMP

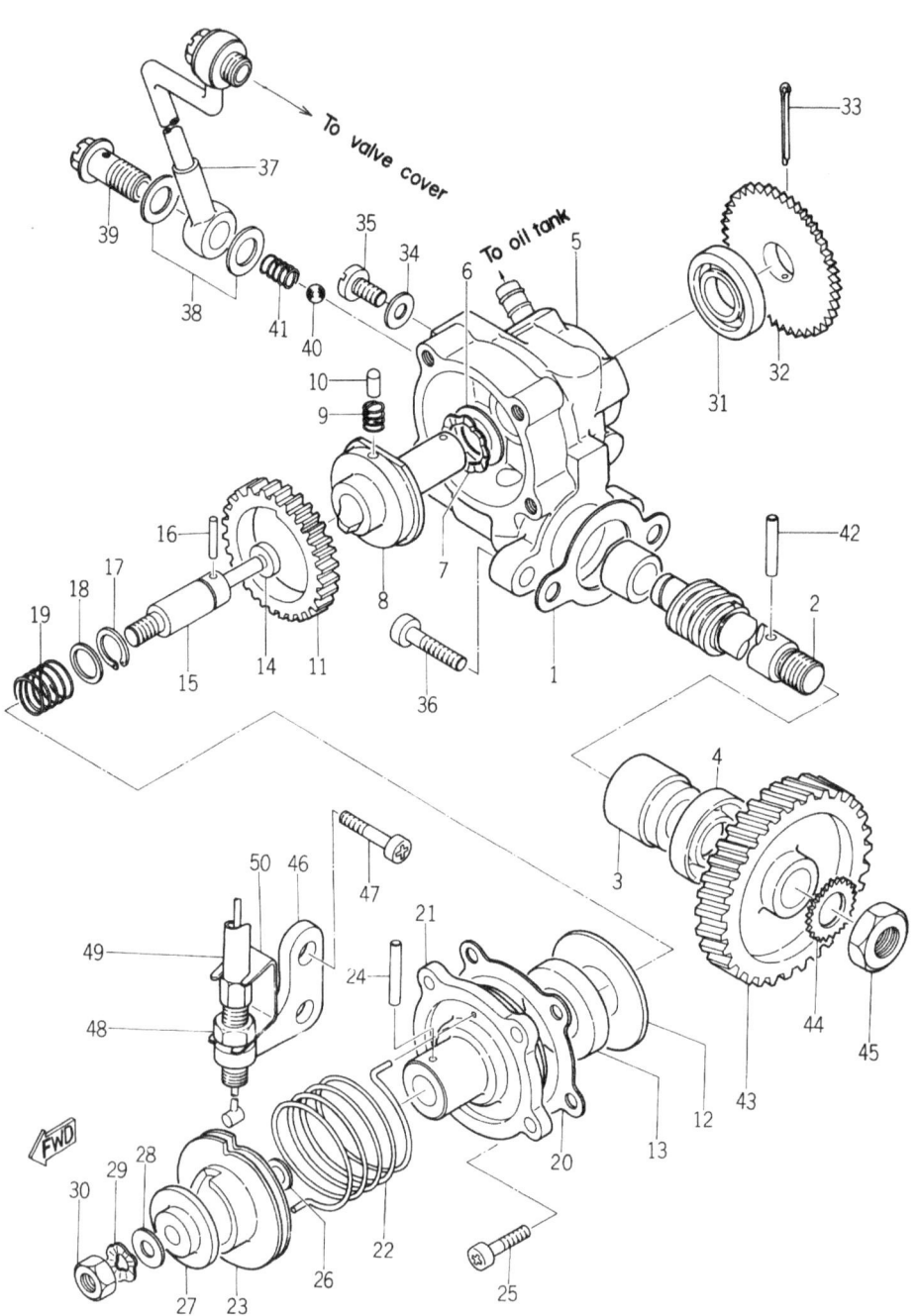

| Ref. No. | Part No. | Part Name | Description | Q'ty | S·R | Remarks |
|---|---|---|---|---|---|---|
| 11- 1 | 126-13116-00 | GASKET, pump case | | 1 | .04 | |
| 11- 2 | 137-13175-00 | SHAFT, worm | | 1 | 2.48 | |
| 11- 3 | 137-13176-00 | METAL, worm shaft outer | | 1 | .60 | |
| 11- 4 | 93101-10002 | **OIL SEAL** | S-10-22-7 | 1 | .40 | |
| 11- 0-1 | 137-13101-00 | OIL PUMP ASS'Y | | 1 | 24.00 | |
| 11- 5 | 137-13110-00 | . PUMP CASE ASS'Y | | 1 | N/A | △ |
| 11- 6 | 137-13148-00 | . PLATE, cam thrust | | 1 | .10 | |
| 11- 7 | 137-13129-00 | . WASHER, wave | | 1 | .10 | |
| 11- 8 | 137-13120-00 | . DISTRIBUTOR ASS'Y | | 1 | N/A | △ |
| 11- 9 | 137-13125-00 | . SPRING, pin return | | 2 | .06 | |
| 11-10 | 93602-04029 | . PIN, dowel | 2-3.8 | 2 | .08 | |
| 11-11 | 137-13124-00 | . GEAR, worm wheel | 36T | 1 | .68 | |
| 11-12 | 137-13127-00 | . PLATE, worm wheel | | 1 | .06 | |
| 11-13 | 93104-14004 | . OIL SEAL | SO-14-25-5 | 1 | .40 | |
| 11-14 | 93104-04001 | . OIL SEAL | SO-4-9-3 | 1 | .16 | |
| 11-15 | 137-13131-00 | . PLUNGER | | 1 | N/A | △ |
| 11-16 | 93603-12030 | . PIN, plunger | | 1 | .06 | |
| 11-17 | 93440-08001 | . CIRCLIP, plunger | | 1 | .10 | |
| 11-18 | 137-13134-00 | . SEAT, spring | | 1 | .02 | |
| 11-19 | 137-13135-00 | . SPRING, plunger return | | 1 | .10 | |
| 11-20 | 137-13142-00 | . GASKET, pump case cover | | 1 | .04 | |
| 11-21 | 137-13141-00 | . COVER, pump case | | 1 | N/A | △ |
| 11-22 | 137-13145-00 | . SPRING, adjust pulley | | 1 | .14 | |
| 11-23 | 137-13144-00 | . PULLEY, adjusting | | 1 | .88 | |
| 11-24 | 91608-20010 | . PIN, spring | | 1 | .06 | |
| 11-25 | 92501-04010 | . SCREW, pan head | | 4 | .02 | |
| 11-26 | 137-13137-00 | . SHIM, plunger | 5.8-10-0.1 | 1 | .06 | |
| 11-27 | 137-13138-00 | .PLATE, adjusting | | 1 | .36 | |
| 11-28 | 137-13147-00 | . SHIM | 5.8-10-0.1 | 2 | .10 | |
| 11-29 | 137-13136-00 | . WASHER, wave | | 1 | .06 | |
| 11-30 | 137-13139-00 | . NUT, adjust plate | | 1 | .02 | |
| 11-31 | 93101-10001 | . OIL SEAL | S-10-21-5 | 1 | .16 | |
| 11-32 | 137-13128-00 | . PLATE, starter | | 1 | .32 | |
| 11-33 | 91401-12018 | . PIN, cotter | 1.2-18 | 1 | .01 | |

# Fig.11 OIL PUMP

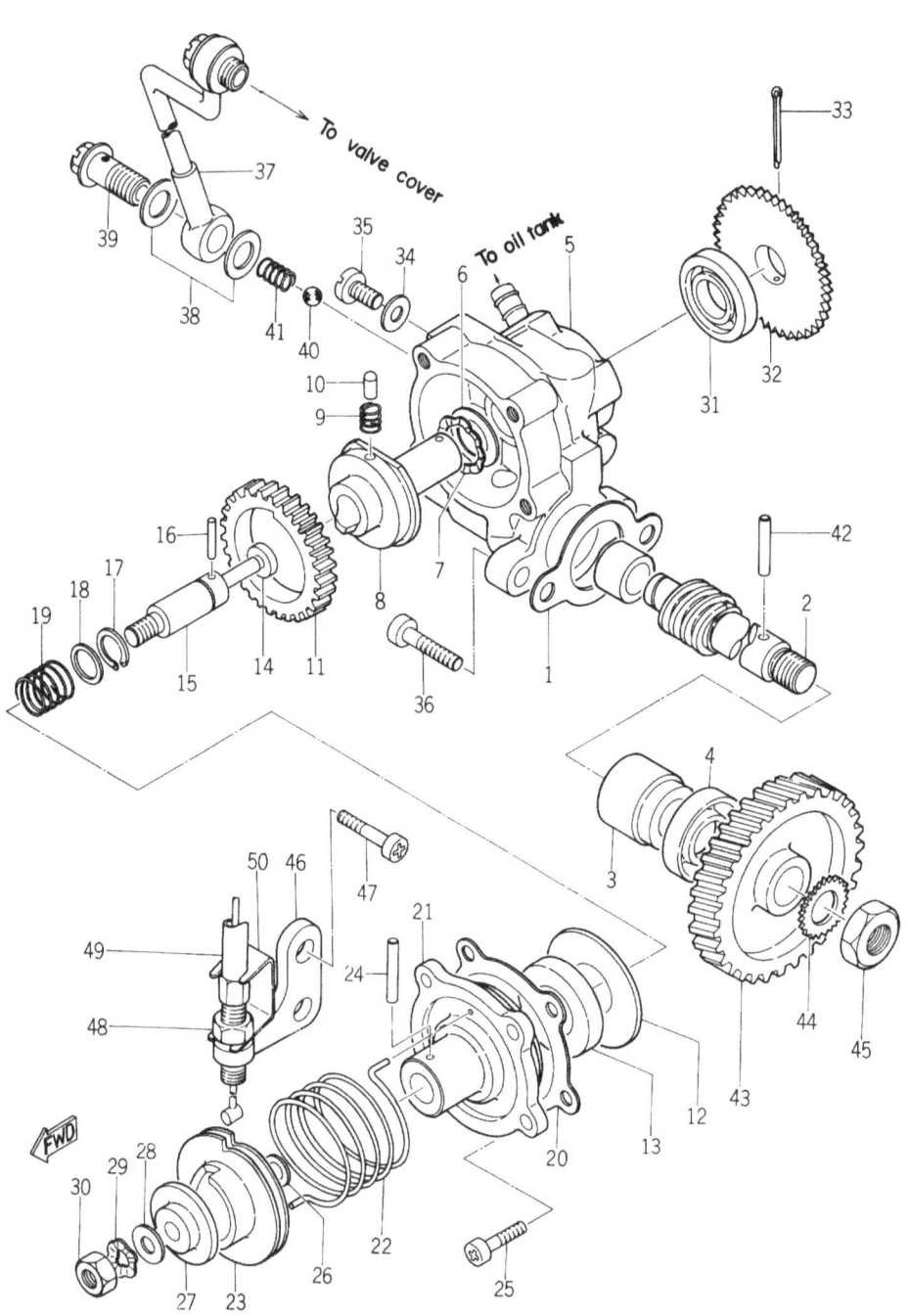

| Ref. No. | Part No. | Part Name | Description | Q'ty | S·R | Remarks |
|---|---|---|---|---|---|---|
| 11-34 | 137-13187-00 | GASKET, breather bolt | 4.2-8.5-0.5 | 1 | .02 | |
| 11-35 | 137-13185-00 | BOLT, breather | | 1 | .12 | |
| 11-36 | 92501-05015 | SCREW, pan head | | 2 | .04 | |
| 11-37 | 137-13161-00 | PIPE, delivery | | 1 | 1.28 | |
| 11-38 | 137-13167-00 | GASKET, banjo bolt | 6-13-0.5 | 4 | .02 | |
| 11-39 | 137-13165-00 | BOLT, banjo | | 2 | .40 | |
| 11-40 | 93505-32002 | BALL | 5/32" | 1 | .02 | ☆ |
| 11-41 | 137-13169-00 | SPRING, check ball | | 1 | .16 | |
| 11-42 | 93603-22028 | PIN, dowel | 3-21.8 | 1 | .04 | |
| 11-43 | 137-13178-00 | GEAR, drive | 23T | 1 | 4.64 | |
| 11-44 | 92901-08400 | WASHER, tooth | | 1 | .04 | |
| 11-45 | 92801-08300 | NUT | | 1 | .04 | |
| 11-46 | 137-26381-00 | HOLDER, wire adjusting | | 1 | .64 | |
| 11-47 | 92501-05008 | SCREW, pan head | | 2 | .04 | |
| 11-48 | 92801-06300 | NUT | | 1 | .01 | |
| 11-49 | 137-26382-00 | BOLT, wire adjusting | | 1 | .24 | |
| 11-50 | 137-26384-00 | CLIP, pump wire | | 1 | .12 | |

# Fig.12 GENERATOR

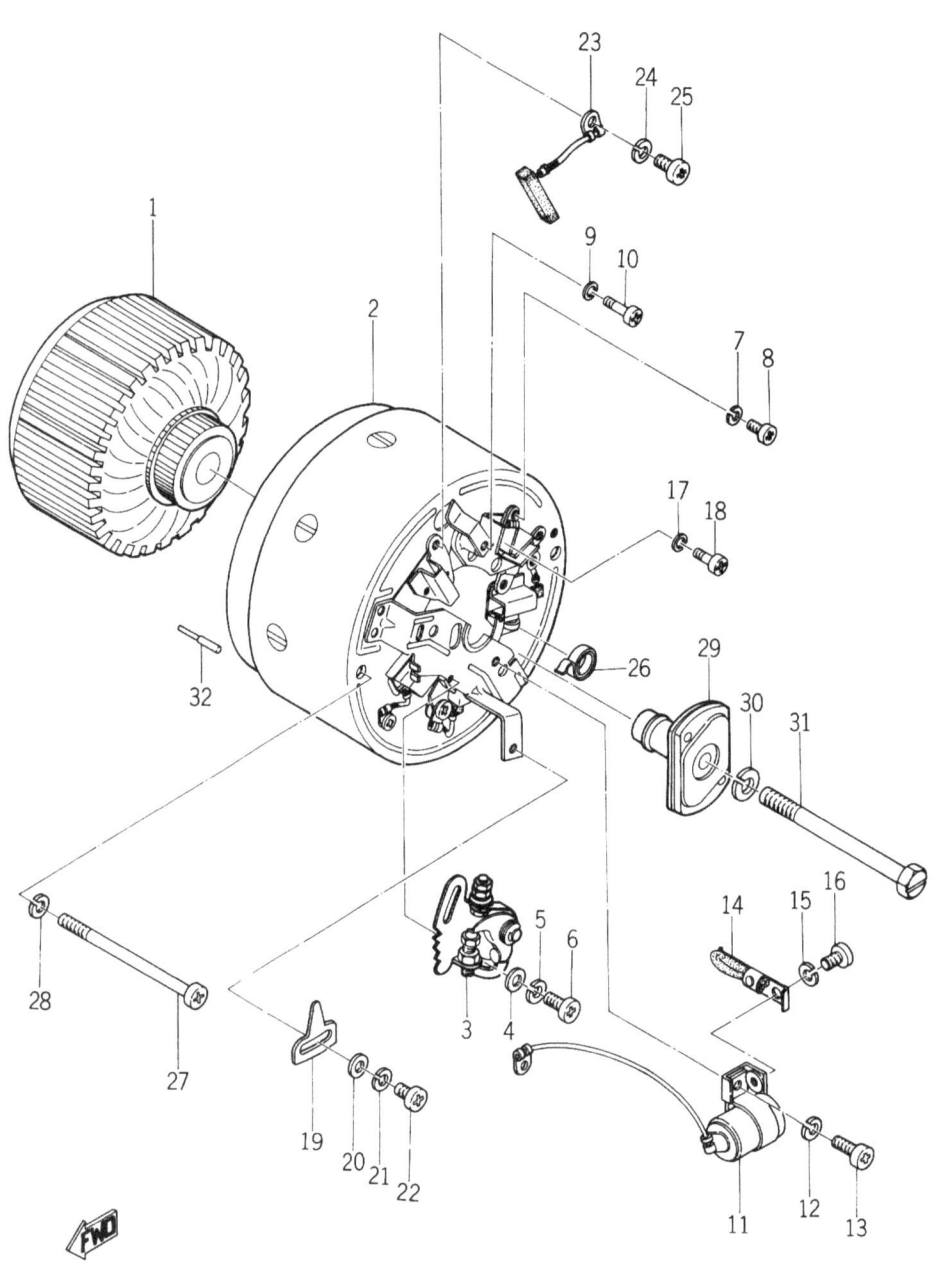

| Ref. No. | Part No. | Part Name | Description | Q'ty | S·R | Remarks |
|---|---|---|---|---|---|---|
| 12- 0-1 | 141-81100-10 | STARTER GENERATOR ASS'Y | | 1 | ✹85.00 | |
| 12- 1 | 141-81155-10 | . ARMATURE | | 1 | ✹31.92 | |
| 12- 2 | 136-81110-10 | . STATOR ASS'Y | | 1 | ✹30.00 | |
| 12- 3 | 136-81121-10 | . . CONTACT BREAKER ASS'Y | | 1 | 3.00 | |
| 12- 4 | 92901-04200 | . . WASHER, plain | | 2 | .01 | |
| 12- 5 | 92901-04100 | . . WASHER, spring | | 2 | .01 | |
| 12- 6 | 92501-04008 | . . SCREW, pan head | | 2 | .04 | |
| 12- 7 | 92901-03100 | . . WASHER, spring | | 2 | .01 | |
| 12- 8 | 92501-03008 | . . SCREW, pan head | | 2 | .04 | |
| 12- 9 | 92901-05100 | . . WASHER, spring | | 1 | .01 | |
| 12-10 | 92501-05008 | . . SCREW, pan head | | 1 | .04 | |
| 12-11 | 148-81126-10 | . . CONDENSER | | 1 | 1.20 | |
| 12-12 | 92901-04100 | . . WASHER, spring | | 2 | .01 | |
| 12-13 | 92501-04008 | . . SCREW, pan head | | 2 | .04 | |
| 12-14 | 141-81131-10 | . . LUBRICATOR | | 1 | .35 | |
| 12-15 | 92901-04100 | . . WASHER, spring | | 1 | .01 | |
| 12-16 | 92501-04008 | . . SCREW, pan head | | 1 | .04 | |
| 12-17 | 92901-04100 | . . WASHER, spring | | 4 | .01 | |
| 12-18 | 92501-04008 | . . SCREW, pan head | | 4 | .04 | |
| 12-19 | 141-81132-10 | . . PLATE, timing | | 1 | .11 | |
| 12-20 | 92901-04200 | . . WASHER, plain | | 1 | .01 | |
| 12-21 | 92901-04100 | . . WASHER, spring | | 1 | .01 | |
| 12-22 | 92501-04008 | . . SCREW, pan head | | 1 | .04 | |
| 12-23 | 141-81111-10 | . . BRUSH | | 4 | 1.16 | |
| 12-24 | 92901-04100 | . . WASHER, spring | | 3 | .01 | |
| 12-25 | 92501-04008 | . . SCREW, pan head | | 3 | .04 | |
| 12-26 | 141-81113-10 | . . SPRING, brush | | 4 | .48 | |
| 12-27 | 136-81135-10 | . SCREW, stator | | 2 | .20 | |
| 12-28 | 92901-05100 | . WASHER, spring | | 2 | .01 | |
| 12-29 | 141-81153-10 | . GOVERNOR ASS'Y | | 1 | 4.24 | |
| 12-30 | 92901-08100 | . WASHER, spring | | 1 | .01 | |
| 12-31 | 141-81152-10 | . BOLT (7∅) | | 1 | .36 | |
| 12-32 | 93603-14026 | PIN, dowel | 3-14 | 1 | .04 | |

# CHASSIS

MEMO

## Fig. 13 FRAME

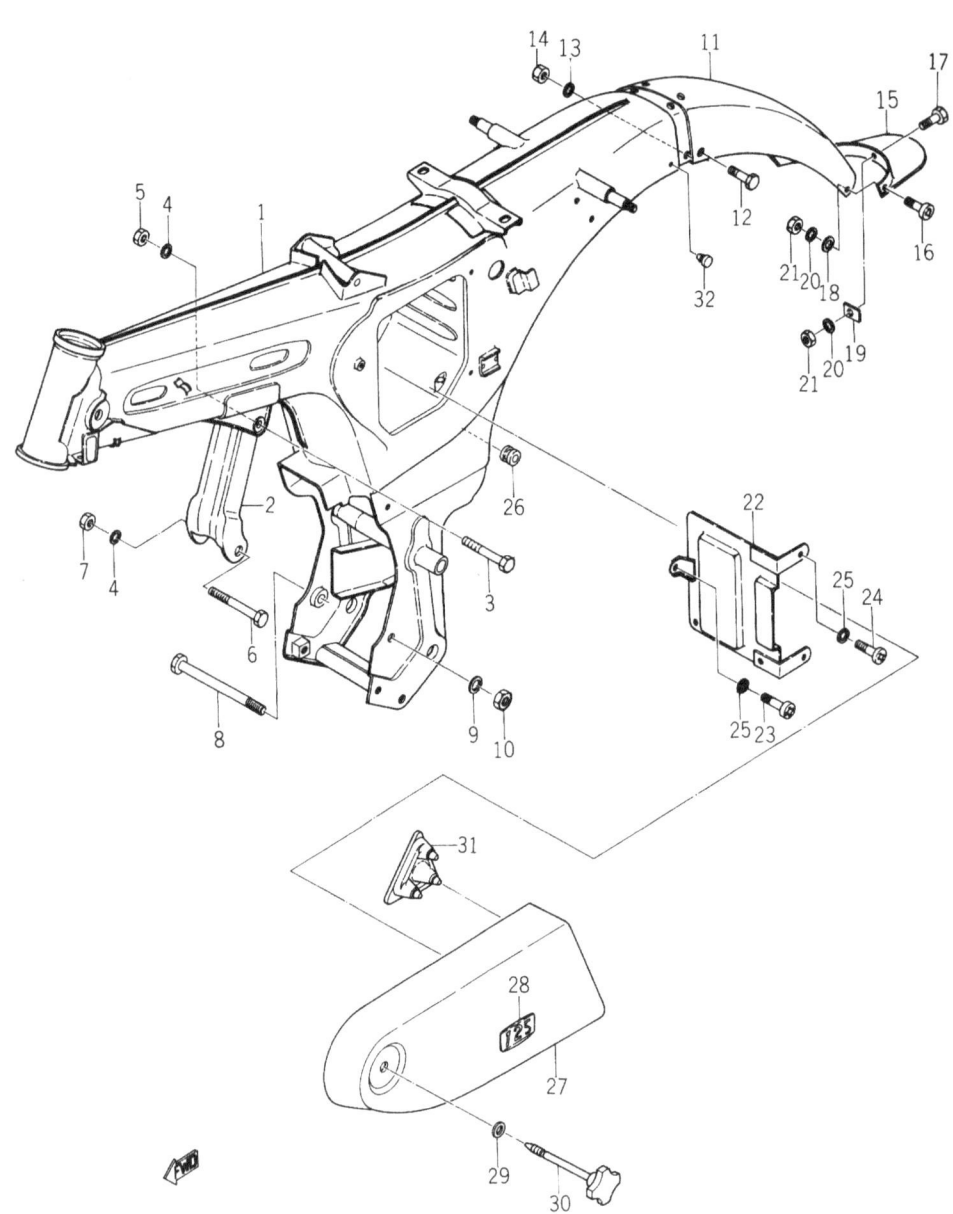

| Ref. No. | Part No. | Part Name | Description | Q'ty | S·R | Remarks |
|---|---|---|---|---|---|---|
| 13- 1 | 137-21110-00 | FRAME COMP | | 1 | 80.00 | ⊙ ~ No. 173000 |
| 13- 1-1 | 137-21110-08 | FRAME COMP | | 1 | 80.00 | ⊙ No. 173001~ |
| 13- 2 | 137-21283-00 | SUPPORT, engine | | 1 | 1.76 | ⊙ |
| 13- 3 | 91203-08060 | BOLT | | 1 | .24 | |
| 13- 4 | 92901-08100 | WASHER, spring | | 2 | .01 | |
| 13- 5 | 92803-08100 | NUT | | 1 | .04 | |
| 13- 6 | 137-21481-00 | BOLT, mounting | | 1 | .20 | |
| 13- 7 | 92801-08100 | NUT | | 1 | .04 | |
| 13- 8 | 91101-08130 | BOLT | | 2 | .40 | |
| 13- 9 | 92901-08100 | WASHER, spring | | 2 | .01 | |
| 13-10 | 92801-08100 | NUT | | 2 | .04 | |
| 13-11 | 137-21610-60 | REAR FENDER COMP | | 1 | 8.00 | ⊙ ~ No. 173000 |
| 13-11-1 | 137-21610-61 | REAR FENDER COMP | | 1 | 8.00 | ⊙ No. 173001~ |
| 13-12 | 91201-08015 | BOLT | | 2 | .10 | |
| 13-13 | 92901-08100 | WASHER, spring | | 2 | .01 | |
| 13-14 | 92801-08100 | NUT | | 2 | .04 | |
| 13-15 | 137-21612-02 | FLAP, rear fender | | 1 | 2.08 | |
| 13-16 | 92503-06015 | SCREW, pan head | | 2 | .06 | |
| 13-17 | 91201-06012 | BOLT | | 1 | .04 | |
| 13-18 | 137-21623-01 | PLATE, flap fitting (1) | | 2 | .20 | |
| 13-19 | 137-21624-00 | PLATE, flap fitting (2) | | 1 | .08 | |
| 13-20 | 92901-06100 | WASHER, spring | | 3 | .01 | |
| 13-21 | 92801-06100 | NUT | | 3 | .01 | |
| 13-22 | 137-81915-00 | PLATE, regulator fitting | | 1 | 1.44 | |
| 13-23 | 92501-06010 | SCREW, pan head | | 1 | .04 | |
| 13-24 | 92501-06012 | SCREW, pan head | | 2 | .04 | |
| 13-25 | 92901-06100 | WASHER, spring | | 3 | .01 | |
| 13-26 | 135-82595-00 | GROMMET | | 1 | .04 | |
| 13-27 | 137-21711-00 | COVER, side (L.H) | | 1 | 5.52 | |
| 13-28 | 137-21786-00 | EMBLEM | | 1 | .24 | |
| 13-29 | 122-21715-00 | WASHER, special | | 1 | .04 | |
| 13-30 | 137-21714-00 | KNOB, side cover | | 1 | .72 | |
| 13-31 | 137-21719-00 | GROMMET, side cover seal | | 1 | 1.08 | |
| 13-32 | 101-21790-00 | PLUG, blind | | 2 | .03 | |

## Fig. 14 REAR ARM AND CHAIN CASE

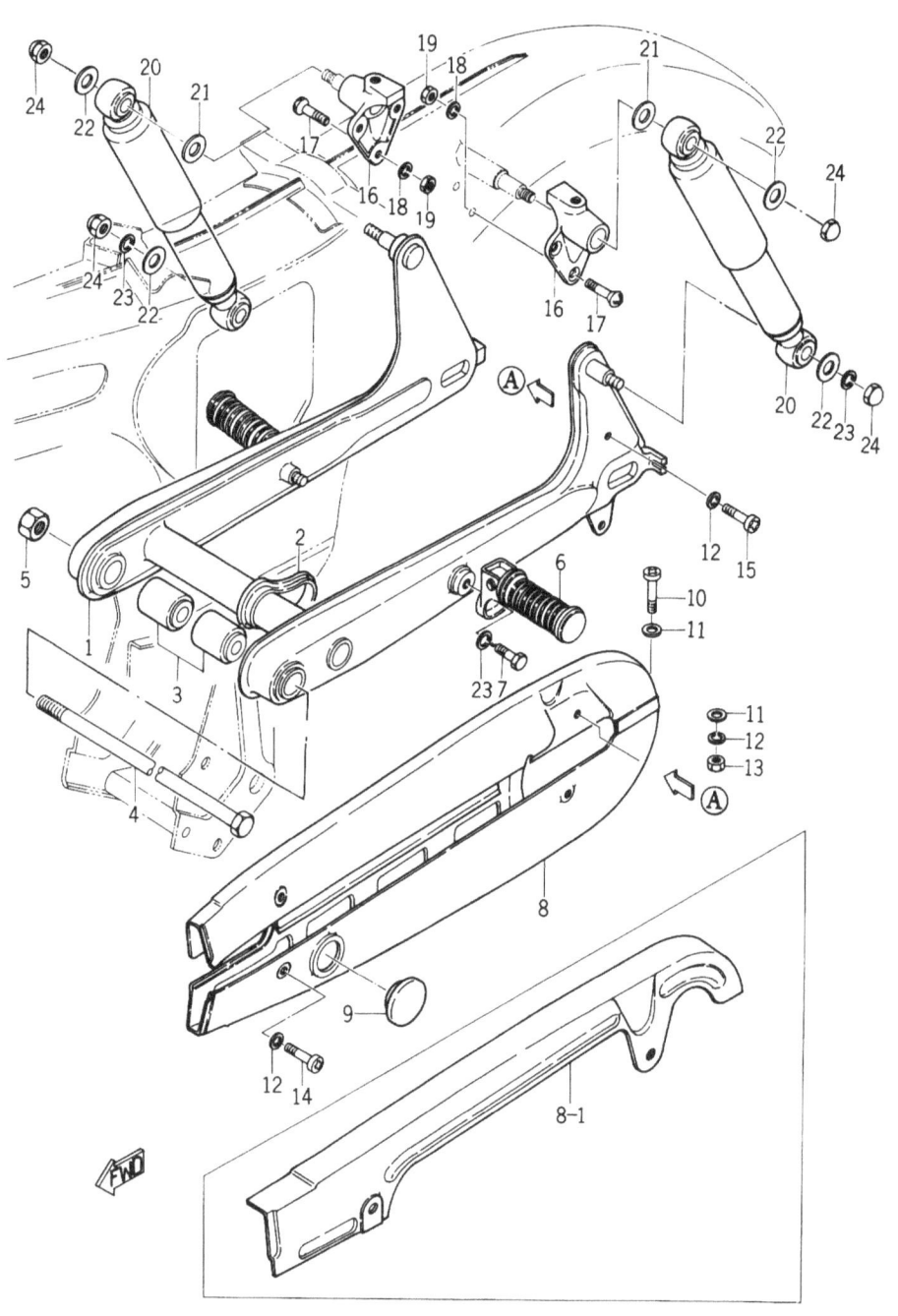

| Ref. No. | Part No. | Part Name | Description | Q'ty | S·R | Remarks |
|---|---|---|---|---|---|---|
| 14- 1 | 137-22110-60 | REAR ARM COMP | | 1 | 20.00 | ⊙ |
| 14- 2 | 137-22151-00 | SEAL, guard | | 1 | .40 | |
| 14- 3 | 137-22123-00 | BUSHING, rear arm | | 2 | 1.20 | |
| 14- 4 | 137-22141-00 | SHAFT, pivot | | 1 | 2.40 | |
| 14- 5 | 92803-14200 | NUT | | 1 | .16 | |
| 14- 6 | 120-27430-00 | REAR FOOT REST ASS'Y | | 2 | 2.20 | |
| 14- 6-1 | 120-27433-00 | . COVER, rear foot rest | | 2 | .32 | |
| 14- 7 | 91201-10045 | BOLT | | 2 | .20 | |
| 14- 8 | 137-22310-00 | CHAIN CASE ASS'Y | | 1 | 10.00 | |
| 14- 8-1 | 137-22311-60 | CHAIN CASE, half | | 1 | 3.20 | |
| 14- 9 | 148-22315-00 | CAP | | 1 | .12 | |
| 14-10 | 92501-06045 | SCREW, pan head | | 1 | .10 | |
| 14-11 | 92901-06200 | WASHER, plain | | 2 | .01 | |
| 14-12 | 92901-06100 | WASHER, spring | | 5 | .01 | |
| 14-13 | 92801-06100 | NUT | | 1 | .01 | |
| 14-14 | 92501-06010 | SCREW, pan head | | 3 | .04 | |
| 14-15 | 92501-06020 | SCREW, pan head | | 1 | .04 | |
| 14-16 | 137-21381-00 | BRACKET, rear cushion | | 2 | 2.16 | |
| 14-17 | 92603-06018 | SCREW, oval head | | 6 | .06 | |
| 14-18 | 92901-06100 | WASHER, spring | | 6 | .01 | |
| 14-19 | 92801-06100 | NUT | | 6 | .01 | |
| 14-20 | 137-22210-00 | REAR CUSHION ASS'Y | | 2 | 16.00 | ⊙ |
| 14-21 | 135-22243-00 | WASHER, rear cushion | | 2 | .08 | |
| 14-22 | 136-22243-00 | WASHER, rear cushion | | 4 | .08 | |
| 14-23 | 92903-10100 | WASHER, spring | | 4 | .04 | |
| 14-24 | 92803-10700 | NUT, crown | | 4 | .20 | |

## Fig.15 STAND AND BRAKE PEDAL

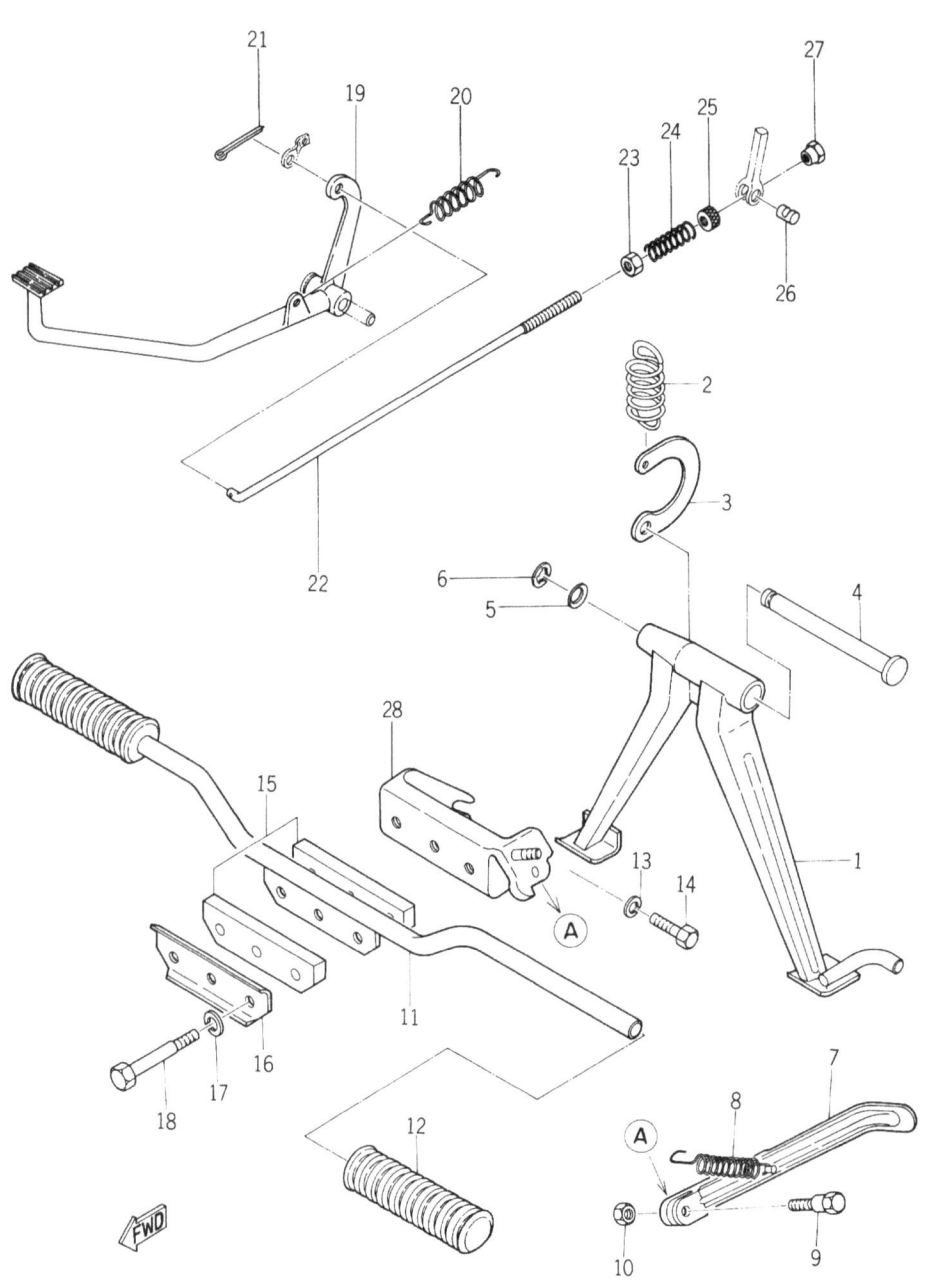

| Ref. No. | Part No. | Part Name | Description | Q'ty | S·R | Remarks |
|---|---|---|---|---|---|---|
| 15- 1 | 137-27111-00 | STAND, main | | 1 | 7.20 | |
| 15- 2 | 136-27116-00 | SPRING, main stand | | 1 | .40 | |
| 15- 3 | 137-27115-00 | LINK, main stand | | 1 | .32 | |
| 15- 4 | 137-27112-01 | SHAFT, main stand | | 1 | 1.28 | |
| 15- 5 | 137-27219-00 | WASHER, wave | | 1 | .12 | |
| 15- 6 | 93430-12008 | CIRCLIP | E12 | 1 | .12 | |
| 15- 7 | 137-27311-01 | STAND, side | | 1 | 3.60 | |
| 15- 8 | 136-27316-00 | SPRING, side stand | | 1 | .32 | |
| 15- 9 | 137-27317-00 | BOLT, side stand | | 1 | .16 | |
| 15-10 | 92801-08300 | NUT | | 1 | .04 | |
| 15-11 | 137-27411-00 | ARM, foot rest | | 1 | 4.00 | |
| 15-12 | 136-27413-00 | COVER, foot rest | | 2 | .60 | |
| 15-13 | 92901-08100 | WASHER, spring | | 3 | .01 | |
| 15-14 | 91202-08018 | BOLT | | 3 | .10 | |
| 15-15 | 137-27414-00 | DAMPER, foot rest | | 2 | .20 | |
| 15-16 | 137-27417-00 | WASHER, foot rest | | 1 | .40 | |
| 15-17 | 92901-10100 | WASHER, spring | | 3 | .01 | |
| 15-18 | 137-27416-00 | BOLT, foot rest | | 3 | .32 | |
| 15-19 | 137-27211-00 | PEDAL, brake | | 1 | 6.40 | |
| 15-20 | 137-27216-00 | SPRING, brake pedal | | 1 | .28 | |
| 15-21 | 91401-20012 | PIN, cotter | | 1 | .01 | |
| 15-22 | 137-27231-00 | ROD, brake | | 1 | .48 | |
| 15-23 | 92801-06100 | NUT | | 1 | .01 | |
| 15-24 | 148-27236-00 | SPRING, brake rod | | 1 | .08 | |
| 15-25 | 148-27239-00 | SEAT, spring | | 1 | .16 | |
| 15-26 | 148-27237-00 | PIN, clevis | | 1 | .12 | |
| 15-27 | 109-27238-00 | NUT, rod adjusting | | 1 | .32 | |
| 15-28 | 137-27410-01 | FOOT REST ASS'Y | | 1 | 3.60 | |

## Fig. 16 HANDLE AND FRONT FENDER

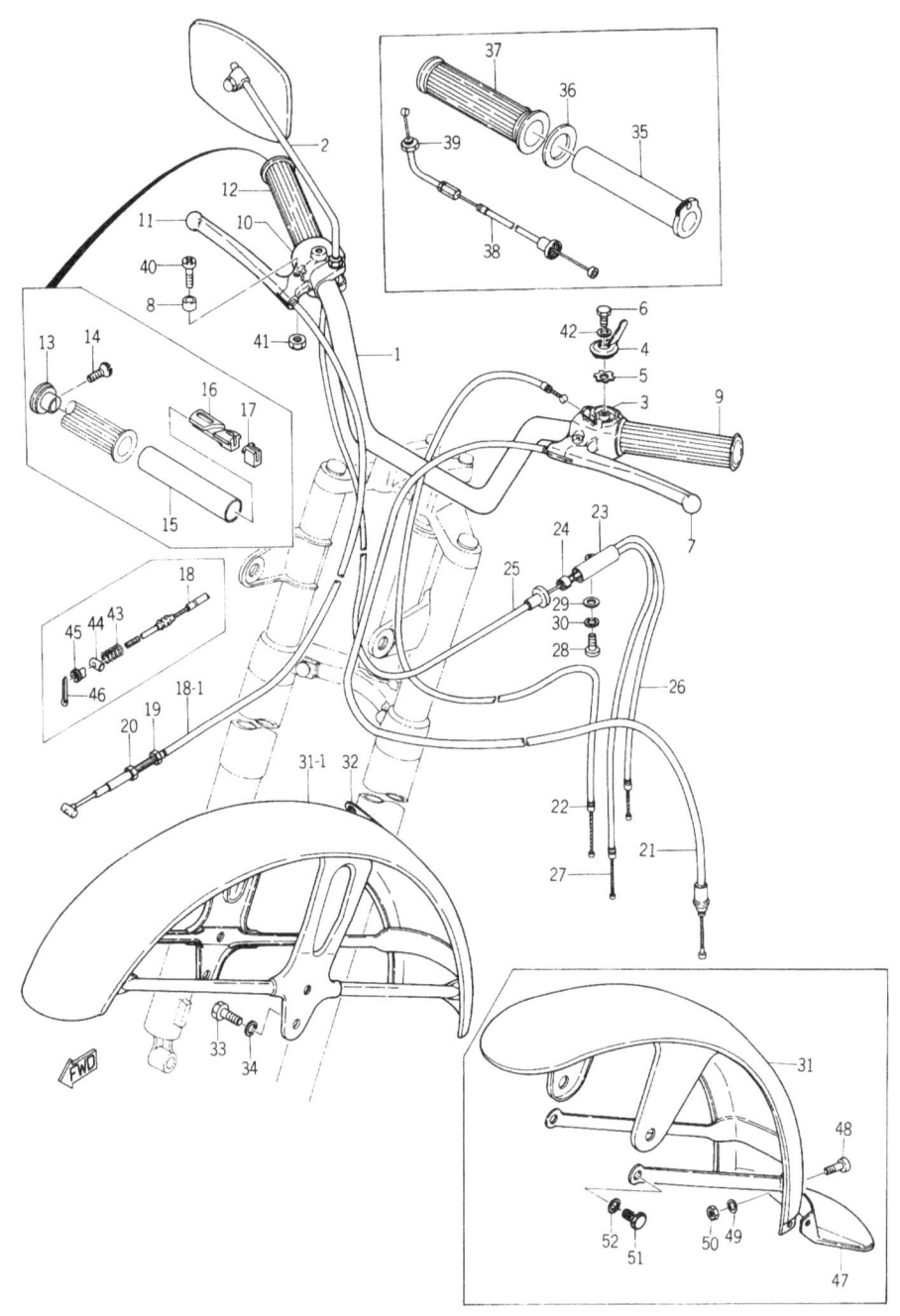

| Ref. No. | Part No. | Part Name | Description | Q'ty | S·R | Remarks |
|---|---|---|---|---|---|---|
| 16- 1 | 137-26111-11 | HANDLE | | 1 | 6.00 | ~ No. 173000 |
| 16- 1-1 | 137-26111-60 | HANDLE | | 1 | 6.00 | No. 173001 ~ |
| 16- 2 | 137-26290-00 | BACK MIRROR ASS'Y | | 1 | 2.70 | ~ No. 173000 |
| 16- 2-1 | 137-26290-01 | BACK MIRROR ASS'Y | | 1 | 2.70 | No. 173001 ~ |
| 16- 3 | 137-82610-11 | LEVER HOLDER ASS'Y (L.H) | | 1 | 7.20 | |
| 16- 4 | 137-83941-01 | LEVER, starter | | 1 | .80 | |
| 16- 5 | 137-83944-00 | WASHER, spring | | 1 | .16 | |
| 16- 6 | 137-83945-00 | BOLT, lever fitting | | 1 | .10 | |
| 16- 7 | 137-83912-00 | LEVER (L.H) | | 1 | 1.60 | ~ No. 173000 |
| 16- 7-1 | 137-83912-01 | LEVER (L.H) | | 1 | 1.60 | No. 173001 ~ |
| 16- 8 | 137-83913-00 | COLLAR, lever | | 2 | .16 | |
| 16- 9 | 136-26241-00 | GRIP, handle (L.H) | | 1 | .72 | |
| 16-10 | 137-82620-10 | LEVER HOLDER ASS'Y (R.H) | | 1 | 7.20 | ~ No. 173000 |
| 16-10-1 | 137-82620-60 | LEVER HOLDER ASS'Y (R.H) | | 1 | 7.20 | No. 173001 ~ |
| 16-11 | 137-83922-00 | LEVER (R.H) | | 1 | 1.60 | ~ No. 173000 |
| 16-11-1 | 137-83922-01 | LEVER (R.H) | | 1 | 1.60 | No. 173001 ~ |
| 16-12 | 136-26242-00 | GRIP, handle (R.H) | | 1 | .40 | |
| 16-13 | 137-26246-00 | END, grip | | 1 | .48 | |
| 16-14 | 92101-05010 | SCREW, oval head | | 1 | .04 | |
| 16-15 | 148-26243-00 | TUBE, guide slider | | 1 | .80 | |
| 16-16 | 137-26244-00 | SLIDER, throttle | | 1 | .20 | |
| 16-17 | 135-26245-00 | STOPPER, throttle wire | | 1 | .12 | |
| 16-18 | 137-26341-1Z | WIRE, brake | | 1 | 1.60 | ~ No. 164104 |
| 16-18-1 | 109-26341-10 | WIRE, brake | | 1 | 1.60 | No. 164105 ~ |
| 16-19 | 109-26345-00 | BOLT, wire adjusting | | 1 | .40 | |
| 16-20 | 109-26344-00 | NUT, wire adjusting | | 1 | .24 | |
| 16-21 | 137-26335-10 | WIRE, clutch | | 1 | 2.08 | |
| 16-22 | 137-26331-11 | WIRE, starter | | 1 | .72 | |
| 16-23 | 137-26261-01 | CYLINDER | | 1 | .80 | |
| 16-24 | 137-26263-01 | PIECE, connecting | | 1 | .36 | |
| 16-25 | 137-26311-11 | WIRE, throttle (1) | | 1 | .84 | |
| 16-26 | 137-26312-00 | WIRE, throttle (2) | | 1 | .44 | |
| 16-27 | 137-26321-00 | WIRE, oil pump | | 1 | .96 | |
| 16-28 | 92501-06012 | SCREW, pan head | | 1 | .04 | |

## Fig.16 HANDLE AND FRONT FENDER

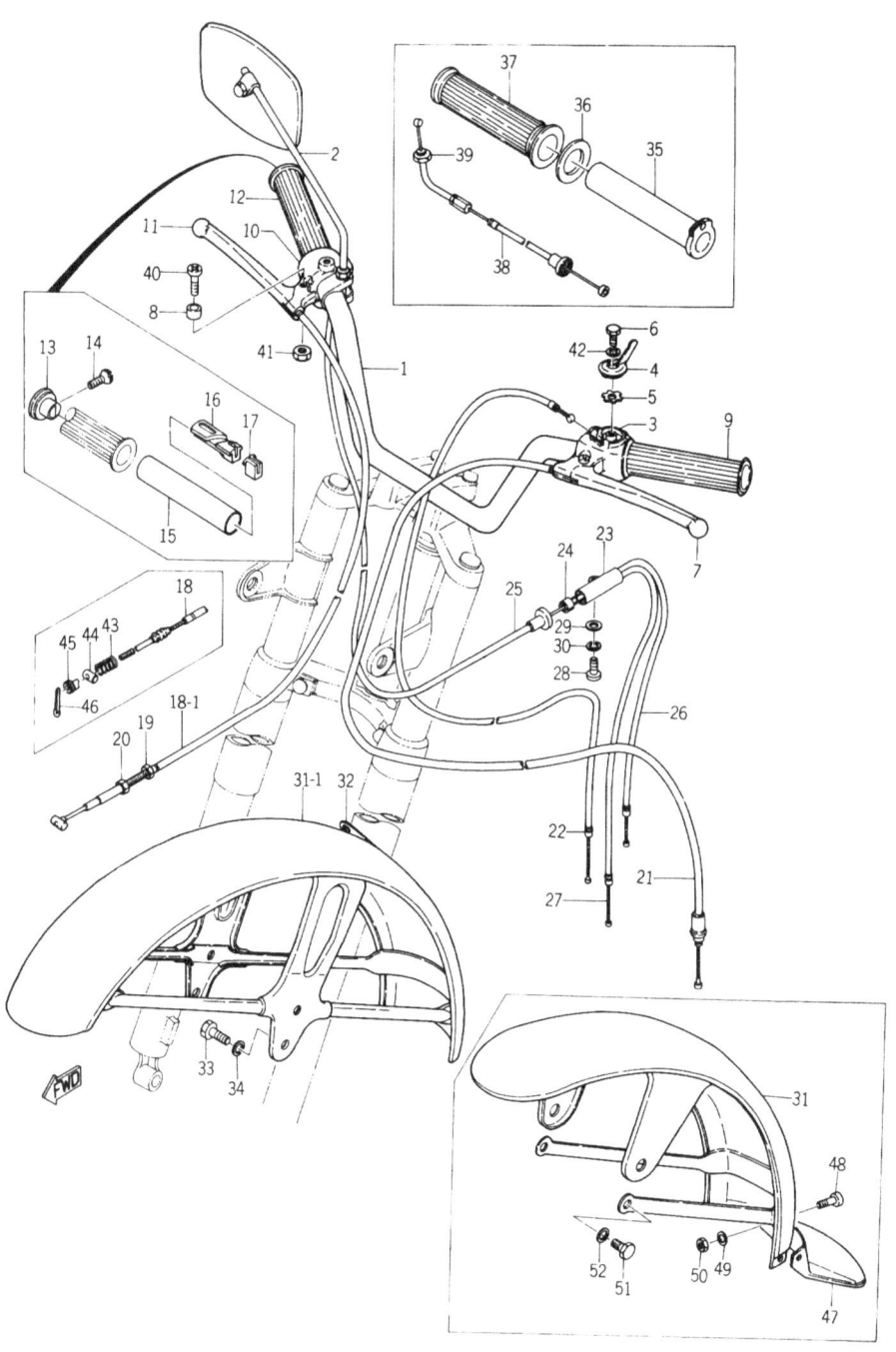

| Ref. No. | Part No. | Part Name | Description | Q'ty | S·R | Remarks |
|---|---|---|---|---|---|---|
| 16-29 | 92901-06200 | WASHER, plain | | 1 | .01 | |
| 16-30 | 92901-06100 | WASHER, spring | | 1 | .01 | |
| 16-31 | 137-21510-03 | FRONT FENDER COMP | | 1 | 14.80 | ⊙ |
| 16-31-1 | 137-21510-60 | FRONT FENDER COMP | | 1 | 14.80 | |
| 16-32 | 137-21517-00 | PAD, wire | | 1 | .20 | |
| 16-33 | 91201-08012 | BOLT | | 4 | .10 | |
| 16-34 | 92901-08100 | WASHER, spring | | 4 | .01 | |
| 16-35 | 137-26243-60 | TUBE, guide | | 1 | .80 | No. 173001~ |
| 16-36 | 150-26249-00 | RING, leaf | | 1 | .08 | No. 173001~ |
| 16-37 | 137-26242-60 | GRIP (R.H) | | 1 | .40 | No. 173001~ |
| 16-38 | 137-26311-60 | WIRE, throttle (1) | | 1 | 1.44 | No. 173001~ |
| 16-39 | 156-26251-00 | NUT, adjusting | | 1 | .24 | No. 173001~ |
| 16-40 | 92503-05020 | SCREW, pan head | | 2 | .06 | |
| 16-41 | 92801-05100 | NUT | | 2 | .01 | |
| 16-42 | 92901-06200 | WASHER, plain | | 1 | .01 | |
| 16-43 | 136-26348-00 | SPRING, wire adjusting | | 1 | .80 | |
| 16-44 | 136-26349-00 | PIN, clevis | | 1 | .24 | |
| 16-45 | 136-26344-00 | NUT, wire adjusting | | 1 | .24 | |
| 16-46 | 91401-10012 | PIN, cotter | | 1 | .01 | |
| 16-47 | 137-21521-00 | FLAP, front fender | | 1 | 1.12 | |
| 16-48 | 92503-06010 | SCREW, pan head | | 3 | .04 | |
| 16-49 | 92901-06100 | WASHER, spring | | 3 | .01 | |
| 16-50 | 92801-06300 | NUT | | 3 | .01 | |
| 16-51 | 91201-06010 | BOLT | | 2 | .04 | |
| 16-52 | 92901-06100 | WASHER, spring | | 2 | .01 | |

# Fig.17 FRONT FORK

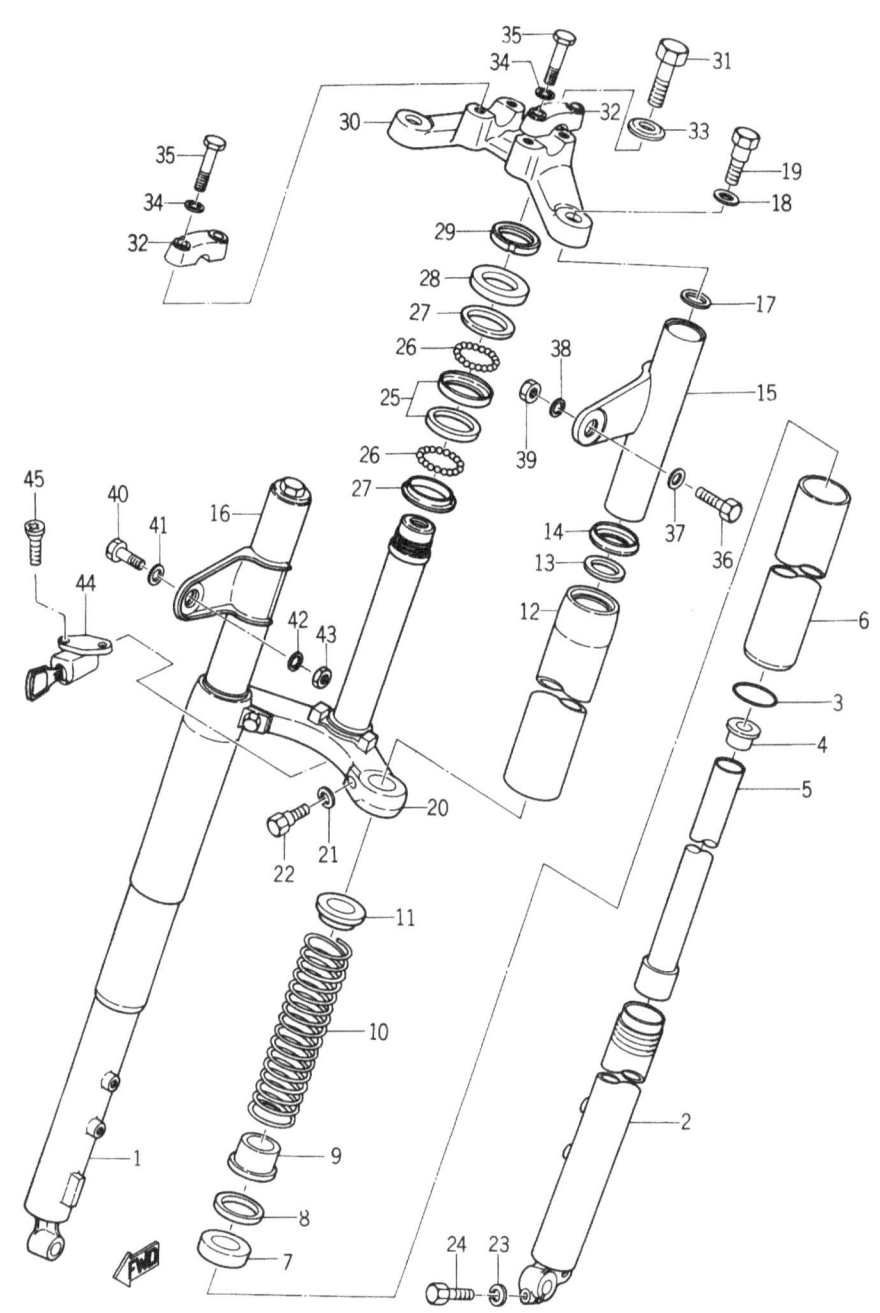

| Ref. No. | Part No. | Part Name | Description | Q'ty | S·R | Remarks |
|---|---|---|---|---|---|---|
| 17- 0-1 | 137-23100-60 | FRONT FORK ASS'Y | | 1 | 88.00 | ⊙ |
| 17- 1 | 137-23136-60 | . TUBE, outer (R.H) | | 1 | 10.00 | ⊙ |
| 17- 2 | 137-23126-60 | . TUBE, outer (L.H) | | 1 | 10.00 | ⊙ |
| 17- 3 | 137-23147-00 | . O-RING | | 2 | .28 | |
| 17- 4 | 137-23125-00 | . METAL, slide | | 2 | 1.20 | |
| 17- 5 | 137-23124-00 | . TUBE, inner | | 2 | 12.80 | |
| 17- 6 | 137-23127-00 | . NUT, outer | | 2 | 4.40 | |
| 17- 7 | 137-23145-00 | . OIL SEAL | | 2 | 1.44 | |
| 17- 8 | 137-23146-00 | . WASHER, oil seal | | 2 | .36 | |
| 17- 9 | 137-23143-00 | . SEAT, spring under | | 2 | .72 | |
| 17-10 | 137-23141-00 | . SPRING, fork | | 2 | 1.92 | |
| 17-11 | 137-23142-00 | . SEAT, spring upper | | 2 | .36 | |
| 17-12 | 137-23123-00 | . COVER, under | | 2 | 3.20 | ⊙ |
| 17-13 | 137-23163-00 | . PACKING | | 2 | .20 | |
| 17-14 | 137-23116-00 | . GUIDE, cover under | | 2 | .48 | |
| 17-15 | 137-23121-60 | . COVER, upper (L.H) | | 1 | 3.20 | ⊙ |
| 17-16 | 137-23131-00 | . COVER, upper (R.H) | | 1 | 3.20 | ⊙ |
| 17-17 | 137-23114-00 | . PACKING | | 2 | .28 | |
| 17-18 | 137-23112-00 | . WASHER, cap | | 2 | .36 | |
| 17-19 | 137-23111-00 | . BOLT, cap | | 2 | .40 | |
| 17-20 | 137-23340-00 | . UNDER BRACKET COMP | | 1 | 16.00 | |
| 17-21 | 92901-10100 | . WASHER, spring | | 2 | .01 | |
| 17-22 | 137-23346-00 | . BOLT, under bracket | | 2 | .48 | |
| 17-23 | 92901-08100 | . WASHER, spring | | 1 | .01 | |
| 17-24 | 91201-08030 | . BOLT | | 1 | .12 | |
| 17-25 | 156-23412-00 | RACE, ball (2) | | 2 | 1.04 | |
| 17-26 | 93501-04004 | BALL | 1/4" | 38 | .02 | ☆ |
| 17-27 | 156-23411-00 | RACE, ball (1) | | 2 | 1.04 | |
| 17-28 | 136-23415-00 | COVER, ball race | | 1 | .14 | |
| 17-29 | 137-23454-00 | NUT, fitting | | 1 | .84 | |
| 17-30 | 137-23435-00 | CROWN, handle | | 1 | 12.00 | ~No.135325 |
| 17-30-1 | 137-23435-01 | CROWN, handle | | 1 | 12.00 | No.135326~ |
| 17-31 | 122-23452-00 | BOLT, fitting | | 1 | .24 | |
| 17-32 | 137-23441-00 | HOLDER, handle upper | | 2 | .96 | ~No.135325 |

# Fig. 17 FRONT FORK

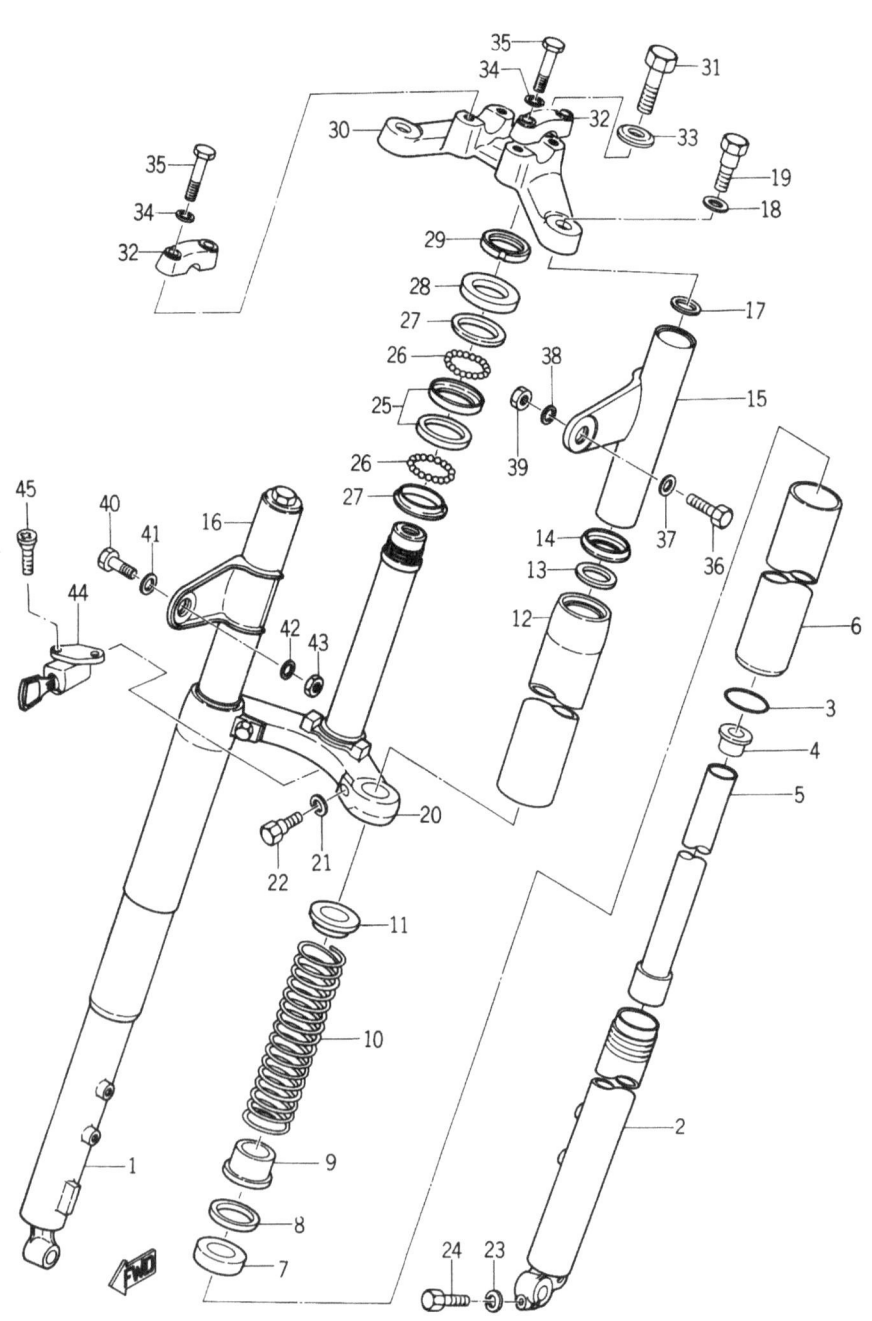

| Ref. No. | Part No. | Part Name | Description | Q'ty | S·R | Remarks |
|---|---|---|---|---|---|---|
| 17-32-1 | 137-23441-01 | HOLDER, handle upper | | 2 | .96 | No. 135326~ |
| 17-33 | 164-23443-00 | WASHER, crown | | 1 | .32 | |
| 17-34 | 92901-06100 | WASHER, spring | | 4 | .01 | ~No. 135325 |
| 17-34-1 | 92901-08100 | WASHER, spring | | 4 | .01 | No. 135326~ |
| 17-35 | 91103-06035 | BOLT | | 4 | .16 | ~No. 135325 |
| 17-35-1 | 91103-08035 | BOLT | | 4 | .16 | No. 135326~ |
| 17-36 | 91204-08030 | BOLT | | 1 | .16 | |
| 17-37 | 92901-08200 | WASHER, plain | | 1 | .01 | |
| 17-38 | 92901-08100 | WASHER, spring | | 1 | .01 | |
| 17-39 | 92801-08300 | NUT | | 1 | .04 | |
| 17-40 | 91203-08030 | BOLT | | 1 | .16 | |
| 17-41 | 92903-08200 | WASHER, plain | | 1 | .01 | |
| 17-42 | 92901-08100 | WASHER, spring | | 1 | .01 | |
| 17-43 | 92801-08300 | NUT | | 1 | .04 | |
| 17-44 | 137-23480-00 | STEERING LOCK ASS'Y | | 1 | 3.60 | |
| 17-45 | 92701-06015 | SCREW, flat head | | 2 | .04 | |

# Fig. 18 TANK

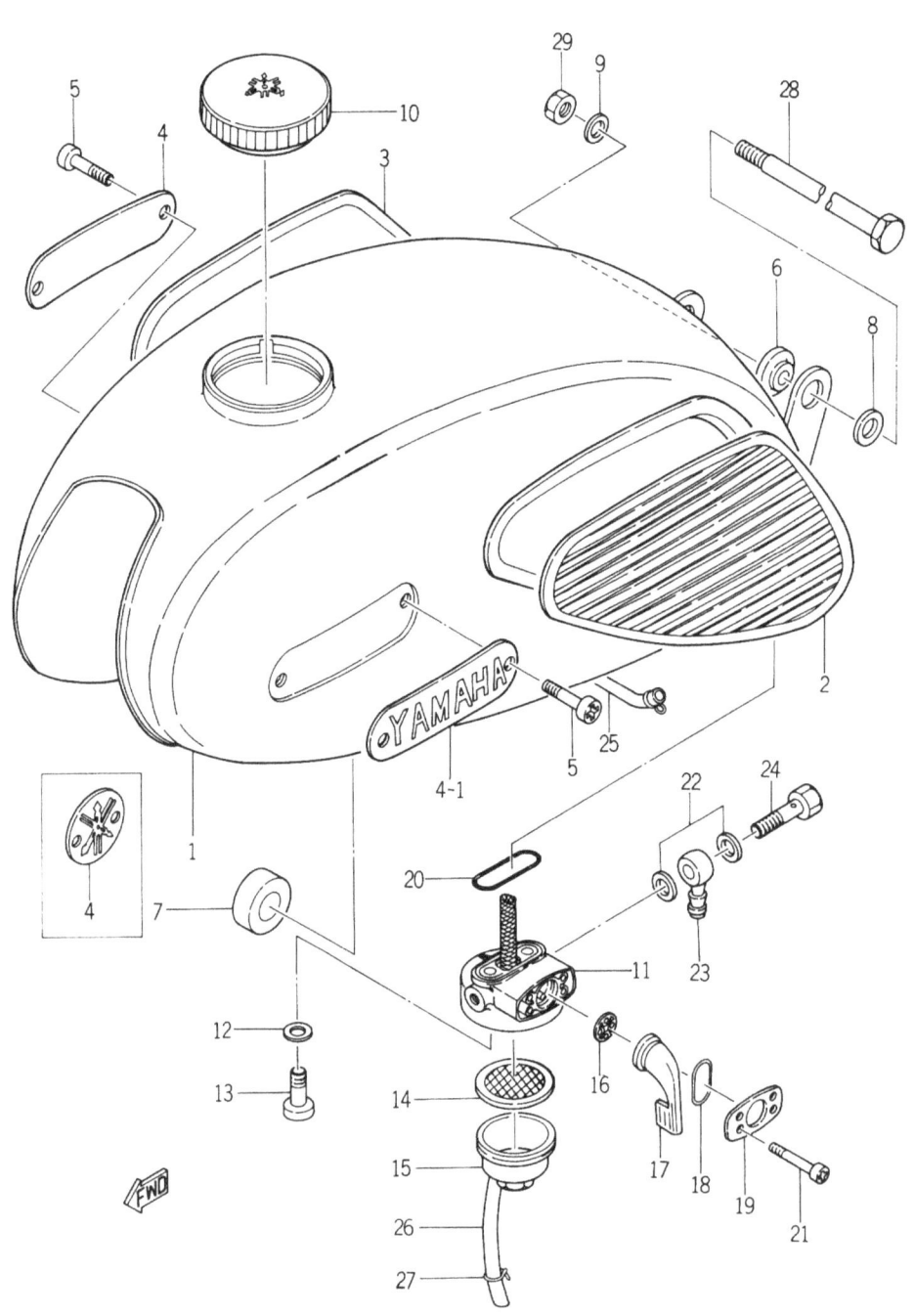

# 18

| Ref. No. | Part No. | Part Name | Description | Q'ty | S·R | Remarks |
|---|---|---|---|---|---|---|
| 18- 1 | 137-24110-01 | FUEL TANK COMP | | 1 | 36.00 | |
| 18- 2 | 137-24171-00 | GRIP, knee (L.H) | | 1 | 2.00 | |
| 18- 3 | 137-24172-00 | GRIP, knee (R.H) | | 1 | 2.00 | |
| 18- 4 | 137-24161-00 | EMBLEM | | 2 | .80 | ~ No. 173000 |
| 18- 4-1 | 132-24161-00 | EMBLEM | | 2 | 1.20 | No. 173001 ~ |
| 18- 5 | 92501-04008 | SCREW, pan head | | 4 | .04 | |
| 18- 6 | 137-24182-00 | DAMPER, tank locating (2) | | 2 | .44 | |
| 18- 7 | 137-24181-00 | DAMPER, tank locating (1) | | 2 | .36 | |
| 18- 8 | 137-24186-00 | WASHER, special | 8.5⌀ | 1 | .06 | |
| 18- 9 | 137-24187-00 | WASHER, special | 6.5⌀ | 1 | .06 | |
| 18-10 | 148-24610-00 | CAP ASS'Y | | 1 | 1.44 | |
| 18- 0-1 | 137-24500-00 | FUEL COCK ASS'Y | | 1 | 3.84 | |
| 18-11 | | . BODY, fuel cock | | 1 | N/A | △ |
| 18-12 | 137-24513-00 | . GASKET, cock fitting | | 2 | .10 | |
| 18-13 | 92501-06030 | . SCREW, pan head | | 2 | .04 | |
| 18-14 | 137-24515-00 | . NET, filter | | 1 | .24 | |
| 18-15 | 137-24521-00 | . CUP, filter | | 1 | .80 | |
| 18-16 | 137-24523-00 | . VALVE | | 1 | .20 | |
| 18-17 | 137-24524-00 | . LEVER, cock | | 1 | .44 | |
| 18-18 | 137-24518-00 | . WASHER, wave | | 1 | .04 | |
| 18-19 | 137-24525-00 | . PLATE, lever fitting | | 1 | .16 | |
| 18-20 | 137-24512-00 | . GASKET, body | | 1 | .20 | |
| 18-21 | 92501-03005 | . SCREW, pan head | | 4 | .04 | |
| 18-22 | 137-24528-00 | GASKET, fuel pipe | | 2 | .04 | |
| 18-23 | 101-24526-00 | COLLAR, banjo bolt | | 1 | .80 | |
| 18-24 | 102-24527-00 | BOLT, banjo | | 1 | .20 | |
| 18-25 | 137-24331-00 | PIPE, level | | 1 | .20 | |
| 18-26 | 137-24311-00 | PIPE, fuel | | 1 | .52 | |
| 18-27 | 101-24356-00 | CLIP, pipe | | 4 | .04 | |
| 18-28 | 137-24176-00 | BOLT, tank fitting | | 1 | .44 | |
| 18-29 | 92801-06100 | NUT | | 1 | .01 | |

50

# Fig. 19 OIL TANK

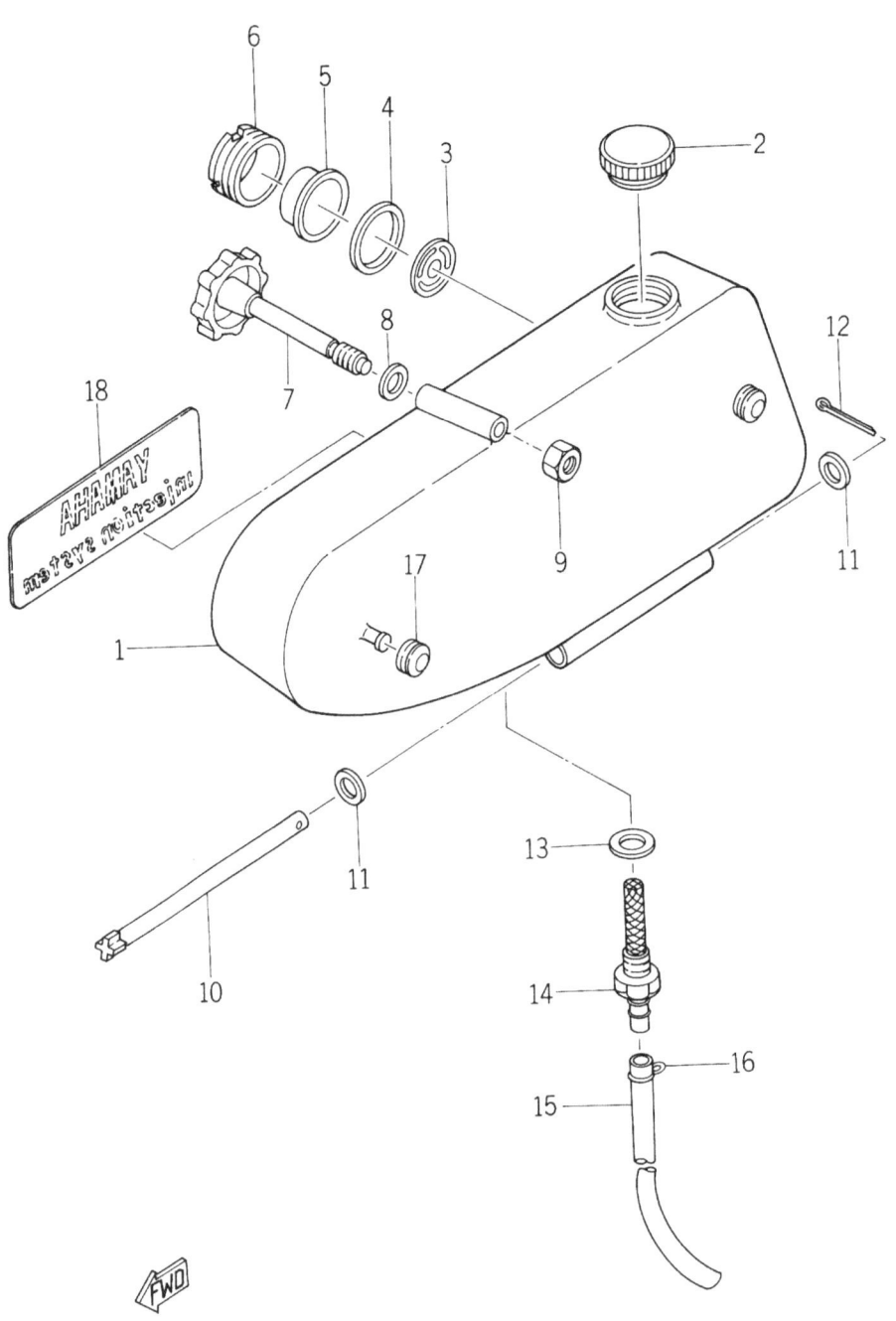

| Ref. No. | Part No. | Part Name | Description | Q'ty | S·R | Remarks |
|---|---|---|---|---|---|---|
| 19- 1 | 137-21751-02 | TANK, oil | | 1 | 12.00 | ⊙ |
| 19- 2 | 137-21770-61 | OIL TANK CAP ASS'Y | | 1 | 2.00 | |
| 19- 3 | 137-21761-00 | GAUGE, level | | 1 | .06 | |
| 19- 4 | 137-21763-00 | GASKET, level gauge | | 1 | .16 | |
| 19- 5 | 137-21764-00 | LENS, level gauge | | 1 | .20 | |
| 19- 6 | 137-21762-00 | NUT, level gauge | | 1 | .76 | |
| 19- 7 | 137-21714-00 | KNOB, side cover | | 1 | .72 | |
| 19- 8 | 92901-06200 | WASHER, plain | | 1 | .01 | |
| 19- 9 | 92801-06300 | NUT | | 2 | .01 | |
| 19-10 | 137-21795-00 | PIN, tank fitting | | 1 | .16 | |
| 19-11 | 92901-05200 | WASHER, plain | | 2 | .01 | |
| 19-12 | 91401-12012 | PIN, cotter | | 1 | .01 | |
| 19-13 | 137-21767-00 | GASKET, union | | 1 | .02 | |
| 19-14 | 137-21768-01 | SCREW, union | | 1 | 1.00 | |
| 19-15 | 137-24319-00 | PIPE, oil | | 1 | 1.00 | |
| 19-16 | 101-24356-00 | CLIP, pipe | | 2 | .04 | |
| 19-17 | 137-21778-00 | DAMPER, oil tank | | 2 | .20 | |
| 19-18 | 137-21782-60 | EMBLEM, injection | | 1 | .36 | |

## Fig. 20 SEAT AND CARRIER

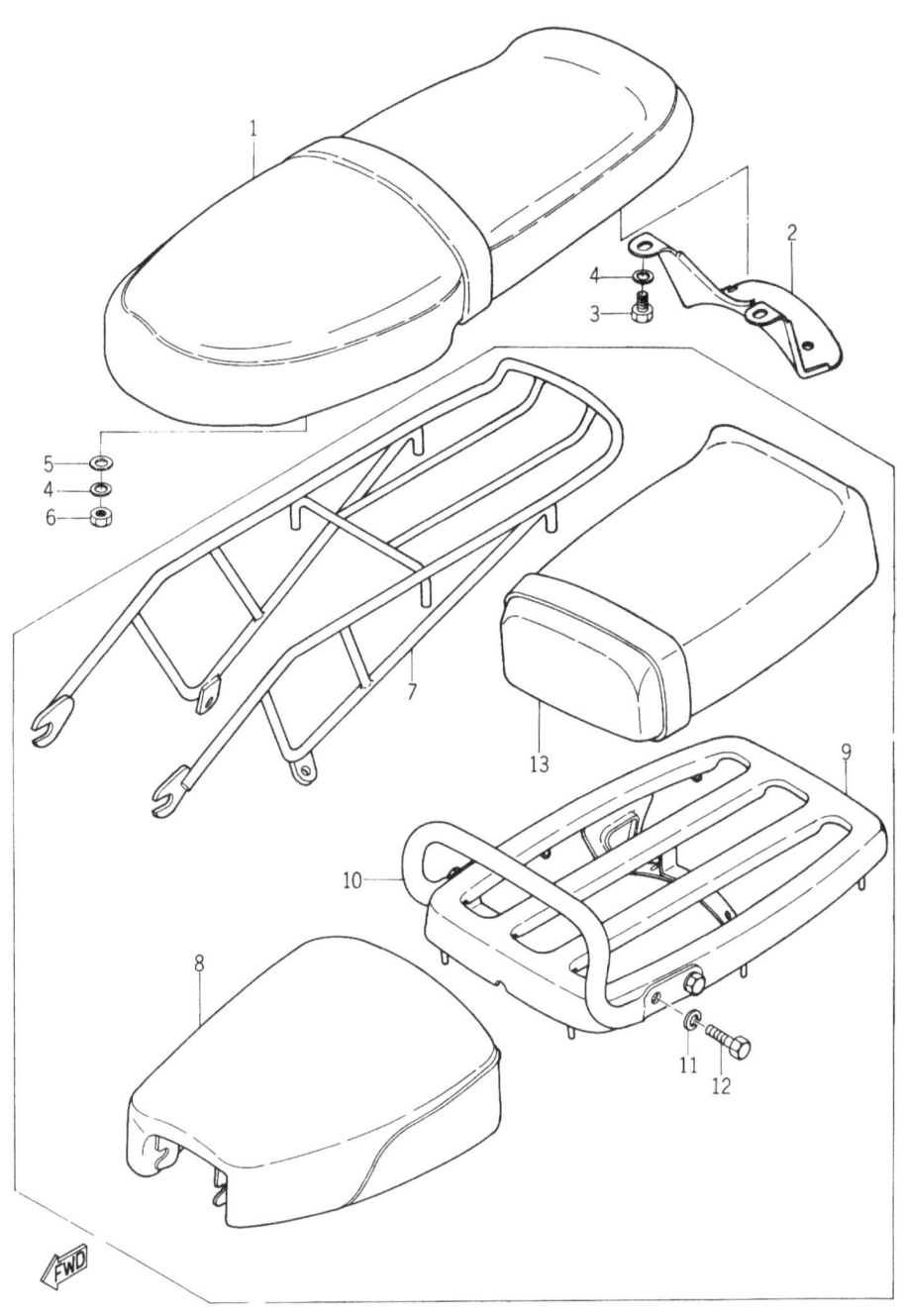

| Ref. No. | Part No. | Part Name | Description | Q'ty | S·R | Remarks |
|---|---|---|---|---|---|---|
| 20- 1 | 137-24730-00 | DOUBLE SEAT ASS'Y | | 1 | 32.00 | |
| 20- 1-1 | 137-24731-00 | . COVER, seat | | 1 | 7.00 | |
| 20- 2 | 137-24738-00 | BRACKET, double seat | | 1 | 2.00 | |
| 20- 3 | 91201-08015 | BOLT | | 2 | .10 | |
| 20- 4 | 92901-08100 | WASHER, spring | | 4 | .01 | |
| 20- 5 | 92901-08200 | WASHER, plain | | 2 | .01 | |
| 20- 6 | 92801-08100 | NUT | | 2 | .04 | |
| | | OPTIONAL PARTS | | | | |
| 20- 7 | 137-24830-00 | SUB CARRIER ASS'Y | | 1 | 6.80 | |
| 20- 8 | 137-24710-00 | SINGLE SEAT ASS'Y | | 1 | 14.40 | |
| 20- 8-1 | 137-24711-00 | . COVER, single seat | | 1 | 5.00 | |
| 20- 9 | 137-24810-00 | CARRIER ASS'Y | | 1 | 8.80 | ⊙ |
| 20-10 | 137-24812-00 | HANDLE | | 1 | 2.00 | |
| 20-11 | 92901-06100 | WASHER, spring | | 4 | .01 | |
| 20-12 | 91203-06012 | BOLT | | 4 | .06 | |
| 20-13 | 136-24750-00 | TANDEM SEAT ASS'Y | | 1 | 14.40 | |
| 20-13-1 | 136-24751-00 | . COVER, seat | | 1 | 5.00 | |

## Fig.21 FRONT WHEEL

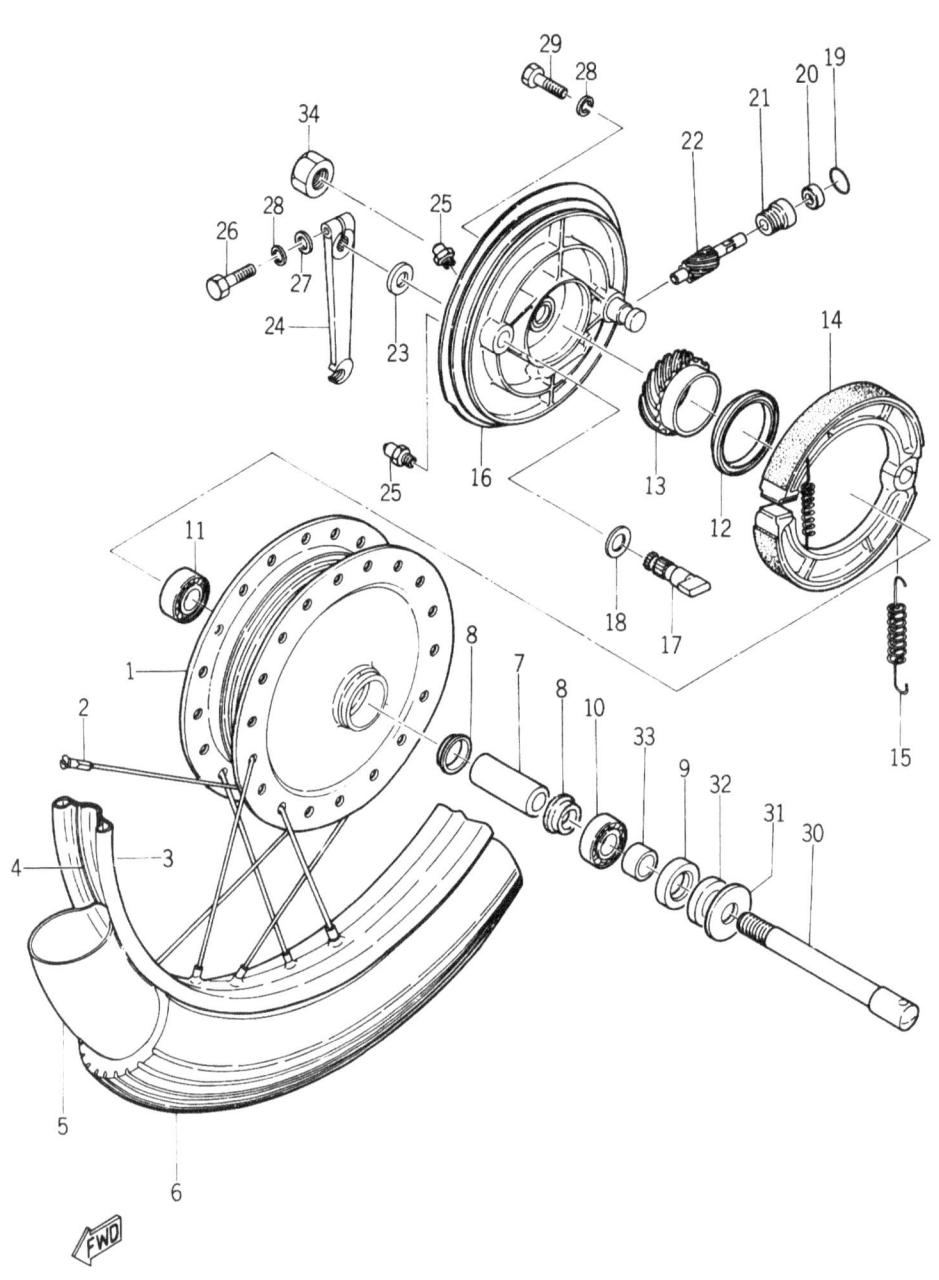

| Ref. No. | Part No. | Part Name | Description | Q'ty | S·R | Remarks |
|---|---|---|---|---|---|---|
| 21- 1 | 136-25111-02 | HUB, front | | 1 | 19.20 | |
| 21- 2 | 136-25104-00 | SPOKE SET | | 1 | 4.32 | |
| 21- 3 | 94416-16008 | RIM | 1.60A-16 | 1 | 7.04 | |
| 21- 4 | 94330-16009 | BAND, rim | 3.00-16 | 1 | .50 | |
| 21- 5 | 94230-16011 | TUBE | 3.00-16 | 1 | 3.50 | ☆ |
| 21- 6 | 94130-16027 | TYRE, front | 3.00-16-4PR | 1 | 16.94 | ☆ |
| 21- 7 | 136-25117-00 | SPACER, bearing | | 1 | .88 | |
| 21- 8 | 136-25115-00 | FLANGE, spacer | | 2 | .04 | |
| 21- 9 | 93102-20009 | OIL SEAL | SD-20-35-7 | 1 | .48 | |
| 21-10 | 93306-20201 | BEARING | 6202 | 1 | 1.76 | ☆ |
| 21-11 | 93306-20203 | BEARING | 6202RS | 1 | 2.00 | ☆ |
| 21-12 | 93107-48002 | OIL SEAL | OS-47.5-60-7 | 1 | .76 | |
| 21-13 | 135-25135-00 | GEAR, drive | | 1 | 3.20 | |
| 21-14 | 136-25130-00 | BRAKE SHOE COMP | | 2 | 2.40 | |
| 21-15 | 137-25133-00 | SPRING, brake shoe return | | 2 | .12 | |
| 21-16 | 137-25121-00 | PLATE, brake shoe | | 1 | 8.80 | ~No.150640 |
| 21-16-1 | 137-25121-01 | PLATE, brake shoe | | 1 | 8.80 | No.150641~ |
| 21-17 | 136-25151-01 | CAM, shaft | | 1 | 2.24 | |
| 21-18 | 137-25153-00 | SHIM, cam shaft | | 1 | .04 | |
| 21-19 | 93210-13017 | O-RING | 2.4-13.4 | 1 | .10 | |
| 21-20 | 93104-07003 | OIL SEAL | SO-7-14-4 | 1 | .16 | |
| 21-21 | 109-25136-00 | BUSHING | | 1 | 1.04 | |
| 21-22 | 136-25138-00 | GEAR, meter | | 1 | 1.60 | |
| 21-23 | 137-25159-00 | SEAL, cam shaft | | 1 | .12 | |
| 21-24 | 136-25155-00 | LEVER, cam shaft | | 1 | 2.20 | ~No.15640 |
| 21-24-1 | 137-25155-60 | LEVER, cam shaft | | 1 | 2.20 | No.15641~ |
| 21-25 | 93700-06001 | NIPPLE, grease | | 2 | .10 | |
| 21-26 | 91203-06020 | BOLT | | 1 | .06 | |
| 21-27 | 92901-06200 | WASHER, plain | | 1 | .01 | |
| 21-28 | 92901-06100 | WASHER, spring | | 2 | .01 | |
| 21-29 | 91201-06025 | BOLT | | 1 | .06 | |
| 21-30 | 141-25181-00 | SHAFT, front wheel | | 1 | 3.20 | |
| 21-31 | 136-25127-00 | COVER, plate | | 1 | .16 | |
| 21-32 | 136-25129-00 | SEAL, dust | | 1 | .08 | |
| 21-33 | 136-25183-00 | COLLAR, wheel shaft | | 1 | .32 | |
| 21-34 | 92803-14200 | NUT | | 1 | .16 | |

# Fig.22 REAR WHEEL

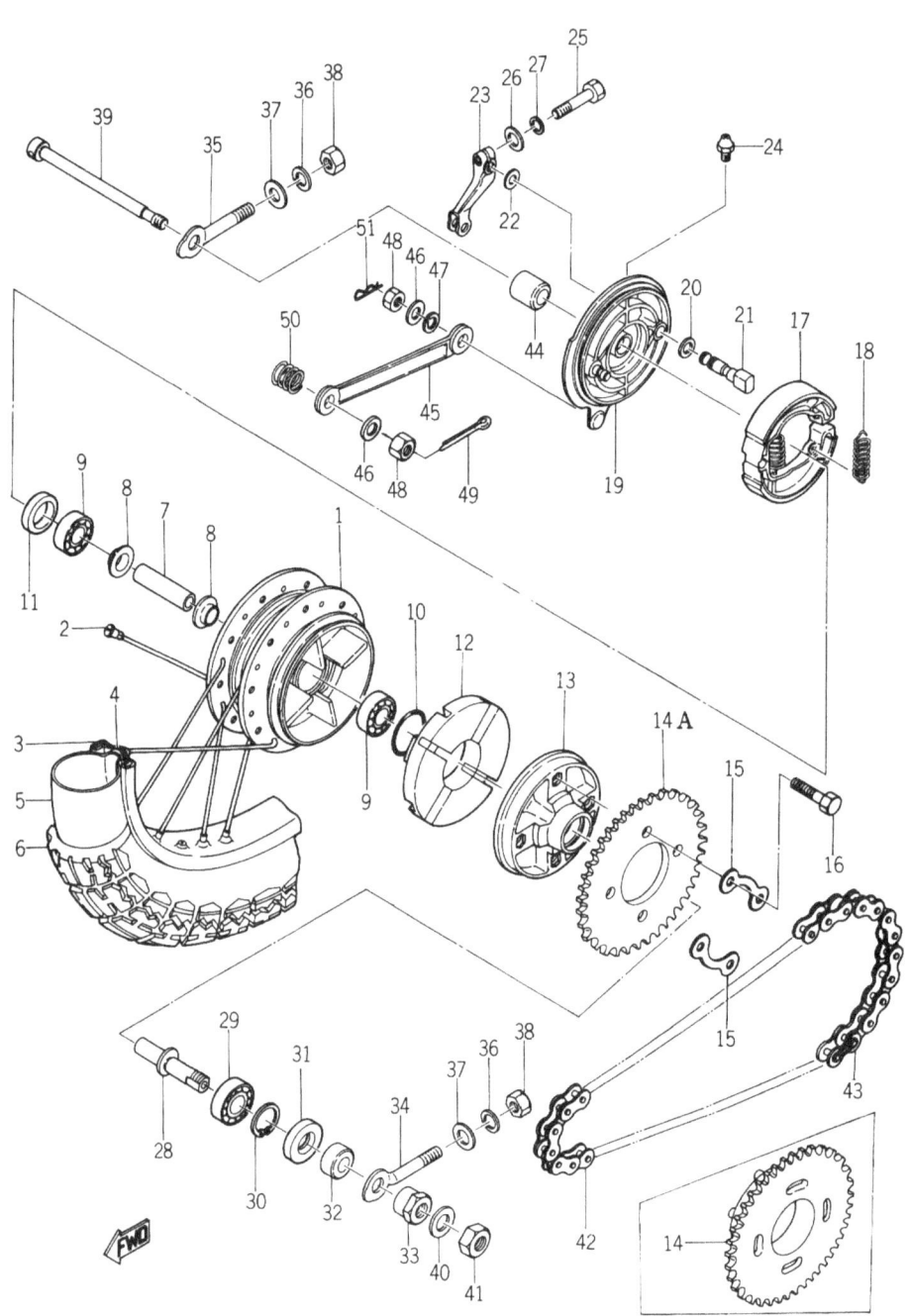

| Ref. No. | Part No. | Part Name | Description | Q'ty | S·R | Remarks |
|---|---|---|---|---|---|---|
| 22- 1 | 136-25311-02 | HUB, rear | | 1 | 20.80 | |
| 22- 2 | 136-25304-00 | REAR SPOKE SET | | 1 | 4.32 | |
| 22- 3 | 94416-16008 | RIM | 1.60A-16 | 1 | 7.04 | |
| 22- 4 | 94330-16009 | BAND, rim | 3.00-16 | 1 | .50 | |
| 22- 5 | 94230-16011 | TUBE | 3.00-16 | 1 | 3.50 | ☆ |
| 22- 6 | 94130-16028 | TIRE, rear | 3.00-16 -4PR | 1 | 16.94 | ☆ |
| 22- 7 | 136-25317-00 | SPACER, bearing | | 1 | .80 | |
| 22- 8 | 136-25115-00 | FLANGE, spacer | | 2 | .04 | |
| 22- 9 | 93306-20203 | BEARING | 6202RS | 2 | 2.00 | ☆ |
| 22-10 | 93210-43043 | O-RING | 3-42.5 | 1 | .16 | |
| 22-11 | 93101-42018 | OIL SEAL | S-42-56-6 | 1 | .64 | |
| 22-12 | 136-25364-01 | DAMPER, clutch | | 1 | 2.40 | |
| 22-13 | 137-25366-00 | CLUTCH, hub | | 1 | 4.80 | No. 197577〜 |
| 22-14 | 137-25439-00 | GEAR, sprocket wheel | 39T | 1 | 11.20 | 〜No. 197576 |
| 22-14A | 174-25437-31 | GEAR, sprocket wheel | 37T | 1 | 5.60 | No. 197577〜 |
| 22-14-1 | 174-25439-31 | GEAR, sprocket wheel | 39T | 1 | 5.60 | No. 197577〜 |
| 22-14-2 | 174-25441-31 | GEAR, sprocket wheel | 41T | 1 | 5.60 | No. 197577〜 |
| 22-15 | 148-25412-00 | WASHER, lock | | 2 | .08 | |
| 22-16 | 141-25411-00 | BOLT, fitting | | 4 | .12 | |
| 22-17 | 136-25130-00 | BRAKE SHOE COMP | | 2 | 2.40 | |
| 22-18 | 137-25133-00 | SPRING, brake return | | 2 | .12 | |
| 22-19 | 136-25321-01 | PLATE, brake shoe rear | | 1 | 8.80 | |
| 22-20 | 136-25153-00 | SHIM, cam shaft | | 1 | .04 | |
| 22-21 | 136-25351-01 | CAM, shaft | | 1 | 2.24 | |
| 22-22 | 137-25159-00 | SEAL, cam shaft | | 1 | .12 | |
| 22-23 | 137-25355-60 | LEVER, cam shaft brake | | 1 | 2.08 | |
| 22-24 | 93700-06001 | NIPPLE, grease | | 1 | .10 | |
| 22-25 | 91203-06020 | BOLT | | 1 | .06 | |
| 22-26 | 92901-06200 | WASHER, plain | | 1 | .01 | |
| 22-27 | 92901-06100 | WASHER, spring | | 1 | .01 | |
| 22-28 | 137-25387-00 | SHAFT, sprocket | | 1 | 2.24 | |
| 22-29 | 93306-00405 | BEARING | 6004D | 1 | 2.60 | ☆ |
| 22-30 | 93420-42007 | CIRCLIP | R42 | 1 | .40 | |
| 22-31 | 93106-30004 | OIL SEAL | DD-30-42-8 | 1 | .48 | |
| 22-32 | 137-25386-00 | COLLAR, sprocket shaft | | 1 | .28 | |

# Fig.22 REAR WHEEL

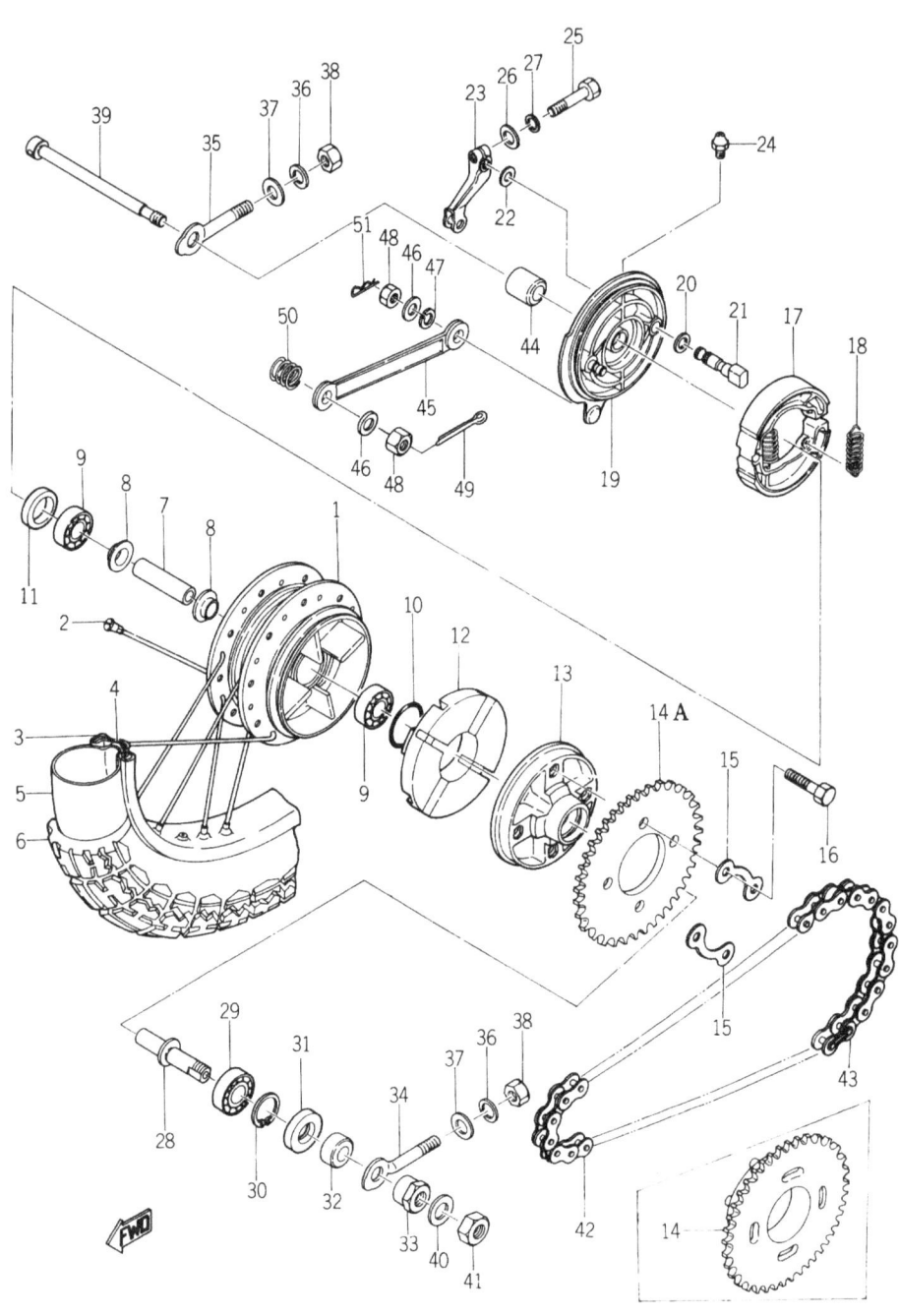

| Ref. No. | Part No. | Part Name | Description | Q'ty | S·R | Remarks |
|---|---|---|---|---|---|---|
| 22-33 | 137-25385-00 | NUT, sprocket shaft | | 1 | .88 | |
| 22-34 | 137-25388-00 | PULLER, chain | | 1 | .64 | |
| 22-35 | 137-25389-00 | PULLER, chain | | 1 | .64 | |
| 22-36 | 92901-06100 | WASHER, spring | | 2 | .01 | |
| 22-37 | 92901-06200 | WASHER, plain | | 2 | .01 | |
| 22-38 | 92801-06100 | NUT | | 2 | .01 | |
| 22-39 | 137-25381-00 | SHAFT, wheel | | 1 | 2.40 | |
| 22-40 | 136-25384-00 | WASHER, special | | 1 | .12 | |
| 22-41 | 92803-14200 | NUT | | 1 | .16 | |
| 22-42 | 94501-28108 | CHAIN | DK428 | 1 | 8.00 | |
| 22-43 | 94604-28001 | . JOINT, chain | | 1 | .56 | |
| 22-44 | 137-25383-00 | COLLAR, wheel shaft | | 1 | .88 | |
| 22-45 | 136-25371-00 | BAR, tension | | 1 | 1.04 | |
| 22-46 | 92901-10200 | WASHER, plain | | 2 | .01 | |
| 22-47 | 92901-12100 | WASHER, spring | | 1 | .04 | |
| 22-48 | 92801-10300 | NUT | | 2 | .04 | |
| 22-49 | 91401-20015 | PIN, cotter | | 1 | .01 | |
| 22-50 | 102-25374-00 | SPRING, tension bar | | 1 | .06 | |
| 22-51 | 136-25375-00 | CLIP, tension bar | | 1 | .06 | |

## Fig.23 HEAD LAMP AND TAIL LAMP

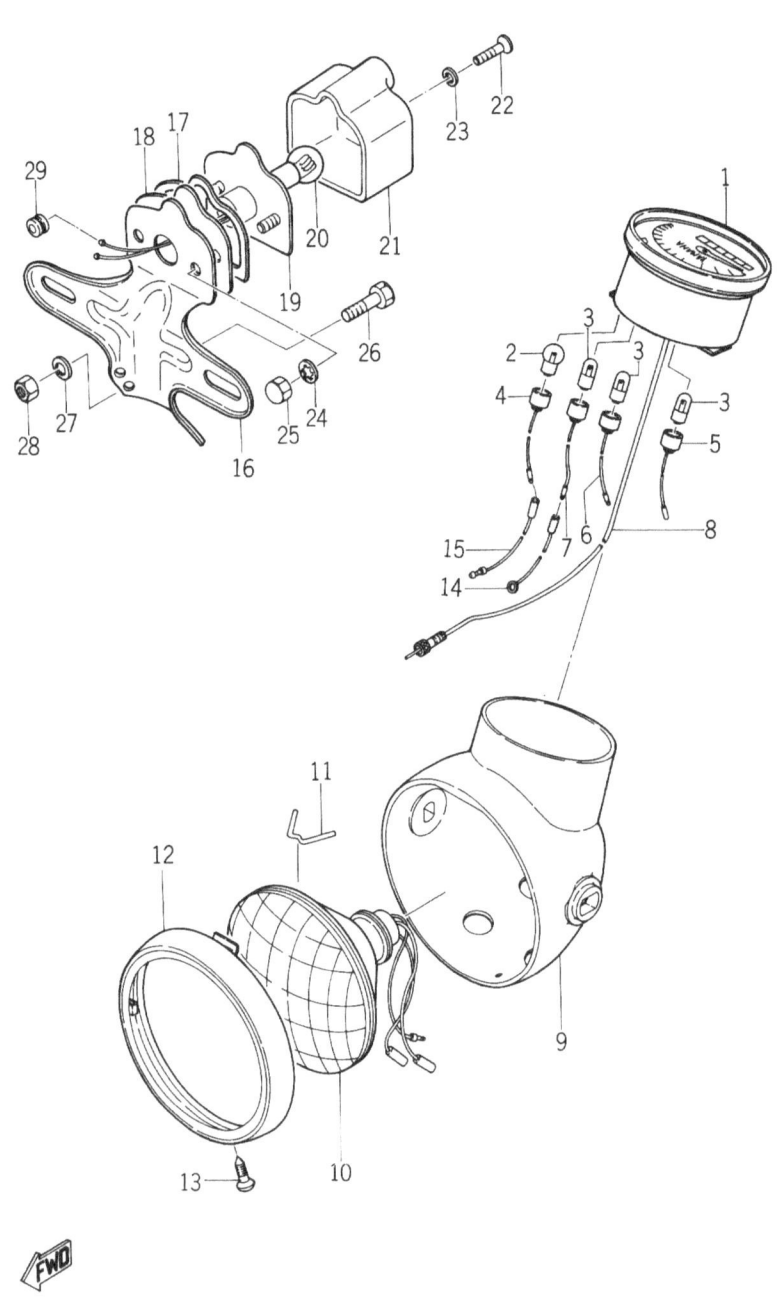

| Ref. No. | Part No. | Part Name | Description | Q'ty | S·R | Remarks |
|---|---|---|---|---|---|---|
| 23- 1 | 140-83510-40 | SPEEDOMETER ASS'Y | | 1 | 18.40 | |
| 23- 2 | 123-83516-20 | . BULB, meter | 12V/3W | 1 | .16 | ☆ |
| 23- 3 | 102-83517-20 | . BULB, pilot | 12V/2W | 3 | .16 | ☆ |
| 23- 4 | 136-83536-20 | . SOCKET, meter | | 1 | 1.20 | |
| 23- 5 | 136-83537-20 | . SOCKET, neutral | | 1 | 1.20 | |
| 23- 6 | 136-83539-20 | . SOCKET, charge | | 1 | 1.20 | |
| 23- 7 | 136-83538-20 | . SOCKET, flasher | | 1 | 1.20 | |
| 23- 8 | 137-83550-10 | SPEEDOMETER CABLE ASS'Y | | 1 | 1.60 | |
| 23- 0-1 | 137-84300-60 | HEAD LAMP ASS'Y | | 1 | 18.40 | ⊙ |
| 23- 9 | 136-84311-00 | . BODY, head lamp | | 1 | 9.60 | ⊙ |
| 23-10 | 137-84320-60 | . LENS ASS'Y | | 1 | 4.60 | |
| 23-11 | 136-84324-00 | . SPRING, reflector set | | 3 | .04 | |
| 23-12 | 136-84315-60 | . RIM, head lamp | | 1 | 4.00 | |
| 23-13 | 150-84125-00 | . SCREW, rim fitting | | 1 | .04 | |
| 23-14 | 122-84148-00 | WIRE, lead (1) | | 1 | .16 | |
| 23-15 | 122-84149-00 | WIRE, lead (2) | | 1 | .20 | |
| 23-16 | 137-84751-60 | BRACKET, licence | | 1 | 2.72 | |
| 23- 0-2 | 137-84710-60 | TAIL LAMP UNIT ASS'Y | | 1 | 6.64 | |
| 23-17 | 124-84512-60 | . SEAT, base | | 1 | 1.06 | |
| 23-18 | 124-84516-60 | . COVER, tail lamp | | 1 | .73 | |
| 23-19 | 137-84711-60 | . BASE, tail lamp | | 1 | 2.80 | |
| 23-20 | 137-84714-60 | . BULB, tail lamp | 12V 25/8W | 1 | .70 | ☆ |
| 23-21 | 124-84521-60 | . LENS, tail lamp | | 1 | 2.00 | |
| 23-22 | 92503-04015 | . SCREW, pan head | | 2 | .04 | |
| 23-23 | 124-84522-60 | . WASHER, lens fitting | | 2 | .01 | |
| 23-24 | 92903-06300 | . WASHER, tooth | | 2 | .04 | |
| 23-25 | 92803-06700 | . NUT, crown | | 2 | .12 | |
| 23-26 | 91201-06012 | BOLT | | 4 | .06 | |
| 23-27 | 92901-06100 | WASHER, spring | | 4 | .01 | |
| 23-28 | 92801-06100 | NUT | | 4 | .01 | |
| 23-29 | 152-84518-00 | GROMMET, tail lamp cord | | 1 | .04 | |

## Fig.24 ELECTRICAL SYSTEM

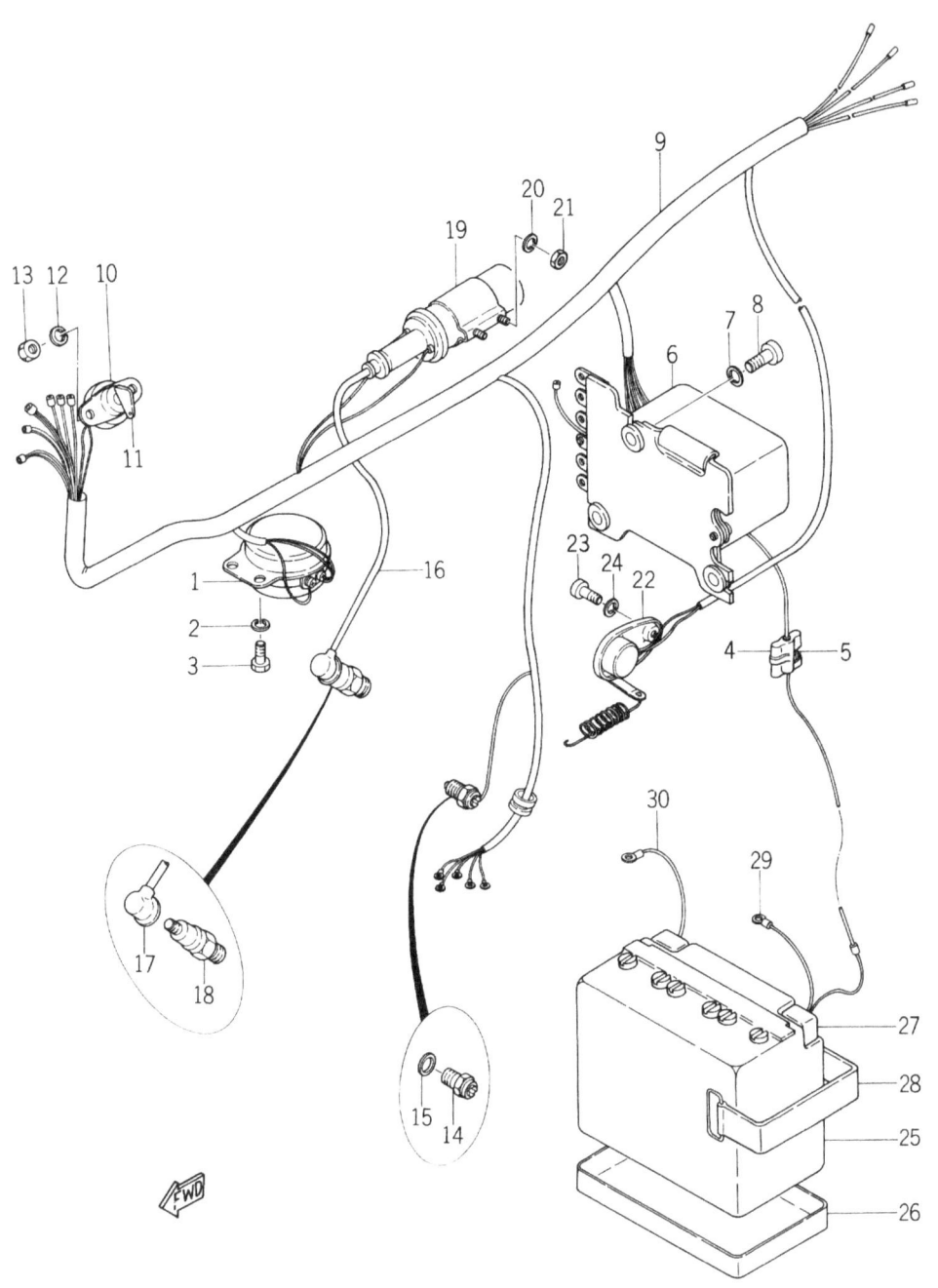

| Ref. No. | Part No. | Part Name | Description | Q'ty | S·R | Remarks |
|---|---|---|---|---|---|---|
| 24- 1 | 137-83371-20 | HORN | | 1 | 5.28 | |
| 24- 2 | 92901-08100 | WASHER, spring | | 2 | .01 | |
| 24- 3 | 91201-08020 | BOLT | | 2 | .10 | |
| 24- 4 | 148-82150-00 | FUSE HOLDER ASS'Y | | 1 | .72 | |
| 24- 5 | 148-82151-00 | . FUSE | | 3 | .10 | |
| 24- 6 | 137-81910-10 | VOLTAGE REGULATOR ASS'Y | | 1 | 26.10 | ~ No. 173000 |
| 24- 6-1 | 137-81910-11 | VOLTAGE REGULATOR ASS'Y | | 1 | 26.10 | No. 173001 ~ |
| 24- 7 | 92901-06100 | WASHER, spring | | 3 | .01 | |
| 24- 8 | 92501-06015 | SCREW, pan head | | 3 | .04 | |
| 24- 9 | 137-82590-12 | WIRE HARNESS ASS'Y | | 1 | 8.00 | |
| 24-10 | 136-82510-10 | MAIN SWITCH ASS'Y | | 1 | 5.20 | |
| 24-11 | 136-82511-00 | . KEY, main switch | | 2 | .50 | |
| 24-12 | 92901-04100 | WASHER, spring | | 2 | .01 | |
| 24-13 | 92801-04100 | NUT | | 2 | .01 | |
| 24-14 | 136-82540-00 | NEUTRAL SWITCH ASS'Y | | 1 | 1.20 | |
| 24-15 | 136-82543-00 | GASKET | 12-18-1 | 1 | .02 | |
| 24-16 | 137-82341-00 | CORD, high tension | | 1 | .96 | |
| 24-17 | 166-82370-20 | PLUG CAP ASS'Y | | 1 | .56 | |
| 24-18 | 94700-00002 | PLUG, spark | B6H | 1 | 1.00 | |
| 24-18-1 | 94700-00003 | PLUG, spark | B7H | 1 | 1.00 | |
| 24-19 | 148-82310-60 | IGNITION COIL ASS'Y | | 1 | 8.00 | |
| 24-20 | 92901-06100 | WASHER, spring | | 2 | .01 | |
| 24-21 | 91801-06100 | NUT | | 2 | .01 | |
| 24-22 | 137-82530-00 | STOP SWITCH ASS'Y | | 1 | 2.32 | |
| 24-23 | 92503-05008 | SCREW, pan head | | 1 | .06 | |
| 24-24 | 92903-05100 | WASHER, spring | | 1 | .01 | |
| 24-25 | 137-82110-60 | BATTERY ASS'Y | | 1 | ✽14.00 | |
| 24-26 | 137-82122-00 | SEAT, battery | | 1 | .48 | |
| 24-27 | 137-82119-00 | COVER, lead wire | | 1 | .56 | |
| 24-28 | 137-82131-01 | BAND, battery | | 1 | .72 | |
| 24-29 | 137-82115-00 | WIRE, plus lead | | 1 | .64 | |
| 24-30 | 123-82116-00 | WIRE, minus lead | | 1 | .48 | |

## Fig. 25 LEG SHIELD AND TOOLS

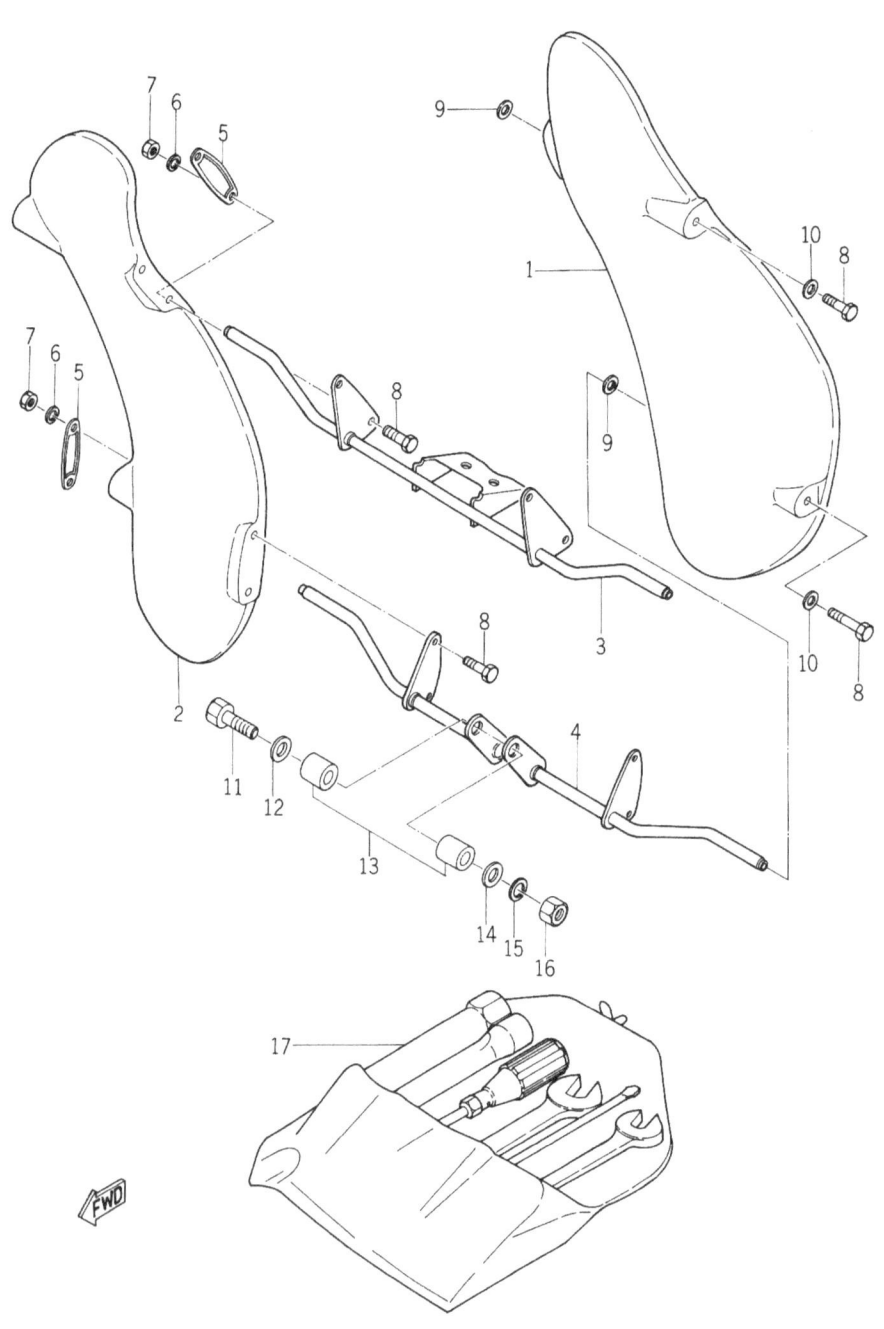

| Ref. No. | Part No. | Part Name | Description | Q'ty | S·R | Remarks |
|---|---|---|---|---|---|---|
| 25- 0-1 | 137-28300-00 | LEG SHIELD ASS'Y | | 1 | 19.20 | |
| 25- 1 | 137-28311-00 | . LEG SHIELD (L.H) | | 1 | 5.76 | |
| 25- 2 | 137-28312-00 | . LEG SHIELD (R.H) | | 1 | | |
| 25- 0-2 | 137-28320-00 | . LEG SHIELD STAY SET | | 1 | 13.20 | |
| 25- 3 | 137-28321-03 | .. STAY, leg shield, upper | | 1 | N/A | △ |
| 25- 4 | 137-28322-03 | .. STAY, leg shield, under | | 1 | N/A | △ |
| 25- 5 | 136-28323-00 | .. WASHER, leg shield | | 4 | N/A | △ |
| 25- 6 | 92903-06100 | .. WASHER, spring | | 8 | .01 | |
| 25- 7 | 92803-06100 | .. NUT | | 8 | .04 | |
| 25- 8 | 91103-06015 | .. BOLT | | 12 | .06 | |
| 25- 9 | 136-28323-00 | .. WASHER, leg shield | | 4 | N/A | △ |
| 25-10 | 137-28323-00 | .. WASHER | | 4 | N/A | △ |
| 25-11 | 137-28331-00 | .. BOLT, fitting | | 1 | N/A | △ |
| 25-12 | 137-24186-00 | .. WASHER, special | 8.5φ | 1 | N/A | △ |
| 25-13 | 137-28327-00 | .. DAMPER, washer | | 2 | N/A | △ |
| 25-14 | 137-24187-00 | .. WASHER, special | 6.5φ | 1 | N/A | △ |
| 25-15 | 92901-06100 | .. WASHER, spring | | 1 | .01 | |
| 25-16 | 92801-06100 | .. NUT | | 1 | .01 | |
| 25-17 | 137-28100-00 | TOOL ASS'Y | | 1 | 8.00 | ☆ |

# MEMO

First edition, Dec., '67.

# YAMAHA YA6 PARTS LIST

( IBM  New Number )

# YAMAHA MOTOR CO.,LTD.

HAMAKITA JAPAN

## VELOCEPRESS MANUALS - MOTORCYCLE

1930'S BRITISH MOTORCYCLE CARBS & ELEC COMPONENTS (BOOK OF)
1930'S BRITISH MOTORCYCLE ENGINES (OVERHAUL & MAINTENANCE)
1930'S BRITISH MOTORCYCLE GEARBOXES & CLUTCHES (BOOK OF)
AJS 1932-1948 SINGLES & TWINS 250cc THRU 1000cc (BOOK OF)
AJS 1945-1960 SINGLES 350cc & 500cc MODELS 16 & 18 (BOOK OF)
AJS 1955-1965 SINGLES 350cc & 500cc (BOOK OF)
ARIEL UP TO 1932 (BOOK OF)
ARIEL 1932-1939 PREWAR MODELS (BOOK OF)
ARIEL 1933-1951 (WORKSHOP MANUAL)
ARIEL 1939-1960 4 STROKE SINGLES (BOOK OF)
ARIEL 1958-1964 LEADER & ARROW (BOOK OF)
BMW R26 R27 (1956-1967) FACTORY WORKSHOP MANUAL
BMW R50 R50S R60 R69S (1955-1969) FACTORY WORKSHOP MANUAL
BRIDGESTONE 90 SERIES FACTORY WSM & PARTS CATALOGUE
BRIDGESTONE 175 SERIES FACTORY WSM & PARTS CATALOGUE
BSA BANTAM ALL MODELS FROM 1948 ONWARDS (BOOK OF)
BSA SINGLES & V-TWINS UP TO 1927 (BOOK OF)
BSA SINGLES & V-TWINS UP TO 1930 (BOOK OF)
BSA SINGLES & V-TWINS UP TO 1935 (BOOK OF)
BSA SINGLES & V-TWINS 1936-1939 (BOOK OF)
BSA OHV & SV SINGLES 250-600cc 1945-1959 (BOOK OF)
BSA OHV & SV SINGLES 250cc (ONLY) 1954-1970 (BOOK OF)
BSA OHV SINGLES 350 & 500cc 1955-1967 (BOOK OF)
BSA TWINS 1948-1962 (BOOK OF)
BSA TWINS 1962-1969 (SECOND BOOK OF)
CYCLEMOTOR (BOOK OF)
DOUGLAS 1929-1939 PREWAR ALL MODELS (BOOK OF)
DOUGLAS 1948-1957 POSTWAR ALL MODELS FACTORY SHOP MANUAL
DUCATI 160cc, 250cc & 350cc OHC MODELS FACTORY SHOP MANUAL
HONDA 50 ALL MODELS UP TO 1970 INC MONKEY & TRAIL (BOOK OF)
HONDA 90 ALL MODELS UP TO 1966 (BOOK OF)
HONDA 125-150cc TWINS C/CS/CB/CA FACTORY WORKSHOP MANUAL
HONDA 250-305 TWINS C/CS/CB FACTORY WORKSHOP MANUAL
HONDA 450 CB/CL 1965-1974 K0 TO K7 WORKSHOP MANUAL
HONDA C100 SUPER CUB FACTORY WORKSHOP MANUAL
HONDA C110 SPORT CUB 1962-1969 FACTORY WORKSHOP MANUAL
HONDA TWINS & SINGLES 50cc THRU 305cc 1960-1966 (BOOK OF)
HONDA TWINS ALL MODELS 125cc THRU 450cc UP TO 1968 (BOOK OF)
J.A.P. ENGINES 1927-1952 & MOTORCYCLES 1934-1952 (BOOK OF)
LAMBRETTA 1947-1957 ALL 125 & 150cc MODELS (BOOK OF)
LAMBRETTA 1957-1970 LI & TV MODELS (SECOND BOOK OF)
MATCHLESS 1931-1939 ALL MODELS 250cc THRU 990cc (BOOK OF)
MATCHLESS 1945-1956 350 & 500cc SINGLES (BOOK OF)
MATCHLESS 1955-1966 350 & 500cc SINGLES (BOOK OF)
NEW IMPERIAL ALL SV & OHV FROM 1935 ONWARDS (BOOK OF)
NORTON 1932-1939 PREWAR MODELS (BOOK OF)
NORTON 1932-1947 (BOOK OF)
NORTON 1938-1956 (BOOK OF)
NORTON 1955-1963 MODELS 19, 50 & ES2 (BOOK OF)
NORTON 1955-1965 DOMINATOR TWINS (BOOK OF)
NORTON 1957-1970 TWINS FACTORY WORKSHOP MANUAL
NSU PRIMA 1956-1964 ALL MODELS (BOOK OF)
NSU QUICKLY 1953-1963 ALL MODELS (BOOK OF)
PANTHER 1932-1958 LIGHTWEIGHT MODELS 250 & 350cc (BOOK OF)
PANTHER 1938-1966 HEAVYWEIGHT MODELS 600 & 650cc (BOOK OF)
RALEIGH MOPEDS 1960-1969 (BOOK OF)
RALEIGH MOTORCYCLES 1919-1933 (BOOK OF)
ROYAL ENFIELD 1934-1946 SINGLES & V TWINS (BOOK OF)
ROYAL ENFIELD 1937-1953 SINGLES & V TWINS (BOOK OF)
ROYAL ENFIELD 1946-1962 SINGLES (BOOK OF)
ROYAL ENFIELD 1958-1966 250cc & 350cc SINGLES (SECOND BOOK OF)
ROYAL ENFIELD 736cc INTERCEPTOR FACTORY WORKSHOP MANUAL
RUDGE 1933-1939 (BOOK OF)
SUNBEAM 1928-1939 (BOOK OF)
SUNBEAM 1946-1957 S7 & S8 (BOOK OF)
SUZUKI 50cc & 80cc UP TO 1966 (BOOK OF)
SUZUKI T10 1963-1967 FACTORY WORKSHOP MANUAL
SUZUKI T20 & T200 1965-1969 FACTORY WORKSHOP MANUAL
SUZUKI TWINS 1962 ONWARDS 125-500cc WORKSHOP MANUAL
TRIUMPH 1935-1939 PREWAR MODELS (BOOK OF)
TRIUMPH 1935-1949 (BOOK OF)
TRIUMPH 1937-1951 (WORKSHOP MANUAL)
TRIUMPH 1945-1955 FACTORY WORKSHOP MANUAL
TRIUMPH 1945-1958 TWINS (BOOK OF)
TRIUMPH 1956-1969 TWINS (BOOK OF)
VELOCETTE 1925-1970 ALL SINGLES & TWINS (BOOK OF)
VESPA 1951-1961 (BOOK OF)
VESPA 1955-1963 125 & 150cc & GS MODELS (SECOND BOOK OF)
VESPA 1955-1968 GS & SS (BOOK OF)
VESPA 1963-1972 90, 125 & 150cc (THIRD BOOK OF)
VILLIERS ENGINE UP TO 1959 INC. 3 WHEELERS (BOOK OF)
VILLIERS ENGINE UP TO 1969 (BOOK OF)
VINCENT 1935-1955 (WORKSHOP MANUAL)
YAMAHA 1961-1967 YA5 & YA6 (WORKSHOP MANUAL & ILL PARTS LIST)
YAMAHA 1971-1972 JT1& JT2 (WORKSHOP MANUAL & ILL PARTS LIST)

## VELOCEPRESS TECHNICAL BOOKS – MOTORCYCLE

CATALOG OF BRITISH MOTORCYCLES (1951 MODELS)
INDIAN PONYBIKE, BOY RACER & PAPOOSE ILL PARTS LIST & SALES LIT
MOTORCYCLE ENGINEERING (P.E. Irving)
SPEED AND HOW TO OBTAIN IT (Motor Cycle Magazine UK)
TUNING FOR SPEED (P.E. Irving)

## VELOCEPRESS MANUALS - THREE WHEELER'S

BSA THREE WHEELER (BOOK OF)
VINTAGE MORGAN THREE WHEELER (BOOK OF)

## VELOCEPRESS MANUALS - AUTOMOBILE

ALFA ROMEO GIULIA WORKSHOP MANUAL 1300 TO 2000cc 1962-1975
ALFA ROMEO GIULIA TECH MANUAL CARBURETED CARS FROM 1962
ALFA ROMEO GIULIA TECH MANUAL FUEL INJECTED CARS FROM 1969
AUSTIN-HEALEY 6-CYLINDER WORKSHOP MANUAL
AUSTIN-HEALEY SPRITE & MG MIDGET WORKSHOP MANUAL 1958-1971
BMW 600 LIMOUSINE FACTORY WORKSHOP MANUAL
BMW 600 LIMOUSINE OWNERS HAND BOOK & SERVICE MANUAL
BMW 2000 & 2002 1966-1976 WORKSHOP MANUAL
BMW ISETTA FACTORY WORKSHOP MANUAL
CORVAIR 1960-1969 WORKSHOP MANUAL
CORVETTE V8 1955-1962 WORKSHOP MANUAL
FIAT 500 FACTORY WORKSHOP MANUAL 1957-1973
FIAT 600, 600D & MULTIPLA FACTORY WORKSHOP MANUAL 1955-1969
JAGUAR E-TYPE 3.8 & 4.2 SERIES 1 & 2 WORKSHOP MANUAL
JAGUAR MK 7, 8, 9 & XK120, 140, 150 WORKSHOP MANUAL 1948-1961
METROPOLITAN FACTORY WORKSHOP MANUAL
MGA & MGB OWNERS HANDBOOK & WORKSHOP MANUAL
MG MIDGET TC, TD, TF & TF1500 WORKSHOP MANUAL
PORSCHE 356 1948-1965 WORKSHOP MANUAL
PORSCHE 911 2.0, 2.2, 2.4 LITRE 1964-1973
PORSCHE 912 WORKSHOP MANUAL
TRIUMPH TR2, TR3, TR4 1953-1965 WORKSHOP MANUAL
VOLKSWAGEN TRANSPORTER, TRUCKS & WAGONS 1950-1979 WSM
VOLVO 1944-1968 ALL MODELS WORKSHOP MANUAL

## VELOCEPRESS TECHNICAL BOOKS - AUTOMOBILE

FERRARI 250/GT SERVICE AND MAINTENANCE
FERRARI GUIDE TO PERFORMANCE
FERRARI OWNER'S HANDBOOK
FERRARI TUNING TIPS & MAINTENANCE TECHNIQUES
HOW TO BUILD A FIBERGLASS CAR
HOW TO BUILD A RACING CAR
HOW TO RESTORE THE MODEL 'A' FORD
MASERATI OWNER'S HANDBOOK
OBERT'S FIAT GUIDE
PERFORMANCE TUNING THE SUNBEAM TIGER
SOUPING THE VOLKSWAGEN
SOLEX CARBURETORS (EMPHASIS ON UK & EU AUTOMOBILES)
SU CARBURETORS (EMPHASIS ON UK AUTOMOBILES)
WEBER CARBURETORS (EMPHASIS ON ALFA & FIAT)

## VELOCEPRESS BOOKS & GUIDES - AUTOMOBILE

ABARTH BUYERS GUIDE
COMPLETE CATALOG OF JAPANESE MOTOR VEHICLES
FERRARI 308 SERIES BUYER'S AND OWNER'S GUIDE
FERRARI BERLINETTA LUSSO
FERRARI BROCHURES AND SALES LITERATURE 1946-1967
FERRARI BROCHURES AND SALES LITERATURE 1968-1989
FERRARI OPP, MAINTENANCE & SERVICE H/BOOKS 1948-1963
FERRARI SERIAL NUMBERS PART I - ODD NUMBERS TO 21399
FERRARI SERIAL NUMBERS PART II - EVEN NUMBERS TO 1050
FERRARI SPYDER CALIFORNIA
HENRY'S FABULOUS MODEL "A" FORD
MASERATI BROCHURES AND SALES LITERATURE

## VELOCEPRESS BOOKS – RACING

CARRERA PANAMERICANA - MEXICAN ROAD RACE (BOOK OF)
DIALED IN - THE JAN OPPERMAN STORY
IF HEMINGWAY HAD WRITTEN A RACING NOVEL
VEDA ORR'S NEW REVISED HOT ROD PICTORIAL

## AUTOBOOKS WORKSHOP MANUALS & BROOKLANDS ROAD TEST PORTFOLIOS

FOR A COMPLETE LISTING OF THE AUTOBOOKS & BROOKLANDS TITLES THAT WE CURRENTLY HAVE AVAILABLE, PLEASE VISIT OUR WEBSITE.

www.VelocePress.com

www.ingramcontent.com/pod-product-compliance
Lightning Source LLC
Chambersburg PA
CBHW080424230426
43662CB00015B/2206